venice

FODOR'S TRAVEL PUBLICATIONS

NEW YORK • TORONTO • LONDON • SYDNEY • AUCKLAND

WWW.FODORS.COM

Contents

KEY TO SYMBOLS

- Map reference
- Address
- Telephone number
- Opening times
- Admission prices
- Bus number
- Train station
- Vaporetto/boat
- Driving directions
- Tourist office
- Tours
- Guidebook
- Restaurant
- Café
- Bar
- Shop
- Toilets
- Number of rooms
- No smoking
- Air-conditioning
- Swimming pool
- Gym
- Other useful information
- Shopping
- Entertainment
- Nightlife
- Sports
- Activities
- Health and Beauty
- For Children
- Cross reference
- Walk/drive start point

HOW TO USE THIS BOOK

Understanding Venice is an introduction to the city, its geography, economy and people. **Living Venice** gives an insight into the city today, while **The Story of Venice** takes you through its past.

For detailed advice on getting to Venice—and getting around once you are there—turn to **On the Move**. For useful practical information, from weather forecasts to emergency services, turn to **Planning.**

Venice's key attractions are listed alpabetically in **The Sights** and are located on the maps on pages 58–63. The key sightseeing areas are described on pages 64–68 and are circled in blue on the map on the inside front cover.

Turn to **What to Do** for information on shops, entertainment, nightlife, sport, health and beauty, children's activities and festivals and events. Entries are listed by theme and then alphabetically. Shops are located on the maps on pages 184–189 and entertainment venues on the maps on pages 202–207. The top shopping areas are described on pages 179–183 and are circled in green on the map on the inside front cover.

Out and About offers walks around Venice and Murano, and excursions that encourage you to explore farther afield.

Eating and **Staying** give you selected restaurants and hotels, listed alphabetically. Restaurants are located on the maps on pages 252–257 and hotels on the maps on pages 270–275.

Map references refer to the locator maps within the book or the street atlas at the end. For example, the Palazzo Ducale has the grid reference ⊞ 61 H10, indicating the page on which the map is found (61) and the grid square in which the palace sits (H10). The grid on the locator maps within the book is the same as the grid on the atlas at the back of the book.

UNDERSTANDING VENICE

Venice is truly unique, a city built on water, threaded by canals, where water, stone and art combine to form a dazzling backdrop to an unparalleled way of life. Once mistress of the seas and controller of the Eastern trade routes, Venice used her riches to embellish her canals, streets and squares with churches and palaces, whose interiors house some of the greatest mosaics, paintings and sculpture to be found anywhere on earth. The march of history left this beautiful city stranded far from its former pre-eminence; Italian unification relegated Venice's political role to that of a small—and shrinking—regional city; the ever-increasing problems of pollution, decay and winter flooding place huge strains on the authorities responsible for keeping Venice functioning; and the summer visitors almost swamp the city. Despite everything, Venice continues to survive as a living, and still incomparably beautiful entity, with new conservation plans in the pipeline and a burgeoning international cultural role.

The Rialto Bridge illuminated at night, one of Venice's quintessential sights

LAYOUT OF THE CITY

Venice is divided into six *sestieri* (wards/sixths), three of which lie on each side of the Grand Canal. Within each of these are several parishes, whose main church generally overlooks the area's central square, known in Venice as a *campo*. From each *campo* streets fan out, crossing, by means of bridges, the myriad canals that are Venice's alternative highways. Streets and canals are lined with *palazzi*, the mansions of the rich, whose architecture spans the full range of Venetian styles—Veneto-Byzantine, Venetian Gothic, Renaissance and baroque. Finding your way through this labyrinth of passages and alleys

more than an historic theme park. Under Mayor Paolo Costa (▷ 23), who stood down in 2005, great strides were made on all fronts; with his encouragement the city council, businesses and cultural associations started massive investment designed to give Venice 21st-century airport and port facilities, better communications within the city and a far larger range of cultural events. Steps were taken to solve the problems brought by the vast numbers of day-trippers—as many as 150,000 visit daily during the peak months, over-whelming the city while contributing little to the economy. The city council must also take into account the demands and needs of the other

Detail on Palazzo Ducale (left); a gondolier in traditional uniform (middle); Piazza San Marco (right)

may be a challenge, but it's also one of the great Venetian pleasures, with countless glimpses of everyday life and serendipitous discoveries along the way. The *sestieri* of San Marco, Cannaregio and Castello lie north of the Grand Canal; to the south are San Polo, Santa Croce and Dorsoduro. South of the city the lagoon opens out towards the islands of the Lido and Pellestrina, long thin land strips that provide the bulwark against the open seas of the Adriatic. North from the city, the lagoon, scattered with islands, stretches peace-fully towards the mainland, the *terra ferma*.

CLIMATE

Lying at the head of the Adriatic and backed by the foothills of the Alps, Venice has a climate as much influenced by central European weather systems as by those of the Mediterranean. Winters range from wet and foggy to bitingly cold, while summer is marked by periods of great heat punctuated by violent and dramatic storms. The city's maritime position contributes frequent high humidity, mist and damp, though there are days of clear brilliance, when the snow-capped Alps are clearly visible to the north and the air is fresh. October and November are the wettest months (around 80 mm/3 inches of rain), July and August the hottest (26–28°C/79–82°F), making spring and autumn the best time to visit the city.

POLITICS AND ECONOMY

Politics and economics are inextricably linked, with the city authorities attempting a delicate jug-gling act between the demands made on the city's infrastructure by visitors and the need for some sort of economic diversification away from tourism. There is also the pressing requirement to provide modern services for the Venetians them-selves, without whom the city would be little

areas of the municipality, Mestre and the estuar-ine settlements, whose inhabitants far outnumber those of the historic centre. Venice has constantly reinvented itself through the years, and the grow-ing numbers of 'serious' visitors, businesspeople and cultural enthusiasts, may mark another role in the story of this city.

SOCIETY—PEOPLE AND LANGUAGE

Away from the major sights, everyday life goes on. The Venetians have had well over a thousand years of sightseers flocking to their city, and are quite accustomed to spellbound foreigners on every corner. Stunned by the physical actuality of the city, many tourists fail to grasp that, despite a population drop of over 100,000 since 1950, Venice is still a functioning, prosperous provincial city, with a population of around 65,000 and all the facilities needed for their 21st-century lives. These numbers are swelled by a sizeable student presence, a growing band of devoted part-time foreign residents, and a daily influx of thousands of commuters from the mainland. The nature of the city makes it not only one of the safest in Europe, but also one of the most intimate, where neighbourhoods have a village atmosphere and everyone knows everyone else. Venetians are civic-minded, tolerant and hard-working, attributes that have served them well throughout the cen-turies; though they have catered to outsiders they've never surrendered their own identity. They are helped by the existence of the Venetian dialect, a wonderfully vibrant tongue with which few foreigners come to terms. Characterized by sing-song rhythms, elisions, slurred vowels and softened consonants, it's rich in specialized vocabulary, stingingly pithy proverbs and down-to-earth wit, a language that cuts across all social boundaries and binds Venetian society together.

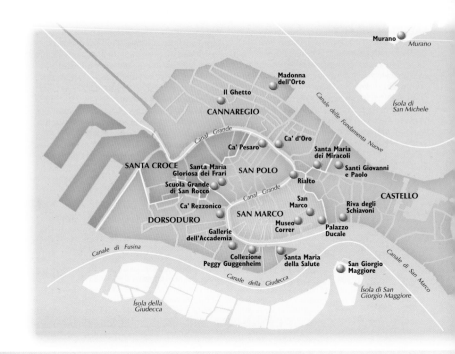

Murano
Murano

Madonna
dell'Orto

Il Ghetto

CANNAREGIO

Ísola di
San Michele

Canale delle Fondamenta Nuove

Canal Grande

Ca' Pesaro

Ca' d'Oro

Santa Maria
dei Miracoli

SANTA CROCE

Santa Maria
Gloriosa dei Frari

SAN POLO

Santi Giovanni
e Paolo

Scuola Grande
di San Rocco

Rialto

Canal Grande

CASTELLO

Ca' Rezzonico

San
Marco

Riva degli
Schiavoni

DORSODURO

SAN MARCO

Gallerie
dell'Accademia

Museo
Correr

Palazzo
Ducale

Canale di Fusina

Collezione
Peggy Guggenheim

Santa Maria
della Salute

San Giorgio
Maggiore

Canale di San Marco

Canale della Giudecca

Ísola di San
Giorgio Maggiore

Ísola della
Giudecca

*Map showing the layout of Venice's six sestieri (wards/sixths; above)
Panoramic view of the island of Burano from Torcello (below)*

Torcello

Ísola di
San Pietro

Ísola di
Sant'Elena

THE SESTIERI AND SHAPE OF THE CITY— THE ISLANDS AND THE GRAND CANAL

Venice is a mosaic of over 120 islands, linked by more than 400 bridges that span the canals between them. Since the 12th century, the city has been divided into six *sestieri*, each with its own distinct character. **San Marco**, **Castello** and **Cannaregio** lie to the north of the Grand Canal and are called the *sestieri de citra*, literally meaning 'on this side', referring to the Grand Canal. **San Polo**, **Santa Croce** and **Dorsoduro** lie to the south, and are known as the *sestieri de ultra*, 'on that side'. They are the most important political, economic and religious districts. **San Marco**, which includes the island of **San Giorgio Maggiore**, was the seat of Venice's secular power, home to the administration, the mint and the law courts, all grouped around the Piazza di San Marco, the only open space in Venice to qualify for the name Piazza. East of here, **Castello** was the original religious hub, where the city's cathedral, San Pietro in Castello, was sited, away from the central powerhouse of the Piazza. West of San Marco lies **Cannaregio**, developed through reclamation of sandbanks and lagoon shoals and historically one of the early city's most important areas, which borders with San Marco at the **Rialto**, medieval Europe's greatest financial and commercial centre. Across the Grand Canal lie San Polo and Santa Croce and Dorsoduro, which includes, administratively, the island of the **Giudecca**, to the south of the Canale della Giudecca. **San Polo** and **Santa Croce**'s boundaries are blurred, rather than being separated by canals; both were settled and were of major economic importance in early Venice. **Dorsoduro**, home to some superb churches and museums, has always been an immensely varied *sestiere*, firmly working-class to the north and west, elegant and well-heeled to the east and along the Grand Canal.

UNDERSTANDING
THE LAGOON

**Since earliest times, the history of Venice has also been the history
of the lagoon. The two are interdependent; the city has been much
influenced by the ebb and flow of the tides in and out of the lagoon,
and the lagoon inhabitants, who look on Venice as the metropolis,
depend on the city for their livelihood.**

*Beach huts on the Lido (left); view from the Giardini Biennale (middle left); rowing Venetian style
(middle right); vineyard on Sant'Erasmo (right); canal signs (top right)*

THE LAGOON

The Venetian lagoon is a small inland sea whose
waters are both brackish and salty. It covers an
area of 550sq km (212sq miles), is 50km
(31 miles) in length and ranges in width from
8–14km (5–9 miles). The lagoon is protected
from the open sea by a chain of narrow strips of
land; the curving peninsula of Punta Sabbioni to
the north, and the islands of the Lido and
Pellestrina to the south. Twice daily, tides surge
through the gaps between these outer barriers,
cleansing the lagoon waters and the canals that
thread the lagoon itself. The largest of these channels follow the original paths of rivers that once
flowed through the lagoon, which were diverted
during the huge engineering works undertaken
from the 15th to 17th centuries. These works
maintained a vital balance between allowing the
tides to cleanse the lagoon, and keeping out the
full force of the sea. Maintaining this equilibrium
has always been the primary preoccupation of
the city. During the last 60 years of industrial
development on the land around the lagoon,
huge damage was done to this delicate balance,
which is only now beginning to be addressed.

THE LAGOON LANDS

Over half of the area of the lagoon is permanently
covered with water. The rest is a shifting landscape of islands, marshlands, shoals and mudflats, some firm enough to be used for cultivation
and settlement, other areas only emerging from
the sea at the lowest of tides. The firmest areas
are the islands proper, a group of which contains
Venice itself. The rest divides into *barene*, shoals
or strips of land, covered with vegetation, which
are only water covered at exceptionally high tides;
velme, muddy, algae-cloaked stretches that

emerge at low tide; and *valli di pesca chiuse*,
areas mainly in the north and southwest of the
lagoon where most of the fish farms are located.
The *valli* have both permanent bodies of water
and shoals, ideal for farming and are surrounded
by embankments to protect them from the ebb
and flow of the tide. The best way to grasp the
diversity of the lagoon is from the air on the
approach to the airport, from where the marshes,
shoals and water spread like a patchwork below.

THE LAGOON ISLANDS

The lagoon is scattered with islands, many of
which were once inhabited, served as hospitals or
military installations or housed religious communities. San Giorgio Maggiore and the Giudecca
lie close to the south of the city; San Michele,
the cemetery island, and Murano, the heart of
Venice's glass-blowing industry, are a short hop to
the north. Further north are the islands of Burano,
Mazzorbo and Torcello, a once important trio of
settlements. The 'barrier' islands of the Lido and
Pellestrina guard the lagoon entrances; of the
two, the Lido is far more developed, due mainly
to its 19th-century role as one of Europe's most
fashionable resorts. Pellestrina, to the south, is
still a lonely fishing community, a narrow strip of
sandy land that feels a thousand miles from central Venice. Other important islands include
bucolic Sant'Erasmo, a large agricultural island
that still supplies many of the city's vegetables,
and San Francesco del Deserto and San Lazzaro
degli Armeni, both still retaining a monastic role.
Smaller islands still in use are San Servolo, once
a psychiatric hospital and now part of Venice
International University; San Clemente, one of
Venice's classiest hotels; and Sant'Andrea, a
fortress island undergoing a lengthy restoration.

Beneath the surface the water depth varies tremendously, and the lagoon is navigable only along channels, many of which have to be dredged constantly to prevent them silting up. These are marked by various types of beacons and bollards, each of which follows a precise code of reference. Without them, the lagoon would be totally impassable. The pilings are driven deep into the bed of the lagoon and need replacing every 20 years. They provide attractive perches for the lagoon's birdlife, and the submerged parts support thriving colonies of anemones, barnacles, mussels, limpets, crabs, tiny fish and various seaweeds. The main types are:

Bricola – the massive groups of timber bound with iron hoops. These mark the limits of navigable channels and those along the main routes are illuminated at night.

Dama – generally a group of three large timbers. They mark the entrance to a channel or a junction between two navigable waterways.

Palina – the single poles, seen mainly along the city's canals, which are used as mooring posts. They are often painted with coloured stripes, which signify that the pole belongs to a specific family.

BOATS

Transport throughout the lagoon relies on boats, many of which are unique to Venice. As well as the ubiquitous *vaporetti*, taxis and goods barges, motorized boats include specifically modified vessels which act as refuse barges, fire engines, refrigerated transport, police boats and ambulances. In addition there is a variety of uniquely Venetian boats, whose design has evolved over the centuries for differing and specific uses in the shallow lagoon waters. Prime among these is the gondola (▷ 48–49); others include:

Topo – a sailing boat originating in Chioggia. They differ in size and were used for fishing. The middle part of the deck is left open to the hold so the catch can be thrown in.

Puparin – an asymmetrical 10m-long (33ft) general-purpose boat, rowed from a small platform at the stern.

Sanpierota – a small, exceptionally stable craft, much used by families for excursions.

Caorlina – a streamlined rowing boat for six oarsmen now mainly used for racing.

S'ciopin – a water-hugging small boat, once used for duck shooting; the shallow draft makes it ideal for lagoon use.

Sandalo – a single-handed rowing boat propelled by a standing oarsman using crossed oars.

Mascareta – a light rowing skiff, usually used by women.

Gondolino – a very fast racing gondola, propelled by two oarsmen.

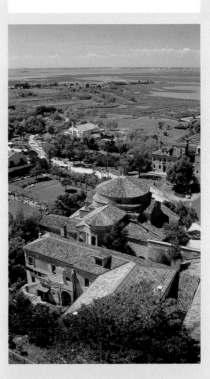

View from the bell-tower of the Basilica di Santa Maria Assunta on Torcello

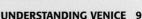

THE BEST OF VENICE

BEST VIEWS

Two bird's-eye views: from the top of the Campanile on Piazza San Marco, and from the campanile of San Giorgio Maggiore.
The **panorama** of the Bacino di San Marco from the Molo.
The **view** down the Grand Canal towards the Salute from the Accademia Bridge.
The **silhouetted buildings** of Dorsoduro from the Giudecca.
The **view** towards San Marco and the mouth of the Grand Canal from San Giorgio Maggiore.

BEST CHURCHES

Basilica di San Marco (▷ 134–139): the spiritual heart of Venice and one of Europe's most sublime medieval buildings.
Madonna dell'Orto (▷ 106–107): a perfect Venetian Gothic church, packed with paintings by Tintoretto.
San Giorgio Maggiore (▷ 130–131): rational, intellectual and beautiful Palladian architecture at its finest.
Santa Maria dei Miracoli (▷ 148–149): a serene Renaissance jewel in polychrome marble.
Santa Maria Assunta on Torcello (▷ 174): the oldest church in the lagoon, whose interior is adorned with superb mosaics.
Santa Maria Gloriosa dei Frari (▷ 144–147): a lofty church, that's home to two superb works by Titian and one of Giovanni Bellini's greatest paintings.
Santi Giovanni e Paolo (▷ 132–133): a Gothic church that holds the best of Venetian church monuments and is the burial place of many doges.

Views of the Basilica di San Marco (above and below); exterior of San Giorgio Maggiore (left)

BEST *PALAZZI*

Palazzo Ducale (▷ 112–117): the ultimate expression of the might and power of independent Venice, and an incredible palace packed with artistic treasures.
Ca' d'Oro (▷ 70–71): the most beautiful of all the Gothic *palazzi* on the Grand Canal.
Ca' Rezzonico (▷ 74–75): a splendid High Renaissance *palazzo* that gives an insight into sumptuous 18th-century Venetian life.

BEST PAINTINGS AND PICTURE CYCLES

Feast in the House of Levi (▷ 96–97): a massive Veronese, packed with drama, in the Accademia.
La Tempesta (▷ 96): an enigmatic masterpiece by Giorgione in the Accademia.
Madonna and Child with Saints (▷ 144): a glowing altarpiece by Giovanni Bellini in the sacristy of the Frari.
Miracle of St. Mark Feeding the Slave (▷ 97): a tour-de-force of perspective and drama by Tintoretto in the Accademia.
Presentation of the Virgin (▷ 107): a wonderfully calm and reverential painting by Tintoretto in Madonna dell'Orto.
San Sebastiano (▷ 157): a glorious cycle of dazzling paintings by Paolo Veronese.
Scuola di San Giorgio degli Schiavoni (▷ 163): a picture cycle by Vittore Carpaccio that's packed with charm and incident.
Scuola Grande di San Rocco (▷ 164–167): a staggering picture cycle by Tintoretto in a purpose-built *scuola grande*.
Story of St. Ursula (▷ 98–99): a narrative picture cycle by Carpaccio in the Accademia.
The Assumption of the Virgin (▷ 146): a ground-breaking work by Titian above the high altar in the Frari.
The Miracle of the Relic of the Cross (▷ 98): a picture cycle with wonderful scenes of 16th-century Venice by Gentile Bellini, Carpaccio and others in the Accademia.

The Palazzo Ducale as seen from across the lagoon (above)

Ceiling painting in the Church of San Sebastiano (above)

BEST VENETIAN SPECIALITY SHOPS

Anticlea Antiquariato (▷ 196): a treasure house of antique beads for earrings and necklaces to be made up on the spot.

Bevilacqua (▷ 197): traditional Venetian brocades, velvets, taffetas and damasks and home accessories such as curtain ties, swags and key tassels.

Bottega Veneta (▷ 198): mouth-wateringly supple and highly stylish leather goods.

Ebrû (▷ 191): marbled paper products in a rainbow of colours.

Gaggio (▷ 197): sumptuous hand-printed silk velvet cushions, wall-hangings, lengths and scarves.

Gilberto Penzo (▷ 191): intricate models of every type of Venetian boat and build-it-yourself miniature gondola kits.

Legatoria Piazzesi (▷ 192): elegant block-printed and marbled paper and paper products.

Mazzega (▷ 195): traditional, hand-blown Venetian glass.

MondoNovo (▷ 190): the very best in handmade traditional and modern Carnival masks.

Pauly (▷ 195): beautiful Murano glass with a modern twist.

Perle e Dintorni (▷ 197): a huge range of modern glass beads and ready-made jewellery.

Venetia Studium (▷ 197): Fortuny-style pleated silk and figured velvet scarves, pillows and bags.

Exquisite Venetian glassware from Murano (top and above); typical Venetian mask (top right); Campo San Polo (below)

BEST *CAMPI* – VENICE'S BEST SQUARES

Campo San Giacomo dell'Orio (▷ 79).
Campo San Polo (▷ 80–81).
Campo Santa Margherita (▷ 80).
Campo Santa Maria Formosa (▷ 143).
Campo Santo Stefano (▷ 81).

BEST ROMANTIC PLACES

The **Punta della Dogana:** come at night for floodlit views, twinkling lights and the slap of water on stone.

The bench by the water on **Campo San Vio** in Dorsoduro: a grandstand seat overlooking the Grand Canal.

The double seat of a **gondola**.

The **Fondamenta della Sensa** in Cannaregio: the perfect quiet quayside for strolling hand-in-hand.

BEST PLACES TO EAT

The height of romance— newlyweds on a gondola

Sample Venetian cooking at its best here

Alla Maddalena (▷ 258): a waterside setting on the tiny island of Mazzorbo makes this the nicest place for lunch if you're visiting the northern lagoon islands.

Alle Testiere (▷ 259): a tiny restaurant that has a high reputation with the Venetians for its innovative cuisine.

Alla Zucca (▷ 260): the best place in Venice for vegetarians.

Corte Sconta (▷ 262): the first of Venice's new-style restaurants is still rightly acclaimed for its food and ambience 20-plus years down the line.

Dal Pampo (Osteria Sant'Elena) (▷ 263): one of Venice's best traditional local restaurants, tucked away off the tourist route in Sant'Elena.

Fiaschetteria Toscana (▷ 263): famous, high-class restaurant where the food and service are consistently good.

Osteria Oliva Nera (▷ 265): Venetian cooking with a twist has established the reputation of one of Venice's foremost new-style restaurants.

Vini da Gigio (▷ 265): the best place to sample the finest Venetian cooking and superb wines at excellent prices.

BEST PLACES TO STAY

Ca' Maria Adele (▷ 277): tiny and sybaritic, this hotel is the top choice for romantics.

Cipriani (▷ 277): world-class luxury hotel set in extensive gardens on the Giudecca.

Danieli (▷ 278): one of Italy's great hotels is housed in a 15th-century *palazzo* overlooking St. Mark's Basin.

Dinesen (▷ 278): a beautiful, quiet, mid-range hotel, with spacious rooms, tucked away on one of Dorsoduro's prettiest canals.

Gritti Palace (▷ 279–280): luxury hotel with superb public rooms and bedrooms situated five minutes from the Piazza San Marco on the Grand Canal.

Locanda San Barnaba (▷ 281): an excellent hotel in the mid-price range with a courtyard garden and a good position a short walk from Ca' Rezzonico *vaporetto* stop.

Novecento (▷ 282): new-wave boutique hotel with every modern comfort set on a quiet alley 10 minutes from Piazza San Marco.

San Clemente Palace (▷ 284): get away from the city at this luxury hotel on the tiny island of San Clemente—linked to the centre by private launch.

The swimming pool of the Hotel Cipriani

DON'T MISS BEST EXPERIENCES

Take *vaporetto* No. 1 down the Grand Canal (▷ 82–91) to drink in the procession of *palazzi* on the world's most beautiful man-made waterway.

Take the lift up the Campanile di San Marco (▷ 139). The views over the city and lagoon are wonderful and it's a great way to get your bearings.

Browse the food stalls of the Rialto markets (▷ 120–121), the best place for a take on local life as you watch the shoppers and admire the super-fresh fish, fruit and vegetables.

Don't miss the bronze horses when you visit the Basilica di San Marco (▷ 136). Dating from classical times, they're the oldest equestrian bronze group in the world.

Splash out on a drink at Florian's or Quadri's in the Piazza San Marco (▷ 76)—listen to the band and relax in the surroundings of what Napoleon called the 'greatest drawing room in Europe'.

Buy an ice-cream at Nico's (▷ 220) and stroll along the Zattere in the late afternoon; soft evening light and views over the water to the Giudecca add to the charms of the city's most sheltered promenade.

Head for the Giardini Pubblici (▷ 104) for green space and room to stretch you legs.

Cross the Grand Canal on a *traghetto* (▷ 53), one of the gondola ferries that have transported Venetians for over a thousand years—and do it standing up.

Get away from the crowds; head for northern Cannaregio (▷ 106–107) and the church of Madonna dell'Orto.

Spend a day exploring the lagoon islands of Murano, Burano and Torcello (▷ 170, 172–173, 174): leave early and take a picnic to eat in the tranquil little park on Mazzorbo.

Watch the glass blowers at work in one of Murano's factories (▷ 172–173).

Visit the Ca' Rezzonico (▷ 74–75) to get an idea of the scale of luxury enjoyed by the patrician classes in 18th-century Venice.

Join the well-heeled Venetians in and around Calle Vallaresso (▷ 179), home to the big Italian retail names—Armani, Fendi, Bottega Veneta and Gucci.

Visit Campo Santa Margherita (▷ 80) in the morning to sit at a café table and soak up local life—market stallholders, students, schoolchildren and housewives going about their business.

Along the Grand Canal near San Silvestro

Stallholder at Rialto's popular market

The bronze horses in the Basilica di San Marco

Caffè Quadri—all neoclassical design and chandeliers

Living Venice

A vegetable stall boat in the Dorsoduro (left); canalside dining in the Ostreghe (right)

Decorated gondolas at their moorings (above); visitors on the Cannaregio Canal (right); fine artwork on a traditionally carved gondola (below)

Venice's Canals

Street Traffic

Venice's canals are used for delivering everything. Barges and smaller boats penetrate the side canals, offloading food, stores and equipment. From here, everything is transported on trolleys. Workers arrive by water, barges make daily refuse collections and the emergency services use the canal network for all their calls; around 300 fires are extinguished annually from the fire boats, and the white ambulance boats have their own water entrance to the main hospital on the Fondamente Nuove. Beneath the surface, pipes convey fresh water, gas is delivered and wastewater empties into the canals. Most sewage nowadays is collected in *pozzi neri* (black wells), the septic tanks that are periodically emptied by specially designed barges.

Arriving in Venice in 1947, Robert Benchley cabled home: 'Streets full of water; please advise'. He had a point, for the most essential fact about Venice is that there are no roads, and the city's main arteries are waterways. Alleys, quaysides and squares exist, but the main street is the Grand Canal, from which radiates a 17km (28-mile) long spider's web of 177 lesser canals, varying in length, width and depth. They follow the old natural watercourses, which meandered through the islets of the lagoon before Venice was founded, and from their earliest days were integral to the everyday life of the city.

Everything in the city, old or new, transient or permanent, at some stage has to travel by water. Until the 19th century boats plied incessantly through the Canale di Cannaregio from the mainland or docked in the Bacino; today most of the city's essentials are offloaded from trucks, trains and container ships in the dispiriting and frenzied surroundings of Piazzale Roma and transferred to the ubiquitous barges for onward transport on the canal network. Nowhere in Venice is more than a few metres from a canal, and the city itself is in reality a collection of 118 separate islands, linked by bridges. Beneath these glide every conceivable sort of craft; gondolas—the city's symbol—grimy barges and refuse collectors, police boats and sleek white taxis, ambulances and fire-engines, and myriad small craft. Water dictates the pace of life, and the Venetian existence, governed by boats and tides, is unlike that of any other city in the world.

A wedding party transported in style (left); taking refuge from the rain (right)

One of Venice's many gondoliers on the Grand Canal

Crossing the Rio di Sant'Anna (below, left); keeping the canals clean is a never-ending task in the city (below)

Bridges

The canals are crossed by around 400 bridges, many of them dating from the Middle Ages. With a few exceptions, they have single semi-circular arches, and are high enough to provide a passage for gondolas and barges, while two of those on the Grand Canal, the Scalzi and the Accademia bridges, were specifically designed to allow enough height for *vaporetti*. Early bridges were wood, later replaced by stone and brick constructions whose foundations rest on wooden piles hammered into each bank. Temporary bridges are built for two of Venice's main festivals; one across the Giudecca Canal for the feast of the Redentore in July, and the other across the Grand Canal to the church of the Salute in November. The average Venetian crosses 40 to 50 bridges daily, climbing and descending the equivalent of 120m (400ft) each way.

Keeping it Clean

The tide is the first line of defence in keeping the canal system fresh, with the incessant twice-daily tides sweeping constantly in to fill and empty even the narrowest waterways. This is augmented by the regular dredging of the side canals, usually every 2 to 3 years, a noxious process whereby each end of the canal is sealed off with boarding and the canal pumped dry. Repairs are then made to the side walls, the bottom scraped of mud and deposits, and any pipe system below water level inspected and repaired if necessary. Despite this cleaning, high summer temperatures inevitably bring an unforgettable, and quintessentially Venetian, smell to many of the smaller side canals. Out in the lagoon, threaded by deepwater channels, dredgers are constantly at work removing the build-ups of silt and sand that the tides bring in.

Boats

The thoroughbred, streamlined gondola, Venice's 1,000-year-old city boat, is queen of the canals, but over the centuries Venice's boats have evolved to the point where there's a specialized craft for every conceivable function. Traditional boats, redolent with history and all rowed in the traditional Venetian manner, standing up, include the little *sandolo*, designed in the 13th century; the *mascareta*, rowed mainly by women; and the fast-moving *gondolino*, a greyhound of a craft. Modern boats are legion, the *vaporetti*, the public transport vessels, and the barges being the real workhorses. Specialized motor boats serve as taxis, police boats, ambulances, fireboats and hearses, while out in the lagoon there are pleasure craft, fishing boats and beautiful, flat-bottomed, wooden sailing boats with square sails and a 10cm (4-inch) draught called *topi*.

Storming the Decks

There was a lagoon-wide alert in winter 2004 when ACTV, the transport authority, realized a No. 51 *vaporetto* was missing from its berth near St. Mark's Basin. The vessel was tracked by global positioning technology moving at full throttle across the lagoon. Fearing a terrorist attack on the petrochemical works at Marghera, the police gave chase, upon which the *vaporetto*'s mystery thief attempted to ram the much smaller police vessel. Officers eventually forced it into a U-turn, then stormed the ship and overwhelmed a man. He proved to be an extremely drunk, 36-year-old illegal Russian immigrant named Viktor Sobolev, who had taken the *vaporetto* because, in his own words, he 'missed being at sea'. He was charged with aggravated theft, resisting police officers, being without immigration papers, and breaking various navigation laws.

Venice has acted to save places such as Piazza San Marco (above) for residents and visitors alike (right)

A dilapidated façade, which is typical of canalside building (left)

A large crane out in the lagoon, part of the MoSE project (right)

The Trouble with
Venice

Venice is 123cm (48 inches) lower in the water than in 1900, *acqua alta* ('high water', or flood) hits the city an average of 130 days a year, water levels in the Adriatic will rise 25–60cm (10–23 inches) by 2100, and experts believe the city will be uninhabitable within a hundred years unless new methods of protection from the water are installed. The causes are legion, but most vital of all for the city's survival is the equilibrium of the lagoon, a fragile environment that was actively destroyed during the boom years following World War II. The juggling act of balancing erosion and sedimentation was seriously threatened by indiscriminate tapping of the aquifers beneath the lagoon, undermining the very foundations of the city. Pollution levels rocketed, with more than 3.5 million tonnes of waste being dumped daily into the lagoon. Channels 18m (59ft) were gouged into the lagoon bed for petrol tankers and cruise ships, landfill sites proliferated, and the lagoon became deeper, saltier and dirtier. Meanwhile, global warming steadily drove the sea levels higher. Every year the *acqua alta* situation worsened, causing huge damage to the city's buildings and fabric, exacerbated by the destruction of precious stonework by the chemicals from the refineries and industry of the mainland. The worst of these practices has now been halted, and construction has started on the MoSE project; it remains to be seen whether help is coming too late.

Erosion on a statue of the Lion of St. Mark, outside San Nicolò dei Mendicoli

Holding Back the Waters

After years of investigation, wrangling and procrastination, work started on the controversial, but vital, MoSE project in 2003. This will consist of 79 hinged floodgates lying flat on the seabed across the three main lagoon entry channels. When damagingly high tides are forecast they will be pumped full of air and will rise to an angle of 30 degrees to hold back the sea and prevent flooding in the city, returning to the bottom once the danger is past. Opinion polls show Venetians broadly in favour, but environmentalists are still campaigning for more gradualist measures, such as raising pavements and dealing with the legacy of industrial pollution, all, in fact, part of the overall plan. The barrier is scheduled for completion in 2011 at a cost of approximately €4 billion, and will cost €8 million a year to maintain.

Pollution is an ongoing issue (above); gondoliers take matters into their own hands by striking (below)

Dredging the canal in the Cannaregio district (above); smoke from factories causes damage to stonework (right); the Mestre plant (below)

Gondoliers on Strike

Gondoliers have long protested aganist the *moto ondoso* (motor wash) caused by motor boats and transport barges. It is a major contributor to ever more water-logged foundations of city buildings and excessive wear and tear on traditional boats. Protests are frequent, and by 2005, when legislation also came in to limit gondolas' operational hours, said to be the cause of increasing numbers of collisions on the Grand Canal, enough was enough. On 14 February, St. Valentine's Day, all 400 Venetian gondoliers started a three-day strike against what they saw as unfair measures to reduce accidents and to draw the world's attention to the perils of vibration— tough indeed on lovers hoping for a gondola ride on the most romantic day of the year.

Depopulation

Since 1946 about 110,000 people have left Venice to live on the mainland, leaving a population of around 60,000. This beautiful city is inconvenient and slow, housing is both expensive to buy and to maintain, and, with the closure of major city businesses—2,000 jobs alone went when Assicurazione Generali moved its headquarters—there is little work outside the tourist and service industries. The population drop has deprived those who've hung on of local shops, tradesmen, workmen and entertainment. The housing issue is being addressed by new construction, particularly on the Giudecca, but prices are high, and many new flats are snapped up by well-heeled out-of-town-ers, who spend little time in the city. A 2005 UNESCO report stated 'Venice is becoming a museum-city, and is no longer a residential one'.

Mestre and Marghera

Mestre-Marghera is one of the largest industrial complexes in Italy, with oil refineries and chemical plants—and it's just across the lagoon from Venice. Chemical pollution has fallen by 80 per cent since legislation in the 1970s, but the industrial zone is still a major source of pollution. Westerly winds blow the waste onto the historic quarter where the combination of gaseous acid with humidity and salt wreaks havoc. The surface amount eaten away annually is 6 per cent of marble and stone, 5 per cent of frescoes and 3 per cent of paintings on canvas and wood. In addition, giant tankers daily use the channels through the lagoon to ferry over 12 million tons of chemicals and crude oil annually, and conservationists believe it's only a matter of time before a major shipping disaster totally destroys the ecological balance of the lagoon itself.

A Case History

The church of Santa Maria dei Miracoli (below) was first restored in the 1860s, when the marble facing was removed, cleaned and reattached with cement. By 1970 the underlying brickwork was waterlogged as the cement crumbled, and more work was needed. This restoration was only a temporary measure, as the marble itself was subsequently attacked by mineral salts, and in 1987 yet more work was needed. All walls were desalinated, cleaned and consolidated, crumbling stucco and masonry repaired using traditional techniques and materials, and iron supports replaced with steel ones. The work took over 10 years and cost $3 million, and, on the scale of Venetian restoration projects, was not considered a hugely difficult or expensive job.

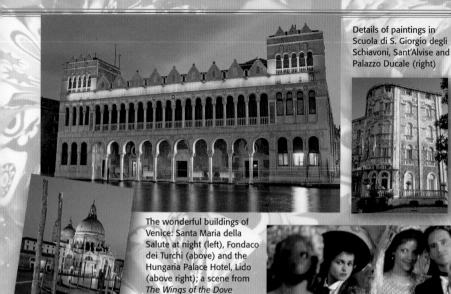

Details of paintings in Scuola di S. Giorgio degli Schiavoni, Sant'Alvise and Palazzo Ducale (right)

The wonderful buildings of Venice: Santa Maria della Salute at night (left), Fondaco dei Turchi (above) and the Hungaria Palace Hotel, Lido (above right); a scene from *The Wings of the Dove* (right); the logo of the Venice in Peril group (below)

Art and Architecture

Today's Grand Tourists

Visitors have been gazing open-mouthed at Venice's treasures for centuries, and those on the Grand Tour have been replaced by earnest academics and their flocks. Well-to-do parents still send their offspring to Venice for crash courses in art history; some, like John Halls', are firmly aimed at students taking a year off, others, like the Venice International University offerings, target undergraduates from all over the world. Budding academics have a great choice of libraries for research into the city's art: the Archivio di Stato, with over 300 rooms of documents, the Fondazione Giorgio Cini, and the library of the Architectural Faculty of the University, one of the best in Italy.

In no other city are art and architecture as central to the essence of a place as they are in Venice. Every corner of this unique city contains buildings, paintings and sculpture that combine to form one of the world's most astonishing urban landscapes. Water, stone and light are the keynotes, overlaid with colour, shape and texture. Eastern influences shaped the unique Veneto-Gothic design of the early churches and palaces, the most individual architectural style the city ever produced, which segued in the 15th century into Venice's own take on the Renaissance. Two centuries later the classical forms of the High Renaissance evolved into the triumphantly opulent forms of baroque, studding the city with buildings and churches of mind-blowing ostentation. Down the line, artists were at work decorating the interior of these buildings; first, in the 11th and 12th centuries with glittering mosaics, and later with paintings on wood and then canvas. Technical expertise, rich hues, daring perspective and luminous light are the hallmarks of Venetian painting, found in the pictures in civic buildings, museums and churches throughout the city. Artists also celebrated the physical reality of their city and its inhabitants with a glorious procession of paintings of the city and its waters, piercing portraits of its citizens through the ages, and wonderfully quirky scenes of everyday life in the style known as *genre* painting. Trade and commerce may have given Venice its power and wealth, but it's the art, whether of paint, stone or gilded wood, that has created the physical reality of the city and still inspires people today.

Death in Venice (above); painting on the canal (left); floodwaters outside San Marco (below)

A Touch of the New

There's a dearth of modern buildings in Venice. The reasons are myriad; the physical reality of the city, the difficulties of construction, the lack of space. But things are changing in the 21st century, with international architects making their mark. First on the scene was the 2002 high-tech airport terminal, designed by local architect Giampolo Mar, followed in 2004 by plans for the fourth bridge over the Grand Canal, the work of Spanish super-star Santiago Calatrava. San Michele cemetery is expanding under the direction of UK-based David Chipperfield, and the giant talent of Frank Gehry—responsible for Bilbao's famed Guggenheim—won him the prize for the 'Venice Gateway' competition, which will see the construction of an exciting, convention, hotel and boat terminal complex on the edge of the lagoon.

Art Round Every Corner

Venice's museums are packed with great paintings, but the attraction for many visitors may well be a little something to take home – and there's plenty on offer. Pavement artists of varying talent are everywhere, knocking off canal scenes, lurid sunsets, gondolas and gondoliers and a hundred versions of the Bridge of Sighs. These artists congregate en masse at the Giardini ex Reali and along the Riva degli Schiavoni, where they exhibit their finished work and sketch out the work on progress. Most use vividly bright oils as a medium, though a few go for charcoal or watercolour, and will happily run up a special commission. Many of the subjects are pure pastiche, including canals that don't exist and buildings in the wrong place, but they're only following in a great Venetian tradition—Canaletto was guilty of the very same offence.

On Set

Venice is one of the world's great movie locations, and the city has played starring and cameo roles in a string of films of varying artistic merit. It's the atmosphere, both voluptuous and sinister, that shines in Nicolas Roeg's 1973 adaptation of Daphne du Maurier's Don't Look Now, while David Lean's 1955 Summertime, starring Katharine Hepburn, captures the romance of Venice, and Visconti's Death in Venice its air of mist-laden nostalgia. But, above all, Venice sparkles in a costume drama, whether it's The Wings of the Dove, with Helena Bonham Carter making yet another corseted appearance, the decadent Comfort of Strangers, directed by Paul Schrader, or 2005's Casanova, the tale of the great lover, with Venice wonderfully restored to its 18th-century appearance and Heath Ledger, Sienna Miller and Jeremy Irons adding the vital touch of star quality.

Saving Venice

The catastrophic floods of 1966 drew the world's spotlight on the perilous state of Venice and her treasurers and was the impetus for one of the most audacious international conservation projects ever launched—a scheme to save not just a single building, but an entire city. Today, over two dozen international organizations, under the umbrella guidance of UNESCO, work to raise funds for restoration and conservation. Topping the list are the British-based Venice in Peril fund, founded in the immediate aftermath of the 1966 floods as the result of an urgent phone call from the Italian director Franco Zeffirelli, and Save Venice Inc, operating with US money. All these private committees work closely with the Italian government and city authorities; Italy itself has provided over 90 per cent of the money so far expended on the city.

Venetians processing across the pontoon bridge, in celebration of the Festa del Redentore (above)
The red and gold flag of San Marco, an area of the city vital to its festivals (right)
A traditional mask worn during Carnevale (below)

Venice's
Festivals

Once the 18th-century party capital of Europe, Venice still knows how to celebrate in style. There's a year-round procession of big-scale pageantry and fun, much of it aimed firmly at the Venetians themselves—though free-spending foreigners are always welcome. Historically festivals have always been part of city life, used by the powers-that-be in the great days of the Republic to bolster the power and prestige of the State, celebrate the feast days of local saints, give thanks for plague deliverances, and allow the citizenry to let off steam. Unsurprisingly, the feasts still dearest to the natives' hearts are those associated with water, which range from the superb Grand Canal pageantry of the Regata Storica and its accompanying races, to the chaotic fun of the Vogalonga (Long Row). Culture gets a good look-in during the summer and autumn, when the internationally high-profile Biennale and the Film Festival bring in the artistic world's movers, shakers and beautiful people, while winter brings the start of the opera season and music in churches across the city. Things really get going in late winter, when Carnevale draws costumed and masked revellers from all over the world to pose against the magnificent backdrop of Venice itself. On a lower key, the year's rhythm is punctuated by more Venetian events—local saint's days, the city marathon, which crosses the lagoon and ends at the Riva degli Schiavoni, and open-air film events and children's traditional festivities.

The Maritime Celebrations

The first Sunday after Ascension sees the Vogalonga, the Long Row, a 33km (20.5-mile) row from St. Mark's Basin through the lagoon and back via the Canale di Cannaregio and the Grand Canal. Founded to encourage Venetian-style rowing—standing—the event now attracts entries from all over Europe and great effort goes into decorating some of the boats. The best place to watch is in Cannaregio, where the boats re-enter the bottle-neck canal accompanied by cheering crowds. The Regata Storica in September is a far grander event, with a spectacular procession of ornate boats, rowed by costumed oarsmen, down the Grand Canal. Venetians love the races that follow, a series of four events for different boats that finishes at the Volta, the big curve on the Grand Canal at Ca' Foscari, where the prize-giving takes place.

The Marriage of Venice to the Sea (left and below)

Gold-leafing a Carnevale mask (above); a sailing regatta on Venice's lagoon (below)

Extravagant costumes on display (below)

The Plague Festivals

In 1576, Venice celebrated deliverance from a major plague outbreak with the construction of the church of Il Redentore (The Redeemer). Ever since, the third week of July sees the construction of a pontoon bridge across the Giudecca Canal to link the church with the main city, across which people process in the run-up to the Saturday celebrations. During the afternoon hundreds of boats, laden with people, mass on the water to picnic and party while awaiting the firework finale. Another pontoon bridge goes up in November, this time across the Grand Canal to the church of the Salute, built after the 1631 plague. On 21 July, the Patriarch, the Cardinal of Venice, crosses the bridge from the Salute and processes to San Marco. People flock to the church to buy candles and enjoy the goodies sold at the stalls en route.

Carnevale

Carnevale officially starts from 10 days before *martedi grasso* (Shrove Tuesday), so exact dates depend on when Easter falls. Well before the opening, traditional carnival goods appear in *pasticcerie*, such as *fritelle*, a fried spiced or cream-filled doughnut. The first Saturday sees a masked procession and party in the Piazza San Marco, followed the next day by the highlight of the first week, the *volo dell'angelo* (flight of the Angel), when a female acrobat swoops down a wire from the top of the Campanile to the Piazza below. *Giovedi grasso* (Thursday) sees the competition for the best costume, Friday a masked open-air ball in the Piazza, and Saturday a masked gondola procession along the Grand Canal. Carnevale culminates on Shrove Tuesday with clowns, acrobats and fireworks in the Piazza, and celebrations, parties and entertainment all over the city.

Biennale and Film Festival

The Biennale D'Arte Contemporanea was established in 1895 to showcase contemporary art, and now alternates with the Biennale d'Architettura Contemporanea, highlighting modern architecture, held in even-numbered years. Both attract visitors and exhibitors from all over the world, who showcase their work in the Giardini, and in the Arsenale buildings. The Biennale runs concurrently with the Mostra Internazionale D'Arte Cinematografica, better known as the Venice Film Festival, held on the Lido. This major event runs for two weeks, showing films in three venues, the main one being the Palazzo del Cinema, and awarding a prestigious prize. In recent years, it's worked hard to attract the big-name stars, moving away from its art-house image, though the prizes still go to the non-commercial, indie offerings.

Out and About

Two events provide the counterbalance to a series of festivals that are heavy on tradition and culture; Su e Zo per I Ponti (Up and Down the Bridges) and the Venice Marathon. Su e Zo originated over 20 years ago as an attempt to raise awareness of Venice, and consists of navigating your way through the city by means of a map and a list of checkpoints to tick off. There's a slew of opportunities for eating and drinking, both in the city's *bacari*, and at temporary official watering holes along the way—after the sixth refreshment stop, finishing the course tends to lose its importance. The October Marathon is a different story. This 42km 195m (26.2-mile) run starts on *terra firma* on the Riviera del Brenta, with runners crossing the lagoon via the Ponte della Libertà, running through the city to cross the Grand Canal on a pontoon bridge and finishing on the Riva dei Sette Martiri.

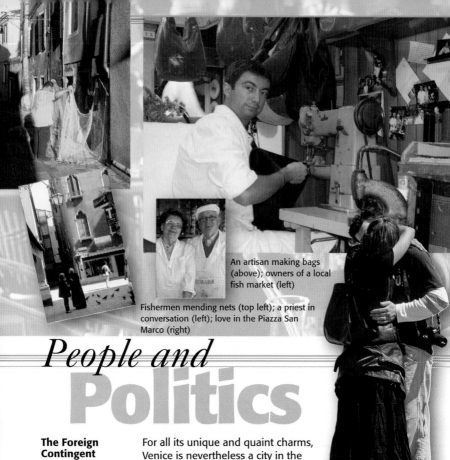

An artisan making bags (above); owners of a local fish market (left)

Fishermen mending nets (top left); a priest in conversation (left); love in the Piazza San Marco (right)

People and
Politics

The Foreign Contingent

Venice has a large, and diverse, foreign population. Numerically high on the list are the academics, writers, researchers and students immersed in studying the city's past and preserving Venice for the future, but there's an increasing number of foreigners who are prepared to pay highly for a holiday home. Demand for property is high, but it's a double-edged sword; foreigners have the desire, and money, to live in, and thus preserve, old buildings, but their homes are often empty for months on end and rising prices prevent those younger Venetians who do want to stay in the city from buying. Property on the Grand Canal or in smart Dorsoduro will fetch anything up to €1.5 million plus, and even working-class Castello has seen dramatic increases.

For all its unique and quaint charms, Venice is nevertheless a city in the modern world, and there's a determination to make a mark and to hold its own against the vibrant economies of the prosperous towns of the Veneto. This is a decidedly left-leaning city in a region that's increasingly conservative, and its dynamic mayor, Paolo Costa, used this attitude to full advantage when he was the moving force behind a highly publicized letter, signed by mayors from all over the world, that urged President George Bush to change his stance on the Kyoto Treaty. In the run-up to the 2004 Iraq War, Venetians were outspoken in their criticism of British and American policy, an attitude that was perhaps a legacy of the city's Centro Pace (Peace Centre), founded by the city council in 1983 and now including over 35 member organizations. Living in a treasure house that attracts over 12 million visitors annually has brought a tolerance at grass-roots level to the Venetian character—quite an achievement when its citizens have to run their lives constantly impeded by hordes of spellbound tourists. This is helped by the recognition of the part played by the numerous international organizations working to preserve the city, who pump money into restoration projects. Venice has been welcoming foreigners for centuries, and lessons continue to be learnt, with an increasing effort by the council, businesses and cultural associations to deal with the impact of the vast numbers of day-trippers by promoting the city as a vibrant cultural centre, rather than a historic theme park.

Stopping for a chat (left); visitors at the Peggy Guggenheim Collection (top left); Communist party HQ (above); a political rally (top right); Paolo Costa (right)

A Small-town City

Tourists may travel thousands of miles to marvel at Venice, but its inhabitants are firmly wedded to their own home patch, their *sestiere*. There are still plenty of Venetians who rarely get as far as St Mark's Square and whose lives are focused on their own *campo* and *calli*. Living in a carless society, where everyone walks or takes a boat, brings a unique sense of community. Locals shop locally, bump into friends regularly and nurture a network of local concerns, bringing a marvellously village-like feeling to the city. Venice is remarkably safe and, give or take a pickpocket or two, crime rates are low; children can play and walk to school unattended and the streets are safe at night. Provincial it may be, but provincialism has its charms.

Failing the Test

They say gondoliers are born not made and it certainly helps to be both Venetian and male. In October 2004, Alexandra Hai, a would-be gondolier, originally from Hamburg, failed the basic gondolier exam for the third time. She had moved to Venice ten years previously, found work on the *vaporetti* with ACTV, and spent years learning how to row a gondola. After her first failure, in 1996, she won an appeal on the ground there were no women on the examining board—since then there have been two. To no avail, for her performance on the 800m (2,625ft) test course on the Rio del Vin, unfamiliar territory to her, was less than perfect and Alexandra abandoned her dream, with a lingering suspicion that her sex and her foreign status had more than a little to do with her failure.

The CVN

Venice's biggest political hot potato is solving the ongoing problem of simply staying afloat. This means not only preventing further water damage within the city, but also safeguarding the lagoon environment, and the job is the responsibility of the Consorzio Venezia Nuovo. This body is funded by the Ministry of Public Works and the Venetian Water Authority and it's constituted so it can plan, organize and manage operations from start to finish. Its biggest initiative is the MoSE project, but it's also behind the funding and construction of higher-level canalside *fondamente*, silt dredging, reinforcing 46km (28.5 miles) of sea walls and ruling on the transit of big oil tankers through the lagoon. Some of its decisions have been contentious, but, as work on sea defences progresses, the benefits are starting to be seen.

Paolo Costa

Mayor Paolo Costa, who led the administration from 2000 to 2005, was born, educated and worked in Venice. As a rising star, his path then led him away from the city and its university, where he was professor, to spells overseas before entering politics. He was a Minister in the government from 1996 to 1998, and was elected to the European Parliament in 1999, combining this with serving on the city council back home. He was elected mayor of Venice in 2000, and it's the combination of a passionate love for his native city and experience in high places that has made him one of the smartest cookies in Italy's local government scene. Not all Venetians love him, and he's certainly stirred up the conservationists, but no one denies his desire to breathe new life into his city, and it remains to be seen whether Massimo Cacciari, his successor, follows in his footsteps.

Performers at the Biennale festival (left); Marco Polo airport (above left); a cruise ship at the Stazione Marittima (above right); visitors at San Marco (below)

The Future of
Venice

Venetians are nothing if not determined—the mere existence of the lagoon city is proof of that. The problems are immense, but Venice has succeeded in selling itself as the property of the whole world, and its millions of admirers feel they have a stake in its future. Far-sighted planning and the desire for change into a cultural centre on a 21st-century scale may well provide yet another makeover in the city's long history. Venetians are well aware they have to help themselves but know, too, they can count on the world's support to look to the future on a foundation of a glorious past. The authorities are finally addressing the problem of depopulation and excess visitors, though global warming remains the major threat. Even here, a strong recognition that action is needed may have emerged in the nick of time.

Venice featured heavily in *The Wings of the Dove*

Sublagunare—a Metro for Venice

Mayor Paolo Costa's vision of the future includes the *sublagunare*, an underground railway running deep beneath the lagoon that will link the city to the mainland, and thus, he hopes, create jobs and encourage people to continue to live in the city. The line would start near the airport and run for 8km (5 miles), via the island of Murano, to a terminus at the Arsenale on the north side of Venice. The single line, with passing places in stations, would have trains running on rubber to reduce harmful vibrations and tunnels would lead out to the stations, themselves situated 45m (147ft) from the canal sides. Opinions of the project are mixed, with critics pointing out that tourists will always want to arrive by boat in Venice.

City of the Arts

Venice's future may well lie as a big-time player in the world cultural league. First steps to realizing this came in 1999 when the Biennale enlarged its scope to include not only the visual arts, architecture and film, but the performing arts as well, with international big names in theatre, music and dance visiting the city. If plans for the further revamp of the Arsenale, Venice's historic shipyards, go ahead, the area will become a huge cultural and exhibition space; parts are already used during the Biennale. Across St. Mark's Basin, the Fondazione Cini, on the island of San Giorgio Maggiore, is continuing to enlarge its schedule of cultural conferences, and has restored and reopened the beautiful open-air Teatro Verde as a summer performance venue.

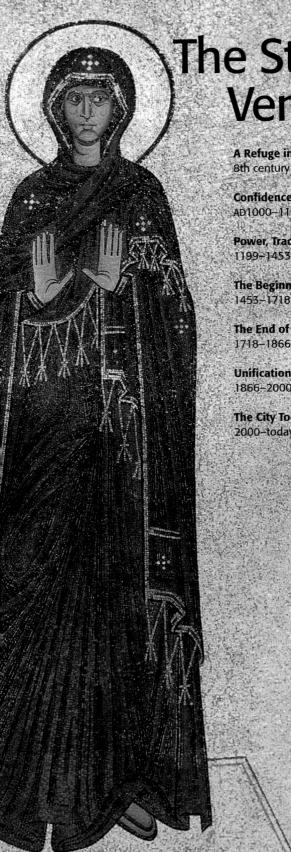

The Story of Venice

A Refuge in the Waters

Angelo Participazio

In 810 Pepin the Frank, son of Charlemagne, invaded Lombardy and swept through the mainland towns to besiege the lagoon communities, including Malamocco, the Venetians' main settlement. Things looked bad until a great leader, Angelo Participazio, emerged. He abandoned Malamocco, moving the capital to the Riva Alto, a settlement in the heart of the lagoon. From here, he sent his fleet first to head towards the Frankish ships massed outside the lagoon, then to feign terror and retreat into the shallow waters around the Rialto. The Franks, scenting cowardice, followed, only to run aground on the myriad sandbanks, allowing the Venetians to pick them off at their leisure and secure the lagoon. Angelo was elected doge, and it was during his reign that work started on the Doge's Palace and the lagoon communities were first formally called Venetia.

Venice, according to legend, was founded at midday on Friday 25 March, 421; historical reality is less exact. As early as the 8th century BC there was some settlement of the lagoon by the Venetii and Euganei tribes from the adjoining mainland, and by 250BC Rome had conquered northeast Italy and founded important colonies at Padua, Verona and Aquileia. These thriving cities viewed the muddy islets of the lagoon as a place apart, attractive only for short fishing and hunting forays. Attitudes changed around 375, when the barbarian Huns and Visigoths swept south to threaten the rich cities of the Veneto. The terrified inhabitants fled to the lagoon, establishing settlements on the marshy islands, which were to become a lagoon duchy called Venetia. Vital to this was the stabilization of the existing land to make building possible, the control of the rivers, which threatened to silt up the navigable channels, and the regulation of the tides to safeguard the settlements. Once this equilibrium of the lagoon waters was achieved, the embryonic state could thrive while the rest of Europe entered its darkest age. Politically and commercially, the early Venetians looked east to the more stable Byzantine Empire, gradually attaining sufficient autonomy to elect their first duke, or doge, in 697. The ninth century saw the construction of St. Mark's Basilica and the Doge's Palace, funded by a booming economy based on trade and shipping. By the start of the 11th century Venice, standing at the crossroads between East and West, was established as a major mercantile power with a growing empire.

8th century BC

Attila, leader of the Huns (top); an intricate mosaic in Basilica di San Marco (left); the four arches from Verona's Arena date from the 1st century (right)

The Lions of Venice

The lion is the symbol of St. Mark and, like the saint, has become inextricably associated with Venice itself. St. Mark's lion still appears on the city's flag, on all official documents, on billboards and souvenir shops, and, in early times, was carved on the prows of warships; lions still guard the gates of the Arsenale. The Venetian lion, often winged, frequently appears with his paw on an open book—St. Mark's Gospel—engraved with the words 'Pax tibi, Marce' (Peace be with you, Mark). There are hundreds of stone lions throughout the city, including 75 alone on the main entrance, the Porta della Carta, to the Palazzo Ducale. Live lions were sometimes kept in the city gardens and their cubs fed at the expense of the state.

A Premier League Saint

The rising star of 9th-century Venice needed a first-class saint to rival Rome's great patron, St. Peter the Apostle. The Venetians chose St. Mark the Evangelist, whose remains lay in Alexandria in Egypt. To bolster the claim, stories were told of a visit to the lagoon by St. Mark and St. Paul, where they beheld a vision of Jesus appearing to Mark and saying 'Pax tibi Marcus Evangelista meus' (peace be to you Mark, my evangelist). Despite this, the Christians of Alexandria were unwilling to give up St. Mark, so smuggling was the only answer. In 828, two merchants sailed to Egypt, seized St. Mark's body and, burying it under a cargo of pork to stop the Muslims and Jews searching too closely, brought the saint to his new home.

St. Theodore and the Crocodile

Venice's first patron, St. Theodore, still occupies his perch on a column in the Piazzetta. He was born in Asia Minor, converted to Christianity, and became a brave soldier in the Roman army. Stationed in a remote mountain town in Persia, he slew a demon-possessed dragon with a bad habit of devouring local children, and generally annoyed his pagan superiors with his piety and good works. In 313 he was beheaded, canonized as a martyr and buried in Egypt. From here, his remains were shipped to southern Italy, where he came to the attention of the Venetians, who adopted him as their patron, using the dragon, now in the guise of a crocodile, as his symbol. St. Theodore's position was short-lived; with the rise of Venetian power the city dumped him in lieu of a higher-profile saint.

A golden lion of St. Mark on the exterior of San Marco (left); the Doge on his way to espouse the sea (right)

Marriage to the Sea

The lagoon and Adriatic were vital to the city's wealth and safety, and Venice's reliance on the sea was first celebrated in 997 in a symbolic ceremony of marriage, which was enacted annually on Ascension Day until the fall of the Republic. The doge proceeded in the magnificent state barge called the *Bucintoro*, after Alexander the Great's horse, Bucephalus, to the Porto di Lido, the channel onto the open sea, where he threw a gold ring into the waters with the words 'I wed thee, oh Sea, in sign of perpetual dominion', a clear reminder to other nations of Venice's domination of the Adriatic. Hymns were sung before the procession returned to the Rialto for celebrations, leaving the spectators free to dive in and recover the ring, a case of finders, keepers.

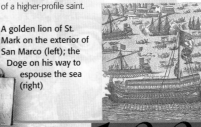

St. Theodore and his crocodile still survey Venice from a column in the Piazzetta (right)

Two of the Palazzo Ducale's Four Moors, or tetrarchs, from the 4th century (left)

Confidence and
Expansion

With its growing merchant power, Venice was ready for expansion. The century started well with the defeat of the Adriatic pirates by Doge Pietro Orseolo in 1000, a victory that brought much of Dalmatia, the northeastern coast of the Adriatic, under Venetian control. Further south, the Normans still held sway, and looked increasingly aggressively towards the failing Byzantine Empire. In 1081, the Byzantine emperor appealed to Venice for help, and Venetian ships played a key role in the ensuing naval battles. Venice triumphed, establishing itself as the protector of the Empire, and securing the Adriatic shipping lines and advantageous trading rights with Byzantium, enshrined in the Golden Bull of 1082, a charter of alliance between Venice and the Byzantine emperor. Further opportunities for trade and territorial expansion came with the proclamation in 1095 of the First Crusade, a pan-Christian expedition to free the Holy Land from Muslim occupation. The Venetians provided transport ships and finance, neatly reaping a profit while appearing piously to support this Christian enterprise, and extending the city's influence in the Aegean and Black Sea. Back home, the city flourished. In 1171, the six *sestieri*, the wards into which Venice is divided, were established. Fire destroyed the 9th-century Basilica di San Marco, but work started on a new structure, which was inaugurated in 1094. Churches such as San Giacomo al Rialto and San Nicolò dei Mendicoli were built, and the first grand *palazzi* went up around the growing commercial centre of the Rialto.

The Peace of Venice

In 1177, Venice achieved a major diplomatic coup when it persuaded the warring Pope Alexander III and the Holy Roman Emperor Frederick Barbarossa to meet in Venice. Worn out and almost bankrupt by years of struggle, the two made peace in Venice. It was the end of Frederick's attempt to establish his supremacy over the Pope, and he asked for forgiveness and received absolution at San Marco. Alexander was so delighted with his reception he gave Doge Zani a golden rose and a golden ring, which was used in the ceremony of the Marriage to the Sea.

AD 1000

Mosaics on the cupolas of Basilica di San Marco were created, in part, by Byzantine craftsmen (top left); Barbarossa (above)

The cupolas of San Marco (below); a Medieval Arabian perfumier at work (right)

Pope Alexander III presents the sword of office to Doge Ziani (right)

Ships and Shipbuilding

Venice's mastery of ship-building began early, with craftsmen being sent abroad to Dalmatia and Istria to learn construction techniques in the 7th century. By 1104 the Arsenale, the city's shipyards, were functioning initially as an arms and repair depot, with private yards responsible for the actual building. In emergencies workers were requisitioned by the doge, and shipbuilding became increasingly focused in one place. Teams of men, the *arsenalotti*, composed of carpenters, sawyers, caulkers and apprentices, worked together under a foreman, and could build up to six large galleys every two years. The merchant galleys were fast and light. They sailed in convoy and specialized in transporting valuable cargoes of spices, silks, furs, gold, ivory and amber.

First Among Equals

The first doges were presented to the people, in theory their electors, as *primus inter pares*, first among equals. In practise, early doges were despotic and thus prone to meet calamitous ends—of the 50 holding office up to 1172, 20 were exiled, murdered or deposed. In 1044 laws were drawn up to limit their power and they were barred from naming their successors. The Senate, a distinct council, evolved to supervise the doge's activities, and a complex electoral system was established. The doges ruled for life, leading to repeated elections of elderly men who, it was felt, would have less time to build up their own power. The average election age was 72, and by about 1200 the role of the doge was similar to that of a modern president.

The *Maggior Consiglio*

In 1172 power passed from the doge to the *Maggior Consiglio*, the Great Council, founded by 35 members of Venice's leading patrician families. The council was responsible for legislation, and, by 1297 had grown to number over 500, prompting the *Serrata del Maggior Consiglio* (the Closing of the Great Council), which limited membership to those on the original list of 500. This evolved in 1315 into the *Libro d'Oro*, the Golden Book, a closed register of noble families, from whose ranks were drawn council members and officers of state. From these names, too, the *Senato* and *Collegio* members were drawn, augmented by provincial and religious representatives. These two bodies remained virtually unaltered for more than 500 years.

The Art of Mosaic

The glowing mosaic decoration of San Marco is a legacy of Byzantium, where this Greco-Roman skill continued throughout the Dark Ages. Mosaics are designed to cover large surfaces like a skin, and are composed of thousands of tiny pieces of tinted glass, fitted together to form a picture. They are created by first plastering the area to be covered, then tracing the design in fine detail on this surface. Each day, a layer of cement is applied and the *tesserae*, glass pieces, embedded in it. Glass of all hues is used, including gold and silver, made by applying the metals in leaf form to transparent glass, then fusing them with an over layer. The glass shards are deliberately set at different angles so the light will be refracted in varying ways.

The gondola repair yard at San Trovaso (left)

The main cupola at San Marco depicts the Ascension (right)

1199

Mosaic detail in the cathedral of Santa Maria Assunta (below and right)

Power, Trade and Wealth

In 1199 the Fourth Crusade was called, and by 1202 Crusaders from all over Europe were mustering in Venice to requisition ships and supplies, for which they were unable to pay in full. This provided Venice with the opportunity to persuade the Crusaders to let Venice both lead the expedition and make a detour to Constantinople, Christian capital of the Eastern Empire. Led by Doge Enrico Dandolo, the Crusaders attacked Constantinople in 1204, looted and sacked the city and carved up the Empire, Venice keeping every strategic port and island and gaining complete domination of the eastern Mediterranean trade routes. Sixty years later, aided by Genoa, the Byzantine emperor evicted the Venetians from Constantinople, leading to a Venetian-Genoese conflict that was finally resolved in 1381 with a decisive Venetian victory at the Battle of Chioggia. This heralded an era of unrivalled wealth and expansion, hardly dented by the 1348 Black Death, which left two thirds of the city's population dead. It was during the 14th and 15th centuries that Venice assumed the architectural appearance it has today, with a reputation as the richest city in Christendom. At this time, too, the state increased its hold over the citizens, with measures to ensure that power remained in the hands of the elite and the institution of the Council of Ten, an all-powerful, secret commission whose spies were everywhere. It was a golden age, but for the blow inflicted in 1453, when Constantinople, the great trade centre, fell to the Turks and became a Muslim city.

1199

Trade brought a range of goods to the city, such as spices (top left); Enrico Dandolo (1107–1205, right)

Doge Enrico Dandolo

Enrico Dandolo was nearing 90 and practically blind when the Crusaders approached him for help with the Fourth Crusade. He drove a hard bargain; for 85,000 silver marks he agreed to ship 33,500 men and their equipment to the Holy Land and to supply Venetian soldiers and warships for the expedition, with the proviso that he would lead the force. The Crusaders had not the money to pay, and found themselves blocked in the lagoon until they agreed to attack some ports on the Dalmatian coast and then detour to the Christian city of Constantinople. Dandolo himself led the attack, and encouraged the troops to plunder and destroy, thus making Venice 'Lords and Masters of a Quarter and a Half-quarter of the Roman Empire'.

A map of Venetian lands (below); the four bronze horses of San Marco (bottom)

Loading supplies in Venice before the Fourth Crusade

Marco Polo

In 1269 Marco Polo, a member of a family of merchant adventurers, left Venice to travel overland to Asia in pursuit of trade—sugar, spice, silk and cotton. Travelling along the Silk Road, he reached the court of the great Kublai Khan, ruler of the Mongol Empire, in 1274, and remained in China for 17 years, serving the Khan as governor and emissary. He was a great favourite, amply rewarded with money and precious jewels. These accompanied him home in 1292, via a route that took him south to Sumatra and Sri Lanka. He arrived, unrecognized, back in Venice in 1295, dictating his memoirs of 'a million wonders' while languishing in jail as a prisoner of war of the Genoese, and dying in 1324. His house, in the aptly named Corta Seconda del Milion, is still marked by a plaque.

Marco Polo
(1254–1324)

Black Death

The first major outbreak of plague, in the shape of the Black Death, hit Venice in 1348. The disease originated in Mongolia and may have spread to Europe along the trade routes, or, as is more likely, was carried back by Genoese sailors. Called the Black Death because of the skin discolouration and black buboes that appeared in the groin, the plague, fatal in 99 per cent of all cases, took 37 days to incubate and kill. In Venice, 60 per cent of the population died over the course of 18 months, with deaths running at 500 to 600 a day at the height of the epidemic. Victims were buried on the now vanished island of San Marco in Boccalama. The Venetians learned a lot from this first epidemic and later isolated incoming ships and established quarantine islands in the lagoon.

The Tiepolo Conspiracy

Following the closure of the Maggior Consiglio in 1297, many of the mercantile class were indignant to have missed their chance to participate in government. None more so than Baiamonte Tiepolo, who, in 1310, banded together with two conspirators to lead a revolt. The timing went wrong, his associates were captured, and Tiepolo was left marching through the main shopping street with a train of rebels. As they progressed, legend tells that an old woman, leaning from her window, dislodged a stone, which hit Tiepolo's standard-bearer on the head. Panic ensued, Tiepolo's troops fled and the rebellion failed. Tiepolo was sent into exile and his *palazzo* razed, and fear of a future conspiracy led to the establishment of the Council of Ten.

The Council of Ten

Venice's most feared and powerful institution, the Council of Ten, was founded in 1310 to deal with insurrection and conspiracy. It had virtually unlimited powers, running the Inquisition, controlling the police and running a network of spies. These were helped by ordinary citizens who were encouraged to denounce each other through anonymous letters, posted in the lion's head boxes that are still scattered about the city. No one was beyond the Council's reach, not even the Doge. In 1355 Doge Marin Falier was executed following an attempt to increase his powers and establish his family as hereditary leaders, the last attempt to attack the principle of rule by the Senate and Councils. In the series of dogal portraits in the Hall of the Maggior Consiglio, Falier is conspicuously absent, his place forever shrouded in a black cloth, with no likeness beneath.

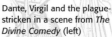

Dante, Virgil and the plague-stricken in a scene from *The Divine Comedy* (left)

1453

The Doge Marin Falier (1274–1355, left); boxes used for citizens' denunciations were disguised with grotesque heads (below)

DENONTIE SECRETE
NTRO CHI OCCVLTER
RATIE ET OFFICII
O COLLVDERA PER
NASCONDER LA VERA

The Beginning of the End

In 1544 Venice signed a peace treaty with Francesco Sforza of Milan, a move that marked the end of the Republic's annexation of territory in mainland Italy, begun in the 15th century. Venice now held much of the modern Veneto region, Udine and Friuli, Verona and its hinterland. This inland empire was to remain intact for nearly 300 years and did something to alleviate the gradual loss of overseas political and trading power. The first blow abroad had come in 1453 with the fall of Constantinople, causing the loss of Venice's crucial trading privileges, and in 1489 Vasco da Gama reached Calcutta by sea, putting an end to the Republic's monopoly of far Eastern trade. Such was the city's accumulated wealth that the economic effects of these events were at first barely felt, and the 16th century saw an explosion of the decorative and performing arts within the city. But these riches fuelled dislike among the other European powers and the early 16th century was a story of warfare. By mid-century, mutual fear of the Ottomans united the European powers, led by Venice, and the Turks' advance was temporarily halted by their naval defeat at the Battle of Lepanto in 1571. This proved to be a hollow victory, swiftly followed by the secession of all the Venetian Mediterranean possessions to the Turks. The 17th century saw a succession of attempts to regain territory and solve the growing economic and commercial crisis, but the trend was towards steady decline, and by 1718 Venice was virtually bankrupt and its government inert.

1453

Statue of Veronese in San Sebastiano (top); Caterina Cornaro (right)

Caterina Cornaro, Queen of Cyprus

Caterina Cornaro, a pawn in the hands of the Senate, was a member of the Corner family, a powerful clan with strong interests in Cyprus. With the Turks pressing hard in the eastern Mediterranean, the island was seen as a strategically vital Venetian possession and its loyalty was bolstered by the marriage of Caterina to the King of Cyprus in 1472. Only a year later he died and she was forced to surrender the island first to Venetian control, and then to the doge, abdicating in 1489. Caterina was given a hypocritically triumphant welcome back in Venice and then presented with the lordship of the town of Ásolo, where she held a cultured and sophisticated court until her death in 1510.

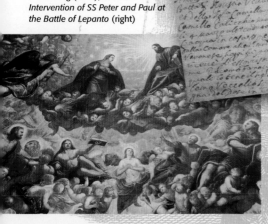

Paradise by Tintoretto in the Palazzo Ducale (below); a record of Vivaldi's christening (inset); *The Miraculous Intervention of SS Peter and Paul at the Battle of Lepanto* (right)

Marcantonio Bragadino

Bragadino was a Venetian general captured by the Turks in Cyprus in 1571. Besieged for 11 months, he surrendered under the promise of safe passage for him and his men. Instead, the Turks slaughtered his men and then cut off Bragadino's nose and ears, before thrice withholding execution at the last moment. He was then paraded, laden with earth, around the Turkish camp, being forced to kiss the ground each time he passed the Pasha's tent, a regime only interrupted by hours spent suspended from the yards of a ship. He was finally chained to a stake and slowly skinned alive, the Turks stuffing his skin with straw and sending it back to Venice. Bragadino's skin is still preserved in an urn on his monument in the church of Santi Giovanni e Paolo.

Doge Giovanni Mocenigo (1478–85)

The Battle of Lepanto

Virtually unknown until 1300, by the 16th century the Ottoman Turks were a constant threat, and in 1570 an alliance of Venice, Spain and the Papal Sates mustered a huge fleet of 208 war galleys to sail against them to avenge previous defeats. Under the command of John of Austria, half-brother to Philip II of Spain, the fleet sailed to the Gulf of Corinth and encountered the Turkish force off Lepanto on 7 October 1571. It was the largest naval battle ever fought in the Mediterranean and a resounding victory for Venice and her allies, with 117 galleys captured. Back home, the news was greeted with an orgy of self-congratulation, but it was a shallow victory and the Turks remained as strong as ever. In 1573 Cyprus was handed to the Turks, and Crete, the final Venetian possession, fell in 1669.

Life on the Mainland

Land on the newly acquired Venetian *terra firma* rapidly became a must-have for the aristocracy during the 16th century. Rents and farming filled the coffers and the countryside was a welcome escape from the city. Access from Venice to the cool hills was easy along the Brenta, and it was in the hinterland of this river that many families built their summer villas. The architect of choice was Palladio, who designed a staggering variety of classically influenced summer palaces in the provinces of Vicenza, Padua and Treviso. Best-known are the Villa Malcontenta, modeled on a Greek temple and the inspiration for thousands of other buildings, the beautifully set Villa Barbaro, inspired by traditional Veneto farm buildings, and the Villa Rotonda, a pleasure palace built for a retired cleric.

The Venetian Renaissance

Despite a waning economy, the 16th and 17th centuries saw an explosion of art, architecture and music in Venice. The Renaissance started later here than in Tuscany, with the first clutch of big-name painters—the Bellinis, Cima da Conegliano and Carpaccio—active from the mid-15th century. They laid the foundations for the superstars of the 16th century; Giorgione, Titian, Tintoretto and Veronese, who worked all over the city, their paintings remaining in their original homes to this day. On the architectural front, Venice turned its back on its own unique Veneto-Gothic style and embraced classical ideals. The buildings designed by Palladio, Sanmicheli, Sansovino and Scamozzi illustrate this new style, and were, and still are, the perfect backdrop for the music of the Gabriellis and Venice's lauded composer, Antonio Vivaldi.

Madonna with Saints by Giovanni Bellini, in the church of San Zaccaria, is a masterpiece of perspective

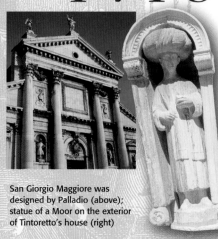

San Giorgio Maggiore was designed by Palladio (above); statue of a Moor on the exterior of Tintoretto's house (right)

The End of the Republic

By 1718 the writing was on the wall for Venice as a political power. The city was still rich, but the funds were in the hands of patrician families rather than the state, and it was the aristocracy who fuelled Venice's reputation as the party capital of Europe. This was the era of hedonistic living, when Carnevale ran for months at a time, playboys, embodied by that great lover, Casanova, roamed the streets, and fortunes were squandered in the city's gambling houses. The state, meanwhile, turned its last efforts against the perpetual threat of seas and tides, building the vast *murazzi* to protect the lagoon against the Adriatic tides. By the 1790s Venice was bankrupt and politically stagnant. When Napoleon invaded in 1797, there was no money left; the last doge, Lodovico Manin, was deposed and the once mighty Senate voted itself out of existence. Between 1797 and 1815, Venice was first Austrian, then French, then, with the fall of Napoleon, Austrian again. In 1848, two years after the construction of the railway bridge linking Venice to the mainland, there was a brief resurgence of the old independent spirit, when a lawyer, Daniele Manin—no relation to the last doge— led a revolt against the occupying Austrians. An independent republican government was set up which held the city in a state of siege for five heroic months. The uprising failed, and the Austrians renewed their grip on what was an increasingly provincial city. In 1866, the Austrians, badly weakened by defeats by the Prussians elsewhere in Europe, handed over the city of Venice to the newly formed united Italian State.

1718

Napoleon was eager for Venice's wealth (top); part of the sea walls (right)

Murazzi (the Sea Walls)

The construction of the great *murazzi*, sea walls, on the barrier island of Pellestrina was the last great engineering work undertaken by the Republic. The maintenance of the water level in the lagoon had been a Venetian preoccupation since the city's foundation, and a special government department, the Magistrati alle Acque, was responsible for lagoon management. Sandy, low-lying Pellestrina had long been a weak link in the lagoon's defences and these great ramparts, 14m (46ft) wide and rising to 4.5m (14.75ft) above the mean tide level, were the final solution. Beautifully built of Istrian stone, they were erected between 1744 and 1782. They still stand, a monument to the everlasting struggle to keep the sea out and the city protected.

Cover of a play about Casanova (left); Venetian dramatist Goldoni (above)

Giacomo Casanova

Casanova, history's most noted libertine, was born in Venice in 1725, a man whose aim, as he wrote in his memoirs, was 'always to indulge my senses; I never knew anything of greater importance'. His life story is a monument to this philosophy, encompassing constant sexual adventures, gambling, drunkenness and other bad behaviour, which led, in 1755, to accusations of witchcraft and imprisonment in the Palazzo Ducale. From here he escaped by climbing through a hole in the ceiling and over the rooftops to emerge in the Piazza looking, in his own words, 'like a man of quality who had been beaten up in a brothel'. The next years were spent in exile, constantly on the move, one step ahead of creditors and enraged husbands. In 1774 he moved back to Venice, working as a government spy, but 10 years later, under threat of a libel suit, fled to Bohemia, where he died 1798.

The Bucintoro returning to the Molo, by Canaletto (below)

The Downside of Pleasure

The great pox, syphilis, had first arrived in the city in 1450, and 18th-century Venice was one of the first states to try and control the disease by mandatory registration of brothels and prostitutes. Young visiting foreigners, as keen on nightlife and bedroom games as art and architecture, could buy a guidebook to the city brothels, and the Rio della Sensa, in Cannaregio, was famed for its daily afternoon procession of gondolas carrying the city's loveliest prostitutes. Prostitutes and courtesans with the disease were quarantined and given the dreaded mercury treatment—which often killed them—but ordinary citizens' behaviour was unchecked and by the 18th century it's estimated that around 20 per cent of Venice's population suffered from syphilis, including that great lover Casanova. A special hospital, the Incurabile, was built on the Zattere for those suffering from the horrific late stage of the disease.

Music was a large part of the Carnevale (right)

Non-stop Party Time

Traditionally a festival held in the run-up to the penance-filled days of Lent, by the 17th and 18th centuries Venetian Carnevale, Carnival, was occupying six months of the year, a non-stop round of parties and gambling, where, safe behind the universally worn masks, aristocrats and common people could mix and indulge in behaviour whose licentiousness was a byword throughout Europe. Elaborate stages were set up in the Piazza for acrobats, tumblers and wrestlers, there was bear baiting in San Polo and bull fighting in Santo Stefano, while dancing and drinking went on around the clock. Small wonder John Evelyn, the diarist, wrote in 1646 '...'tis impossible to recount the universal madnesses of this place during this time of license'.

The Last Doge

In January 1789 Lodovico Manin, a member of a recently ennobled mainland family, was elected as the 120th doge. Rather than interrupt Carnevale, his accession was barely announced by the Senate, though one of the patrician Grand Council, Gradenigo, remarked, 'I have made a Friulian doge; the Republic is dead'. His words were prophetic; in 1797, Napoleon, conqueror of most of Italy and anxious to plunder Venice's wealth, attacked the city and Manin was deposed. He went quietly, removing his doge's cap, the symbol of the thousand-year old Republic, and handing it to his valet with the words, 'Take this, I shall not be needing it again'. He is buried in the church of the Scalzi beneath a slab marked simply 'Cineres Manini' ('The Ashes of Manin').

Daniele Manin led a revolt against the Austrians (above)

1866

The opening of the Ponte dell'Accademia, 1854 (left); paintings by Tiepolo in the church of Sant'Alvise (below)

Unification to the
Millennium

Venice saw its fortunes improve with some economic success in the shape of a revival of shipbuilding in the Arsenale and an upswing in glass production on Murano. The opening of the Suez Canal in 1869 brought renewed trade, and tourist numbers increased steadily, with luxury hotels opening in the city and on the newly fashionable Lido. This modest boom was halted by the outbreak of World War I, during which the Austrians pushed south through the Veneto almost to the borders of the lagoon. Shipbuilding was hard hit due to the proximity to the enemy front, a blow from which it never recovered, and many shipyard workers were reduced to poverty. Against this background, the climate was ripe for the success of Fascism in the 1930s, and government funds financed the development of new industrial initiatives at Porto Marghera on the adjoining mainland. World War II left Venice virtually untouched, but the post-war years saw the mainland industries boom, bringing growing problems from pollution, and causing an exodus from the city as workers for the new factories moved to the mainland; between 1946 and 2000 the population fell from 170,000 to around 58,000. Meanwhile tourism mushroomed, putting a huge strain on the city's infrastructure, as did the increasing problems brought by pollution, the 1966 floods and ever more frequent high tides flooding the city. By the 1990s questions about Venice's future role were high on the agenda, as ever-increasing numbers of international bodies became aware of the need to safeguard this unique city.

The Lagoon Bridges

Venice was first directly linked to the mainland in 1846 when the rail bridge was built across the lagoon and Santa Lucia station was built. Physically, as well as psychologically, the bridge ended Venice's isolation, with easy, fast access to the mainland, and the transportation of goods now simpler. As road transport became increasingly common, it was inevitable that a road link be built, and a 3,657m-long (11,004ft), 222-arched viaduct bridge, the Ponte della Libertà, was constructed and opened in 1932. It was over this bridge that the Allies raced in 1945 to liberate the city; a story has the Allied tanks crossing the flyover to reach the bridge and seeing the Germans retreating on the road beneath.

1866

A bust of Verdi (1813–1901) at the Giardini Biennale (top)

The fashionable Lido of the 1920s (below); a 19th-century image of the lagoon (right); the Pink Floyd concert (bottom right)

The Regina Margherita

In 1881, the first mechanically propelled public transport vessel, a steamship named the *Regina Margherita* (*Queen Margaret*), arrived in Venice. Gondoliers were up in arms, horrified at the competition, but the Venetians soon took the newcomer—reliable and cheap—to their hearts, and the following year a licence was granted to a French company to carry passengers on the Grand Canal. Its eight boats were built in France, sailing right round Italy to Venice, where they soon won the affectionate diminutive of *vaporetti* (little steamers), the name still given to the modern diesel-powered craft. Today, the *vaporetti* are run by ACTV, a company that carries approximately 180 million passengers annually and employs more than 3,000 personnel.

The 1966 Floods

For centuries, Venice was prone to flooding when a combination of seasonal variation in the sea level, low atmospheric pressure and the southerly sirocco wind combined to trap water in the lagoon. Due to changes in the environment of the lagoon, these high waters increased in frequency, but remained largely ignored, throughout the 20th century. On 4 November 1966, at the same time as the disastrous floods in Florence, the city suffered the worst floods it has ever seen. Water flooded the Piazza to a height of 1.2m (4ft) and 100 per cent of the city streets were flooded, with over 5,000 Venetians losing their homes and countless works of art damaged and destroyed. The flood finally forced international and national recognition of the peril facing the city.

Pink Floyd in Venice

In 1989 the Venetian authorities gave permission for rock group Pink Floyd to give a free concert as part of the celebrations for the 15 July Festa del Redentore. It was a terrible mistake. Over 200,000 fans flooded into the city, many of them camping out for two days before the concert in a city that was totally unprepared, lacking even public lavatories and litter disposal for such an influx. During the concert, performed on a pontoon off the Piazzetta, fans climbed on lampposts and the Palazzo Ducale itself, damaging precious 10th-century stonework. When they left, the army had to be called in for a 3-day clean-up, and a 3-year repair to the Palazzo damage totalled nearly $46,000. The city council, faced with the wrath of citizens, art historians and conservationists, resigned en masse.

The Fenice Fire

During the night of 29 January 1996, fire broke out in Venice's beautiful opera house, La Fenice. With the nearest canal, which would have provided water for the fire fighters, closed for dredging, the blaze rapidly took hold, with flames clearly visible from the mainland, six miles away. All that remained by morning was a blackened shell. Over a year later, two electricians were arrested and accused of starting the fire in an attempt to avoid a 50 million lire fine for failing to complete a rewiring job on time. Rumour labelled the pair as fall guys for a more sinister explanation, compounded by a series of court cases over insurance and the rebuilding plan. La Fenice, triumphantly rebuilt, finally reopened for the 2004–2005 season.

English poet Robert Browning (1812–89) died in Venice (left)

Wagner claimed the horn prelude to the third act of *Tristan and Isolde* was inspired by the gondolier's cry (left)

Elizabeth Taylor and Claudia Cardinale at the 1967 Film Festival (left); La Fenice's phoenix (above); Palazzo Ducale in the 1890s (below)

The City Today

In terms of conservation, Venice entered the 21st century with a renewed determination to tackle the environmental problems that had spiralled during the second half of the 20th century, with initiatives launched for safeguarding the lagoon and tackling the ever-growing problem of *acqua alta*. Set against this is an awareness of the toll taken by the 12 million annual visitors, 80 per cent of whom are daytrippers, who contribute virtually nothing economically but impose a heavy load on the city's fragile infrastructure; tour buses and boats are now charged an admission fee. The authorities, too, are committed to strengthening the port facilities, one of the world's largest cruise-ship docks, while expanding the airport complex and providing further parking. Whether the proposed *sublagunare*, the under lagoon rail link, ever makes it past the planning stage remains to be seen, but this exciting project could be the factor that ends the continuing drift by Venetians to mainland living.

The Fourth Bridge

The Grand Canal finally got the go-ahead for a fourth bridge in 2004, when work started on the hot-shot Spanish architect Santiago Calatrava's elegant Istrian stone and glass arch across the canal. Designed to be floodlit, the bridge was conceived as a 'carpet of light that reflects on the expanse of water', a fitting foil to the Canal's other three bridges. However, there were stormy waters ahead. No sooner were the plans made public than disabled groups were up in arms, pointing out that the 80m (262ft) bridge, scheduled to cost the city €5 million, made no provision for disabled access. Calatrava was forced to modify his design, proposing ramps and an elevator running across the outside of the bridge.

Ship Aground

On 11 May 2004, the *Mona Lisa*, a 200m (656ft) German-operated cruise ship, ran aground in thick fog in the waters of St. Mark's Basin, a stone's throw from the Piazza itself. Tugboats swarmed in to rescue the 1,000 passengers, none of whom were hurt, and to tow the vessel off the mud in the narrow channel. Venice's dynamic mayor, Paolo Costa, used the incident to draw attention to the growing concerns about the size and numbers of the cruise ships now sailing to the heart of the city: '…disastrous and unimaginable consequences were avoided, but steps must be taken to eliminate the danger of a ship landing up in St. Mark's Square', suggesting they should anchor further out, near the Lido.

2000–today

Watching the rising waters (top); the busy Rio dei Santi Apostoli in Cannaregio (left); a cruise ship at Piazza San Marco (above); officials trying to avoid the high water (right)

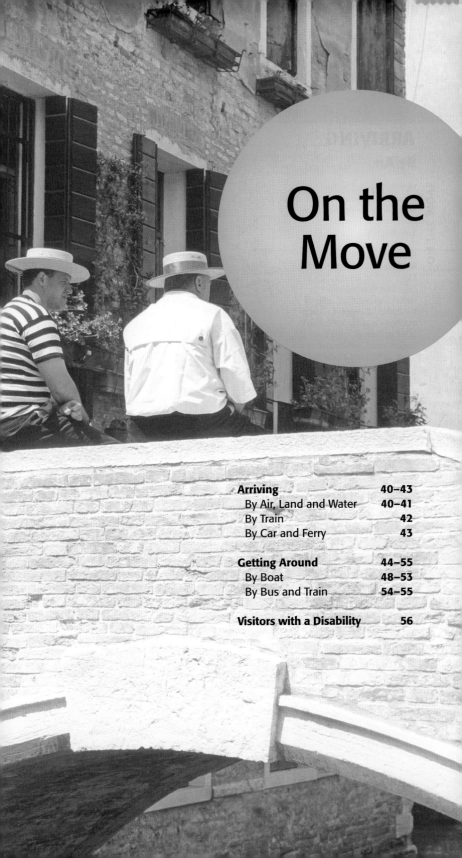

On the Move

ARRIVING

By Air

ON THE MOVE

Venice is served by two airports: the Aeroporto di Venezia Marco Polo and the Aeroporto di Treviso Sant'Angelo.

AEROPORTO DI VENEZIA MARCO POLO (VCE)

Marco Polo, at Tessera, 7km (4 miles) from central Venice by water on the northern edge of the lagoon, underwent a major expansion and modernization in 2002 and is now Italy's third-busiest airport, handling internal Italian traffic, international flights from all over Europe and a daily New York flight.

The ground floor of the single terminal handles arrivals *(arrivi)*, and has cash dispensers *(bancomat)*, a currency exchange desk *(cambio)*, toilets and public telephones. There are car rental facilities, hotel information and reservation desk, and transport, taxi and tourist information desks. A bar serves coffee, drinks and light refreshments, and a news kiosk, Hub, sells newspapers, books, magazines, snacks, drinks and souvenirs.

TRANSFERS FROM THE AIRPORT TO THE CITY

There are two options for getting into Venice: by land, using the route across the causeway to Piazzale Roma, and by water, across the lagoon.

By Land

The land route to Venice is inexpensive and takes between

20 and 40 minutes, depending on traffic. The quickest way is to take a taxi at the rank outside the arrivals area; the journey time is approximately 20 minutes and costs around €27.

Two bus services connect the airport with Piazzale Roma. ATVO runs a fast coach service (blue buses) to and from Piazzale Roma that coincides with most incoming flights. The service starts at 6.06am and, from 10.20am, runs half-hourly until 12.10am. The journey takes 20 to 35 minutes, depending on traffic. Tickets (€3.20) are available from the ATVO desk in the concourse to the left of the exit from the baggage reclaim area, and must be bought before boarding. Buses leave from the stop to the right of the exit from the arrivals area.

ACTV (Azienda Comunale per il Trasporto di Venezia, pronounced AhCheeTayVoo), Venice's public transport company, has a regular public service (white buses) between Marco Polo and Piazzale Roma. Bus No. 5 runs from 4.40am until midnight, with departures half-hourly from 6.10am and a journey time of 25 to 40 minutes. Tickets (€2.20) are

available from the ATVO kiosk in the concourse to the left of the exit from the baggage reclaim area, and buses leave from the stop to the left of the exit from the arrivals hall. Validate your ticket on boarding by punching it in one of the yellow boxes on the bus.

On arrival at Piazzale Roma, unless your hotel is within walking distance, you must

GETTING TO CENTRAL VENICE FROM THE AIRPORT				
	MARCO POLO		**TREVISO SANT'ANGELO**	
	Via Luigi Broglio, Tessera		Via Noalese, Treviso	
	Tel 041 260 6111		Tel 0422 315 1312	
	(central operator);			
	041 260 9260 (flight info)			
TAXI	€27	20 minutes		
BUS				
ATVO	€3.20	20–35 minutes	€5.20	45 minutes
ACTV	€2.20	25–40 minutes		
WATER TAXI	€90+	30–40 minutes		
BOAT				
Alilaguna	€10	75–90 minutes		

AIRLINES			
Alitalia	tel 0870 544 8259 (UK),	tel 8488 6543 (Italy)	www.alitalia.co.uk
British Airways	tel 0870 850 9850 (UK),	tel 199 712266 (Italy)	www.ba.com
Delta	tel 800/241-4141 (US)		www.delta-air-com
Easyjet	tel 0905 821 0905 (UK),	tel 848 887766 (Italy)	www.easyjet.com
Ryanair	tel 0871 246 0000 (UK),	tel 899 899844 (Italy)	www.ryanair.com

transfer to the ACTV *vaporetto* service for onward travel by boat. The ACTV ticket offices are near the Grand Canal and are clearly marked. Once you have bought your ticket, go down the steps to the *imbarcarderi* (landing stages) along the quayside (*fondamenta*) to your left to board the boats.

By Water

There are two options: a regular boat service, run by Alilaguna, or a water taxi. To get to the boats, exit the arrivals hall and take the shuttle bus (*navetta*) which runs regularly every 5 minutes to the lagoon edge. If you want to walk down, it's a 7- to 12-minute walk, turning left outside the terminal building.

The Società Alilaguna (tel 041 523 5775, www.alilaguna.com) runs an hourly boat service from Marco Polo to the city. There are two lines: the Linea Alilaguna Rossa, which goes via Murano, the Lido, Arsenale and San Marco to the Zattere; and the Linea Alilaguna Blu, which travels via Murano, the Fondamente Nuove and the Lido to San Zaccaria and San Marco. Choose the service that will take you as near as

possible to your hotel; you may find that you will have to connect with an ACTV *vaporetto* for the last stages. The Rossa services start at 6.15am; thereafter the boat leaves at 7.15, then hourly at 10 minutes past the hour until just after midnight. The Blu boats start at 9.40am and runs hourly until 40 minutes past midnight. Tickets cost €10 and can be bough on board; the journey time is around 75 to 90 minutes.

Water taxis are run by the Consorzio Motoscafi Venezia (tel 041 541 5084), whose desk is to the left of the exit from the baggage reclaim area in the arrivals hall. The main advantage of a water taxi is the sheer pleasure of the lagoon trip and the fact that taxis are able to deliver you, and your luggage, to the nearest water access point to your hotel, cutting out a walk over bridges with all your bags from the nearest *vaporetto* stop. The disadvantage is the price; they cost upwards of €90, depending on the number of people in your party and your end destination. If there are four or more of you, it's worth considering. The journey across the lagoon takes about 15 to 20 minutes.

AEROPORTO DI TREVISO SANT'ANGELO (TSF)

Treviso airport is 26km (16 miles) north of Venice and is served from the UK by Ryanair. It has one terminal with a currency exchange desk (*cambio*), transport information desk, lavatories and car rental facilities. The snack bar is in the departure area. ATVO runs a bus service that connects with flight arrivals to Piazzale Roma via Mestre railway station. The journey time is around 45 minutes and a single ticket costs €5.20. Buy your ticket from the *cambio* in the arrivals hall and board the bus in the parking area outside the departures hall. Once at Piazzale Roma, walk to your hotel or transfer to the ACTV *vaporetto* service (see above).

GETTING TO YOUR HOTEL

Before you leave, ask your hotel to send you details of how to reach them. You need to know the nearest *vaporetto* stop, the name of the street as well as the *numero civico* (▷ 44–45), and the nearest landmark, such as a *campo*, church or museum. If you have a lot of heavy luggage, you can have it delivered to your hotel by porter. This is charged per piece and must be booked in advance at Cooperativa Trasbagagli; tel 041 522 3590 (Piazzale Roma) or 041 715 272 (Ferrovia) between 8am and 6pm.

RETURNING HOME

ATVO, ACTV and Alilaguna all run between the city and Marco Polo airport. ATVO buses run from 5am to 8.40pm and ACTV services from 4.40am to midnight. The Alilaguna Rossa service starts at 4.20am from the Zattere and runs until 10.35pm, and the Blu service from 8.20am to 11.20pm from San Marco. Both land and water taxis operate a 24-hour service. Note that buses to Treviso leave well in advance of flights to allow for delays, so check the timetable carefully on your arrival at Treviso.

ON THE MOVE

By Train

From the UK you can travel by train to Venice, routing, via the Channel Tunnel, through Paris. The choice of routes and fares is highly complex, but it's best to use the Eurostar service as far as Paris Gare du Nord, then transfer to Paris Bercy for the journey south. The old train and ferry route from London to Paris is now little used, and consequently badly timetabled.

Eurostar trains depart from Waterloo station and arrive in Paris in under 3 hours. Check in 30 minutes before departure; you are allowed two suitcases and one item of hand luggage. Label all bags clearly with your name, address and seat number. You need your passport to clear immigration and customs.

● The total journey time from Waterloo to Venezia Santa Lucia is 26 hours 30 minutes.
● Return ticket prices range from £200 to £300 and include the cost of a couchette.

Eurostar and other fast European trains have facilities which include:
● 1st- and 2nd-class seating
● Sleeping cars
● Bar/restaurant cars
● Trolley service on daytime trains
● Baby-changing facilities on daytime trains
● Air-conditioning
● Telephones
● Toilets in each carriage (car) including some that are wheelchair accessible

Note that if you are arriving in Venice by train from elsewhere in Italy some trains terminate in Venezia Mestre. If this is so, you need to change to a local train for the 10-minute hop across the lagoon. Trains from Mestre to Venice leave approximately every 10 minutes.

Fast train in the station at Venice

Sleeper accommodation varies from 3-, 4- and 6-berth couchettes to single and double sleepers with integral shower and lavatory. Your choice of accommodation will be reflected in the ticket price.

The Orient Express, the ultimate luxury train ride to Venice, operates from March to November, and runs from Victoria station (London) to Venezia Santa Lucia. The journey time is 31 hours and tickets cost between £1,350 (single) and £2,015 (return/round-trip).

RAIL PASSES

If you are coming to Venice by train, or combining your visit with other European or Italian destinations, you may wnat to consider investing in some type of rail pass.

Inter-Rail Passes are valid for one month's unlimited rail travel within a specific zone; Italy is in Zone G, together with Turkey, Greece and Slovenia. You must be an EU citizen or have lived in Europe for six months to be eligible. The full fare is around

€350 for adults and €300 for those under 26. The ticket gives you discounts on cross-Channel services, including Eurostar.

Eurail Passes are available for North American visitors. They allow several days consecutive travel, or a certain number of days within a fixed time period in up to 17 countries. There are many combinations to choose from; check out www.raileurope.com for further information.

Trenitalia Passes, valid from 10 to 14 days, allow unlimited travel during a 2-month period (adult €360, child age 4–12 €180). There is also a **Saver Pass** available to groups of 2 to 5 people travelling together (10 days: adult €300, child €150).

Before you invest in a pass, bear in mind that train travel is cheap in Italy—a return (round-trip) ticket from Venice to Florence costs about €40—so if you're only planning one or two train journeys during your stay, it will probably work out cheaper to buy single tickets.

TRAIN INFORMATION AND TICKETS		
Eurostar	tel 0870 518 6186	www.eurostar.com
Rail Europe	tel 0870 584 8848	www.raileurope.co.uk
Trenitalia	tel 892021	www.trenitalia.com
Venice-Simplon-Orient-Express	tel 020 7805 5100	www.orient-express.com

By Car

If you're considering driving to Venice, bear in mind that you will have to organize and pay for parking while you are in the city. Information on how the parking areas work is on page 55.

You will need the following:
● Valid driver's licence
● Original vehicle registration document
● Motor insurance document (at least third-party insurance is compulsory)
● Passport
● A warning triangle
● A distinguishing nationality sticker if you do not have euro-plates
● A reflective vest in case of emergencies (this is compulsory)
● A set of replacement bulbs
● If you're driving in winter you may need winter tyres or snow chains for the Alpine passes

BEFORE YOU GO
● Check what you must do to adjust your headlights for driving on the right. For newer cars, this adjustment may have to be made by a mechanic, so allow time for this.
● Remove any device to detect radar speed traps as they are banned in most European countries. Even if not in use,

possession of such a device will incur a fine and may result in the confiscation of the car.
● Contact your car insurer or broker at least one month before taking your car to Italy.
● Have the car serviced and the tyres checked.
● Ensure you have adequate breakdown assistance cover. Contact driving organizations such as the AA in the UK (tel 0800 444500, www.theAA.com). In case of breakdown on non-motorway roads in Italy, you can get assistance from the Automobile Club d'Italia (ACI) by calling 803 116, or if you are using a foreign network mobile on 800 116 800. This is not a free service.

From the UK, you can cross the Channel either by ferry or through the Channel tunnel. Heading for Venice, the main routes south to Italy run through France, Switzerland and Germany. All cross the Alps; the main passes are the St. Gotthard, the Great St. Bernard, Fréjus and Mont Blanc. The St. Gotthard tunnel is free; the cost range for the others is from €15 to €30. To reach the tunnels from Calais, take the E15 and E17 to Reims, then pick up the motorways towards the different passes. Alternatively you could drive east through Switzerland into Austria

and cross the Alps from Innsbruck via the E45 motorway through the Brenner Pass. The E45 runs south to Verona, where you join the E70 to Venice.

There are toll-roads all along the routes south. You should allow between 11 to 15 hours driving time to reach the north Italian border.

By Ferry

If you are travelling to or from Greece, there are two Greek ferry lines serving Venice. ANEK Lines has four weekly sailings (Monday, Wednesday, Friday, Saturday) from Corfu and Patras, with a journey time of 27 and 36 hours respectively; Minoan Lines covers the same destinations on a daily basis, with Corfu trips taking 19 hours and Patras 29.

The agent for both is Paleologos s.a., 5 25th August Street, 71202 Heraklion, Crete, tel (30) 2810 346185 or 2810 330598; fax (30) 2810 346208; www.minoan.com

Ferries and cruise ships dock at the Stazione Marittima in the heart of the Venice.

A Greek ferry enters the Giudecca Canal

GETTING AROUND

The best way to move around Venice is on foot; this is how the Venetians themselves get from place to place, combining walking with the judicious use of public transport in the shape of *vaporetti* (water buses) and *traghetti* (cross-Grand Canal ferries). Every Venetian carries in his head a mental map of the city, which he'll consult for main routes, short cuts and transport before he begins his journey. Visitors won't reach this state of expertise, but the satisfaction of rounding a corner, crossing a bridge and finding you're exactly where you want to be is huge, and the discoveries that walking brings are one of the intrinsic pleasures of the city.

Which way to San Marco?

Venice is divided in to six *sestieri*, which roughly translates as 'quarters' or 'city wards'. Three—San Marco, Cannaregio and Castello—lie to the north of the Grand Canal, and three—San Polo, Santa Croce and Dorsoduro—to the south. The Grand Canal sweeps in a sinuous curve between the two halves of the city, crossed by three bridges, the Scalzi, the Rialto and the Accademia, whose spans divide the Canal into three roughly equal sections. Myriad smaller canals (*rii*) branch off the Grand Canal, snaking their way through

the city to form a spider's web of waterways. These are crossed by 400 or so bridges, linking neighbourhoods, streets and *campi* (squares). Making sense of this labyrinth and finding your way around is a challenge, and this section will help you to understand it better.

Vaporetti

The *vaporetti* (▷ 48, 50–52) can be a real help in getting round the city, and are a huge attraction to most visitors, but a glance at a map will show that, time-wise, they are often the slowest way to move about Venice. If you want to go from

the Piazza San Marco to the Rialto, it's tempting to wait for a *vaporetto* and take the 8-stop, 20-minute boat trip. But if you cut through the streets running north out of the Piazza you can be at the Rialto in around 10 minutes. Along the Grand Canal, it's over 20 minutes and 8 stops from the station to the *vaporetto* stop nearest the Frari church; the journey on foot takes around 10 minutes. The outer edges of Venice, up by the Fondamente Nuove in Cannaregio, and down by the Zattere in Dorsoduro take even longer to reach by *vaporetto*, and may involve complicated routes and changes of boats. So it makes sense, once you've begun to get your city bearings, to think twice before you automatically head for the *vaporetto*, and perhaps only use them for longer journeys; it is often quicker on foot, and you'll certainly see more of the city.

Walking

Venice is a small city; roughly 3km (2 miles) long and a little less across at its widest point. Brisk walking—once you know the way—will take you from end to end in around an hour. Like all cities, it has its main through routes, important thoroughfares that link the city's major focus points. For many years, these routes have been helpfully signposted by the city council, and you'll see yellow signs, above head height, indicating the route to five central hubs; San Marco, the Rialto, the Accademia, Ferrovia (the station), and Piazzale Roma, where the causeway to the mainland starts. Follow these yellow signs, no matter how narrow and unlikely

the street looks as a route, and they will take you to these end points. For the first couple of days, this will probably be all the help you need, but once you decide to explore further you will need to use your map. Spend a few minutes before you set out studying it and working out your route, and accept, too, that you will inevitably get lost, go round in circles or end up somewhere completely different from where you intended. If this happens, console yourself with the thought that this is how you start to get to know one of the world's most topographically challenging cities.

● Follow the yellow signs for main cross-city routes.
● Remember that just because a street is very narrow it doesn't mean it's not an important route.
● Make a point of noticing key landmarks—churches, distinctive shop fronts, *campi*—so you can retrace your steps if necessary.
● Follow the crowds; even if you're lost in an out of the way corner, you'll be surprised how soon one person becomes two,

then three, then six, until you're suddenly back on a main thoroughfare.
● Follow the disembarking crowds at *vaporetti* stops, some of which appear to be in the middle of nowhere; the other passengers will lead you to sights and through routes.
● Wear comfortable shoes; street surfaces are hard and the bridges provide a surprising amount of climbing.

Traghetti

Traghetti (gondola ferries) ply back and forth from one side of the Grand Canal to the other at seven fixed points (for how they work see page 53). Think of them as bridges, and it becomes clear they will save both time and unnecessary mileage. All have been operating for hundreds of years, and they exist primarily for the convenience of locals, but, once you're familiar with the system, judicious use of the *traghetti* will help get you quickly from point to point.

FINDING AN ADDRESS

Every *calle* and *campo* in Venice is clearly marked above eye-level with its name, written in black on a white background. These signs are called *nissioeto* and are written in Venetian dialect. The spelling therefore differs, sometimes considerably, from that marked on all maps of Venice, which always use normal

Italian. However, written postal addresses for the city do not always give street names. The Venetian practice is to give the *sestiere* name, followed by its number, the *numero civico*. Venice is divided into six *sestieri*; San Marco, Cannaregio and Castello, to the north of the Grand Canal, and San Polo, Santa Croce and Dorsoduro to the south. In each of the six *sestieri*, *numeri civici* start at No. 1 and progress, seemingly at random and without logic, throughout the *sestiere* until every building has been covered; in the case of San Marco, this is over 5,000. Your hotel's address therefore may officially read as San Marco 4563 or Dorsoduro 3118, with no indication of where in the *sestiere* it is. For this reason, it is essential to make certain you are given either the name of the street, or a local landmark, such

Campo dei Gesuiti

MOST USEFUL TRAGHETTI

Pescheria to Santa Sofia: connects the Rialto area with the Strada Nova. If you're staying near the Rialto, use it to access the Strada Nova, to join the walking route north via Santi Apostoli to the Fondamente Nuove (for boats to San Michele, Murano and Burano), to walk to Santi Giovanni e Paolo, Santa Maria dei Miracoli, the Ca' d'Oro and northern Cannaregio. From the Strada Nova side, it connects with the Rialto and the markets and the Campo San Polo area.

San Tomà to Ca' Garzoni: if you're staying in San Polo use it as the quickest way to San Marco by cutting through to Campo Santo Stefano and picking up the yellow signs from there. From the San Marco side, this *traghetto* gives easy access to the Frari and the Scuola Grande di San Rocco, and is a 5- to 10-mimute walk from Campo Santa Margherita and Campo San Polo.

Ca' Rezzonico to San Samuele: useful link from Dorsoduro to San Marco and vice versa, but operates only in the mornings.

Santa Maria della Salute to Santa Maria del Giglio: from San Marco, this is the quickest way to reach the church of the Salute and the Collezione Peggy Guggenheim. If you're staying in eastern Dorsoduro it provides a quick link to the Piazza San Marco, by way of Calle XXII Marzo, and to the Rialto via Campo Sant'Angelo and Campo Manin; alternatively use the Dogana *traghetto* for the Piazza.

ON THE MOVE

as a church, important *campo*, or even a shop, to help you locate the address. In this book, we have indicated street names in the Sights and Listings sections to make things easier. If you need to find somewhere and don't have the street name, invest in the comprehensive *Calli, Campielli e Canali* street guide. This gives the street name for every *sestiere* number, and marks them on clear maps, along with historical information about every building in Italian and English. It is available at good bookshops throughout the city (Edizioni Helvetia €19).

RULES OF THE ROAD

Venetians have considerable patience with visitors, but remember that locals live and work in the city and you should observe a few rules:
● Street traffic has to flow in both directions, so keep to the right and allow room for overtaking.
● Don't obstruct the middle of busy streets while you take photos or drink in the view.
● Venetians walk briskly so be aware of people behind you trying to pass in narrow streets.
● Pull in while you consult your map.
● Don't clutter up busy bridges or junctions.

● Avoid the main arteries at rush hour, and the main streets near San Marco and the Rialto at all times to avoid pedestrian traffic jams in high season.

VENETIAN STREET NAMES

Venice's idiosyncratic street names are one of the delights of the city, with the bonus of—just occasionally—providing clues to an address's location and history. Confusingly, you may find the same street name popping up more than once in different areas around the city, so, when checking street names of addresses, make sure you know which particular street of that name it is and in which *sestiere*. Unlike most Italian cities, the key nomenclatures of *Via* and *Piazza* are rare, so it makes sense to get a handle on Venice by coming to grips with its name-system (plurals in brackets).

TYPES OF STREET

Calle (calli): the commonest name for street, the equivalent of

Via in other Italian towns
Campiello (campielli): a small *campo*
Campo (campi): the Venetian name for square, meaning field, comes from its origins as the central cultivated area on one of the islands that made up early Venice
Canale (canali): there are only two canals; the Canal Grande and the Canale di Cannaregio
Corte (corti): an even smaller *campo*
Crosera (crosere): crossroads, usually where important cross-city routes meet
Fondamenta (fondamente): a quayside or street running beside a canal
Lista (liste): a street once occupied by an ambassador's residence
Piazza (piazze): Venice has just one, the Piazza San Marco
Piazzale (piazzali): just one, the Piazzale Roma, where the causeway ends
Piazzetta (piazzette): there are only two; they flank the Basilica di San Marco, the Piazzetta on the water side, and the Piazzetta dei Leoni on the other side
Piscina (piscine): a paved area that was once the site of a pool
Ramo (rami): means branch; hence the name given to narrow side streets which may link two streets or dead end
Rio (rii): the Venetian word for canal
Rio terà (rii terà): a street on the site of a filled-in canal
Riva (rive): a wide *fondamenta*, usually along the Grand Canal, a

MAIN THROUGH ROUTES		
SESTIERE	**FROM WHERE TO WHERE**	**HOW TO WALK IT**
San Marco	Piazza San Marco to the Rialto	Follow yellow Rialto signs
San Marco	Piazza San Marco to Accademia	Follow yellow Accademia signs
San Marco	Rialto to the station	Follow yellow Ferrovia signs
San Marco	Piazza San Marco to Santi Giovanni e Paolo	Santa Maria Formosa, Calle Trevisana (blue sign)
Cannaregio	Rialto to station	Follow yellow Ferrovia signs
Cannaregio	Rialto to Fdta Nove	Santi Apostoli, Gesuiti, Fondamenta Nove
Dorsoduro	Accademia to the Rialto	Follow yellow Rialto signs
San Polo	Rialto to the station	Follow yellow Ferrovia signs
San Polo	Rialto to Piazzale Roma	Follow yellow Piazzale Roma signs

major *rio* or open water
Ruga (ruge): a street with shops
Sacca (sacce): originally a lagoon inlet
Salizzada (salizzade): the most important street in a neighbourhood, the word means 'paved'
Sotoportego (sotoportegi): a covered street or archway
Via (vie): Venice has two, both laid out in the 19th century; Via Garibaldi in Castello, and Via (Calle) XXII Marzo in San Marco

MAPS
There is a street map of Venice at the back of this guide (▷ 303–317) and a *vaporetto* map in the inside back cover. Venice's APT has a free street map at all its offices and also sells, as do many newsstands and bookshops, other street maps of the city. These vary greatly in accuracy, and it's generally accepted by the Venetians themselves that there's no such thing as a faultlessly accurate map of the city.

ACQUA ALTA
The *acqua alta*, high water, is becoming increasingly common between September and April. This occurs when higher than average tides coincide with low atmospheric pressure and a wind driving against the tidal outflow from the lagoon. Tides 100cm (3.2ft) above average will flood 3.5 per cent of central Venice; 110cm (3.6ft) puts 11.7 per cent

of the city under water, 120cm (3.9ft) 35 per cent, 130cm (4.2ft) 68.7, and 140cm (4.5ft) will make over 90 per cent of the city impassable for 2 to 3 hours each side of high tide. The worst months are October and November, but it can occur at any time during the late autumn and winter months.

● Two to three hours before an exceptionally high tide sirens around the city sound five 10-second wailing blasts. These may go off in the middle of the night.
● The water will gradually make its way through the city streets and into buildings, oozing up through the pavements and overflowing the *fondamente*.
● The city council will erect the *passarelle*, the raised walkways kept permanently on hand throughout the winter months, on major flood-prone routes. If the water rises above 130cm (4.2ft), these too will float, so in such circumstances it's better to head for somewhere dry and sit it out.
● *Acqua alta* normally lasts for three days.

HOW TO COPE WITH ACQUA ALTA
● You can get advance information on tides by logging onto www. comune.venezia.it/maree/previsione; by calling 041 241 1996 to hear a taped 36-hour tide forecast, or by picking up a text message from your mobile by sending the word MAREA to 339 99 41041.

Living with the acqua alta—*pedestrians on the* passarelle

● If tide levels are high, it's worth either bringing Wellington boots *(stivali)* with you, or investing in a pair while you're in Venice. The disposable plastic leggings sold by street traders are not recommended, as they let in water and quickly fall to pieces.
● Use the *passarelle* (raised walkways) to move around the city; wait your turn to get on them and walk carefully along the planks, keeping to the right. Venetians are polite and helpful to each other during *acqua alta* and expect visitors to be the same.
● Never splash; the *calli* may be under water, but they're still public streets and Venetians will not appreciate getting any wetter than is absolutely unavoidable.
● Remember that during *acqua alta* you cannot see where the pavement stops and the canal begins
● *Vaporetti* continue to function up to a tide level of around 125cm (4.1ft); all stops have maps showing flood-prone areas, and the routes covered by the *passarelle*.
● You can get a copy of the *acqua alta* map from the tourist offices.
● Shops, bars and restaurants may temporarily close during *acqua alta* in order to try to keep water out, or pump it out; be patient—things will quickly get back to normal.

By Boat

Although many journeys around Venice are quicker on foot, there's no doubt that for most visitors the *vaporetti* or waterbuses are a big draw. Until you start to get your city bearings, they can prove a lifeline, depositing you, from all over the city and lagoon, back on the familiar territory of the streets surrounding your hotel. They also provide a moving grandstand from which to drink in the beauty of the city—the palaces, the churches, the lagoon views—while the steady stream of local passengers will give you a real insight into the actuality of living in Venice.

Strictly speaking, the public service boats used by ACTV are not all *vaporetti*, the diminutive name used by all Venetians and coined over a century ago when the first 'little steamers' appeared in Venice. ACTV has three types of boat:

● **Vaporetti:** large, relatively slow vessels with rounded sterns, one large cabin and ample standing and luggage space on the foredeck. They cover the Grand Canal and Lido routes.

● **Motoscafi:** smaller, lower and faster boats with cabins fore and aft of the bridge and some outside seating at the back. They serve the stops on the periphery of the city and run to the Giudecca, San Giorgio and Murano.

● **Motonavi:** double-decker steamers that cross the lagoon to Burano, Torcello, Punta Sabbione and the Lido. The upper deck has plenty of outside seating.

There are three other types of public service vessel you will come across:

● **Water taxis:** these are sleek, brown-and-white motorboats with comfortable cabins. Authorized taxis show a black registration number on a yellow background. They can take you all over the city via both the Grand Canal and many of the smaller *rii*.

● **Gondole:** Venice's own boats are by now almost solely devoted to tourism and few people use them to get around the city. In fact, they are the only boats that can penetrate even the narrowest and shallowest canals.

● **Traghetti:** these are inexpensive gondolas which cross the Grand Canal backwards and forwards at fixed points. They are extremely useful when moving about Venice on foot as they dispense with the need to take *vaporetti* or go out of your way to cross one of the Grand Canal bridges.

Water taxi—expensive but quick (below);
Taking the traghetto (above and middle right) across to the other side;
A gondola on the Grand Canal— the ultimate Venetian experience (below right)

Vaporetto *is the best way to travel the canal (above and right); island ferry (below)*

VAPORETTI ROUTES

If you are going to be using the *vaporetti* a lot, it's worth investing in the ACTV *Orario* (Timetable), from the tourist information offices, the main ACTV/VeLa office at Piazzale Roma or any large ACTV booth (€0.60). It's worth noting that ACTV is notorious for sudden timetable changes and for changing or eliminating routes, services and numbers. Details of any changes to the services, including strikes, are posted in the cabins of the landing stages.

THE MAIN ROUTES

● **No. 1:** slow route from Piazzale Roma down the Grand Canal and east along the Riva

Detail from the vaporetto *map*

degli Schiavoni to the Giardini, Sant'Elena and the Lido; boats stop at every landing stage. Also operates in reverse.

● **No. 82:** a faster service with fewer stops from San Marco (Vallaresso) up the Grand Canal to Piazzale Roma, then around the southwestern edge of the city with stops at the Tronchetto parking areas, the islands of Sacca Fisola, Giudecca and San Giorgio Maggiore and back to San Marco. From Jun–Sep the service extends to the Lido. Also operates in reverse.

● **No. 41 and 42:** service running anticlockwise and clockwise around the outer edge of the main city from Murano, with stops on the northern side of the city, Piazzale Roma, the Giudecca, San Marco and Sant'Elena.

● **No. 51 and 52:** service running anti-clockwise and clockwise from the Lido along the northern city edge and down the Canale di Cannaregio to the station and Piazzale Roma. It then returns to the Lido via the Canale della

Giudecca, stopping at the Zattere and Sant'Elena.

● **No. 61 and 62:** fast service from Piazzale Roma to the Lido via the Zattere and Giardini.

● **DM:** the Diretto Murano is a non-stop service linking Piazzale Roma and Ferrovia with the island of Murano.

● **LN:** lagoon service (Laguna Nord) from the Fondamente Nuove to Murano, Mazzorbo and Burano, which returns via Treporti, Punta Sabbione and the Lido to San Zaccaria.

● **T:** Burano–Torcello service. Other routes serve the islands of Pellestrina, Vignole, Sant'Erasmo, San Servolo and San Lazzaro.

Routes are clearly marked on vaporetti *and departure quays*

MAIN *VAPORETTI* STOPS

Piazzale Roma is the stop for the causeway to the mainland

Ferrovia is the stop for the station

Rialto is the stop for the Rialto

San Marco (Vallaresso), San Marco and San Zaccaria are the stops nearest to the Piazza San Marco

Piazzale Roma, Ferrovia and the Fondamente Nuove can be used to reach Murano

Fondamente Nuove is the departure stop for Burano and Torcello

Pietà also serves departures for Burano and Torcello

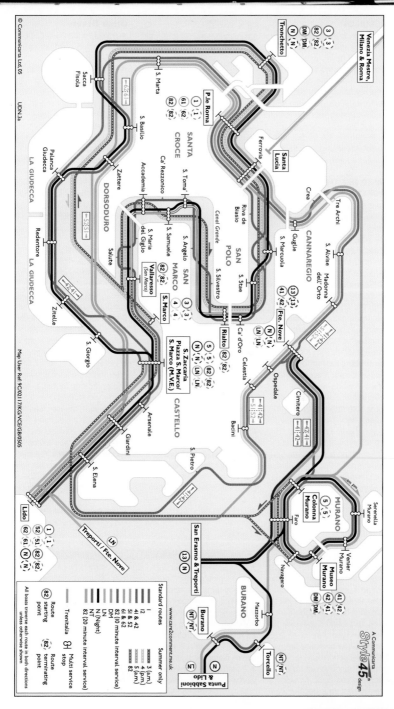

TIMETABLES

Vaporetti run to strict timetables, which are clearly displayed at all stops. On the main routes, services start around 5am and run to midnight or just after, when a regular night service (N), following the route of the No. 82, takes over. During the day, the No. 1 and No. 82 run every 10 minutes; the 41, 42, 51, 52, and 62 every 20 minutes; and the DM, LN and T half-hourly.

HOW TO USE THE VAPORETTI

If you're a stranger to Venice, the main pitfall of first using the *vaporetto* system is taking the wrong boat going in the wrong direction. As a general rule, if you're on the north side of the Grand Canal boats heading left are travelling towards San Marco, those heading right will take you towards the station or Piazzale Roma. Main stops have two *imbarcaderi* (landing stages), one for each direction; both will be clearly marked with a route board showing the number of the *vaporetto* and the direction in which it will be heading. Smaller *imbarcaderi* serve boats going in both directions. If this is the case, check the destination board on the side of the boat which will indicate the number, final destination and stops *en route*. If you're still unsure, listen to the crewperson in charge of embarking who will shout out the final destination.

● Buy your ticket before boarding and make sure it is validated.
● As the boat arrives, stand back and allow passengers to disembark first.
● Board the boat, moving aft into the cabin if directed by the crew.
● Keep an eye open for the stop before yours and, once this is passed, start to work your way forwards for your own disembarkation, moving past other passengers by saying *permesso*. *Vaporetti* can be jam-packed and you don't want to be carried past your stop.

You must validate your ticket

● Luggage should be stored where directed by the crew.
● Bear in mind *vaporetti* are extremely crowded during Venetian commuting hours, and at all times during the height of the tourist season.

TICKETS
Biglietti a tempo

For visitors, by far the best ticketing option is to invest in one of ACTV's *biglietti a tempo* (Travel Cards). These are valid for 90 minutes, 24 or 72 hours and cost respectively €5, €10.50 and €22. They can be purchased at ACTV/VeLa's main office at Piazzale Roma, the ticket booths at main stops and *tabacchi* (tobacconist shops) showing the ACTV logo. If the ticket is not already validated, you must do so by inserting it into the orange punch box at the *imbarcadero*. Validity starts from the moment it is punched.

Other Tickets

● A single ticket costs €3.50 and is not valid for the Grand Canal.
● A single 90-minute ticket that includes the Grand Canal routes costs €5.
● Tickets valid for two trips (not including the Grand Canal services) cost €6.
● Tickets for a return journey on No. 3 and 4 *vaporetti* (from Tronchetto parking to San Marco via the Grand Canal) cost €7.
● If you board without a ticket, ask a member of the crew for one immediately. Ticket inspections are frequent and the on-the-spot fine is €30.

Abbonamenti

If you are staying for a week or more, or planning to return to Venice frequently, it's worth considering a *tessera di abbonamento*. This is a three-year travel card which entitles you to buy tickets on all ACTV water and land routes at the same tariff as that paid by Venetian residents, which will offer you considerable savings. The application form is available from main ACTV and VeLa offices. Fill in the form and take it, along with a passport-sized photo, to the office, where, on payment of €8, you will be issued with the card. You can then buy a monthly ticket, valid on all routes, for €25. Holders of *abbonamenti* can also buy single tickets for €1 or a book of 10 (*carnet*) for €9. The card is renewable after 3 years for a fee of €5.

TIPS

● If you're in Venice for 3 to 4 days and want to buy a 72-hour pass, it's worth working out when to buy it. You may find that you won't be using the *vaporetti* for your first or last day, so fit your boat travel into the middle three days to save money.
● New No. 1 *vaporetti* are gradually being introduced. The new boats no longer have the much-sought after front seats which give such superb views of the Grand Canal. If you're planning on using the No. 1 to sightsee, wait until one of the older type *vaporetti* comes along and try for a front seat.
● If you're planning a day to the lagoon islands use the timetable to plan your trip so you won't waste time waiting for infrequent boats.

HOW TO USE THE TRAGHETTI

The *traghetti* are the best way of crossing from one side of the Grand Canal to the other; they're also a quintessential Venetian experience and a bargain way to have a gondola ride. The service is run by the gondoliers' cooperative in conjunction with the city council; fares are a standard €0.50 per crossing.

● *Traghetti* are marked by green *traghetto* boards with the name of the service.
● If there is a gondola waiting you can board at once; the service will leave when the gondolier has enough passengers or feels those on board have been waiting long enough.
● Hand your money to the gondolier as you board—the right change is always appreciated.
● Move towards the back of the boat and remain standing. It's customary to stand so as many passengers can ride as possible, though you can sit down if the gondola isn't crowded.
● As you disembark, the gondolier will give you a helping hand if required.

WATER TAXIS

For moving to and from the airport and around the city, fast water taxis, seating up to eight people, are a solution. They are organized by the Cooperativa San Marco, which operates the

Taking a traghetto *across the canal can save a lot of walking*

TRAGHETTI STATIONS	
STATION	**TIMES**
San Marco to Punta di Dogana	daily 9–12, 2–6
Giglio to Salute	daily 8–6
San Samuele to Ca' Rezzonico	Mon– Sat 7.30am–1.30 pm
Ca' Garzoni to San Tomà	Mon–Sat 7.30 am–8.30 pm; Sun 8am–7.30
Riva del Carbon to Riva del Vin	Mon–Sat 8am–2pm
Santa Sofia to Pescheria	Mon–Sat 7.30am–8.30 pm; Sun 8–7
San Marcuola to Fontego dei Turchi	Mon–Sat 9–12.30

services both from ranks and via a telephone switchboard. Your hotel will order a taxi in advance to take you to the airport or around the city; it will arrive at the nearest *fondamenta* to your hotel. The main drawback is the cost; taxis are inordinately expensive. You can expect to pay between €90 and €100 for the trip into Venice from the airport; shorter, city rides will cost almost the same. Taxis charge a night supplement between 10pm and 7am of €8.
Bookings: tel 041 522 2303 www.motoscafi.com

GONDOLAS

Gondolas today are almost solely used for tourist trips, the ultimate Venetian romantic experience. If you're planning a trip, you can discuss the itinerary beforehand with the gondolier; the route will depend on where you're boarding, but most gondola trips will cover either the Bacino di San Marco and some side canals, or a section of the Grand Canal and some smaller *rii*. Fares are set by the *Istituzione per la Conservazione della gondola e*

tutela del gondoliere (Gondola Board), tel 041 528 5075, www.gondolavenezia.it. Gondolas can carry up to six passengers; there are no discounts for fewer numbers. Expect to pay: Between 8am and 8pm €65 for 50 minutes + €35 for each additional 25 minutes; between 8pm and 8am €80 for 50 minutes + € 40 for each additional 25 minutes.
If you're in Venice on a package holiday, a gondola ride may be included in the deal.

GONDOLA STATIONS
Bacino Orseolo (behind the Piazza San Marco)
Campo San Moisè (in front of the Grunwald hotel)
Ferrovia (railway station)
Piazzetta San Marco
Piazzale Roma
Riva degli Schiavoni (in front of Hotel Danieli)
Riva del Carbon (south end of Rialto bridge)
San Tomà (near vaporetto stop)
Santa Maria del Giglio (next to vaporetto stop)
Vallaresso (next to vaporetto stop)

By Bus

If you're planning to visit other towns in the Veneto, you'll find many are easily accessible in a day by bus or train from central Venice. Both forms of transport are cheap, frequent and reliable, and you can find full travel information at either the ACTV and VeLa offices in Piazzale Roma or Santa Lucia station on the Grand Canal.

BUSES

The white land buses serving the Venice area are run by ACTV to Mestre and Marghera on the mainland; ACTV also operates the island bus services on the Lido and Pellestrina and in the town of Chioggia.

● Buses for the mainland depart from Piazzale Roma.
● Lido and Pellestrina buses leave from outside the *vaporetto* stop on the Lido.
● Tickets cost €1 and are valid for 60 minutes, during which time you may use several buses, though not for a return journey.
● Buy the ticket before boarding and validate it on the bus by punching it in one of the yellow boxes.
● 24- and 72-hour travel passes are valid for Lido and Pellestrina buses.
● Tickets are available at the ACTV office at Piazzale Roma, ACTV ticket booths and *tabacchi* showing the ACTV logo.
● Buses leave from designated stands at Piazzale Rome; these are clearly marked with service numbers, final destinations, departure times and stops en route.
● Avoid bus travel at peak morning (7.30–9) and evening (6–8) travel times.
● Board the bus through the front or rear doors (marked *entrata*) and leave from the middle (*uscita*).
● Night buses from Mestre, Marghera, the Lido and Pellestrina connect with the N nighttime *vaporetto* service.

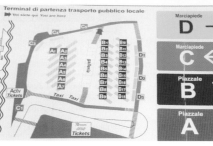

Farther Afield

● ACTV buses connect Venice and Padova (Padua), stopping at several Palladian villas along the route; details from ACTV office, Piazzale Roma.
● SITA blue buses leave from Piazzale Roma and go directly to Padova along the motorway; details from the VeLa office at Piazzale Roma or tel 049 820 6811.
● FTV buses connect Padova and Vicenza, leaving from outside the railway station; details on 0444 223 111.

By Train

Few stations are as beautifully sited as Venezia Santa Lucia, where you exit the station to find yourself on the edge of the Grand Canal, an unforgettable arrival that outclasses Piazzale Roma in every way. Italian trains are excellent and, if you're sightseeing outside Venice, the most convenient form of transport. Verona is 90 minutes by train from the city,

Detailed bus information at Piazzale Roma

while Padova and Vicenza are close enough to make a day-trip to them both feasible.

TYPES OF TRAIN

Eurostar Italia (ES): a superfast service (250kph/155mph) connecting main Italian cities (eg Venice to Verona, Venice to Florence). First-class tickets are available and include newspapers and refreshments. All trains have a restaurant car and trolley service. You should book ahead, either at the station; via Trenitalia agents; by telephone on 892021; or online at www.trenitalia.com.
Intercity (IC): high-speed trains connecting the main cities and important regional towns. Advance reservations are recommended (see above).
Treni Espressi (E): long-distance express trains; use them if you are moving on from Venice to another part of Italy.
Diretti (D): trains calling at larger stations only; useful from Venice for Padova and Verona.

CAR PARKS		
NAME	**ADDRESS**	**TEL/FAX**
Autorimessa Comunale	Piazzale Roma, Santa Croce 365B	041 272 7211/041 723131; www.asmvenezia.it, www.urbislimen.net
Marco Polo Park	Marco Polo Airport, Via Luigi Broglio, Tessera	041 541 5913; www.veniceairport.it/parcheggi
Park Terminal Fusina	Via Moranzani 79, Fusina	041 523 1337, 041 241 0261; www.terminalfusina.it
Tronchetto	Isola Nuova del Tronchetto	041 520 7555, 041 528 5750; www.veniceparking.it

TIP

• If you speak Italian, there is an excellent, automated train information line; dial 041 258 0136 and follow the instructions. www.trenitalia.com

Regionali (R): local trains that stop at every station within a 100km (62-mile) radius of their departure station. They are very slow, and it's often worth waiting a few minutes for a faster train. No seat reservations and smoking is not permitted.

TICKETS

• Italian trains have first- and second-class tickets, which are calculated by the kilometre. A single second-class ticket between Venice and Padova costs around €5.50.
• Supplements are charged for the faster services, such as Intercity and Eurocity. These come in the form of a separate ticket and must be shown to the ticket inspector.
• There are no discounts for return (round-trip) tickets.
• Children aged 4–12 travel at a 50 per cent discount of the normal fare; children under 4 travel free.
• Tickets are valid for 6 months, but must be used within 6 hours of being validated.

AT THE STATION

• The ticket office is on the left of the front concourse of Santa Lucia station. There are separate windows for advance booking, and a useful travel information office, where English is spoken, to the right just before the entrance to the platforms.
• Ask for either *andata* (one-way) or *andata e ritorno* (return/round-trip). The distance and price are displayed on an electronic board next to the booking clerk. If you plan to travel by a fast train remember to ask for the supplement.
• Payment is normally by cash, though you can use a credit card for longer, more expensive journeys.
• Check your train's departure time and platform on the board; all platforms also have clear timetables for both arriving and departing trains (*arrivi* and *partenze*), and there is an information board, showing the next train's destination and departure time, at the head of each platform.
• Trains are numbered and almost always leave from the same platform.
• Validate your ticket by inserting it in one of the yellow boxes found at various points around the station and on the platforms. Failure to do this incurs an on-the-spot fine of around €17.

PARKING IN VENICE

If you arrive by car, you must leave your vehicle in one of the parking areas around the city, which are connected to Venice proper by public transport. Costs are high, and mount up if you're staying for more than two to three days in the city. However, many Venetian hotels offer their guests discounts at parking areas, so it's worth checking when you make your hotel reservation.

Before you decide where to park, it's worth thinking about ease of access to the city as well as the cost. The multilevel parking areas at Piazzale Roma, at the end of the causeway, are virtually in the city itself, less than a 5-minute walk from the *vaporetto* stop. The artificial island of Tronchetto, northwest of Piazzale Roma, is equally convenient and is served by its own *vaporetto* service, which connects with central Venice via the Grand Canal, though the walk to the *embarcaderi* is longer than at Piazzale Roma. Both these options are expensive. Across the lagoon on the mainland, the Fusina parking areas are cheaper, and have the convenience of an hourly boat service across the lagoon to the Zattere. Marco Polo airport has plenty of parking at competitive rates; if you park here, use the city transfer routes outlined on pages 40–41. There is additional, and very cheap parking, around the station in Mestre, but finding a space can be difficult and parking cannot be pre-booked.

The best way to pre-book parking is online; follow the instructions on screen to send an email. The parking area will then confirm your reservation. You can pay by credit card or cash, and will be charged for each whole day or fraction of to the nearest hour. If your hotel negotiates reduced parking costs for you they will send you the necessary vouchers and paperwork.

PRICE	HOW TO GET THERE	ONWARD TRAVEL	OPEN
€19 per day	Cross causeway and follow signs to Piazzale Roma	*Vaporetto* 1, 82, 41, 42, 51, 52 at Piazzale Roma	Open 24 hours a day
€12 per day, reduced rates for longer periods		Follow airport signs from A4, bus 5 to Piazzale Roma, then *vaporetto*	Open 24 hours a day
€10 up to 12 hours, €15 up to 24 hours	Exit A4 onto SS309 towards Ravenna and follow signs	Boat from Fusina to Zattere (Oct–end May 8–8; Jun–end Sep 8am–10pm)	Open Oct–end May 8am–9.30pm; Jun–end Sep 8am–11.30pm
€19 per day	Cross causeway and follow signs to Tronchetto	*Vaporetto* 82, 3, 4 at Tronchetto	Open 24 hours a day

VISITORS WITH A DISABILITY

Unfortunately Venice presents particular problems for people with mobility disabilities, who will need the help of able-bodied companions to get around. Even with assistance, some areas of the city will be inaccessible, due particularly to the bridges. However, with some judicious planning, there's no reason why people with physical disabilities cannot experience at least some of Venice's special delights.

TRANSPORT INFORMATION FOR VISITORS WITH DISABILITIES

Marco Polo Airport
tel 041 260 9260
ACTV tel 0421 383672

ARRIVING

Contact your airline to let them know what assistance you will need. Marco Polo airport has wheelchair access to all facilities, and airport buses, in theory, take wheelchairs. At Piazzale Roma, access to the *imbarcadero* for the No. 1 *vaporetto* service is straightforward.

CHOOSING A HOTEL

Elevators are rare in Venetian buildings, but the more expensive hotels have them, and some have wheelchair accessible rooms on the ground floor. Make sure there are no bridges between your hotel and the nearest *vaporetto* stop, preferably on the route of the No. 1 *vaporetto*, as these are easily accessible with wheelchairs.

INFORMATION

Informahandicap provides information on disabled travel in Venice and the Veneto. In conjunction with the tourist board, it produces a booklet listing hotels, restaurants and museums with disabled facilities, and the tourist offices have a map with wheelchair-accessible routes. Both maps and booklets are obtainable from:

Informahandicap
Piazzale Candiani 5, Mestre
Tel 041 274 8144 (Venezia);
041 274 6144 (Mestre)
www.comune.venezia.it/handicap

Before you go, you could also contact:

Tourism for All
The Hawkins Suite, Enham Place, Enham Alamegn, Andover SP11 6JS
Tel 0845 124 9971
www.tourismforall.org.uk

A UK-based company that produces publications and iinformation on accessibility.

RADAR
12 City Forum, 250 City Road, London EC1V 8AF
Tel 020 7250 3222
www.radar.org.uk

SATH
347 5th Avenue, Suite 610, New York City, NY 10016
Tel 212/447-7284
www.sath.org

GETTING AROUND

You will find *vaporetto* crews helpful when boarding and disembarking. Standard *vaporetti* and *motonavi* (▷ 48–49) have a large flat deck area and easy boarding; they operate on lines 1, 82, 3, 4, 5, LN, T and N.

Venice has several bridges with wheelchair ramps. These are automated and need a key to operate them, available from tourist offices.

Visitors with visual disabilities should note that not all canals have railings or walls at the water's edge.

SIGHTSEEING

There has been an improvement in accessibility in recent years, and many Venetian museums now have good access within the building. However, access to the building is a different matter, and you will not be able to visit all the main sights. This is true of many churches with great art, as many are some distance from *vaporetti* stops and only accessible over several bridges. See panel for easily accessible areas and main sights.

EASILY ACCESSIBLE AREAS AND MAIN SIGHTS
(no bridges from *vaporetto*)

	Vaporetto No. and Stop
Basilica dei Frari	1, San Tomà
Basilica di San Marco	1, San Marco (Vall)
Burano	LN, Burano
Ca' d'Oro (ask at the entrance to use the elevator)	1, Ca d'Oro
Campo Santo Stefano	1, San Samuele
Gallerie dell'Accademia (ask at the entrance to use the elevator)	1, 82 Accademia
Murano	LN, Murano Faro
Museo Civico Correr (ask at the entrance to use the elevator)	1, San Marco (Vall)
Museo del Costume	1, San Stae
Palazzo Ducale (ask at the entrance to use the elevator)	1, San Marco (Vall)
Piazza San Marco	1, San Marco (Vall)
Rialto markets	1, San Silvestro
Scuola Grande di San Rocco	1, San Tomà
Zattere	1, Accademia

Other major sights may only involve negotiating as few as one or two bridges; careful study of the map will help you decide which to tackle.

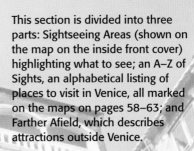

This section is divided into three parts: Sightseeing Areas (shown on the map on the inside front cover) highlighting what to see; an A–Z of Sights, an alphabetical listing of places to visit in Venice, all marked on the maps on pages 58–63; and Farther Afield, which describes attractions outside Venice.

The Sights

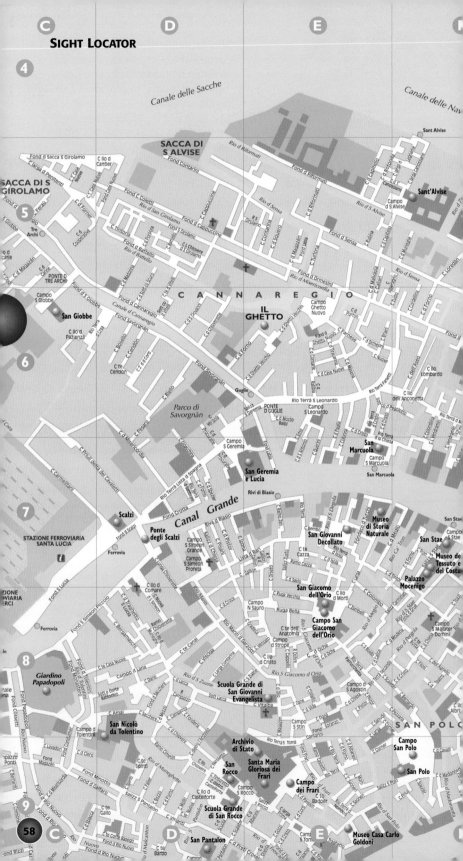

C **D** **E** **F**

4

Canale delle Sacche

Canale delle Nav

Sant'Alvise

SACCA DI
S ALVISE

Fond Contarini

Rio d Riformati

Rio d Riformati

Sant'Alvise
Campo
d S Alvise

SACCA DI S
GIROLAMO

Fond d Sacca S Girolamo

C llo d
Cantier

C llo d
Pazienza

Fond C Coletti

Rio di San Girolamo

Fond d Cappuccine

Rio d Sensa

Rio d S Sensa

Rio d Sensa

Tre Archi

Fond d Battello

Rio d Battello

C I Chiovere
d Girolamo

Fond d Ormesini

Rio d Ormesini

Fond d Misericordia

San Giobbe

C A N N A R E G I O

Campo
S Giobbe

PONTE D
TRE ARCHI

Canale di Cannaregio

Fond d Cannaregio

**IL
GHETTO**

Campo
Ghetto
Nuovo

C llo
dell'Anconetta

C llo
Lombardo

Guglie

Parco di
Savorgnàn

Rio Terrà S Leonardo

PONTE
D'GUGLIE

Campo
S Leonardo

**San
Marcuola**

Campo
S Marcuola

San Marcuola

Scalzi

Canal Grande

STAZIONE FERROVIARIA
SANTA LUCIA

Ponte
degli Scalzi

Campo
S Simeon
Grande

Rivi di Biasio

Campo
S Simeon
Profeta

**San Giovanni
Decollato**

**Museo
di Storia
Naturale**

San Stae

Campo
S Stae

San Stae

Ferrovia

**Museo de
Tessuto e
del Costu**

Ferrovia

Campo
N Sauro

**San Giacomo
dell'Orio**

Ruga Bella

**Palazzo
Mocenigo**

**ZIONE
OVIARIA
ERCI**

Campo
N Sauro

**Campo San
Giacomo
dell'Orio**

Campo
S M Mater
Domini

**Giardino
Papadopoli**

Campo d
S Agostin

SAN POLO

Campo d
Tolentino

**Scuola Grande di
San Giovanni
Evangelista**

**Campo
San Polo**

**San Nicolò
da Tolentino**

**Archivio
di Stato**

Campo
S Stin

San Polo

**San
Rocco**

**Santa Maria
Gloriosa dei
Frari**

**Campo
dei Frari**

Rio Terrà Tomà

9

**Scuola Grande
di San Rocco**

C **D** **San Pantalon** **E**

58

**Museo Casa Carlo
Goldoni**

SIGHT LOCATOR

60

J   K   L   M

8

Barbaria delle Tole

Rio d S Giovanni Laterano

C larga S Lorenzo

9

Campo San Lorenzo

Scuola di San Giorgio degli Schiavoni

Celestia

San Francesco della Vigna

Campo della Confraternita

Campo d'Celestia

Campo S Giustina

Campo d'Gatte

Campo S Ternita

Rio di Colesta

Canale delle Galeazze

Darse Grand

San Giorgio degli Greci

San Zaccaria

Santa Maria della Visitazione-La Pietà

Riva degli Schiavoni

10

San Giovanni in Bragora

Campo Bandiera e Moro

Arsenale

Fond del Fronte

Campo Arsenale

Darsena Arsenale Vecchio

C A S T E

Riva degli schiavoni

Arsenale

Riva Ca' di Dio

Museo Storico Navale

Campo S Biagio

Riva S Biagio

Campo della Tana

Rio della Tana

Fond della Tana

Corte Nuova

C d Preti

Fond del

C S Francesco di Paolo

11

Via Giuseppe Garibaldi

Riva dei Sette Martiri

Canale   di   San   Marco

Bacino

San Giorgio Maggiore

12

Giardi

Bacino di San Giorgio

Ísola di San Giorgio Maggiore

13

SIGHT LOCATOR

J   K   L   M

San Marco and San Giorgio Maggiore

HOW TO GET THERE

🚤 1 (down Grand Canal) stopping at Rialto, Giglio, San Marco (Vallaresso), San Zaccaria; 82 (down Grand Canal) stopping at Rialto, San Samuele, San Marco (Vallaresso), San Zaccaria; 41, 42 to Piazza San Marco via Giudecca Canal; 82 from San Zaccaria to San Giorgio Maggiore

San Marco is the busiest of Venice's six *sestieri* (wards). The area's focal point, the

The Basilica di San Marco in Piazza San Marco

Piazza San Marco, is dominated by the Basilica di San Marco, the Campanile and the Palazzo Ducale. These lie close to the Riva degli Schiavoni and the Bacino di San Marco (St Mark's Basin), bounded to the south by the island of San Giorgio Maggiore and opening westwards into the sweep of the Grand Canal. Since the Middle Ages, the area's shopping heartland has been the Mercerie, a string of narrow alleys linking the Piazza with the Rialto and its famous bridge, while another main route through the area runs west from the Piazza through wider streets to the Accademia

bridge across the Grand Canal. For a change of pace, board a *vaporetto* and head across to the island of San Giorgio Maggiore and its great church.

THE MAIN SIGHTS

San Marco's main sights are the main sights of Venice itself, with the Piazza San Marco and its surrounding buildings drawing every visitor to the city. Be selective and concentrate on what interests you most.

Museo Correr

A museum devoted to the history of Venice, with an art gallery, an archaeological collection and the Biblioteca Nazionale Marciana, the city's historic library (▷ 108–109).

Palazzo Ducale

This huge complex is a superlative example of Venetian architecture. Don't miss the Doge's Apartments or the Sala del Maggiore Consiglio, with its lavishly decorated gilded ceiling (▷ 112–117).

Piazza San Marco

The heart of San Marco contains the vast Piazza, dominated by the Basilica di San Marco, the soaring Campanile (bell-tower) and the Piazzetta (▷ 139–140).

Riva degli Schiavoni

The wide quayside area fronting the Palazzo Ducale has superb views over St. Mark's Basin (▷ 122–123).

San Giorgio Maggiore

One of Palladio's finest churches, set on its own island, with fabulous city views from the top of its campanile (▷ 130–131).

Santo Stefano

An historic 14th- to 15th-century church overlooking the second-largest *campo* in the *sestiere* (▷ 159).

OTHER PLACES TO VISIT

Between the Piazza and the Accademia are the churches of San Moisè and Santa Maria del Giglio (▷ 142), while the famous opera house, Teatro La

The Gothic exterior of the Palazzo Ducale (Doge's Palace)

Fenice (▷ 168), also lies on this route. Further north are some fine *palazzi*, notably the Contarini del Bovolo, with its spiral exterior stair, and the Grassi (▷ 118), venue for spectacular temporary exhibitions. There's more art at the Museo Diocesano d'Arte Sacra (▷ 105), while the Museo Fortuny (▷ 110) showcases sumptuous fabrics hanging in a unique setting.

WHERE TO EAT

There are dozens of possibilities in San Marco, with those in or near the Piazza being the most expensive. Head west or north to find places used by the Venetians themselves.

Castello

HOW TO GET THERE

📧 1 to San Zaccaria, Arsenale, Giardini, Sant'Elena; 41, 42, 51, 52 to San Zaccaria, Arsenale, Giardini, Sant'Elena, San Pietro, Bacini, Celestia, Ospedale

Castello, which gets its name from the fortress *(castello)* that once stood here, is the biggest Venetian *sestiere* (ward), stretching from San Marco in the west to the islands of San Pietro and Sant'Elena in the east. It was once both the city's industrial powerhouse, with the Arsenale producing fleets of ships, and home to Venice's religious heart, the island of San Pietro; San Marco only became the city's cathedral in 1807. It's a varied area, with a long southern waterfront over-looking St. Mark's Basin and a northern quayside that looks towards the main lagoon islands and the distant Alps. To the east lies the *fondamenta*

The Riva degli Schiavoni, looking towards Piazza San Marco

of the Riva degli Schiavoni, while western Castello runs from the Arsenale to Sant'Elena. Packed between these boundaries are churches and museums, but the area's strongest allure perhaps lies in its vibrant working-class streets and busy *campi*, its wide waterside promenades, and the artisan and work shops in the narrow streets.

THE MAIN SIGHTS

With the exception of Santi Giovanni e Paolo, in the north of Castello, the major attractions lie on or not far from the Riva degli Schiavoni, so you could work your way east from San Marco.

Campo Santi Giovanni e Paolo

This *campo* in northern Castello is home to a remarkable equestrian statue by Andrea Verrocchio (▷ 133), a superb Renaissance façade (▷ 133) and a huge Gothic church (▷ 132–133) that's the burial place of many of the city's doges and heroes.

Museo Storico Navale

A collection of all things nautical pertaining to Venice illustrates perfectly the city's historic relationship with the sea (▷ 111).

Riva degli Schiavoni

A wide quayside with superb views over St. Mark's Basin, that stretches, under different names, from the Palazzo Ducale to the Giardini Pubblici in the east of the *sestiere* (▷ 122–123).

Scuola di San Giorgio degli Schiavoni

The tiny headquarters of one of Venice's charitable confraternities is beautifully decorated with fine paintings by Vittore Carpaccio (▷ 163).

Santa Maria Formosa

This 15th-century church (▷ 143) stands in an attractive square (▷ 80) that's the heart of western and northern Castello and a through route to the whole *sestiere*.

San Zaccaria

An ancient church that show-cases some of the best of Venetian early Renaissance art and contains the only crypt in Venice (▷ 160).

OTHER PLACES TO VISIT

Western Castello has a couple of interesting museums, such as the Museo della Fondazione Querini-Stampalia (▷ 110) and the Museo Diocesano d'Arte

Model of the Bucintoro *in the Museo Storico Navale*

Sacra (▷ 105). In the same area you'll find Santa Maria della Visitazione (▷ 152); San Giorgio degli Greci (▷ 127) and San Giovanni in Bragora (▷ 128). East from here lies the Arsenale (▷ 69), the buildings of the Biennale (▷ 76) and the historic churches of Sant'Elena (▷ 125) and San Pietro di Castello (▷ 153), while to the north lies the Palladian church of San Francesco della Vigna (▷ 125).

WHERE TO EAT

There are plenty of restaurants along Riva degli Schiavoni and the streets behind. Eastern Castello has a good choice around Via Garibaldi.

THE SIGHTS

Cannaregio

HOW TO GET THERE

🚤 1, 82 to Ferrovia, San Marcuola, Ca' d'Oro; 41, 42, 51, 52 to Ferrovia, Guglie, Tre Archi, Sant'Alvise, Orto, Fondamente Nuove

Until the railway link with the mainland was built in 1846, Cannaregio was the entrance to Venice, with every arrival sweeping down the wide Canale di Cannaregio, which runs through the heart of the *sestiere* to join the Canal Grande, the southern boundary. Many visitors still arrive at Cannaregio's Santa Lucia station. From there, the wide Strada Nova, one of the city's main shopping streets, cuts through towards the Rialto. This eastern end of Cannaregio is among the oldest settled parts of Venice, a warren of narrow streets with superb buildings, among them the Ca' d'Oro and the church of Santa

Santa Maria dei Miracoli, while the Ca' d'Oro stands right on the water.

Ca' d'Oro
Medieval Venetians considered the palace of the Ca' d'Oro (Golden House, ▷ 70–71) the most beautiful in the city.

Campo dei Mori
An oddly shaped little waterside *campo* with quirky statues in the backstreets of one of Venice's most tranquil areas (▷ 78).

Il Ghetto
This atmospheric square on a separate island is home to the world's original Ghetto, where you can trace the history of the Jewish community through its buildings and synagogues (▷ 102–103).

Madonna dell'Orto
This superb Gothic building in northern Cannaregio, the burial place of the artist Tintoretto, was his parish church and is adorned with some of his finest paintings (▷ 106–107).

Santa Maria dei Miracoli
A jewel-like Renaissance church that's tucked away from the main city routes, with some of the most delicate stonework in Venice (▷ 148–149).

OTHER PLACES TO VISIT
Cannaregio has some attractive squares, many of which have a fine church as their focal point—head for the Campo dei Gesuiti (▷ 77), also home to the Oratorio dei Crociferi, and the

bustling Campo Santi Apostoli (▷ 79), to get a taste of these. Other churches worth some time include San Giobbe (▷ 127), Sant'Alvise (▷ 124) and the Scalzi (▷ 158). It's worth spending time walking through this

Tintoretto's modest house in the Campo dei Mori

sestiere (▷ 232–233) to soak up its atmosphere of contrasting great sights and quiet side streets and canals, factors that make Cannaregio much more than the sum of its parts.

WHERE TO EAT

There's plenty of choice on the main route from the station to the Rialto in the form of snack bars and restaurants, many of which are definitely aimed at tourists. For something better, choose carefully or head further off the beaten track; behind the Apostoli and along the canals of the Sensa and the Misericordia are a good place to start.

The interior of the church of Santa Maria dei Miracoli

Maria dei Miracoli. To the north, there's contrast in the wide *fondamente* (quaysides) that line a trio of parallel canals, the heart of a quiet area containing the church of Madonna dell'Orto. The canals here constantly buzz with water traffic and a stroll along the *fondamenta* will lead you to the historic Ghetto.

THE MAIN SIGHTS
Cannaregio's highlights are scattered throughout the area, with the church of Madonna dell'Orto and the nearby Campo dei Mori within easy reach of the Ghetto. Closer to the Grand Canal you'll find the Renaissance church of

San Polo and Santa Croce

HOW TO GET THERE

1 to Piazzale Roma, Biasio, San Stae, San Silvestro, San Tomà; 82 to Piazzale Roma, San Tomà; 41, 42, 51, 52, 61, 62 to Piazzale Roma, Santa Marta

Enclosed by a loop of the upper stretches of the Grand Canal, the west-bank *sestieri* of San Polo and Santa Croce are densely populated, workaday districts, full of charm. The big sights lie to the south, along the route running from the Scuola Grande di San Rocco and the adjacent church of Santa Maria Gloriosa dei Frari to the Rialto itself. The latter was first to be settled, and gets its name from the Latin Rivus Altus, meaning high bank, where embryonic islands provided firm ground for the earliest lagoon settlers to build their houses. By the early Middle Ages it was the commercial heart of the city, home

the Rialto and its markets. North from here Ca' Pesaro overlooks the Grand Canal, not far from Campo San Giacomo dell'Orio and its church.

Ca' Pesaro

A superbly restored baroque *palazzo* (▷ 72–73) on the Grand Canal that's home to the Museo d'Arte Moderna and the Museo d'Arte Orientale (▷ 105).

Rialto

The ancient Rivus Altus is one of the oldest parts of Venice and is famed for its bridge and lively markets (▷ 120–121).

San Giacomo dell'Orio

An ancient church (▷ 126) on Campo San Giacomo dell'Orio (▷ 79), packed with quirky architectural details and pictures by Palma il Giovane.

San Polo

This 14th-century Gothic church (▷ 155), with a fine picture cycle by Giambattista Tiepolo, is on Campo San Polo (▷ 80), the largest square on the south side of the Grand Canal.

Santa Maria Gloriosa dei Frari

A cavernous 14th-century Franciscan church (▷ 144–147) on the Campo dei Frari (▷ 76), with works by Giovanni Bellini, and Titian, who is buried here.

Scuola Grande di San Rocco

A pictorial tour de force by Tintoretto, whose paintings are set against a sumptuous architectural interior (▷ 164–167).

Market supplies being offloaded from a barge at the Rialto

to merchants and bankers. It's still a maze of narrow streets and hidden squares, from where you can head north to the topmost point of the Grand Canal and the unalluring surroundings of Piazzale Roma, where the road from the mainland reaches the city. It's better to stick near the water and take in some of the museums, or head here after dark to enjoy dinner.

THE MAIN SIGHTS

If you're heading north through San Polo, the Scuola Grande di San Rocco and the Frari are within yards of each other and a pleasant 20-minute stroll from

OTHER PLACES TO VISIT

For a glimpse of old Venice visit the Museo del Tessuto e del Costume in the lofty Palazzo Mocenigo (▷ 118), or the Museo Casa Carlo Goldoni

Baroque at its finest—a view of the Ca' Pesaro from the canal

(▷ 105). Churches worth a detour include San Giovanni Decollato (▷ 129), San Pantalon (▷ 153), San Stae (▷ 156) and San Rocco (▷ 156). Children can let off steam in the green space of the Giardino Papadopoli (▷ 104) or spot a dinosaur at the Museo di Storia Naturale (▷ 110).

WHERE TO EAT

The Rialto area is one of the best places for bars serving *cicheti*, the tapas-like snacks so popular here. There are serious restaurants, too, while the area nearer San Giacomo dell'Orio has an excellent choice of places to eat.

Map labels

Museo di Storia Naturale
Canal Grande
San Marcuola
San Marcuola
Maddalena
S Fosca
S Felice
Campo S Felice
Rivi di Biasio
San Giovanni Decollato
S Simeon Grande
San Giacomo dell'Orio
San Stae
San Stae
Campo S Stae
Ca' Pesaro
Ca' d'Oro
Palazzo Mocenigo
Museo del Tessuto e del Costume
Ca' d'Oro
Campo S Sofia
Campo N Sauro
Campo San Giacomo dell'Orio
S Maria Mater Domini
San Cassiano
Campo S Cassiano
Campo d'Pescaria
Scuola Grande di San Giovanni Evangelista
Campo d S Agostin
San Giovanni Elemosinario
S Giacomo di Rialto
Archivio di Stato
S Giovanni Evangelista
SAN POLO
S Aponal
Campo Rialto Nuovo
San Rocco
Santa Maria Gloriosa dei Frari
Campo San Polo
Campo S Aponal
Campo S Silvestro
Ponte di Rialto
Campo dei Frari
Campo San Polo
San Polo
San Silvestro
Rialto
Scuola Grande di San Rocco
Museo Carlo Goldoni
S Silvestro
Campo S Tomà
Palazzo Pisani-Moretta
Canal Grande
Campo S Benedetto
S Luca
San Tomà
Sant Angelo
Campo S Benedetto
Campo Manin
Museo Fortuny
Oratio dell'Annunziata

0   200 m
0   200 yds

D8 D9 E7 E10 F6 F10 G7 G9

Dorsoduro and the Giudecca

THE SIGHTS

🚤 1 to Ca' Rezzonico, Accademia and Salute; 51, 52, 61, 62 to Zattere

Dorsoduro is one of Venice's most compelling areas, home to two important galleries and some superb art-filled churches. It is bounded to the north by the Grand Canal and to the south by the Giudecca canal. Campo Santa Margherita

A view across the water to Santa Maria della Salute

is the hub, from where you can head south and parallel with the Grand Canal to the church of the Salute, set virtually at the end of this tapering stretch of land. South from here, the long waterfront known as the Zattere runs west; off it are fashionable residential streets, peaceful canals and picturesque squares. Dorsoduro's west end lies in one of the oldest parts of the city; here the streets around the church of San Nicolò dei Mendicoli contrast with the bustle around the Stazione Marittima, where the huge cruise liners dock, just across the water from the island of Giudecca.

THE MAIN SIGHTS
You can take in most of Dorsoduro's main attractions by heading south from Campo Santa Margherita; Ca' Rezzonico, the Accademia, the Guggenheim and Santa Maria della Salute lie along this route. Head west for the quieter backstreets and the churches of San Sebastiano and San Nicolò dei Mendicoli.

Ca' Rezzonico
A sumptuous *palazzo* housing furniture, pictures and *objets d'art* evoking 18th-century patrician life in Venice (▷ 74–75).

Collezione Peggy Guggenheim
An important collection of 20th-century art, amassed by the millionairess Peggy Guggenheim (▷ 92–93).

Gallerie dell'Accademia
Venice's most important gallery provides an essential overview of Venetian painting, with superb examples by the most outstanding painters of the 14th to 18th centuries (▷ 94–100).

San Nicolò dei Mendicoli
Tucked away in a quiet corner is one of the city's oldest churches, still retaining its Veneto-Byzantine structure (▷ 154).

San Sebastiano
Known as Veronese's church, San Sebastiano (▷ 157) shimmers with a luminous series of works by this great artist, who is buried in the church.

Santa Maria della Salute
The baroque domes of the great plague church of Santa Maria della Salute (▷ 150–151) punc-

tuate the skyline at the entrance to the Grand Canal, while the marbles and fine paintings of the interior are drenched in light.

OTHER PLACES TO VISIT
Don't miss Campo Santa Margherita (▷ 80) and its surrounding area, packed with good shops and fine churches, such as the Angelo Raffaele (▷ 69), the Carmini (▷ 142) and San

Looking over the Redentore church from the Lagoon

Trovaso (▷ 158). From San Trovaso it's a few steps to the Squero di San Trovaso (▷ 168), a working gondola yard, and the Zattere *fondamenta* (▷ 168), perfect for a stroll with a view. From here, you can take the *vaporetto* across to La Giudecca with its superb Palladian church, Il Redentore (▷ 119).

WHERE TO EAT
Dorsoduro has a wide choice of bars and restaurants, mostly around the Accademia northwards. Eating places along the Zattere are great for dining al fresco, and you'll find a good choice of price ranges around Campo Santa Margherita.

Detail from the carved relief on the pulpit of Angelo Raffaele, a 17th-century church built on the site of one dating from the 8th

St. Mark's lion stands proudly above the Arsenale's main portal

ANGELO RAFFAELE

🗺 310 C10 • Campo Angelo Raffaele, Dorsoduro ☎ 041 522 8548 🕐 Daily 9–12, 3–5 💰 Free 🚤 Ca' Rezzonico, San Basilio

The church of the Angelo Raffaele is one of the city's oldest foundations, traditionally established in the 8th century, though today's structure, in the shape of a Greek cross, dates from the 17th century. It's tucked away in a secluded part of Dorsoduro, standing in a spacious *campo* and fronted by a *rio*, and is one of only two Venetian churches that you can walk the whole way around outside. Visitor numbers have risen dramatically since the success of Salley Vickers' book *Miss Garnet's Angel* (published 2000); the church plays a starring role in the novel. The façade is flanked by two bell-towers, visible over much of eastern Dorsoduro, and above the main door is a statue of the Archangel Raphael, holding the hand of the boy Tobiolo and accompanied by a dog. Inside, the ceiling fresco by Gaspare Diziani shows *St. Michael Driving Out Lucifer*, but the real gems are on the organ loft. Five panels painted by Gianantonio Guardi (1699–1760) show scenes from the apocryphal story of *Tobias and the Angel*, miracles of liveliness, charm and luminosity. Elsewhere in the church are other sculptures and images of the Archangel with Tobias and his dog; Tobias is always pictured holding a fish, which plays a key role in the biblical story.

ARCHIVIO DI STATO

🗺 58 E9 • Campo dei Frari, San Polo 3002 ☎ 041 522 2281 🕐 Mon, Fri–Sat 8.30–2, Tue–Thu 8.30–6 💰 Free to students and academics; small variable charge for exhibitions 🚤 San Tomà www.archivi.beniculturali.it

The smooth running of the Venetian state depended on an efficient bureaucratic administration. There were records of Council meetings to be kept, trade treaties to be made, ambassadors to be briefed, the Arsenale to run, spies' and informers' information to be collated, and an eye kept on suspicious characters at home and abroad. Everything was written down, and nothing was thrown away. This vast mountain of paperwork, going back to the 9th century, still exists; it's known as the Archivio di Stato (State Archive) and has been housed since the early 1800s in the monastery adjoining the Frari. Laid out the paperwork would stretch over 70km (43 miles). Much is of interest only to scholars, but the Archive occasionally stages exhibitions on aspects of Venetian history using its materials. If you want to look for something, you must request the files in the morning; a knowledge of Latin is useful and it helps to be able to decipher medieval and Renaissance handwriting.

ARSENALE

🗺 62 L10 • Campo dell'Arsenale, Castello 🚤 Arsenale

The Arsenale, whose name derives from the Arabic 'Dar Sina'a', the place of industry, was Venice's industrial powerhouse, an ultra-efficient shipbuilding production line that built the galleys that made Venetian seapower a reality. The wealth of the city, its *palazzi*, churches, sumptuous art and sculpture, all derived from the profits of its trade and empire—profits dependent on its merchant and war fleets. For a taste of what made the Republic tick, there's nowhere better than this huge, and now virtually deserted,

complex. Shipbuilding started here in the 12th century; by the 15th over 16,000 people were employed here and the workers were capable of assembling a galley in just a few hours, using the world's first production line. The interior of the Arsenale is still occupied by the Italian Navy, and is off-limits as a military zone, but it's worth heading to the main gates to see as much as you can. The gateway, designed by Antonio Gambello in 1460, is the first example of Renaissance classical architecture in the city. The capitals on its columns are Veneto-Byzantine; the lions guarding it a mixed bunch. Two were looted from Athens in 1687—one of them has runic inscriptions on its side, probably carved by a Norse mercenary in service with the Byzantine empire. Just off the Campo della Tana, on the other side of the canal, is the huge building which once housed the rope works, the Corderia. It's used during the Biennale (▷ 21) as an overflow exhibition space, and there are plans for further development of the area as a cultural centre.

BIENNALE INTERNAZIONALE D'ARTE

See page 76.

Naval officers from the Arsenale

Ca' d'Oro

●

Among the finest and most flamboyant of all Gothic *palazzi* in a splendid position on the Grand Canal, this is the perfect place to appreciate how medieval merchant businesses functioned.

Bust of a Young Boy *by Giovanni Romano (15th century)*

Looking out through the Gothic tracery fronting the loggias

The Ca' d'Oro's sparkling façade is a Grand Canal landmark

RATINGS	
Cultural interest	●●●●
Good for kids	●●●
Historic interest	●●●●
Photo stops	●●●●

BASICS

✚ 59 G7 • Calle Ca' d'Oro, Cannaregio 3922

☎ 041 523 8790

◉ Mon 8.15–2, Tue–Sun 8.15–7.15. Closed 1 May

▱ Ca' d'Oro

💵 €5; combined ticket with Accademia and Museo Orientale €11

💿 Guidebook (€8.50) and audiotour (€5) available in Italian, English, French and German

🏛

🏃

www.cadoro.org

Good practical site in Italian only with on-line booking, information on how to get there and details of the shop, but little information on the museum's contents.

SEEING THE CA' D'ORO

For an excellent view of the façade of the Ca' d'Oro, head for the Pescheria (fish market) on the opposite side of the Grand Canal. Once you've had a good look at the exterior, take the *traghetto* Santa Sofia across the water to the building itself. Allow time inside, working your way up from the ground floor, and be sure to linger on the exterior loggias, great places to watch the water traffic. The best time for this is during the morning, when delivery barges and service boats are constantly coming and going. The top floor contains an extensive coin, medal and miniature collection, which is probably only of limited interest to most visitors.

HIGHLIGHTS

THE INTERIOR OF THE CA D'ORO

Medieval Venetian merchants' houses were also their business premises, with goods stored in warehouses on the ground floor and offices leading off the *portego*, a huge reception room running the full depth of the *piano nobile*, the first floor. Today, the Ca' d'Oro's ground floor still reflects this layout, with the main door opening onto the water, warehouse space behind and a tiny pleasure garden and courtyard from where an exterior staircase leads to the upper floors. The rose marble well-head in the courtyard was carved by Bartolomeo Bon in 1472. The upper floors were completely reconstructed during the 1970s restoration, but they retain their open Gothic loggias overlooking the Grand Canal. The galleries contain works of art by Venetian artists such as Gentile Bellini (1429–1507) and Titian (c1487–1576), Florentine and Sienese paintings, Flemish tapestries and ghostly fresco fragments by Titian and Giorgione (c1476/8–1510).

SAN SEBASTIANO

Andrea Mantegna started painting *San Sebastiano* in 1506; it was his last work and remained unfinished at his death. The saint, patron of the sick, was a popular figure in plague-ridden Venice and a subject dear to artists, who used his martyrdom as an opportunity to depict a virtually naked figure—a subject normally tabooed by the ecclesiastical powers. San Sebastiano is seen riddled with arrows, while a guttering

candle in the picture's right-hand corner alludes to the fleeting nature of life. The Latin inscription also refers to man's mortality; it reads 'Only the Divine is eternal, all else is but smoke'.

THE ANNUNCIATION AND THE DEATH OF THE VIRGIN

Two panels from Vittore Carpaccio's picture cycle for the Scuola degli Albanesi are now in the Ca' d'Oro, the *Annunciation* and the *Death of the Virgin*, part of a series that told stories from the life of the Virgin. Both painted in 1504, they are beautifully observed, charming paintings. The *Annunciation* is exquisitely rendered, with the Virgin half-turned away from the angel, as if lost in her own reaction to the momentous news that she is to be the mother of the Saviour.

BACKGROUND

The Ca' d'Oro, Golden House, was built between 1420 and 1434 by Bartolomeo Bon and his associates for the Procurator Marino Contarini, and was intended, like all Venetian domestic buildings, to take the name of its owner. From the moment it was finished it was clear that Ca' Contarini was far too pedestrian a name for this glittering building, whose exterior was adorned with vermilion, ultramarine and gold leaf. Quickly dubbed Ca' d'Oro, the name remains, though the gold leaf has long since disappeared. Over the centuries the interior was drastically altered by successive owners, though the exterior remains the finest Veneto-Byzantine Gothic monument after San Marco. By the mid-19th century, the building was almost in ruins, and the Russian Prince Troubetskoy was able to acquire it cheaply as a gift for his mistress, the famous ballerina Maria Taglioni. Her talents did not extend as far as interior design and her 'restorations' invoked the wrath of English writer John Ruskin, in Venice writing his seminal *Stones of Venice*. In 1894 the building was bought by Baron Franchetti, who reinstalled the stair and well-head in the courtyard and filled the *palazzo* with his collections of paintings, sculpture and coins. In 1916 he left both building and collection to the state and the Ca'd'Oro opened to the public in 1927. There was another lengthy restoration between 1969 and 1984.

The Annunciation *by Vittore Carpaccio (top)*

Brooding lions on the façade of the Ca' d'Oro have watched the water traffic on the Grand Canal for centuries (above)

Ca' Pesaro

This magnificent 17th-century *palazzo* on the Grand Canal has been beautifully
restored to house two important museums and holds paintings and sculpture
covering the main Italian 20th-century movements.

*View of the Ca' Pesaro as seen
from the Grand Canal (above)
Detail of the marble floor
(above right and far right)*

RATINGS	
Cultural interest	● ● ●
Historic interest	● ● ●
Value for money	● ● ● ●

SEEING THE CA' PESARO

The Ca' Pesaro lies a few minutes walk from the *vaporetto* stop
at San Stae; if you're approaching from San Marco you'll be able
to get a look at the ornate façade from the boat, otherwise, to
study it in detail, you'll need to position yourself on the other
side of the Grand Canal. The best place to do this is at the end of
Calle Traghetto on the left of the west end of the Strada Nova.
Once inside, take time to walk through the entrance hall to the
front of the building, with its superb view of the water traffic and
buildings opposite. A grandiose staircase leads to the *piano
nobile* (first-floor state rooms), where the Museo Galleria
Internazionale d'Arte Moderna is situated. The Museo d'Arte
Orientale is on the upper floor. If you're interested in Far Eastern
art allow at least an hour to see this huge collection.

HIGHLIGHTS

THE FAÇADE

It's worth studying the complex architecture of the Grand Canal
façade, a textbook example of baroque, where perfectly balanced
basic architectural elements combine with flamboyant decoration. The
lower plinth, at water level, is decorated with lions' faces and monstrous heads and is surmounted by a rusticated façade with two rows
of windows, punctuated in the middle by twin doorways. These too
are decorated with more statuary and carved swags. Above this, the
first floor alternates deep-set arches and protruding columns, producing a superb chiaroscuro (light and shade) effect that's enhanced by
the play of reflected light from the water. The second floor has more
columns, though the windows are less deeply recessed, and rich
stone ornamentation above the windows. Higher still, a wonderfully
ornate frieze combines horizontal and upright decorative motifs to
pull together the whole architectural ensemble triumphantly.

*A harmonious baroque gateway
is the main land entrance to
the Ca' Pesaro*

THE GROUND FLOOR

The land entrance to the *palazzo* is approached through a courtyard,
whose focal point is a monumental well-head. This space is enclosed
by a terrace and an arcade, which leads into the vast entrance hall.
This runs along the axis of the entire building, a typical layout for
Venetian *palazzi* since the 13th century. Off this were originally store-
rooms and offices; today these side spaces house the museum's café

and shops, leaving the central space wonderfully uncluttered. At the canal end, shallow steps lead down to the water entrance, originally the main means of access.

MUSEO GALLERIA INTERNAZIONALE D'ARTE MODERNA

The *piano nobile* houses the Museo d'Arte Moderna, a well laid out sries of interconnecting rooms (▷ 104–105).

MUSEO D'ARTE ORIENTALE

The second floor is home to the collections of the Museo d'Arte Orientale (▷ 105).

BACKGROUND

The Ca' Pesaro was the home of the wealthy Pesaro family, who made their money from their monopoly of the transport links from the lagoon to the River Brenta. When bought by the family in 1628 it was three separate buildings, and in 1650 Leonardo Pesaro employed Baldassare Longhena to convert all three into one palatial whole. The work occupied the following 50 years and the result is one of the Grand Canal's greatest examples of Venetian baroque architecture, a fitting accompaniment to Longhena's other main Grand Canal buildings, the church of the Salute (▷ 150–151) and Ca' Rezzonico (▷ 74–75). Longhena died in 1682, by which time construction had barely reached the second floor, and Antonio Gaspari was called in to finish the job. He stuck closely to the original plans in most respects and was wholly responsible for the far less flamboyant side façade overlooking the Rio della Pergola.

By the 19th century the palace was the property of the ducal La Masa family from Verona, and in 1889 Felicità Bevilacqua La Masa, the dowager duchess, bequeathed the *palazzo* to the city. She visualized the foundation of an arts centre for struggling young artists, but the city fathers thought otherwise and in 1902 installed a modern art gallery to house works bought from the Biennale. This was joined, after World War I, by the Museo d'Arte Orientale, a vast and eclectic collection of Far Eastern art presented to Venice by Austria in reparation for the damage inflicted by incendiary bombs during the conflict.

BASICS

✚ 59 F7 • Santa Croce 2070–76
☎ 041 524 0662
🕔 Apr–end Oct Tue–Sun 10–6; Nov–Mar Tue–Sun 10–5. Closed 1 May
💶 €5.50, Rolling Venice card holders €3, combined ticket with Ca' d'Oro and Gallerie dell'Accademia €11
🚤 San Stae
📕 Guidebooks €6
☕ Café/bar selling drinks and light snacks
🏬 Good book and giftshop selling art books, museum souvenirs, postcards and posters
♿
www.museicivicivenezia ni.it
Excellent site in English and Italian with full details of all Venices's civic museums.

Statues adorn the courtyard façade of the Ca' Pesaro (above)

Ca' Rezzonico

●

The sumptuous 17th-century Ca' Rezzonico houses a museum of life in the 18th century, Venice's most hedonistic era. Fine furniture, textiles, glass and great paintings are beautifully set in its opulently decorated rooms.

View of the Ca' Rezzonico from the Grand Canal

Gilded chairs line Ca' Rezzonico's walls—a typical 18th-century interior arrangement

Tiepolo's Mondo Novo (New World) *fresco*

RATINGS	
Cultural interest	●●●●○
Good for kids	●●●○
Historic interest	●●●●○
Value for money	●●●●○

BASICS
✚ 60 E10 • Fondamenta Rezzonico, Dorsoduro 3136
☎ 041 241 0100
⏲ Apr–end Oct Wed–Mon 10–6; Oct–end Mar Wed–Mon 10–5. Closed 1 May
💷 €6.50; 'Rolling Venice' card holders €4.50 or cumulative ticket available for Ca' Rezzonico, Palazzo Mocenigo and Museo di Carlo Goldoni €8
🗂 Ca' Rezzonico
🎧 Audioguides (€3) and guidebooks (€12) in Italian, English, French and German
🚻
🍽 Excellent
👫
www.museicivicineveneziani.it Excellent site in English and Italian with full details of all Venices's civic museums.

SEEING THE CA' REZZONICO

The water façade of the Ca' Rezzonico can be seen from Campo San Samuele, on the opposite side of the Grand Canal, or take it in from the *vaporetto*. If you're arriving by boat, you can normally enter the *palazzo* from the water entrance, by crossing the bridge to the right of the *vaporetto pontile*. On foot, the entrance is on the side of the building.

Start your visit by walking up the magnificent stairway to the *piano nobile*, following the designated route; you'll find good information in each room. The second floor contains some very fine pictures, and the third floor is home to a huge, mediocre picture collection bequeathed by Count Egidio Martini in the mid-20th century. This shouldn't detain you, though the 18th-century apothecary's shop is worth a look. Leave time to relax in the pretty garden behind the *palazzo*.

HIGHLIGHTS

THE BALLROOM

The most original architectural feature is the ballroom, approached by a ceremonial stairway and occupying the height of two floors of the building. This design innovation, the brainchild of Giorgio Massari (c1686–1766), was unique in Venice and created an immense space that was the scene of some of the 18th century's grandest entertaining. The sense of grandeur is accentuated by the *trompe l'oeil* architecture painted on the walls, the dizzying ceiling frescoes, the dazzling gilding and stucco decoration, and the florid gilded wood and metal chandeliers, part of the original furnishings of the *palazzo*.

THE PIANO NOBILE

From the ballroom, a series of ornately decorated, interconnected rooms fans out, each furnished with fine contemporary pieces and decorated with rich fabrics and wallhangings. Highlights include the Tiepolo ceiling panels in the Throne Room and Nuptial Room, some stunning *ciocche* (ornate gilded locks and door furniture), Murano glass chandeliers, and the mind-blowing furniture designed by Andrea Brustolon (1662–1732). This furniture maker worked almost exclusively in ebony and boxwood; look out for the extraordinary console-cum-vase stand, all writhing forms, intricate carving and chinoiserie effects, that represents an *Allegory of Hercules*.

THE SECOND-FLOOR GALLERY
The central section of the second floor is occupied by the *portego*, a long room running the full depth of the building and used as a *quadreria*, picture gallery. Pride of place goes to two paintings by Canaletto, the only examples of his work in Venice itself; they show *A View of the Rio dei Mendicanti* and *The Grand Canal from Ca' Balbi*. Don't miss the series of pictures by Francesco Guardi (1712–93) and

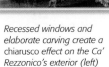

Recessed windows and elaborate carving create a chiarusco *effect on the Ca' Rezzonico's exterior (left)*

Gilded papal throne in the Sala del Trono (above)

Pietro Longhi (1702–85), two of Venice's finest genre painters, who portayed scenes from everyday Venetian life—gambling rooms, bad behaviour in high society, carousing nuns and a charming rhinoceros, painted during a carnival visit to the city.

THE TIEPOLO FRESCOES
Also on the second floor is the beautifully restored cycle of frescoes painted by Giandomenico Tiepolo between 1759 and 1797 for his own villa on the mainland. These are intensely personal works, painted for pleasure, not as a commission, and encompass everything from delicate religious pictures for the chapel to the antics of Punchinello, an ancestor of the puppet Mr. Punch. The most striking work is the surreal *Mondo Novo* (New World) of 1791, showing a crowd, seen from behind, peering into a peepshow.

BACKGROUND
In 1667, the Venetian Procurator Filippo Bon commissioned the Baldassare Longhena to design a major palace for his family on the Grand Canal. Work was soon under way, and by the time of Longhena's death in 1682 the structure was complete as far as the *piano nobile*. His death coincided with a sharp downturn in the Bon family fortune and work on the *palazzo* ceased for the following 70 years. It then came to the attention of the nouveau riche Rezzonico clan, who bought the palace in 1751 and appointed Giorgio Massari, one of Venice's most esteemed architects, to complete it. It was finished in 1756 and remained home to the Rezzonico family until the last member died in 1812. A string of owners followed, among them Pen Browning, whose father, the poet Robert Browning, died here in 1889. It eventually became the property of Count de Minerbi, an Italian member of parliament, who sold it to the Comune di Venezia in 1935. It became the city's museum of 18th-century life, used to display furniture, paintings and *objets d'art* from all over Venice in what became increasingly shabby surroundings. A major restoration was carried out in the late 1990s, and in 2001 this stunningly revamped palace was once more open to the public.

The German Pavilion in the Giardini Pubblici, in Castello

Some of the most famous people in the world have sipped a coffee at Caffè Quadri, under the arcades of the Procuratie Vecchie

BIENNALE INTERNAZIONALE D'ARTE

🕂 63 N12 • Giardini di Castello
☎ 041 521 8711 🕐 Daily 10–6 during the Biennale 💷 €15 🚣 Giardini
www.biennale.org

Founded in 1895 by the mayor of Venice, Riccardo Selvatico, the Esposizione Internazionale di Arte della Biennale di Venezia is a showcase for the best in modern art, alternating in odd-numbered years with the Architectural Biennale, which takes place in even years.

Though spin-off exhibitions take place all over the city, notably in the Corderia (▷ 69; part of the Arsenale complex), the main focus is in the series of permanent pavilions in the Giardini Pubblici, a leafy park at the far eastern end of Castello. Each pavilion was built and is funded by exhibiting countries, and some are architectural works of art in their own right. Pick of the bunch are Alvar Aalto's 1956 Finnish design and the 1961 Scandinavian pavilion by Sverre Fehn.

Criticized in the late 1980s and early 1990s for having lost its edge, the Biennale is now right back with the heavy players on the international contemporary arts scene, and attracts huge crowds during its mid-June to mid-November season. The organization that runs it is also responsible for the city's annual Film Festival (▷ 21) and the architecture, music and dance festivals.

CA D'ORO

See pages 70–71.

CA' PESARO

See pages 72–73.

CA' REZZONICO

See pages 74–75.

CAFFÈ FLORIAN

🕂 61 H10 • Piazza San Marco 56, San Marco ☎ 041 520 5641 🕐 May–end Oct 9:30–midnight; Nov–end Apr Thu–Tue 9:30–midnight 🚣 San Marco (Vallaresso)
www.caffeflorian.com

Sitting with a drink in the Piazza San Marco is as much a part of the Venetian experience as visiting the Basilica or going down the Grand Canal. Café life has been an essential part of the city since the 18th century and still is today, whether you're sitting at an table in the sunshine, or relaxing in the warmth of one of the charming rooms in winter.

The Caffè Florian (▷ 261) has been in business since 1720, when Floriano Francesoni established a coffee-house known as Venezia Trionfante. By the early 1800s it was very popular with Venetians, and it gained the upper hand among the Piazza cafés during the Austrian occupation (1815–1866), when loyal citizens drank here to escape the army officers in Caffè Quadri (see below) across the Piazza. The present warren of intimate and elegant rooms dates from 1859, while marble tables and upholstered benches spill out onto the arcade and into the Piazza. As you listen to the orchestra and sip your inordinately expensive hot chocolate with whipped cream or Bellini (*prosecco* with white peach juice) you'll be in good company—Lord Byron and Goethe were enthusiastic patrons here.

CAFFÈ QUADRI

🕂 61 H10 • Piazza San Marco 120, San Marco ☎ 041 522 2105 🕐 Daily 9am–midnight 🚣 San Marco (Vallaresso)
www.quadrivenice.com

Founded as early as 1638, not long after the introduction into Venice—and thus Europe—of coffee, the coffee-house known as Il Remedio was purchased in 1775 by Giorgio Quadri, who quickly established it as a popular meeting place that attracted society figures and politicians alike. It was the first Venetian café to serve the super-concentrated *caffé alla turca*, the precursor to today's *espresso*. During the Austrian occupation it was a firm favourite with officers from the occupying army, and the then owners, the Vivarini brothers, sought to win back a Venetian clientele with the opening of the upstairs restaurant rooms and the fashionable redecoration of the café itself. The décor remains today; light, bright and elegant, with clear colours and charming stucco and fresco decoration. Outside tables give superb views over the Piazza, the perfect place to view the square while listening to the orchestra and enjoying a drink (▷ 261).

Celebrities have frequented Quadri down the years, and today's habitués range from Pierce Brosnan, Claudia Schiffer and Brad Pitt to Italian heavyweight political players such as Silvio Berlusconi and Giulio Andreotti.

CAMPO DEI FRARI

🕂 60 E9 • Campo dei Frari, San Polo 🚣 San Tomà

The Campo dei Frari gets its name from the great church which dominates the square, Santa Maria Gloriosa dei Frari (▷ 144–147). If you're walking from the Accademia to the Rialto, it's right on the route and the perfect place to pause. Coming from the Accademia, duck under a *portego*, turn right and round the corner and you'll find yourself in the open space around the Frari. It's an oddly shaped *campo*, tucking itself round the

Romantic Caffè Florian has been popular since the 18th century

The Campo dei Gesuiti has been the focus of daily life for generations of Venetian citizens

sheltering walls of the basilica, and is constantly busy with locals and tourists.

Architectural fans can admire the exterior of the Frari, with its rose-red brick walls, lovely stone detailing and campanile soaring up above the paving, from different angles; for the best vantage point, cross the bridge opposite the main entrance and take it all in from the Fondamenta dei Frari.

The building on the right of the west, main door is the Archivio di Stato (▷ 69), home to the archives of the Republic.

CAMPO DEI GESUITI

✚ 59 H7 • Campo dei Gesuiti, Cannaregio ⌨ Fondamente Nuove

If you're walking from the Rialto to the Fondamente Nuove to catch a boat to the islands, you'll find yourself in the Campo dei Gesuiti, a real 'neighbourhood' square used, as it's always been, by local people as a meeting place and somewhere for their children to play.

Unusually long and relatively narrow, it's busy all day with pedestrians hurrying to and from the boats, housewives laden with shopping, and grandmothers supervising noisy children and dogs from the shady benches dotted around. The canal on its south side is exceptionally busy and a great place to watch the variety of goods that arrive in the city and the expertise of the bargemen. Heading north, the big *palazzo* you see on the left is the Palazzo Zen, a Gothic-Renaissance building once decorated with frescoes by Tintoretto (1518–94). Tall, secretive houses line the east side, and at the end, where the *campo* narrows, surges the massive bulk of the church of the Gesuiti (▷ 101).

On the left of the *campo* is the Oratorio dei Crociferi (open

Apr–end Oct Fri–Sat 3.30–6.30pm, €2), a 13th-century foundation similar to a *scuola* (literally 'school'), which was richly frescoed in the late 16th century by Palma il Giovane (1544–1628) with scenes from the history of the Crociferi, a religious order dedicated to the Holy Cross. The paintings, recently restored by the British charity Venice in Peril, were begun in 1581 and finished in 1591 and show the founding of the Order by Pope Anacletus to provide for pilgrims and the sick, the construction of an almshouse for 12 poor women in the 13th century, and the 1581 gift which led to the founding of the Oratory, the present building. The artist included portraits of his contemporaries, along with the commissioner, Father Priamo Balbi, and some of the local housewives who came to pray at the oratory.

CAMPO MANIN

✚ 61 G9 • Campo Manin, San Marco ⌨ Rialto, Sant'Angelo

There aren't many many squares in Venice where 20th-century architecture is the first thing that catches the eye, but yours will be drawn inexorably to the monstrous, less-than-appealing bulk of the 1968 Cassa di Risparmio bank that looms over Campo Manin, designed by Pier Luigi Nervi.

A narrow street and a bridge lead into the square, and there's a real sense of space after the tinny alleys that surround it, an effect due to the enlargement of the *campo* in 1871 to make room for the monument to Daniele Manin, the leader of the 1848 uprising of Venice's citizens against the Austrian occupation.

Statue of Daniele Manin in Campo Manin

The bronze statue in the middle portrays the Venetian hero facing his own house, which still stands beside the left-hand bridge. The uprising was initially successful, a provisional government being set up and new currency printed. But resistance was short-lived, and in 1849, worn down by hunger and disease and bombed from the air by explosives attached to balloons, the Venetians surrendered. Manin died in 1857 in exile in France.

Calle de la Vida, on the left side of the *campo,* leads to the Palazzo Contarini del Bovolo (▷ 118).

RATINGS	
Cultural interest	●●●
Good for kids	●●●
Historic interest	●●●
Photo stops	●●●●

BASICS

✚ 59 F6 • Campo dei Mori, Cannaregio
🚏 Orto

Statue of one of the Moors (above) outside Tintoretto's house on the Fondamenta dei Mori (below)

CAMPO DEI MORI

This attractive and historic square, in a tranquil part of Cannaregio, is just a stone's throw from two fine churches—Sant'Alvise and the Madonna dell'Orto.

The Campo dei Mori lies on the route south from the church of the Madonna dell'Orto (▷ 106–107) towards the city centre. It's in an outlying area of great charm, well away from the main through-routes and sights, so it's better to combine a visit here with other sights in the vicinity. The best way to explore the area might be to follow the walk on pages 236–237.

THE MOORS AND THEIR CAMPO

There are several explanations for the name Campo dei Mori; it may refer to the proximity of the now extinct Fondaco degli Arabi, the trading warehouse run by the Arabs which stood nearby, or more likely to the four 13th-century statues of Moors standing around the square. These wonderfully naïve pieces show turbaned Moors, popularly associated with the Mastelli family, who used to live in the *palazzo* where two of the figures are embedded. They were a Greek trading family who originated in the Morea (the Peloponnese), and were known in the city as the Mori. Three of the statues are said to represent brothers from the family—Rioba, Sandi and Afiani—who arrived in Venice in 1112 and settled; later family members participated in the Fourth Crusade and were probably present at the Sack of Constantinople in 1204. The Venetians have long had a fondness for the statues, particularly the one on the corner house, known as Sior Antonio Rioba, which was in need of a nose job and now sports a replacement iron one. The statue was used as a repository for denunciatory letters destined for the powers-that-be, which were left pinned at his feet, and his name was often used to sign vindictive verses. The fourth Moor, round the corner on the *fondamenta*, is set into the façade of No. 3399, Tintoretto's house. The statue was restored by the British Venice in Peril fund, and was found to have a local 15th-century version of a Roman altar as a column, while a recycled capital from the top of a column had been used as his turban.

The 15th-century Palazzo Duodo, on Campo Sant'Angelo

Campo Santi Apostoli offers fine alfresco dining

Relaxing in the tree-lined Campo San Giacomo dell'Orio

CAMPO SANT'ANGELO

➕ 60 F10 • Campo Sant'Angelo, San Marco 🚤 Sant'Angelo

Lying directly on the route from Campo Santo Stefano (▷ 81) to the Rialto, Campo Sant'Angelo is a wide, airy expanse that makes a good place to pause. Its size is due to the demolition, in 1837, of the church of the Angelo Michele, Sant'Angelo, which stood near the *rio* at the south-west side of the square. The *campo* has two late 15th-century well-heads and is surrounded by patrician houses. The isolated building in the middle of the square is the Oratorio dell'Annunziata, a chapel first built in the 10th century. The present building is one of a series of rebuilds on the site; the interior contains a fine 15th-century Crucifixion. Be sure to take in the view from here of the campanile of Santo Stefano, the most steeply leaning tower in the city.

CAMPO SANTI APOSTOLI

➕ 59 G8 • Campo Santi Apostoli, Cannaregio 🚤 Ca' d'Oro

The wide thoroughfare of the 19th-century Strada Nova, whose creation cut a wide swath through the old streets in this part of Cannaregio, finishes at Campo Santi Apostoli, where the route to the Rialto swings right and back into typically narrow *calli* once more. The *campo* marks a turning point; right to the Rialto, left towards the Fondamente Nuove. It's a busy place, dominated by its church (▷ 124), and very much a cross-roads and the hub of a lively district. There are plenty of interesting local shops, a good corner bar and some shady trees. Pause here to admire the church façade; the campanile was built in 1672 and an old story tells of a sacristan falling from it but

being miraculously caught on the minute hand of the clock. As it reached 6, it placed him gently on a convenient parapet.

CAMPO SAN BARNABA

➕ 60 D10 • Campo San Barnaba, Dorsoduro 🚤 Ca' Rezzonico

Home to one of the world's most photographed vegetable shops—it's on a boat—cosy Campo San Barnaba is a bit of a route hub, with streets leading to many places you may be visiting. The *vaporetto* stop Ca' Rezzonico lies down a narrow alley to the east, and another *calle* heads west to the delights of San Sebastiano (▷ 157) and San Nicolò dei Mendicoli (▷ 154). Southwest lies the Accademia (▷ 94–100) and the spine of Dorsoduro, while the route north will bring you to Campo Santa Margherita (▷ 80), heart of the *sestiere*. There's a fine church, and a clutch of little shops and bars, a great place for watching Venice go by. On the opposite side of the bridge, neatly incised in the

Looking out over Campo San Barnaba

stone, are the imprints of two sets of footprints. These are reminders of the starting points of the officially sanctioned fights that were a means of allowing the working classes to let off steam and channel any aggression towards each other rather than the state. Venice had two main rival factions, the Nicolotti, based near the *campo*, and the Castellani. The rumpus normally started with individual fights between designated champions on various bridges, with eager spectators lining the banks on either side. Once the initial brawl was over, the whole thing degenerated into a free-for-all, the *frotta*. It was normal for as many as 10 people to be killed in these punch-ups, either from their injuries or by falling from the bridge and drowning in the canal. The fights were finally halted in 1705 after a particularly vicious contest. San Barnaba's bridge is still known as the Ponte dei Pugni, the Bridge of Fists.

CAMPO SAN GIACOMO DELL'ORIO

➕ 58 E8 • Campo San Giacomo dell'Orio, Santa Croce 🚤 Biasio

One of Venice's most appealing squares, Campo San Giacomo dell'Orio sprawls round the bulk of its church. Dotted with trees and benches, the *campo* is the focus of local life. The name is a subject of debate; St. James (San Giacomo) is clear enough, but dell'Orio could refer to a laurel tree *(lauro)* that once grew here, or the area might once have been known as San Giacomo dal Rio (St. James of the River). Typical houses surround the square, which stands at the heart of a densely populated residential district, but the church turns its back on these; like so many ancient Venetian churches, the main door faces the water.

The Colleoni statue dominates Campo Santi Giovanni e Paolo

Campo Santa Margherita lies at the heart of Dorsoduro

A graceful façade on Campo Santa Maria Formosa

THE SIGHTS

CAMPO SANTI GIOVANNI E PAOLO

🔢 59 J8 • Campo Santi Giovanni e Paolo, Castello 🚤 Fondamente Nuove

If you're looking for a monumental open space, Campo Santi Giovanni e Paolo, wrapped around three sides of the church (▷ 132–133) with its west side bordered by a busy *rio*, is the richest in Venice after the Piazza. Standing triumphantly above the square is the bronze statue of the *condottiere* Bartolomeo Colleoni (1400–76), a mercenary who left his wealth to the Republic on condition that a monument was erected to him 'outside the Basilica di San Marco'. The city fathers, to whom the cult of anonymity was everything, were horrified. With true Venetian guile they solved the problem by placing the statue outside the Scuola Grande di San Marco, not the Basilica.

The Florentine sculptor Andrea Verrocchio won the commission for the statue in 1481, which was eventually completed after his death in 1488. It's a superb piece, epitomizing the ideal of the commercial soldier's military prowess. Look at Colleoni's coat-of-arms on the pedestal, which feature some pear-shaped objects. These are a play on the soldier's name; Colleoni sounds very like the word *coglioni* (testicles), a fine example of 15th-century humour.

To the west of the *campo*, flanking the church, is the façade of the Scuola itself, decorated with exquisite marble perspectival panels by brothers Tullio (c. 1455–1532) and Antonio Lombardo (c1458–1516). The interior is now home to Venice's major hospital, part of which is attached to the church of the Ospedaletto by Baldassare Longhena (1598–1682) at the east end of the square.

CAMPO SANTA MARGHERITA

🔢 60 D10 • Campo Santa Margherita, Dorsoduro 🚤 Ca' Rezzonico

Campo Santa Margherita has to be one of Venice's most appealing, liveliest squares. Come here at different times of day to experience how the Venetian *campi* can be all things to the people who live around them—babies and grannies, shoppers and old men, students and tourists.

The square stretches out in an oddly shaped rectangle, around which are set lovely old Gothic houses, many dating back to the 14th century. At the north end stands the restored church of Santa Margherita, now part of the University. You can see St. Margaret's dragon on the campanile; she and the beast also feature on the façade of a house at the same end of the square, with the saint standing triumphantly on the monster. Market stalls, trees and benches are dotted around, while just off-centre stands a quirky little building, the Scuola dei Varoteri, once the headquarters of the tanner's guild. Left from here the street curves round towards San Barnaba, while to the right, past the fish stalls, the *campo* leads to the entrance to the Scuola Grande dei Carmini (▷ 161).

CAMPO SANTA MARIA FORMOSA

🔢 61 H9 • Campo Santa Maria Formosa, Castello 🚤 San Zaccaria, Rialto

Every *sestiere* has its own central square, and Campo Santa Maria Formosa is definitely the hub of this part of Castello. Heading from San Marco to the Rialto, or north to Santi Giovanni e Paolo, you're bound to pass through it, so pause and take in the local life. It has a good morning market where stalls groan with fruit and vegetables, a couple of bars and an eclectic mix of both ordinary and palatial buildings. The most noticeable is the Palazzo Priuli on the northeast side, built in the late 16th century. The Veneto-Byzantine Palazzo Vitturi is another stunner—look out for its Byzantine carvings. The *campo* is dominated by the church of Santa Maria Formosa (▷ 143), and has the usual selection of gossiping old ladies on the benches and screaming small children. It's an irregular shape, with *rii* on two sides crossed by a variety of bridges, one leading to the Fondazione Querini Stampalia (▷ 110).

CAMPO SAN POLO

🔢 58 F9 • Campo San Polo, San Polo 🚤 San Silvestro

The largest square on the west bank of the Grand Canal and the largest in the city after the Piazza, Campo San Polo is a a splendid open space, much loved by local kids as a place to practise soccer. Their parents and grandparents enjoy it too, and it's a great place to watch the crowds, sit in the sun and rest on your way from the Rialto to the Accademia. In past centuries it held weekly markets, parades and bull-fighting; today, it comes into its own in summer when it hosts an open-air film festival. Passersby tend to stick to the south side of the *campo*, the main route through to the Rialto, where you'll find the church of San Polo (▷ 155), leaving a huge area free. Wander around to take in the beautiful *palazzi* that overlook the square. The most impressive has to be the double-facaded Palazzo Soranzo on the northeast side. Built in the 14th and 15th centuries, it is unusual in having its main façade on land rather than water. This wasn't

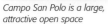

Campo San Polo is a large, attractive open space

Campo San Zaccaria was once described by English writer and caricaturist Max Beerbohm (1872–1956) as melancholy and shabby

always the case; there was originally a canal on this side of the *campo* in front of the *palazzo* and if you look carefully you can see where it was filled in. On the same side as the church stands the Palazzo Corner Mocenigo, designed in 1550 by Veronese Sanmicheli (1484–1559). It was home in 1909 to the disreputable writer Frederick Rolfe (Baron Corvo); he was thrown out when his hosts discovered that his work-in-progress, *The Desire and Pursuit of the Whole*, was a libellous satire on them and their friends.

CAMPO SANTO STEFANO

✚ 60 F10 • Campo Santo Stefano, San Marco ⬛ San Samuele, Accademia

San Marco's second most important square, Campo Santo Stefano is a fine, open, irregular space, enclosed at its north end by the church of the same name (▷ 159), while the southern side leads to the approach to the Accademia bridge. From the *campo* there's a choice of routes—south to Dorsoduro across the Grand Canal, east to the Piazza and north to the Rialto. It's a busy square, but big enough to absorb the crowds easily, with plenty of room to

serve as a playground for local kids and a hangout for students and backpackers. There's an impressive choice of cafés, but connoisseurs head straight for Paolin (▷ 220), which serves some of the city's most delectable ices, while designer-name fans can browse through the fake bags on offer from the African street traders that normally congregate here. It's hard to imagine that this square was one of the main 18th-century bullfighting arenas, a role which was abandoned in 1802 when a bank of seats collapsed, killing a number of spectators. The central statue is of Nicolò Tommaseo (1802–74), a philosopher whose theories were important during the Risorgimento, the Italian movement of unification, and behind is the entrance to the Puntolaguna (▷ 119). At the Canal Grande end you'll see the 17th-century Palazzo Morosini, home to Francesco Morosini, the last doge to serve as the Republic's military commander (1688–94). He's probably better remembered by non-Italians for blowing up the Turkish gunpowder store in the Parthenon, doing more damage in 20 minutes than the wear and tear of the preceding centuries.

CAMPO SAN ZACCARIA

✚ 61 J10 • Campo San Zaccaria, Castello ⬛ San Zaccaria

The best way into Campo San Zaccaria, a quietly elegant square, is by turning off the Riva degli Schiavoni, past some tempting shops and into this wide, open space. The brick façade to the right of the church of San Zaccaria (▷ 160) is that of the 13th-century church that stood here; the next building along was a convent, considered to be the most debauched in Venice, with elegantly dressed nuns entertaining their lovers in the parlour and officiating at some of the city's most fashionable salons. Given that girls were often abandoned in convents by fathers with old titles but no money for dowries, there may be some excuse for their behaviour. The building is now Venice's main *carabinieri* station. San Zaccaria was the scene of the murder of two doges, Pietro Tradonico in 864 and Vitale Michiel II in 1172. The latter brought disgrace to the Republic by failing in his peace negotiations with the Byzantines. Coming home empty-handed, he added insult to injury by bringing the plague with him, and was assassinated as he fled to the church for sanctuary. His killers were never caught, but, hedging their bets, the Senate later decreed that only wooden buildings could be constructed between the *campo* and the Palazzo Ducale, making it easier to flush out would-be murderers. A succession of wooden buildings, which can be seen in many old paintings, remained here for the next 800 years, until the law was rescinded in 1948. They were then replaced by the modern annexe to the Danieli hotel; it remains a moot point whether this is an architectural improvement on the wooden structures.

THE SIGHTS

Sunny Campo Santo Stefano has a clutch of attractive outdoor cafés

Canal Grande

●

Venice's ultimate must-see attraction is the Grand Canal, a magnificent waterway lined with *palazzi* and superb churches that bisects the city and offers constantly changing vistas.

Looking along the Canal towards the Rialto bridge

Covered gondolas bobbing at rest along the Grand Canal

The view from San Giorgio Maggiore

RATINGS	
Cultural interest	●●●●○
Good for kids	●●●●○
Historic interest	●●●●○
Photo stops	●●●●○
Value for money	●●●●○

BASICS
✚ 59 F7 • Venezia
🚏 Start at Piazzale Roma; end at San Marco
🚌 Included in some city tours ▷ 244
🍴 Wide choice

Artist painting the Ponte dell'Accademia (below)
Waiting for the vaporetto *(right)*

SEEING THE CANAL GRANDE

The Grand Canal is Venice's major thoroughfare, a wide waterway running northwest to southeast that was originally the main route for merchant vessels approaching the Rialto. It's almost 4km (2.5 miles) long and varies in width from 30 to 70m (100–230ft), with an average depth of around 5m (16ft).The best, and indeed, only, way to see the whole thing is by water, travelling from Piazzale Roma, where the causeway from the mainland ends, or the Stazione Santa Lucia, all the way to the great set-piece of San Marco. Most visitors do this by taking either the No. 1 or 82 *vaporetto* (or No. 3 and 4 in summer) from Piazzale Roma or Ferrovia as far as Vallaresso/San Marco or San Zaccaria. Other options are by water taxi or gondola; both are very expensive but worth considering, particularly if several people are sharing the cost. There are comparatively few places where you can sit or walk beside the Grand Canal; the best of these include the terrace in front of the station and the *fondamenta* on the opposite bank, the Riva di Biasio, San Marcuola and Santa Sofia, either side of the Rialto bridge, the Accademia and Campo San Vio, along the Salute *fondamenta* and at San Marco.

Bear in mind that the views from the Scalzi, the Rialto and the Accademia bridges are superlative, and that the windows and loggias of museums along the Canal are great vantage points; so if you're visiting the Ca' d'Oro, the Ca' Pesaro, the Collezione Peggy Guggenheim or the Ca' Rezzonico, don't forget to look out of the windows. Last but not least, for a truly watery bird's-eye view, do as the Venetians do and take one of the *traghetti* that ply back and forth across the canal at fixed points. These link crucial city through-routes, saving detours to bridges, and will give you glimpses of the Venetian palaces as they were designed to be seen, from water level. A *vaporetto* trip down the Grand Canal takes around 50 minutes, and you'll need to do it at least twice to see everything properly.

Gondoliers in their summer shirts

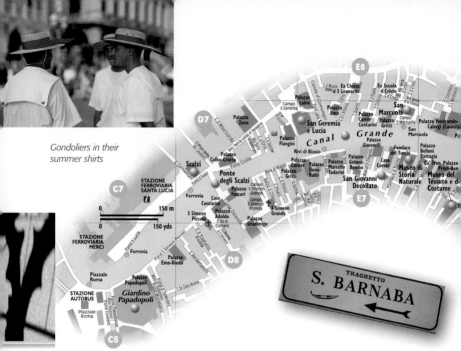

San Marcuola (above); San Simeone Piccolo (below); Casino de Venezia, Palazzo Vendramin-Calergi (below right)

HIGHLIGHTS

PIAZZALE ROMA TO THE CA' D'ORO

A short hop takes you past the entrance of the Rio Nuovo, excavated in 1938, and the park of the Giardino Papadopoli (▷ 104), both on the right, to the Stazione Ferroviaria Santa Lucia, first built by the Austrians in 1846 when the causeway was constructed. Today's structure dates from the 1930s, as does the Scalzi bridge (▷ 119). Opposite the station is the green-domed church of San Simeone Piccolo, built in 1738 in imitation of Rome's Pantheon. Almost opposite, on the left, is the ornate façade of the 1656 Chiesa degli Scalzi (▷ 158), a baroque architectural flourish by Baldassare Longhena, contrasting admirably with the first major palace, the Palazzo Calbo-Crotta, a Byzantine-Gothic structure that now houses a hotel.

Just past this, on the left, is the church of San Geremia e Lucia (▷ 127), right next to the Palazzo Labia, an 18th-century building whose main façade stretches along the Canale di Cannaregio, the gateway to the city before the causeway was built, which joins the Grand Canal at this point. Across the water, on the right, is the Riva di Biasio, named for a butcher executed for reputedly selling human flesh as pork. From here, a string of Gothic *palazzi* line both sides of the water until the San Marcuola *vaporetto* stop (on the left). The

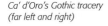
Ca' d'Oro's Gothic tracery
(far left and right)

unfinished brick façade of the church of San Marcuola (▷ 142) is
faced by the impressive, though badly restored, multi-arched Fondaco
dei Turchi (▷ 110), trading headquarters for the Turks in Republican
days, and the Deposito del Megio, once a granary.

Almost opposite this, on the left, is the Palazzo Vendramin-Calergi,
designed at the end of the 15th century by Mauro Codussi, and the
first Grand Canal *palazzo* to be influenced by the classically based
principles of Andrea Palladio (1508–80). It's most famous resident
was the composer Richard Wagner, who rented a suite of rooms and
died here in 1883; today the palace is the winter home of Venice's
Casino. Farther down, on the right, is the dazzling white baroque
façade of the church of San Stae (▷ 156), with Longhena's 1652 Ca'
Pesaro (▷ 72–73), now housing the Museo d'Arte Moderna, a couple
of palaces down. It faces the Palazzo Gussoni-Grimani della Vida, a
mid-16th-century late Gothic palace that, between 1614 and 1618,
was the home to the English ambassador, Sir Henry Wotton. He had
the benefit of the Tintoretto frescoes that once covered the façade,
now long since faded to oblivion. The next important *palazzo* is on
the same side, the beautiful Ca' d'Oro (▷ 70–71), Venice's Veneto-
Byzantine Gothic palace par excellence.

Vaporetto *on the Grand Canal*
(below)

*View over the Grand Canal from
the Ponte di Rialto (below)*

Waiting for the traghetto
(top far right)

The Palazzo Grimani now houses offices of the judiciary (middle far right)

View of the Ponte di Rialto (bottom far right)

CA D'ORO TO SAN TOMÀ

Across the water and a little further down the Grand Canal from the Ca' d'Oro lie the Rialto markets (▷ 120–121), still occupying the same area they did over 700 years ago. The open-arched building with the red awnings is the Pescheria, a neo-Gothic fish market built in 1907, and flanked by the bustling stalls of the fruit and vegetable vendors. The background to their wares is the long arcaded buildings of the Fabbriche Nuove and the Fabbriche Vecchie di Rialto, built in the 15th and 16th centuries by the Republic to house the trade ministry and other commercial administrative departments; the arched porticoes on the ground floor were originally occupied by shops.

Opposite these, on the left, is one of Venice's oldest *palazzi*, the beguiling Ca'

da Mosto, a 13th-century Veneto-Byzantine building with the typically rounded arches of this period. Down from here the canal swings a little, opening up views of the famous Ponte di Rialto (▷ 120). This is flanked by the grandiose Fondaco dei Tedeschi, built as a trade centre and warehouse by the Germans *(tedeschi)*, one of the most powerful and prosperous of all medieval foreign merchant groups in Venice. The present building dates from 1505 and replaced a 13th-century structure; today, it's the main post office. Past the bridge, there's an open *fondamenta* along the water's edge on either side of the Canal, a wharf once used for unloading vital supplies of charcoal, iron and wine and still named for those commodities. The next stretch is packed with superb buildings, great Gothic and Renaissance palaces whose names trumpet the wealth and might of the aristocratic families. On the left, you'll see the adjoining Palazzo Loredan and Palazzo Farsetti, much-restored 13th-century *palazzi* that are now the offices of the Mayor of Venice, and the massive 16th-century Palazzo Grimani, seat of Venice's Appeal Court. This faces the Palazzo Papadopoli, easy to spot with its roof obelisks, while further down, on the same side, a row of Gothic palaces faces the Sant'Angelo *vaporetto* stop. Two of the finest here are the Palazzo Bernardo, whose delicate tracery was copied from the Palazzo Ducale, and the Palazzo Barbarigo della Terrazza, named for its much-envied roof terrace. On the left, opposite the San Tomà *traghetto* and *vaporetto pontile*, is the impressive Palazzo Mocenigo, home for two years to Lord Byron, assorted animals and his mistress from 1816. He had many problems with this fiery lady, a local baker's wife, which culminated in her throwing herself into the Grand Canal after Byron had remonstrated with her for attacking him with a table knife.

Early morning at the Pescheria, Venice's lively fish market (above)

Ca' da Mosto, the oldest palace in Venice (central strip above)

View of the Palazzo Mocenigo, once the home of Lord Byron, from the Canal (below)

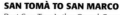

SAN TOMÀ TO SAN MARCO

Past San Tomà, the Grand Canal makes a sweeping bend to the left; this is the Volta del Canal, and it's dominated on the left by the huge Gothic Ca' Foscari part of the university buildings, commissioned in 1437 and still under wraps for what's proving a lengthy restoration. Next to it is the Palazzo Giustinian, another palace that was a temporary home to Richard Wagner (1813–83), who wrote part of his opera *Tristan and Isolde* here. Two doors down is the Ca' Rezzonico (▷ 74–75), which houses Venice's museum of 18th-century life. Facing it, on the opposite side of the canal, is the immaculate Palazzo Grassi, one of the city's most prestigious exhibition centres (▷ 118), while past here don't miss the tiny Palazzo Falier, a 13th-century charmer with two covered balconies, known as *liaghi*. Ahead now is the Ponte dell'Accademia (▷ 119), built in 1932 to provide a

pedestrian link between San Marco and Dorsoduro, and one of the best vantage points for watching boat traffic on the Canal, to say nothing of the incomparable view down towards the Salute.

Immediately below the bridge on the left is the Palazzo Cavalli-Franchetti, a 15th-century building with lovely waterside gardens that was zealously restored in the 19th century. Next to it is the Gothic Palazzo Barbaro, purchased in 1885 by the Curtis family from Boston. They established a salon here, where guests included Henry James, Monet, Whistler, Browning and the society portrait artist John Singer Sargent. Henry James wrote part of *The Aspern Papers* here and used the *palazzo* as a setting for *The Wings of a Dove*. On the right below the bridge, Campo San Vio is one of the few squares actually fronting the canal. Past here is the Palazzo Barbarigo, decorated with garish 19th-century mosaics, and the unfinished Palazzo Venier dei Leoni (▷ 92–93), home to the Collezione Peggy Guggenheim (▷ 92–93). Opposite this, the massive façade of the Palazzo Corner della Ca' Grande, designed by Sansovino in 1545, dwarfs the tiny Casetta della Rose on its left. This pretty little palace, fronted by gardens, was home to the poet Gabriele d'Annunzio (1863–1938) during World War I, overlooked on the opposite bank by the home of his jealous mistress, the actress Eleanora Duse (1858–1924), who took lodgings from where she could keep an eye on his comings and goings.

Back on the right bank, the eye is drawn to the drunkenly leaning Palazzo Dario, one of the canal's treasures. It was designed in the 1480s by Pietro Lombardo, also responsible for Santa Maria dei Miracoli (▷ 148–149), and you can see the similarities in the use of polychrome marble on the façade. The palace is said to be both haunted and cursed, a reputation that was bolstered by the suicide in the 1990s of its owner Raul

The Palazzo Grassi (top left)
Approaching the Ponte dell'Accademia (above)
Looking across to the Palazzo Cavalli-Franchetti (above middle)
The Palazzo Barbarigo (above right)
The Palazzo Corner della Ca' Grande (below)

Taking the traghetto *across to the Pescheria (left)*

Pausing for a break on the Ponte dell'Accademia (below)

Gardini, a businessman heavily implicated in the 1993 *tangentopoli* scandals of corruption in high places. Just past this is the technicolour glitter of the Palazzo Salviati, whose façade was created in 1924 by the glassmakers of the same name, who had a showroom in the building. On your left along this stretch a string of Venice's grandest hotels lines the bank from the *vaporetto* stop of Santa Maria del Giglio onwards—the Gritti, the Europa, the Monaco and others.

Across the water, the end of the Canal is dominated by the bulk of Longhena's plague church of Santa Maria della Salute (▷ 150–151), flanked on one side by the low Gothic ex-convent of San Gregorio, once home to the Woolworth millionairess, Barbara Hutton, and on the other by the row of buildings that culminates in the triumphant final flourish of the Dogana di Mare (▷ 101). Opposite the point, the palaces give way to Harry's Bar and it surrounding glitzy stores, the Giardini ex Reali

(▷ 104), the façade of the Zecca (Mint) and the glories of San Marco and the Palazzo Ducale (▷ 112–117).

(▷ 112–117)

TIPS

- The *vaporetto* is probably the best way of seeing the Grand Canal; gondolas and taxis are the far more expensive options.
- Start your trip at Piazzale Roma or the station, saving San Marco for the end.
- To get the best view on the No. 1, choose one of the older boats that has seating outside at the front.
- Avoid doing the trip during the morning and evening rush hours when *vaporetti* are extremely crowded.
- If time is short, take the No. 82, which has fewer stops than the No. 1.
- The *traghetti* crossings give you superb views from the water at different points along the Grand Canal.

BACKGROUND

The earliest part of Venice to be settled and then developed for commercial purposes was the Rialto, the High Bank, where merchant vessels unloaded their wares. Ships approached it up a wide channel, which soon became the embryonic city's main thoroughfare, known as the Canale Grande. To the Venetians it's the *Canalozzo*, their high street, which divides the city in half, with three *sestieri*, San Marco, Castello and Cannaregio to the north and east, and three, Santa Croce, San Polo and Dorsoduro to the south and west. Along its length, the city's merchants, aristocracy and trading communities built their *palazzi*, headquarters and warehouses, each with its main façade on the water. These were erected and modified over five centuries, and their style covers the entire span of Venetian architectural development, the combination of water, stone and light one of the world's great visual experiences. Bridges were also built across the canal to link the city. The Rialto bridge, from the late 12th century, was the earliest; the Scalzi, by the railway station, and the Accademia were both built in the 1850s during the Austrian occupation. *Traghetti*, gondola ferries, also operate at fixed points along the canal; these have been in operation throughout the city's history.

VAPORETTO STOPS

Piazzale Roma
Ferrovia
Riva de Biasio
San Marcuola
San Stae
Ca' d'Oro
Rialto
San Silvestro
Sant'Angelo
San Tomà
San Samuele
Ca' Rezzonico
Accademia
Giglio
Salute
San Marco (Vallaresso)
San Marco

TAKING A BREAK

To break the journey, you could get off the *vaporetto* at Ca' d'Oro and take the nearby Santa Sofia *traghetto* across the canal to to the Pescheria, walking down through the markets to the Rialto bridge, and across it to re-embark at the Rialto *vaporetto* stop.

Gondolas in the Bacino Orseolo behind the Piazza San Marco, a popular departure point for Grand Canal tours (left)

View of the canal from San Tomà (below)

Collezione Peggy Guggenheim

The perfect antidote to an excess of Byzantine, Gothic, Renaissance and baroque art.

Looking along the Grand Canal from the water-side garden of the Palazzo Venier dei Leoni

Admiring the bronze equestrian statue, Angel of the City, by Marino Marini

RATINGS	
Cultural interest	●●●●●
Specialist shopping	●●●●
Value for money	●●●

BASICS

✚ 60 F11 • Palazzo Venier dei Leoni, Calle San Cristoforo (entrance on Fondamenta Venier), Dorsoduro 701
☎ 041 240 5411 or 041 520 6885
🕐 Aug–end May Wed–Mon 10–6; Jun, Jul Wed–Fri, Sun–Mon 10–6, Sat 10–10
💶 €10, under 12 free
🚤 Accademia/Salute
🎧 Audioguides and guidebooks available in Italian, English, French, German, Spanish and Japanese. For information on guided tours tel 041 240 5400
🚻
🏦 Excellent
🚹🚺
www.guggenheim-venice.it
Comprehensive website giving full information on every aspect of the museum and its collections in Italian and English.

Peggy Guggenheim entertaining on the terrace of the Palazzo Venier dei Leoni (middle right)

Moon Woman by Jackson Pollack (bottom right)

SEEING THE COLLEZIONE PEGGY GUGGENHEIM

The rooms in the gallery are fairly small, so viewing can be a problem; be prepared to wait to see some of the major pieces. The collection, one of the world's most important outside the US, covers all the main 20th-century movements and is beautifully presented. The garden is a delight, with its superb views up and down the Grand Canal.

HIGHLIGHTS

THE GARDEN
The garden is one of its chief pleasures, an oasis of green, cool light and shade, the perfect setting for the sculpture. You can see where Peggy's ashes were interred or walk out to the terrace above the water.

RAIN (MARC CHAGALL)
Painted in 1911, this a typical example of Chagall's naïve, folklore-based art which nevertheless illustrates his awareness of avant-garde French painting, notably Cubism. The references to peasant country life have a dream-like quality.

THE RED TOWER (GIORGIO DE CHIRICO)
The Red Tower (1913) is one of the earliest paintings in what is called the Metaphysical style, where illogical perspective is used to create a sense of unreality. Such paintings were designed to provoke feelings of unease, loneliness and threat.

THE KISS (MAX ERNST)
This picture, which includes a man and woman embracing and two birds, was influenced by the compostion of Leonardo da Vinci's *Madonna with St. Anne* to which Ernst (1891–1976) applied the erotic philosophy of Sigmund Freud, creating the synthesis of reality with instinct that was the hallmark of Surrealism.

MOBILE (ALEXANDER CALDER)
A fine example of Calder's wind-driven mobiles, which he created throughout his working life; this one dates from 1941.

THE ANGEL OF THE CITY (MARINO MARINI)

This bronze equestrian statue by Italy's leading post-war sculptor stands on the terrace of the museum and may have been influenced by ancient Etruscan sculpture.

MOON WOMAN (JACKSON POLLOCK)

Pollock was Peggy Guggenheim's discovery. This early painting (1942) shows stylistic elements which were to develop into his instantly recognizable drip painting, seen in the nearby *Alchemy*.

SACRIFICE (MARK ROTHKO)

This seminal watercolour (1946), shows Rothko moving from a Surrealist point of departure towards the large bands of 'floating' colour that typifies his greatest work.

The light-drenched main rooms of the *palazzo* are approached through a garden court where sculpture by artists such as Giacometti (1901–66) and Henry Moore (1898–1986) are displayed. The interior rooms still combine Peggy Guggenheim's furniture and memorabilia with her collection; look out especially for the magnificent silver bed-head by Alexander Calder. The art collection covers all the major names and movements of the early to mid-20th century: Cubism, Surrealism, Abstract Expressionism and Constructivism represented by Picasso, Chagall, Magritte, Salvador Dalí, Brancusi, Mark Rothko, Jackson Pollock, Klee, Ernst, Calder, Cornell and Miró.

TIPS

● Be prepared for year-round crowds, with the summer months bringing the worst.
● The museum café is one of the best in Venice, so plan your visit to include lunch or tea time.
● There's a superb museum shop with a wide range of books and gifts.

THE SIGHTS

BACKGROUND

The Palazzo Venier dei Leoni is one of the Grand Canal's most eccentric buildings, an unfinished palace known by Venetians as *il palazzo non finito*. What exists was constructed by the Venier family, one of the oldest Venetian noble clans. Work started on the building, designed by Lorenzo Boschetti, in 1748, but never progressed further than the first floor. Its distinctive appearance appealed to Peggy Guggenheim, who realized its potential as a showcase for her modern art collection and purchased it in 1948. She had started amassing contemporary art in the 1920s, buying from and dealing in the works of a whole generation of innovative abstract and surrealist artists and marrying Max Ernst, one of the great exponents. In 1949 she staged the first exhibition in the garden of the *palazzo*, utilizing more of the interior as exhibition space over the years, though she continued to live in the palace. In 1969 she donated both the *palazzo* and her collection to her uncle's foundation, the Solomon R. Guggenheim Foundation, which, since her death in 1979, has administered and expanded the house and museum. Her ashes were interred in a corner of the garden, near the graves of her dogs.

Gallerie dell'Accademia

The Accademia contains a comprehensive and specialist collection of all that's best in Venetian painting. It's world-class, yet intimate, tracing the development of Venetian art from the 14th to the 18th century.

RATINGS	
Cultural interest	●●●●●
Value for money	●●●●●
Walkability	●●●●

Room 10 is filled with paintings by Tintoretto and Veronese (top)

Coronation of the Virgin relief over the door (above)

SEEING THE GALLERIE DELL'ACCADEMIA

For an overview of the development of Venetian painting, head for the Gallerie dell'Accademia, the city's main gallery, a splendid collection where you can compare works by all the great masters and revel in the richness of colour and light that typifies Venetian painting. Five hundred years of Venetian painting are covered by the Accademia's 24 more or less chronologically arranged rooms, where you can see the obsession with colour, texture and light emerge, and trace the development of technical mastery of composition, perspective and anatomy.

A major plus is that the Gallery is surprisingly small, so there's little chance of mental indigestion or total exhaustion; allow a

couple of hours for a thorough visit. Floor plans and guidebooks are available at the front desk, and enthusiasts can also pick up an audioguide here. The well-organized, well-lit rooms all have information boards in several languages. Venetian painting can be overwhelming in its richness and complexity, so if you're not a gallery fan at home, you may get little out of the Accademia.

HIGHLIGHTS

CORONATION OF THE VIRGIN (ROOM 1)

Early Venetian painting bridged the gap between mosaics and true panel painting, and Paolo Veneziano (c1290–1362) was the prime exponent of this trend. His stylized and immobile figures reflect Byzantium, while the luminous colours of his work herald the future Venetian obsession with colour and light. No painting better illustrates this than *The Coronation of the Virgin*, dated around 1350, a huge gold-ground polyptych where the central scene of Christ, the Virgin and angels is surrounded by panels showing scenes from the lives of Christ and the saints, notably St. Francis of Assisi.

SAN GIOBBE ALTARPIECE (ROOM 2)

The dramatic advances in perspective and the handling of space, form and light that marked the Renaissance came later to Venice than elsewhere in Italy and developed highly individually. By the mid-15th century the Bellini family had developed the concept of the *sacra conversazione*, a unified composition of the Madonna and saints, of which the San Giobbe Altarpiece by Giovanni is a superb example. It was painted for the church of the same name in 1478, probably as a plague offering, the naked figure of St. Sebastian being normally

BASICS

✚ 60 E11 • Campo della Carità, Dorsoduro 1050

☎ 041 520 0345

🕓 Mon 8.15–2, Tue–Sun 8.15–7.15 (last entrance 6.30). Closed 1 May

💶 € 6.50, EU citizens 18–25 €3.25, EU citizens under 18 and over 65 free, non-EU citizens under 12 free. Combined ticket with Ca d'Oro and Museo d'Arte Orientale €11, reduced €5.50. Advance booking Mon–Fri 9–6, Sat 9–2 (tel 041 520 0345 or book on-line (see below)

🚏 Accademia

📖 Illustrated guides in Italian, English, French, Spanish, German and Japanese €15.50 and € 8.20

🎧 Audioguides in English, Italian, French and German €3; guided tours in English and Italian, 11–1, 3.30–5, Sun 10–12 (tel 041 522 2247 for further details)

📚 Guidebooks, art books, postcards and gifts

🚻

www.gallerieaccademia.org
Italian website offering on-line booking for the Gallerie and links to a comprehensive site on the museum.

La Tempesta *by Giorgione (top)*

Detail of a ceiling painting by Marco Cozzi (central strip)

associated with sickness. The background, with its coffered ceiling, originally corresponded exactly to the frame and the picture's original setting in the church. This monumental work contrasts with another *sacra conversazione* by the same artist in the next room, *The Madonna with Child with Saints Catherine and Magdalene*, a far more intimate and domestic picture.

LA TEMPESTA (ROOM 5)

Art historians have written and argued about the meaning of *La Tempesta* for decades, interpreting Italy's most enigmatic picture, with its emphasis on landscape and extraordinary light, as myth, allegory or even political statement. Whatever the hidden meaning, if indeed there is one, this painting is one of few works that can be reliably attributed to Giorgione, who died in Venice in 1510 at the age of 32. His work has intense luminosity, and often relies on humanist principles, seen here in the harmony between the human figures and the natural world.

FEAST IN THE HOUSE OF LEVI (ROOM 10)

The huge *Feast in the House of Levi* by Veronese (c1530–88) is unmistakeable; a stupendous set piece where the figures are pictured against a background of classical architecture. The theatricality of the composition is typical of the artist, who was fascinated by the theatre, an interest seen at its height in his work in the church of San Sebastiano (▷ 157). The picture was painted in 1573 for the refectory of Santi Giovanni e Paolo (▷ 132–133) as a replacement for a *Last Supper* by Titian that had been lost in a fire. The theme was to be the same, but when Veronese delivered the finished work, the Inquisition came down hard, objecting to the inclusion of 'buffoons, drunkards, Germans, dwarves and similar indecencies'. Veronese, who appears in the work as the figure in green to the left of the centre, was ordered to make changes to render the sacred subject more pious; instead, he simply changed the picture's name.

THE MIRACLE OF ST. MARK FREEING THE SLAVE (ROOM 10)

The work of the towering figure of Tintoretto (1518–94) epitomizes the triumphalism of Venetian High Renaissance painting. The blasts of colour, dramatic light and the technical wizardry of his dizzying use of foreshortening is shown to its best advantage in the *Miracle of St. Mark Freeing the Slave*, painted in 1547 for the Scuola Grande di San Marco. It tells the story of a slave, sentenced to torture and blinding by his master for worshipping St. Mark's relics, being freed by the miraculous intervention of the saint. The warm flesh tones and

Room 23, the nave of the former church of Santa Maria della Carità (below middle)

Waiting for the Accademia to open (below)

GALLERIE DELL'ACCADEMIA FLOORPLAN

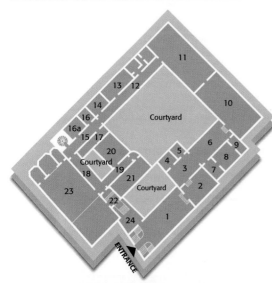

1: 14th–15th c. panel paintings
2: 15th–16th c. Venetian Renaissance altarpieces
3: 16th c. Venetian panel paintings, including G. Bellini
4: Mantegna, Piero della Francesca, Hans Memling
5: G. Bellini, Giorgione
6: 16th c. Venetian paintings, including Veronese, Tintoretto
7: Lorenzo Lotto, Bernardo Licinio
8: Palma il Vecchio, Romanino
9: School of Titian
10: 16th c. Venetian masters, including Veronese, Tintoretto, Titian
11: Tintoretto, Strozzi, Tiepolo
12: Corridor: 18th c. landscapes
13: Bassano, Tintoretto, Titian
14: Early 17th c.
15: Corridor: Tiepolo, Pellegrini Solimena
16: Early work by Tiepolo
16a: Alessandro Longhi, Piazzetta, Galgario
17: Canaletto, Guardi, Tiepolo, Pietro Longhi, Rosalba Carriera
18: 18th c. paintings
19: Bartolomeo Montagna, Giovanni Agostino da Loda, Boccaccino
20: Miracles of the Relic of the True Cross
21: Vittore Carpaccio's Legend of St. Ursula
22: Bookstand
23: Former monastery church: Giovanni Bellini, Antonio and Bartolomeo Vivarini
24: Former Hall of the Carità Brotherhood: Antonio Vivarini, Titian, Giovanni d'Alemagna

Postcards for sale outside the Accademia

Room 1: The primitives—Veneto-Byzantine and International Gothic gold-ground painting, typified by Paolo Veneziano.

Rooms 2–3: 15th-century altarpieces and works by Giovanni Bellini, Cima da Conegliano, Sebastiano del Piombo and Vittore Carpaccio.

Rooms 4–5: Giovanni Bellini *Madonnas*, Piero della Francesca, Cosima Tura, Giorgione and Andrea Mantegna.

minutely rendered fabrics are an admirable foil to the looser treatment of textiles in the artist's much later *Madonna dei Camerlenghi* (1567) in the next room.

PIETÀ (ROOM 10)

Titian's deeply spiritual *Pietà*, painted in 1576 and intended for his own tomb in the Frari, is charged with religious intensity. The picture is imbued with his awareness of the immediacy of death, the paint scratched and scraped onto the canvas. He portrayed himself as Nicodemus, the figure to the right of Christ wearing a red cloak.

SCUOLA GRANDE DI SAN MARCO (ROOM 17)

Venice has few paintings by her great master of cityscapes, Canaletto, and the Accademia contains only one. Bernardo Bellotto was a pupil

Rooms 6 and 10: The Venetian superstars—Titian, Tintoretto, Veronese.

Rooms 7–8: Palma il Vecchio, Lorenzo Lotto.

Room 11: Veronese, Tintoretto, Tiepolo.

Rooms 12 and 13: Tintoretto, Jacopo Bassano, Marco Ricci.

Rooms 14–18: 17th- and 18th-century pictures, portraits and genre paintings by Tiepolo, Canaletto, Bernardo Bellotto, Guardi, Pietro Longhi, Rosalba Carriera.

Rooms 19–20: *Miracles of the Relic of the True Cross* by Gentile Bellini, Vittore Carpaccio and others.

Room 21: *St. Ursula Cycle* by Vittore Carpaccio.

Room 23: Former church of Santa Maria della Carità with 15th-century paintings by Bartolomeo and Alvise Vivarini and Jacopo, Gentile and Giovanni Bellini.

Room 24: Former Albergo room of Santa Maria della Carità with works by Vivarini and Titian.

Titian's Presentation of the Virgin *still hangs in its original position in Room 24 (above left)*
Exterior of the Accademia (above middle)
The Creation of the Animals *by Tintoretto, Room 6 (above right)*
Madonna with Child *by Giovanni Bellini (opposite)*

of the great man, and produced this view—unchanged today—of the façade of the Scuola Grande di San Marco in 1740. It shows afternoon light catching an everyday scene in this northern Venetian *campo*.

THE APOTHECARY (ROOM 17)

Genre painting—the illustration of scenes from everyday life—is a Venetian 18th-century speciality, and this is the most famous example of the work of one of its foremost exponents, Pietro Longhi (1702–85). Signed on the back by the artist, it shows the interior of a pharmacy, with the apothecary himself treating a girl for toothache. An apprentice tends to a cauldron of medicine in one corner and the shelves contain some of the blue-and-white containers for remedies that are still to be seen in the city's museums.

MIRACLES OF THE RELIC OF THE CROSS (ROOM 20)

This cycle of eight paintings by a group of artists that included Gentile Bellini and Vittore Carpaccio, was executed between 1494 and 1510 for the Scuola di San Giovanni Evangelista. The pictures illustrate miraculous episodes focused around a relic of Christ's cross, but the importance of the cycle lies in the pictorial representation of Venice and the wealth of anecdote and decorative detail. Three paintings stand out; the *Miracle of the Cross at the Rialto* (1494) by Vittore Carpaccio, and the *Miracle of the Cross at Ponte San Lorenzo* (1500) and the *Procession in Piazza San Marco* (1496) by Gentile Bellini. The latter shows an instantly recognizable Piazza, with a procession wending its way across the foreground and the Doge's entourage appearing from the Palazzo Ducale. Bellini exercised some license by moving the Campanile over to the right so the whole façade of the Basilica is visible, while the buildings on the right have been replaced by the Procuratie Nuove. In contrast, the Rialto panel, still portraying the original wooden bridge with its movable central section, shows just how much the city has changed in the last 500 years.

ST. URSULA CYCLE (ROOM 21)

Between 1490 and 1494, Vittore Carpaccio painted a narrative cycle of nine pictures for the Scuola di Sant'Orsola. It tells the story of St. Ursula, a Breton princess, who accompanied by her fiancé, Hereus, and an entourage of 11,000 virgins, attempted to cross Europe to Rome, only to be massacred by the Huns near Cologne, exactly as

Miracle of the Relic of the True Cross *by Vittore Carpaccio*

had been foretold in a dream. Like the True Cross cycle, it's packed with intricate detail, much of it a meticulous record of 15th-century costume and interior décor. There are references to contemporary Venetian buildings and the Castel Sant'Angelo in Rome, and Carpaccio's trademark dogs and monkeys appear more than once. Some of the paintings contain several episodes of the story, and the audioguide is useful for sorting out the twists and turns of the tale.

PRESENTATION OF THE VIRGIN (ROOM 24)

Still hanging in its original site in the Scuola Grande di Santa Maria della Carità, now part of the Accademia, the *Presentation of the Virgin* by Titian was painted from 1534 to 1539. It draws heavily on the Venetian narrative tradition, but in a wholly 'modern' way, with landscape, architecture and figures perfectly balanced, while the small figure of the Virgin ascending the stairway is the focal point for the whole composition.

BACKGROUND

The Accademia delle Belle Arti, which houses the Gallerie dell'Accademia, was founded in 1750 as the city's art school. It moved to its present home in 1807 under Napoleon, who, having suppressed dozens of churches and monasteries, needed somewhere to put their artworks. It was envisioned that the paintings would be as much used by art students as admired by the public, and this was the Accademia's initial role. The art school still exists, but today the Accademia is primarily known as one of Europe's finest specialized collections. It is housed in three connected former religious buildings—the Scuola Grande di Santa Maria della Carità, its adjacent church of Santa Maria, and the Monastery of the Lateran Canons.

The Dogana di Mare, the Republic's Sea Customs House, stands at the end of the Grand Canal

The façade of the Gesuati is reminiscent of Palladio's style

DOGANA DI MARE

➕ 61 G11 • Dogana di Mare, Dorsoduro 🚢 Salute

The point where the Giudecca canal merges with the Grand Canal is known as the Punta della Dogana and is occupied by the Dogana di Mare. This replaced the original customs house near San Biagio in the 15th century and was reconstructed from 1677 to 1682 by Giuseppe Benoni. Warehouses stretch along the point, fronted by a portico below a small white tower, which is topped by a gilded bronze globe supported by two atlases and surmounted by a weather vane, designed by Bernardo Falcone to represent Fortune. From this vantage point, every ship approaching the city could be observed, recorded and, if necessary, searched by officers who valued, assessed and taxed cargoes coming into the city. It's perhaps the finest panorama in Venice, with a view sweeping across the Bacino di San Marco and past San Giorgio Maggiore to the Piazza, while to the left the Grand Canal and its *palazzi* stretches west.

GALLERIE DELL'ACCADEMIA

See pages 94–100.

GESUATI

➕ 60 E12 • Zattere ai Gesuati, Dorsoduro 917 ☎ 041 523 0625 🕐 Mon–Sat 10–5, Sun 1–5. Closed Sun in Jul and Aug, 1 Jan, Easter, 15 Aug, 25 Dec 🎫 Chorus Pass (for all churches in Chorus group) €8; single ticket €2.50 🚢 Zattere, Accademia www.chorusvenezia.org

The church of the Gesuati makes a good stopping point on a walk along the Zattere. This wonderfully rococo church, also known as Santa Maria del Rosario, stands four-square on the water-front, its façade designed by Giorgio Massari (1686–1766) and built for the Dominicans between 1726 and 1743. Massari worked frequently with the painter Giambattista Tiepolo (1696–1770), and the Gesuati is a good place to see Tiepolo's dizzyingly foreshortened ceiling frescoes in a setting designed specifically for them. The interior is an intriguing mix of classicism and the sugary elements of rococo, the lines of the columns leading the eye up to the three vertiginous Tiepolo ceiling panels depicting *Scenes from the Life of St. Dominic* (1737–1739). The first altarpiece on the right, showing the *Virgin with Saints Catherine of Siena, Rose of Lima and Agnes* is also by Tiepolo. The third altar has a magnificent and intense *Crucifixion* by Tintoretto (1518–94).

GESUITI

➕ 59 H7 • Campo dei Gesuiti, Cannaregio ☎ 041 528 6579 🕐 Daily 10–12, 3–6 🎫 Free 🚢 Fondamente Nuove

The Jesuit church of Santa Maria Assunta, known as the Gesuiti, lies on the direct route from the Rialto to the Fondamente Nuove. The Jesuits, with their close ties to the Papacy, were never popular in republican Venice, falling out badly with the Serenissima, as the Venetian republic was known, in 1606, when they were expelled from the city in retaliation for Venice's excommunication by the papacy. By 1700 they were once more established and looking round for a new site for a church. The Order purchased an old church, knocked it down and erected a new one, built to a plan by Domenico Rossi between 1715 and 1729. The result was a vast construction of maximum impact, whose mind-bogglingly ornate interior epitomizes the dazzling richness preferred by the Order.

The interior space soars into dim heights, with towering pilasters and a baldachin over the altar modelled on Bernini's version in St. Peter's, while virtually every inch of wall space is festooned with billowing swags of drapery and richly figured damasks. But these swags and drapes, tassels and brocades are actually intricately carved and polished green and white marble, one of the most astounding sights to be found in any Venetian church. Hidden among this are two fine paintings; a night scene by Titian (1478–1576), the *Martyrdom of St. Lawrence*, over the first altar on the left and the *Assumption of the Virgin* by Tintoretto (1518–94) in the left transept. The former, badly lit and hard to discern, shows the saint being roasted on a gridiron amid the taunts of his executioners.

Statue on the façade of the Gesuati

Il Ghetto

The world's first Jewish ghetto was established in Venice in 1516, and is set on its own island in Cannaregio. In this fascinating and thought-provoking enclave you can visit ancient synagogues set in and around a beautiful *campo*.

A street in the Ghetto Vecchio, or Old Ghetto

A wine shop on the Campo Ghetto Nuovo, a separate island at the heart of the Ghetto

A memorial plaque to the victims of the Holocaust

RATINGS	
Cultural interest	● ● ●
Good for kids	● ● ●
Historic interest	● ● ● ● ●
Walkability	● ● ● ●

BASICS

Museo Ebraico and Synagogues
✚ 58 E6 • Campo Ghetto Nuovo, Cannaregio 2902B
☎ 041 715 359 or 041 723 007
🕐 Jun–end Sep Sun–Fri 10–7; Oct–end May Sun–Fri 10–6. May close early on Fri. Closed 1 May and Jewish feast days. Guided tours half-hourly
💶 Adult €6; child (under 12) €6.50
🚤 Guglie, San Marcuola
🎧 Guided tours in Italian, English, French and Spanish
💬
📖 Selection of books on the Ghetto and the Jewish religion, Jewish religious artefacts and gifts
🚻
www.ghetto.it
English-language site giving full background to the Ghetto, synagogues and museums.

SEEING IL GHETTO

The main approach to the Ghetto is through a narrow alley leading off the Fondamenta di Cannaregio. This brings you to the Ghetto Vecchio and over a bridge to the Campo Ghetto Nuovo. Here you'll find the Holocaust Memorial and Museo Ebraica (Jewish Museum), from where the Ghetto tours depart. These leave half-hourly throughout the day and guides will fill you in on the history of the Ghetto while you visit three synagogues. You can then visit the museum and explore the rest of the area, with its fascinating Jewish shops, at your leisure.

HIGHLIGHTS

CAMPO GHETTO NUOVO AND THE HOLOCAUST MEMORIAL

The open space of the Campo Ghetto Nuovo is surrounded by what, for Venice, are extremely tall buildings. Overcrowding was a problem throughout the Ghetto's history, and the authorities only permitted construction of houses one-third higher than in the rest of the city, resulting in very low floors crammed into the available space; seven is usual. These tightly packed buildings surround the *campo* on two sides; the north side is occupied by a purpose-built old people's home. To the left of this is the Holocaust memorial, a series of seven reliefs by Arbit Blatas (1977), with a poem by André Tranc, commemorating the deportation and extermination of the city's Jewish people.

THE SYNAGOGUES

As successive waves of immigrants arrived in the Ghetto from other countries, they built their own synagogues, mainly incorporated into existing buildings, to maintain their individual rites. The Scola Tedesca was founded in 1528 by German Jews, the Scola Canton in 1531 by Ashkenazi French, the Scola Levantina by Jews from the eastern Mediterranean in 1538, the Scola Spagnola followed a Spanish Sephardic settlement in the late 16th century, and the Scola Italiana was established in 1575. As Jewish people were forbidden to work as architects, Christian designers were employed, resulting in strangely Christian-like interiors, with painted wood, stucco and gilt, though there are no figurative images as these are forbidden by Judaism. The syna-

gogues were funded by prosperous members of the community, and the wealth of the different national groups is reflected in the design, with the Scola Levantina and the Scola Spagnola being the most lavish.

The Ghetto has a very lived-in feel to it

BACKGROUND

Jewish people first arrived in Venice in the 1390s and settled in an area of Cannaregio with a foundry, or *geto*, a word that was to give its name to Jewish forced settlement areas throughout the centuries. Jewish people were at first only permitted to reside in Venice for periods of up to 15 days, and their activities were restricted to medicine, money lending—a practice forbidden by the church—and second-hand dealing. They won the right to live full time in the city in 1516, when the Republic instituted the area of the Ghetto as their compulsory place of residence in gratitude for their financial help following the War of the League of Cambrai. Gates, controlled by Christian guards paid for by the Jewish community, were shut between sunset and dawn at the entrance to the Ghetto. Jewish people were compelled to wear distinctive badges or caps, had limited property rights and were subject to a range of financial penalties. Drastic as this sounds, they were probably safer in Venice than elsewhere in Europe and the community was periodically augmented by influxes from more oppressive countries such as Spain and Portugal. They continued their traditional professions of usury and medicine—doctors being the only people allowed to leave at night.

The gates were eventually torn down by Napoleon in 1797, and Jewish people finally achieved full rights as Venetian citizens after the Unification of Italy in 1866. By World War II their position was under threat from Fascism and during 1942 and 1943 many were deported—around 200 died in the death camps. The Jewish population today is small, but the Ghetto is still very much the heart of the community and a place of pilgrimage for Jewish people from many countries, who come to experience the first sad Ghetto in the world.

TIP

● The excellent guided tours (booked at the museum) are the best way to see the Ghetto.

MORE TO SEE

MUSEO EBRAICA

The Jewish Museum was opened in 1955 to display a rich collection of silverware, religious ceremonial objects, textiles, prayer books and documents, dating mainly from the 16th to 19th centuries. The textiles and silverware are particularly impressive, and look for the ornately decorated marriage contracts.

Relaxing in the quiet space of the Giardino Papadopoli

The domes of the Santa Maria della Salute create a stunning skyline as the sun sets

THE SIGHTS

GIARDINI EX REALI

⊞ 61 H10 • Giardini ex Reali, San Marco 🚤 San Marco, San Marco (Vallaresso) 🎫 Free

About the only patch of green in the vicinity of the Piazza San Marco is the Giardini ex Reali, a waterfront oasis of trees behind the Procuratie Nuove. It was created during the Napoleonic occupation, when Eugène Bonaparte, son of Napoleon III, demolished the old state granaries which stood here as part of his scheme to improve the area. He was also responsible for the elegant neoclassical pavilion at the west end, the Casino del Caffè, now home to the excellent main tourist office. Benches are shaded by trees and the view over the Bacino di San Marco is superb, but the downsides are the constant crowds and serried rows of souvenir stalls. It's popular with artists, who sell their watercolours, oils and charcoal sketches. Despite this, the gardens have a certain allure.

GIARDINO PAPADOPOLI

⊞ 58 C8 • Giardino Papadopoli, Santa Croce 🚤 Piazzale Roma 🎫 Free

At the west end of the Grand Canal, a stone's throw from Piazzale Roma with its buses and cars, is the Giardino Papadopoli, once one of the city's largest private gardens. It was created in 1810 with the demolition of a whole group of buildings standing at the junction of the Grand Canal with the Rio dei Tolentini. Among those destroyed were the church and monastery of Santa Croce, which gave the *sestiere* its name. The gardens are bounded on the west side by the Rio Nuovo. Today, the cool gardens are a good place to pause in this crowded urban area—worth bearing in mind if you're waiting for transport to the mainland.

GIARDINI PUBBLICI

⊞ 63 N12 • Riva dei Partigiani, Castello 🚤 Giardini 🎫 Free

After an overdose of architectural grandeur the Giardini Pubblici provide a good antidote. Stretching back from the east end of the Riva in Castello, the gardens were created by Napoleon in the early 19th century. If you've got kids who need some exercise, or want a cool place for a picnic, head here. Much of the area is occupied by the pavilions used during the Biennale (▷ 76); you can see the various buildings partly hidden in the trees, though the area is closed except during the Biennale. The rest of the grassy space is dotted with pine trees and benches and there are wide views over the lagoon. Until the beginning of the 20th century, when the Riva was extended this far east, the only access was from Via Giuseppe Garibaldi through the Giardini Garibaldi. On the waterfront the Riva dei Sette Martiri stretches to the west; cross the first bridge to see the *Donna Partigiana*, a bronze waterside memorial figure to the partisans executed here in 1944. There's more green space to the east, where the Parco delle Rimembranze extends along the waterfront of the Quartiere Sant'Elena, a separate island.

GIUDECCA

⊞ 60 E13 • Giudecca 🚤 Palanca, Redentore, Zitelle

The island of the Giudecca lies south of central Venice across the wide, deepwater Canale della Giudecca. It was once a chain of small islands, settled as early as the 9th century.

From the 13th century it was popular as a place of escape from the summertime heat, and wealthy aristocrats built sumptu-ous *palazzi* here, surrounded by gardens. Later, it became Venice's inner industrial zone, with shipbuilding and factories providing employment throughout the 19th and much of the 20th centuries. Over the past 50 years industry has declined, and the Giudecca today is a largely residential area.

A broad *fondamenta*, with superb views across to Dorsoduro, runs all along the north side of the island. Here stand the main sights—the churches of the Redentore (▷ 119), the Zitelle and Sant' Eufemia. The Zitelle, like the Redentore, was designed by Andrea Palladio in the 16th century, but Sant'Eufemia is far older, its foundation dating from the 9th century. The *fondamenta* is also home to the island's food shops, bars and restaurants, some modest houses and grand 14th-century *palazzi,* and, at the west end, the vast red-brick bulk of the Molino Stucky, a former flour mill built in the 1890s. This is currently being redeveloped as luxury housing and a major hotel. There's more accommodation at the opposite east end of the Giudecca in the shape of the Cipriani (▷ 277), one of the world's most famous hotels.

MADONNA DELL'ORTO

See pages 106–107.

MUSEO D'ARTE MODERNA

⊞ 59 F7 • Ca' Pesaro, Santa Croce 2070–2076 ☎ 041 524 0662 🕐 Apr–end Oct Tue–Sun 10–6; Nov–end Mar Tue–Sun 10–5. Closed 1 May 🎫 €5.50; holders of Rolling Venice card €3 (includes admission to Museo d'Arte Orientale) 🚤 San Stae www.museiciviciveneziani.it

Housed in the stunning Ca' Pesaro (▷ 72–73), the Museum of Modern Art was founded in

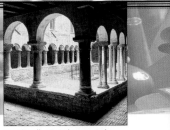

May Morning *by Guglielmo Ciardi (1842–1917) on display in the Museo d'Arte Moderna*

Sant'Apollonia is home to the Museo Diocesano d'Arte Sacra

1902 primarily to exhibit works purchased from the Biennale. Accordingly, much on display is alarmingly pedestrian late 19th- and early 20th-century Italian works by artists such as Filippo de Pisis, Giorgio Morandi and Guglielmo Ciardi. Their winsome lagoon scenes and run-of-the-mill landscapes are a salient reminder that, in its early days, the Biennale was far removed from its present role as a show-case for cutting-edge art. The museum has some foreign artists represented, with single works by Matisse, Klimt, Klee and Chagall and sculpture by Henry Moore. These are well-displayed in spacious first-floor intercon-necting galleries, with some single pieces of sculpture on the ground floor.

MUSEO D'ARTE ORIENTALE

➕ 59 F7 • Ca' Pesaro, Santa Croce 2076 ☎ 041 524 0662 🕓 Apr–end Oct Tue–Sun 10–6; Nov–end Mar Tue–Sun 10–5. Closed 1 May 💶 €5.50; holders of Rolling Venice card €3 (includes admission to Museo d'Arte Moderna) 🚤 San Stae www.museiciviciveneziani.it

Venice's Museum of Oriental Art occupies the top floor of the Ca' Pesaro (▷ 72–73) and is included in the ticket for the Museo d'Arte Moderna (see left). This vast collection of Japanese art is among the largest in the world and was amassed in the 19th century by the Conte de Bardi, who spent two years tour-ing in the Far East. The collection was donated to Venice by the Austrians, as a peace offering for the damage their incendiary bombs had inflicted on the city during World War I. The layout has changed little since the origi-nal installation, and a visit is like stepping back in time, when museums were a positive jumble

of apparently mismatched objects. Connoisseurs of Far Eastern art will find much to admire among the arms, armour, paintings, screens, porcelain, sculpture and musical instru-ments. The lacquerwork, bronzes and porcelain are among the most interesting exhibits, and don't miss the splendid photo-graphs of the noble collector posing in native dress.

MUSEO CASA CARLO GOLDONI

➕ 58 E9 • Calle dei Nomboli, San Polo 2794 ☎ 041 244 0317 🕓 Apr–end Oct Mon–Sat 10–5; Nov–end Mar Mon–Sat 10–4. Closed 1 May 💶 €2.50; holders of Rolling Venice card €1.50 🚤 San Tomà www.museiciviciveneziani.it

The playwright Carlo Goldoni (1707–93) was born in the Ca' Centanni, a 14th-century Venetian-Gothic *palazzo* with an internal courtyard whose stair leads to the *piano nobile*. The building's main role today is that of a theatrical study centre and archive, but it also houses a museum devoted to the life and times of the writer.

Goldoni transformed Venetian theatre by moving away from the much-loved, but narrow, format of the Commedia dell'Arte, which depended solely on the skills of the actor, to plays where the writ-ten text was all-important. His plays describe the daily life of the Venetians, satirizing the laziness of the aristocracy and the man-ners of the day. They were immensely successful, and Goldoni became one of the first authors to make a living from his writing. Three rooms on the *piano nobile* of the *palazzo* are dedicated to his work, prefaced by an informative, multilingual video presentation.

Don't miss the wonderful pup-pet theatre from the Palazzo

Grimani, complete with all the beautifully dressed puppets used in this popular form of 18th-century entertainment.

MUSEO CORRER

See pages 108–109.

MUSEO DIOCESANO D'ARTE SACRA

➕ 61 H10 • Chiostro di Sant'Apollonia, Sant'Apollonia, Castello 4312 ☎ 041 277 0561 🕓 Mon–Sat 10.30am–12.30pm 💶 By donation 🚤 San Zaccaria

Many Venetian churches have closed or been deconsecrated over the years, and the Museum of Sacred Diocesan Art is the repository for many of the treas-ures they once contained. This quirky little museum, tucked off the main route from San Zaccaria to the Piazza, displays an eclectic collection of religious objects and paintings, along with temporary exhibits stored here while restoration is undertaken. Its chief treasure, however, is not its art, but the exquisite cloister of Sant'Apollonia in whose buildings it's housed. This superb, tranquil spot is Venice's only example of Romanesque architecture and dates from the 12th to 13th cen-turies. Rounded arches, supported by an Istrian stone colonnade, surround the central space, beautifully paved with herring-bone brickwork.

Puppet in the Museo Casa Carlo Goldoni

Madonna dell'Orto

This unspoiled and tranquil Gothic church, the burial place of the artist Tintoretto and home to some of his most compelling work, is tucked away in Cannaregio.

Madonna dell'Orto's Gothic façade *The vaulted apse is decorated with works by Tintoretto, who is buried in the church* *A statue of St. Christopher stands over the doorway*

BASICS

➕ 59 G5 • Campo Madonna dell'Orto, Cannaregio
☎ 041 719 933 or 041 275 0462
🕐 Mon–Sat 10–5, Sun 1–5. Closed Sun in Jul, Aug, Easter, 15 Aug
💶 Chorus Pass (for all churches in Chorus group) €8, single ticket €2.50
🚤 Orto
💬 Information sheet and audioguides in Italian, English, French and German
📖 Postcards
www.chorusvenezia.org
Superb site in English and Italian giving comprehensive information about the architecture and art of all the churches in the Chorus group.

SEEING MADONNA DELL'ORTO

Spend a few minutes admiring the façade of Madonna dell'Orto before you enter the church. The simple, airy interior repays a few minutes' appreciation before you move on to take in Tintoretto's frescoes; these are found above the entrance to the Cappella di San Mauro, in the choir and behind the high altar, in the apse and in the Cappella Contarini off the left aisle. Tintoretto is buried in the chapel on the right of the high altar, together with his children. You'll notice a photograph and an empty frame in the first chapel on the left; a superb *Madonna and Child (1480)* by Giovanni Bellini hung here until it was stolen in 1993.

HIGHLIGHTS

THE FAÇADE

The beautiful, predominantly Gothic façade, overlooking its own *campo* and a canal, is built of the same red brick and Istrian stone as Venice's two other major Gothic churches, the Frari and Santi Giovanni e Paolo. Construction here, though, was long drawn out, with the result that the façade is a hybrid, incorporating both Gothic and Renaissance elements. The windows, with their filigree tracery, are clearly Gothic, while the onion-shaped dome of the campanile echoes the earlier Byzantine style. The elegant doorway by Bartolomeo Bon, with its columns and symmetrical lines, is resolutely Renaissance, as is the statue of St. Christopher by Nicolò di Giovanni above. Bridging the stylistic gap are the statues of the Apostles in the false gallery at the top of the aisle wings, thought to be by the Tuscan Dalle Masegne workshop.

THE INTERIOR

The interior is laid out in basilica form, the central nave and its side aisles drawing the eye forwards to the choir and chancel. The overwhelming impression is of space and light, the pointed Gothic arches adding to the feeling of soaring height. The decoration is simple, with Greek marble columns dividing the aisles from the nave, a plain wooden coffered ceiling and a red-and-white *terrazza* tiled floor, the perfect backdrop for the power of the church's stupendous artwork.

THE PAINTINGS

The Madonna dell'Orto was Tintoretto's parish church and the incredible paintings he created for it over a period of some 30 years were his gift to the church; he asked only for money for his materials. On either side of the high altar are the *Making of the Golden Calf* (on the left), and the *Last Judgement* (on the right), dating from 1562–63, while four of the figures of the Virtues, set high behind the altar, are also by the artist. Imbued with religious passion and sincerity, they're full of movement, light and drama. The four carriers of the calf in the *Making of the Golden Calf* have been tentatively identified as Giorgione, Titian, Veronese and Tintoretto (fourth from the left). In the apse the *Beheading of St. Paul* and *St. Peter's Vision of the Cross*

(1566) are again full of movement—look out for the swirling, swooping angels—and provide a contrast with the sublimely mystical *Presentation of the Virgin in the Temple* (1552–53) over the entrance to the Cappella di San Mauro. Tintoretto's final work here, *St. Agnes* (1577), shimmers with radiant blues, and there's another artistic treat in the form of Cima da Conegliano's *St. John the Baptist* (1493) in the first chapel on the right.

The statues in the niches on the façade of the church represent the Twelve Apostles

BACKGROUND

The original church was founded around 1350 and dedicated to St. Christopher, the patron saint of travellers, in the hope he would keep an eye on the ferry service to the northern islands and the gondoliers who ran it from a nearby jetty. Some years later, a statue of the Madonna and Child started to attract attention as a miracle-worker in a nearby vegetable garden *(orto)*. In 1377, St. Christopher was demoted and the Madonna was moved from the *orto* to the church. The statue is still there and can be seen in the Cappella di San Mauro, off the end of the right aisle near the main altar, while St. Christopher now presides over the central door of the façade. The church was rebuilt between 1399 and 1473; Tintoretto's paintings for the choir, apse and side walls cover 30 years of the 16th century.

In 1874 the church was badly restored, with its pavement tombs ripped up, its priceless organ demolished and the Greek marble columns in the nave overpainted. Things were put back to their near-original state and Madonna dell'Orto became the first major restoration to be funded after the 1966 floods by the British Venice in Peril Fund. This was founded by Sir Ashley Clarke, who became its first chairman and was made a freeman of Venice; he is commemorated by a plaque in the chapel to the right of the main altar.

Museo Correr

The Museo Correr, overlooking the Piazza di San Marco, traces the history of the city of Venice. Its huge range of sculpture, paintings and historical objects provides an insight into city life in the great days of the Republic.

The entrance to the Correr is in the arcade of the Ala Napoleonica

Doge Giovanni Mocenigo (1478–85) by Gentile Bellini

Decorative ceiling in the entrance hall of the museum

BASICS

✚ 61 G10 • Ala Napoleonica, Piazza San Marco 52, San Marco

☎ 041 520 9070 (call centre open Mon–Fri 9–6, Sat 9–2) or 041 240 5211

🕐 Apr–end Oct daily 9–7; Nov–end Mar daily 9–5

💷 Museum Card (valid for Museo Correr, Museo Archeologico, Biblioteca Marciana, Palazzo Ducale) adult €11; child (6–14) €3; holders of Rolling Venice card €5.50. No single tickets for the Correr

🚤 San Marco (Vallaresso)

📓 Guidebooks at bookstall; guided tours of Biblioteca Marciana Sat–Sun 10–12, 2–3

🅿

🏛 Guidebooks, art books, posters and museum gifts

🚻

www.museicivicivenezianil.it
Excellent site in English and Italian with full details of all Venices's civic museums.

SEEING THE MUSEO CORRER

The Museo Correr occupies the upper floors of the Ala Napoleonica, the Procuratie Nuove and Sansovino's library building, and is housed in a series of grand and elaborate rooms, many overlooking the Piazza. It's approached up a monumental stairway, which is tucked under the arcade of the Ala Napoleonica at the west end of the Piazza San Marco. The Correr is now directly linked with the Museo Archeologico and the Biblioteca Nazionale Marciana, so you can explore the whole complex on a single ticket. The top floor is home to the Quadreria, a gallery tracing the development of Venetian painting. This is a big museum and you need a whole morning to see everything. You may also find that this is one to leave for the end of your visit, when what you have already learned about the city will help you make sense of many of the displays. If time is short, head for the highlights, leaving time to visit the sumptuous library.

HIGHLIGHTS

THE CANOVA SCULPTURES

The neoclassical rooms of the first floor make the ideal setting for the slickly impressive sculptures by Antonio Canova (1757–1822), considered to be the finest sculptor of his age. He was a poised and technically outstanding sculptor, and you can trace his work process through the *maquettes*, or clay models, that he used as the first drafts for his highly polished works. The focal point of the display is his *Daedalus and Icarus*, created when he was just 22, in which the older man fixes a pair of wings onto the would-be aviator. The collection also includes casts of his work; the black studs on *Paris* were guidelines made by apprentices preparing the marble for the artist.

THE VENETIAN ROOMS

Many of the rooms (6–18) in the Procuratie Nuove are devoted to collections that document Venetian history, covering everything from daily life and local festivals to the workings of the State, the Arsenale, the ducal elections and the great commercial and naval achievements. Don't miss the bird's-eye view of Venice, a huge woodcut that was produced by Jacopo de' Barbari between 1497 and 1500 and is one of the most seminal images of the city. At the far end of the museum, past the picture gallery, there are more enjoyable Venetian displays, with cases devoted to games, pastimes and festivals and a whole exhibit of *zoccoli*, the famous elevated clogs worn by Venetian ladies of leisure. These first appeared in the early 15th century, and by the 17th had reached astounding heights, with women wobbling along supported by two attendants in order to keep their balance.

THE QUADRERIA

Apart from the Accademia (▷ 94–99) Venice has no better and more comprehensive painting collection than the Corter. The great Venetians, such as the Bellinis, are well represented—don't miss the *Portrait of the Doge Giovanni Mocenigo* (1480s) by Gentile Bellini, or the lovely *Madonna and Child* (1470–75) by Giovanni Bellini. Pride of the collection is Vittore Carpaccio's famous *Two Venetian Noblewomen* (1507), which shows two finely dressed ladies sitting on a balcony. For years this picture was known as *The Courtesans*, but it emerged that the sitters had been maligned when the top half of the picture, showing a hunting scene with men and dogs, was traced to the Getty Museum in California. Far from being courtesans awaiting trade, these eminently respectable ladies are merely terminally bored while the boys play. Other treasures include Antonello da Messina's *Pietà* (1475), an early oil painting, and a tranquil and lovely *Madonna* (1525) by Lorenzo Lotto.

BIBLIOTECA NAZIONALE MARCIANA

One of the most outstanding buildings of the ensemble around the Piazzetta (▷ 139–140), the Biblioteca Nazionale Marciana was designed by Sansovino (1486–1570) and completed in 1591. The main hall, among the most beautiful rooms in Venice, is richly decorated with carved and gilded wood, its ceilings covered with allegorical paintings by Veronese, Tintoretto and their followers, while a fresco of *Wisdom* by Titian adorns the ante-room. This grandeur is approached up a magnificent staircase; all gilt and stucco, it's a fitting entrance to one of the Republic's most prestigious buildings. Changing exhibitions of the library's treasures are often held, and there are permanent displays of illuminated manuscripts, early printed books from Venetian presses and historic maps.

Madonna and Child *by Giovanni Bellini (above)*

Daedalus and Icarus *by Antonio Canova (below)*

BACKGROUND

The Museo Correr occupies the buildings around the Piazza which served as Venice's 19th-century royal residence. Until the Napoleonic invasion the west end of the Piazza was occupied by a church which stood between the Procuratie Vecchie and the Procuratie Nuove. This was demolished, and between 1806 and 1814 work started on the Ala Napoleonica. This was finally completed in the mid-19th century, when Venice was under Austrian rule. It served as the royal residence for the Hapsburgs when they visited the city, incorporating a complex that stretched the full length of the Procuratie Nuove as far as the Biblioteca Nazionale Marciana. In 1923, this huge space was opened as the Museo Correr, a museum of the history of Venice, whose core comprises the 16th-, 17th- and 18th-century collections of Teodoro Correr, who gifted them to the city in 1830. The city's archaeological collections were housed in the same complex as a separate museum, and there was public access to the magnificent Libreria Sansoviniana. In the 1960s the third-floor rooms containing the picture collection were revamped and in the late 1990s everything was linked as a single entity, creating one of Venice's biggest museums.

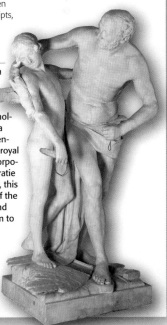

Interior of the Museo della Fondazione Querini Stampalia

The Fondaco dei Turchi contains the Museo di Storia Naturale (Natural History Museum)

THE SIGHTS

MUSEO DELLA FONDAZIONE QUERINI STAMPALIA

🗝 61 J9 • Campiello Querini Stampalia, Castello 5252 ☎ 041 271 1411 🕐 Tue–Thu, Sun 10–6, Fri –Sat 10–10 💶 Adult €6; child (under 11) free; Rolling Venice and Venice Pass holders €4. Includes entrance to the concerts for museum visitors every Fri and Sat at 5 and 8.30 🚤 San Zaccaria www.querinistampalia.it

The Fondazione Querini Stampalia was founded in the 19th century by the aristocrat Giovanni Querini, who bequeathed his *palazzo*, his art collection and considerable funds to the city. His will specified that the money was to be used to open a reading room and library and to promoting 'evening assemblies'. The Foundation has kept the faith in every way, and the Renaissance *palazzo* is busy through the day and into the evenings with students using its excellent facilities, while baroque concerts are a regular weekend feature. Between 1959 and 1963 the ground floor and garden were imaginatively redesigned by Carlo Scarpa to become one of Venice's few truly first-rate examples of modern architecture. This is the perfect foil for the palace's second-floor museum, spread through a series of delightful period rooms. Among the pictures there's a *Presentation in the Temple* by Giovanni Bellini (1430–1516) and two portraits by Palma il Vecchio (1548–1628) of 16th-century members of the Querini family. But the museum's main delight has to be the series of 67 pictures of Venetian festivals, customs and ceremonies by the 18th-century artist Gabriele Bella (active in Venice 1760) and the series of genre paintings of bourgeois life by Pietro Longhi (1702–85). These give charming glimpses into Venetian life, with interior scenes involving hairdressers and tailors and some wonderful portrayals of outdoor pursuits, including a precarious boatload of sportsmen hunting duck.

MUSEO FORTUNY

🗝 61 F9 • Rio Terrà della Mandorla, San Marco 3780 (round corner from main façade) ☎ 041 520 0995 🕐 Varies with exhibitions, but normally Tue–Sun 10–6 💶 €4 🚤 Sant'Angelo www.museiciviciv[eneziani.it

In 1899 the Spanish-born painter, photographer and fabric designer Mariano Fortuny y Madrazo purchased one of the Pesaro family's *palazzi* in San Marco. It dates from the end of the 15th century and is a wonderful example of decorated Gothic, with two inner courtyards and an exterior stair leading to balconies that open into the *piano nobile*. This contains a huge *portego*, the quintessential Venetian central hall. Fortuny decorated the *portego* with textiles and hangings, setting up a workshop to pursue his interest in theatre and design. The two came together in his textiles—both in the pleated silk dresses known as Delphos, which liberated women's bodies, and in the stencilled brocades and velvets he used for interior decoration. Fortuny also produced silk lampshades in his own inimitable and instantly recognizable style. He set up a factory in Venice and his fabrics and clothes were sold all over the world—a small factory on the Giudecca continued production up to the 1980s. Today, Fortuny-style silks and velvets are manufactured by Venetia Studium, with shops all over the city (▷ 197). The Palazzo Fortuny was left to the city in 1956 by the designer's widow and is now used for exhibitions and other cultural events. Though in need of restoration, it's one of the most evocative of all *palazzi*, whose dimly lit interior, pricked with light from pierced lamps and hung with sumptuous textiles, perfectly embodies the voluptuousness of Fortuny's art.

MUSEO DI STORIA NATURALE

🗝 58 E7 • Fondaco dei Turchi, Santa Croce 1730 ☎ 041 275 0206 🕐 Sat–Sun 10–4 💶 Free 🚤 San Stae www.museiciviciveneziani.it

Venice's Natural History Museum is housed in the old Fondaco dei Turchi, the Turks' Warehouse. From 1621 this 13th-century palace-cum-warehouse was rented by the Republic to Ottoman traders to serve as a warehouse, trade and social centre. As trade with the East declined, it fell into disrepair, and by 1880, when the municipality purchased it, was due for a complete overhaul. This 19th-century restoration has been much criticized, but the towers and long water-level arcade give some idea of the building's original appearance. From 1898 to 1922 the Fondaco housed the Correr Museum (▷ 108–109); since then it's been home to a small natural history collection. Downstairs there's an aquarium containing species that live in the Adriatic and some information on the ecology of the lagoon, but the main attraction lies through the inner courtyard. Here you'll find a state-of-the-art exhibition devoted to a hunt for fossilized dinosaurs in Saharan Africa. Huge fossils, known through Tuareg legends, were found during a 1973 expedition, which you can learn about from an Italian-only video. Of more interest to children is the entire dinosaur fossil, rearing up impressively in the upstairs display area.

MUSEO STORICO NAVALE

This superb collection of ships, models and nautical ephemera that places Venice's relationship with the sea in a clear historical context is housed a stone's throw from the Arsenale in an incomparable waterside position.

So entwined were Venetian fortunes with ships and the sea that the Republic established a ship museum as early as the 17th century, when the Casa dei Modelli was set up to display models of ships that were built in the Arsenale. Many of these disappeared during the Napoleonic occupation, but those remaining formed the nucleus of the present museum, set up during the Austrian administration in an old granary building. It came under the directorship of the Italian navy in 1919, and presents a complete overview of Venetian and Italian naval history. Don't expect modern presentation or interactive exhibits; this is an old-fashioned gem that will appeal to adults and children alike, and with over 25,000 exhibits there's something for everyone.

THE COLLECTION'S HIGHLIGHTS

The museum covers every aspect of maritime life, with models and fragments of ships through the ages, nautical and navigational instruments, uniforms, medals, charts and maps, maritime paintings, guns and artillery, Far Eastern vessels, model cruise ships and liners and a huge shell collection. Inevitably, the most interesting exhibits are those that major on Venice itself, particularly the city's traditional and ceremonial vessels. You can admire a scale model of the *Bucintoro*, the gilded barge used by the Doge in the Ascension Day ceremony of the marriage to the sea, and two *cortele*, decorated galley sides, dating from the 16th century; both on the first floor. On the third floor there's an excellent room devoted to the gondola, where you can learn about the boat's history and construction. Here you'll see a 19th-century gondola with the traditional cover, or *felze*, and one of the last privately owned gondolas in Venice, which belonged to Peggy Guggenheim. There's a series of naïf ex voto paintings, mainly from Naples, showing dramatic scenes of shipwrecks and storms at sea. These were commissioned in thanksgiving for deliverance by those rescued from peril on the sea, and were hung in parish churches, normally near the image to which the donor was devoted. There's an annexe, the Padiglione delle Navi (Ships' Pavilion), in an old oar-makers' shed down the *fondamenta* near the entrance to the Arsenale. Here, if it's open, you can see painted fishing boats, a funeral barge and ceremonial galleys.

RATINGS

Cultural interest	●●●
Good for kids	●●●●
Historic interest	●●●●
Value for money	●●●●●

BASICS

✚ 62 L11 • Riva di San Biagio, Castello 2148
☎ 041 520 0276
🕐 Mon–Fri 8.45–1.30, Sat 8.45–1
💶 €1.55
🚤 Arsenale
📖 Floor plan and leaflet only
♿

There's no better place to grasp the relationship between Venice and the sea than a visit to the Naval Museum (above)

A 19th-century gondola on display (below)

Palazzo Ducale

The Palazzo Ducale, once the political and judicial hub of the Venetian Empire and home to the doge, is one of the world's most beautiful buildings. It's the grandest of all Venetian *palazzi* and one of the finest secular buildings of its era.

The magnificent façade of the Palazzo Ducale (Doge's Palace)

Detail of a double grille on the Prigioni Nuove (new prisons)

The Sala Senato, heavily laden with gilt

RATINGS	
Cultural interest	●●●●
Good for kids	●●●
Historic interest	●●●●●
Value for money	●●●●

BASICS

✚ 61 H10 • Piazza San Marco (entrance on Riva degli Schiavoni)

☎ 041 520 9070 (call centre Mon–Fri 9–6, Sat 9–2) 041 271 59 11

🕐 Apr–end Oct daily 9–7; Nov–end Mar daily 9–5

🎫 Museum Card (valid for Palazzo Ducale, Museo Correr, Museo Archeologico, Biblioteca Marciana) adult € 11; child (6–14) €3; holders of Rolling Venice card €5.50. No single tickets for the Palazzo Ducale

🚤 San Marco (Vallaresso), San Zaccaria

📖 Guidebooks in Italian, English, French, German, Spanish and Japanese

🎧 Call 041 520 9070 for details; audio-guides in Italian, English, French, German and Spanish €3. Guided tours of *itinerari segreti* (secret itineraries) daily; book 2 days in advance (tel 041 520 9070), price €12.50

🍴 🏪 🚻

www.museiciviciveneziani.it Excellent site in English and Italian with full details of all Venices's civic museums.

Canal view with Ponte dei Sospiri in the foreground (right)

SEEING THE PALAZZO DUCALE

Built at a time when the rest of Europe cowered behind fortified walls, the fairy-tale façade of the Palazzo Ducale, light, airy and confident, embraces the outside world. It adjoins the Basilica di San Marco at the east end of the Piazza San Marco and overlooks the Piazzetta and the waters of the Bacino di San Marco. It's reached by taking the *vaporetto* from the railway station, a beautiful trip down the Grand Canal of about 35 minutes, or by approaching on foot from wherever you're based; walking from the station takes around 45 minutes. To see it thoroughly you should allow plenty of time, perhaps deciding in advance where you want to linger. The audioguide tour takes around 2 to 3 hours. There are information boards in Italian and English in many of the rooms; if you don't have a guidebook these are well worth reading. There's no ideal time to come, as the Palazzo Ducale is the number-one sight for every visitor to Venice.

HIGHLIGHTS

THE EXTERIOR, THE PORTA DELLA CARTA AND THE COURTYARD

The beautiful pink-and-white façade of the Palazzo Ducale, one of the world's finest examples of Gothic architecture, runs along the Piazzetta and the water's edge. The waterfront façade, finished in 1404, is the older, and its design is echoed by the 15th-century Piazzetta side. Both façades have a ground-floor arcade topped by a gallery supporting the mass of the upper floors, the masonry closing in on the open space as the building heightens. The play of light and shade over solid form and through space adds to the impression of harmony, enhanced by the regularity of the arches and ground-floor columns and pillars, copies of the 14th- and 15th-century originals, which are now housed in the ground-floor Museo dell'Opera.

The main entrance is through the Porta della Carta. This monumental gateway, a superb example of Decorated Gothic at its most ornate, was designed by Bartolomeo and Giovanni Bon in 1438. It was completed during the dogeship of Francesco Foscari (1423–57), who is portrayed kneeling in front of the Lion of St. Mark over the doorway.

From here, a portico leads through to the central courtyard, whose arcade and first-floor gallery echoes the exterior design. Access to the first floor is via the Scala dei Giganti (Giants' Stairway), begun in 1483 by Antonio Rizzo (c1440–99). It was named for the giant statues of Mars and Neptune, designed in 1566 by Jacopo Sansovino, at the top. Sansovino was also responsible for the grandiose Scala d'Oro (Golden Stair), encrusted with dazzling gilt and stucco work, which links this level with the *primo piano nobile*, home to the doge.

THE DOGE'S APARTMENTS

Elected from among the patrician families, the doge held office for life, sitting on all the major councils, a position of such potential power that it was tied up with endless restrictions to prevent its abuse. The rooms are both magnificent and austere, with superb ceilings and huge fireplaces. The finest chamber is the Sala delle Mappe (Map Room), decorated with maps showing the whole of the 16th-century known world, with Venice firmly as the central focus. This leads to the Sala delle Quattro Porte (Room of the Four Doors), a magnificent antechamber with ceiling frescoes by Tintoretto (1518–94), where foreign officials waited to meet the doge and councils.

THE ANTICOLLEGIO, COLLEGIO AND SALA DEL SENATO

The interconnecting trio of rooms known as the Anticollegio, the Collegio and the Sala del Senato are among the most interesting, and certainly the most lavish, in the Palazzo. The Anticollegio, designed by

TIPS
● The visitors' entrance is on the Bacino side.
● Expect parts of the Palazzo Ducale to be closed; a building this age is under constant restoration.
● Winter visitors should dress very warmly; there's no heating in the Palazzo Ducale and it can be extremely cold.
● The Museum Card for the Musei di Piazza San Marco covers entrance to all the museums in the Piazza (Palazzo Ducale, Museo Correr, Museo Archeologico Nazionale and Biblioteca Nazionale Marciana). It costs €11 for adults and €3 for children, and is valid for three months.
● The Museum Pass covers entrance to all the Civic Museums (Musei di Piazza San Marco, Ca' Rezzonico, Palazzo Mocenigo, Museo Casa Carlo Goldoni, Museo del Vetro on Murano and Museo del Merletto on Burano). It is valid for three months and costs €15.50.

Palladio (1508–80), richly stuccoed and decorated with canvases by Tintoretto, served as an inner waiting room for foreign delegations. From here, visitors entered the Collegio, the meeting place of Venice's Cabinet, which, chaired by the doge, presided over the Senate. The latter met in the Sala del Senato, a magnificent room large enough to accommodate this 300-strong body. The decoration of these three chambers was intended to illustrate the story of Venice, while at the same time impressing on foreign emissaries the city's might, power and riches. The panels are in praise to Venice herself, propaganda pieces showing the Serenissima triumphing over all and sundry. Nothing better illustrates this approach than the ceiling panels in the Collegio, where *Justice* and *Peace* are mere side-kicks to Venice, or the ceiling painting in the Sala del Senato, which shows *Venice Triumphant* in a suitably over-the-top gilded, carved surround.

THE SALA DEL MAGGIOR CONSIGLIO
By far the largest room in the *palazzo*, and indeed in the entire city, is the first-floor Sala del Maggior Consiglio, the meeting place for the Great Council—the lower house, made up of over 2,500 aristocratic members. It stretches almost the entire length of the waterfront and is one of the earliest parts of the building. Badbly damaged by fire in 1577, its present decorative scheme is the work of Tintoretto, who devised the complicated iconographical plan, devoted, as elsewhere, to the concept of Venice's prestige. Only the artist's mind-blowing *Paradiso* (1588–92), on the east wall, departs from this theme. The largest oil painting in the world (140sq m/1,500sq ft), it shows the

The magnificent Sala del Maggior Consiglio (top)

Detail of the astrological clock in the Sala del Senato (above)

Statue of Atlas at the foot of the Scala d'Oro (left)

MORE TO SEE

Itinerari Segreti: A behind-the-scenes tour of the Palazzo that takes in the warren of small offices that link the public rooms. It includes fascinating glimpses of the construction of the Palazzo, the torture room where criminals were persuaded to confess and the roof-level prisons from where Casanova escaped.

Museo dell'Opera: A ground-floor museum off the courtyard where more than 40 original

blessed in heaven, as described by Dante in his *Paradiso*. Tintoretto was also responsible for the frieze around the walls, containing portraits of Venice's first 76 doges, best known for the black veil marking Marin Falier's spot; he was executed for conspiring against the State in 1355. The ceiling panels, by Veronese (1528–88) and Palma il Giovane (1548–1628), are further apotheoses of Venice, showing a personification of the city triumphantly crowned while her subjugated enemies struggle beneath her feet.

PONTE DEI SOSPIRI AND THE PRIGIONI NUOVE

Until the 16th century, prisoners of the State served their sentences either in the dreaded *pozzi*, underground cells beneath the palace, or in the attics. This changed after the construction of the Prigioni Nuove (new prisons) in 1598, where even petty criminals enjoyed the com-

capitals from the outer loggia are preserved. Twelve date from the 14th century and are outstanding examples of sculpture, particularly the scene showing the *Creation of Adam and Eve*.

Arco dei Foscari: A late Gothic arch in the courtyard, commissioned by Doge Francesco Foscari in 1438 and designed and built by Antonio Bregno and Antonio Rizzo.

Sala del Magistrato: A small room on the first room where disturbingly bizarre works by Flemish painters, including Hieronymous Bosch, are displayed. They were collected by the Grimani family.

The Armoury: A collection of almost 2,000 weapons, instruments of war and suits of armour; fascinating, but dauntingly large.

forts of what was acknowledged to be Europe's most sophisticated prison accommodation. Access to the new block is across the Rio della Paglia, spanned by the famous Ponte dei Sospiri (Bridge of Sighs), designed by Antonio da Ponte and completed in 1614. By the 19th century the romantic legend was firmly established that, once across, no prisoner ever returned, hence the sighs. In the cell block, dark, narrow corridors and steep stairways link the warren of cells, many of which have their number and capacity painted over the door. Things can't have been too tough; the ground floor's small exercise yard once contained a tavern for the benefit of the inmates.

BACKGROUND

The Palazzo Ducale incorporated both a residence for the doge—the Venetian Republic's head of state—and the offices that housed the machinery of state. Here, in one building, were combined all the offices of government—councils, committee rooms, assembly chambers, diplomatic and foreign offices and the judiciary, as well as the state prisons. From the 14th century, government was in the hands of members of those patrician families whose names were inscribed in the so-called Libro d'Oro (Golden Book), and the building reflects their power, wealth and prestige, as well as that of the Republic itself.

The first governmental building was erected on the site in the 9th century, but it was not until 1340 that the Palazzo began to assume its present shape. In this year work started on a new hall for the Maggior Consiglio (Great Council); it was completed in 1362, the start of a construction process that resulted in much of what we see today.

A serious fire in 1483 caused extensive damage, necessitating rebuilding, but it was decided to repair the damage, rather than build something new, a decision which left the magical fairy-tale Veneto Gothic façade unaltered and was repeated after the further devastating fires of 1574 and 1577. The block across the Canale della Paglia, approached via the Ponte dei Sospiri (Bridge of Sighs) is the exception, being built in the late High Renaissance classical style. Since the fall of the Republic in 1797, the Palazzo Ducale has had many different functions, but still retains a role in the civil administrative life of Venice; as well as being open to the public it houses various city offices.

Detail of a picture frame in the Collegiate rooms (above left)

Statues adorn the exterior of the palace (above middle)

Tintoretto's gargantuan Paradiso, *inspired by Dante (above right)*

Sansovino's Scala d'Oro (left) and detail of the ceiling above the staircase (below)

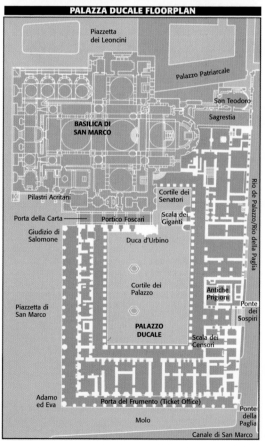

PALAZZA DUCALE FLOORPLAN

Piazzetta dei Leoncini

Palazzo Patriarcale

San Teodoro

Sagrestia

BASILICA DI SAN MARCO

Pilastri Acritani

Porta della Carta — Portico Foscari

Giudizio di Salomone

Duca d'Urbino

Cortile dei Senatori

Scala dei Giganti

Piazzetta di San Marco

Cortile dei Palazzo

Antiche Prigioni

Ponte dei Sospiri

PALAZZO DUCALE

Scala dei Censori

Rio de Palazzo/Rio della Paglia

Adamo ed Eva

Porta del Frumento (Ticket Office)

Ponte della Paglia

Molo

Canale di San Marco

BOCCHE DI LEONE

'Post-boxes' in the shape of grotesque masks and lions' heads are scattered throughout the Palazzo, particularly in the loggia, the Sala della Bussola and the Sala della Quarantia Civil Vecchia. These were used for delivering anonymous accusations from one citizen against another to the Council of Ten, the much feared state inquisition.

The Palazzo Contarini del Bovolo's spiral staircase

The Palazzo Grassi was restored by the Fiat company

Detail of a bedroom ceiling in the Palazzo Mocenigo

THE SIGHTS

MUSEO DEL TESSUTO E DEL COSTUME

✚ 58 F7 • Salizzada San Stae, Santa Croce 1992 ☎ 041 721 798
🕐 Apr–end Oct Tue–Sun 10–5; Nov–end Mar Tue–Sun 10–4. Closed 1 May 💶 Adult €4; students (15–29), Rolling Venice card holders €2.50
🚤 San Stae
www.museiciviciveneziani.it

The Museum of Textiles and Costume occupies the Palazzo Mocenigo and is both a museum and study centre, with an important library and large collection of fabrics and costumes. Some of these are displayed, along with shoes and fashion accessories, in the state rooms of the Palazzo. Venetian fashion was influenced, as elsewhere in Europe, by Paris, and embroidered fabrics, cascades of lace, tight-fitting bodices and puffed skirts were the order of the day for women, while men dressed like peacocks in tailcoats, embroidered waistcoats, breeches, silk stockings and buckled shoes. The major fashion statement for women was the *andrienne*, a pleated tail at the back of the dress that ostensibly allowed greater freedom of movement, but was also a way of displaying expensive and rich decoration. There are good examples of these, along with fans, the typically Venetian lace scarves called *zendale*, purses, high-heeled silk shoes and alarmingly restrictive corsets.

PALAZZO CONTARINI DEL BOVOLO

✚ 61 G10 • Calle dei Risi, San Marco ☎ 041 270 2464 🕐 Apr–end Oct daily 10–6; Nov–end Mar Sat–Sun 10–4
💶 €3 🚤 Rialto

The Gothic Palazzo Contarini del Bovolo is best known for its sinuous exterior staircase. You'll find it in the courtyard of the palace, where it was erected in around 1499 to to link the loggias built on each floor when the owner, Pietro Contarini, enlarged his home. Such staircases are called *scale a chiocciola* (snail stairs) in Italian—the Venetian dialect for snail is *bovolo*. The beautiful red-brick and Istrian stone stair gives access on five different levels to graceful loggias curving around inside a tower that's said to be reminiscent of the tower of Pisa.

PALAZZO DUCALE

See pages 112–117.

PALAZZO GRASSI

✚ 60 E10 • Campo San Samuele, San Marco 3231 ☎ 041 523 1680
🚤 San Samuele
www.palazzograssi.it

You'll notice the façade of the superbly symmetrical Palazzo Grassi on the right-hand side of the Grand Canal, coming from San Marco, between the San Samuele and the San Tomà *vaporetto* stops. Outside, nothing could be more traditionally 18th-century classical than this palace. Inside, it's another story; the interior was converted in the 1980s by Gianni Agnelli of Fiat to become Venice's most high-profile exhibition venue. The *palazzo* was designed by Giorgio Massari (1687–1766) for a newly rich family, and was built between 1748 and 1772. The interior has neclassical elements, with a monumental staircase rising to the frescoed portego on the *piano nobile*, from which richly decorated and stuccoed rooms lead off. The Grassi family died out in the 1830s and, under Fiat ownership, the *palazzo* hosted world-class exhibitions on themes such as the Phoenicians, the Celts, the Maya, the Pharaohs, Andy Warhol and, in 2004–2005, Salvador Dalí. In 2004, following the death of Gianni Agnelli, it was bought by François Pinault, the French millionaire collector and owner of a business empire that includes Gucci, Yves Saint Laurent and Christie's, who plans to move his collection of 20th-century art to Venice.

PALAZZO MOCENIGO

✚ 58 F7 • Salizzada San Stae, Santa Croce 1992 ☎ 041 721 798
🕐 Apr–end Oct Tue–Sun 10–5; Nov–end Mar Tue–Sun 10–4. Closed 25 Dec, 1 Jan, 1 May 💶 Adult €4, child €2.50 🚤 San Stae
www.museiciviciveneziani.it

The Palazzo Mocenigo near San Stae is one of several *palazzi* in the city built by the Mocenigo family, one of the grandest and oldest of the noble Venetian clans, who, between 1414 and 1778, provided the Republic with no fewer than seven doges. The family's grandest palace complex is on the Grand Canal. Situated just behind San Stae, the palace now houses the Museo del Tessuto e Costume (see above) and, even if you're not particularly interested in the history of costume, is worth a visit for a fascinating glimpse of the style in which the 18th-century nobility lived. Set on a narrow *calle* a couple of blocks in from the Grand Canal, it was built in the 17th century, the interior being revamped in the 18th century and still retaining the decorations, fittings and furniture from that era. Many of the paintings, friezes and frescoes are by Jacopo Guarana (1720–1808). In typical Venetian style, the main *portego* runs the length of the building; the rooms off here show signs of the development of neoclassical decoration. They include several living-rooms, whose interior décor is colour-themed, a bedroom, dining room and library, all furnished with contemporary pieces and hung with paintings.

The Nativity *by Francesco Bassano, in Il Redentore*

View along the Grand Canal from the Ponte degli Scalzi

The Ponte dell'Accademia is a copy of the earlier bridge

PONTE DELL'ACCADEMIA

🔲 60 E11 • Ponte dell'Accademia, Dorsoduro 🚤 Accademia

Of the bridges crossing the Canal Grande, the Accademia bridge, lying closest to San Marco, is the widest. The present wooden structure dates from 1984, and is an exact copy of the previous bridge, erected as a temporary measure in 1933. The first Accademia bridge, an ugly cast-iron affair, was built by English engineers in 1854. It was never loved and became obsolete in the 1930s because it was too low to allow a new design of *vaporetto* to pass underneath. A plan was drawn up, both for here and for the station, which had an identical iron bridge. The Canal is much narrower at its west end so money was available for the station bridge to be built in expensive stone, but the price was prohibitive across the far wider stretch of water at the Accademia. A temporary wooden structure was built, intended as a stopgap until funds could be raised for a stone span. No money materialized and by the 1980s the bridge, which was much loved by all Venetians, had reached the point of collapse. New designs were debated in the face of outcry from the conservative citizens; they won the day, and today's bridge is a replica of the last one. It is remarkably graceful, with a double flight of shallow wooden steps approaching the main rise. From the middle of the bridge there are superb views up and down the Grand Canal.

PONTE DEGLI SCALZI

🔲 58 D7 • Ponte degli Scalzi, Cannaregio 🚤 Ferrovia

Until the beginning of the 21st century, the Ponte degli Scalzi, right by the railway station, was the most westerly bridge across the Grand Canal. Today, the New Bridge, designed to provide a pedestrian link between Piazzale Roma and the station, takes that position. The contrast between the two is great, the Ponte degli Scalzi, named for the church on the left, looking far older than its 70 years. It was built in 1934 to replace the original cast-iron one erected by the Austrians between 1858 and 1860. The bridge's approach is right outside the railway station and next to the *vaporetto* stops and souvenir stalls. You may have to fight your way through, but from the bridge you'll get your first 'proper' view down the Grand Canal, and once on the other side, you lose the crowds and can plunge into the warren of streets and *campi* of the *sestiere* of Santa Croce.

PUNTOLAGUNA

🔲 60 F10 • Campo Santo Stefano, San Marco 2949 ☎ 041 529 3582 🕐 Mon–Fri 2.30– 5.30 🎫 Free 🚤 Accademia www.salve.it

If you're interested in what is being done to safeguard Venice and the lagoon, head for the Puntolaguna, a state-of-the-art, multimedia information centre run by the Magistrato alle Acque, Venice's water authority. Workstations allow you access a huge variety of information via CD-ROM, animations and internet sites, and there's a library of videos devoted to the lagoon and its ecosystem. You can pick up information about suggested itineraries for exploring the lagoon, learn more about the MoSE project (▷ 16), consult maps and talk to the enthusiastic and knowledgeable staff. This is a good place to bring children, and the staff run excellent workshops aimed at them, sometimes in English.

IL REDENTORE

🔲 60 F13 • Campo del Redentore, Giudecca 195 ☎ 041 523 1415 🕐 Mon–Sat 10–5, Sun 1–5. Closed Sun in Jul, Aug, Easter, 15 Aug, 🎫 Chorus Pass (for all churches in Chorus group) €8; single ticket €2.50 🚤 Redentore **www.chorusvenezia.org**

Looking across the Giudecca Canal, the eye is immediately drawn to the harmonious façade of Palladio's great church of Il Redentore, with its classical frontage and airy dome. From 1575 to 1576 plague swept the city, eventually killing over 50,000. Once it had abated, the doge and Senate, as an act of thanksgiving, determined to build a church in a prominent site. Andrea Palladio (1508–80) was the obvious choice of architect. Work started in 1577 and was completed 12 years after his death. The exterior has a Greek-temple façade, approached by a flight of steps, with the dome rising behind. Inside, Palladio had to accommodate a choir for the monks, a tribune for the city dignitaries and a simple nave for the common people. He employed the style of architecture used for Roman baths as his solution, producing a sophisticated and harmonious design where the three elements are virtually fused. Paintings were commissioned by the Senate and follow an agreed pattern, including popular topics such as the *Nativity*, the *Baptism of Christ*, the *Deposition*, the *Resurrection* and the *Ascension*. There are two good examples in the sacristy on the right of the choir; a *Madonna and Child* by Alvise Vivarini (c1445–1505) and the *Baptism of Christ* by Veronese (1528–88). Once built, the church became the focus of one of the city's most important feasts, the Festa della Redentore, still celebrated today (▷ 222).

THE SIGHTS

Rialto

●

Venice's most famous bridge spans the Grand Canal at one of the city's longest-settled areas. It's the setting for the oldest and largest market, one of the most vibrant in Italy, and home to an ancient church.

Crossing the Ponte di Rialto towards Campo San Bartolomeo

A stallholder wrapping fish at the Rialto market

Looking down the Grand Canal from the Rialto Bridge

RATINGS	
Good for food and wine	●●●○
Good for kids	●●●●○
Photo stops	●●●●○
Specialist shopping	●●●●○
Walkability	●●●●○

BASICS
✚ 59 G8 • Rialto
🚊 Rialto
🛍 Wide choice

Water taxi by the Rialto Bridge

SEEING THE RIALTO

The Rialto Bridge and its surrounding streets are one of Venice's major must-sees. The first view of the bridge, whether it's from a *vaporetto* on the Grand Canal or emerging from the maze of surrounding streets, is one of those quintessential Venetian moments where surprise and recognition combine. The bridge is the hub of the Rialto, so cross over it, taking in the view, then wander down the *fondamente* on either side to choose the perfect photo angle. Next, visit the church and head for the main fish, fruit and vegetable markets, before exploring the speciality food shops in the narrow streets behind the open market space.

HIGHLIGHTS

PONTE DI RIALTO

The idea of a stone bridge at the Rialto was first broached in 1557 and the design was thrown open to competition, with big names such as Michelangelo, Palladio and Sansovino submitting plans. The prize was awarded to Antonio da Ponte, for his revolutionary single-span solution. Given the site's difficulties, the bridge went up in record time, and was opened in 1591. The portico now houses shops, and was a later addition. The *fondamente*, stretching below the bridge on either side of the water, are named for their original functions as unloading wharfs; the San Marco side is the Riva del Ferro, so called for the iron once unloaded here, while the Riva del Vin opposite recalls the thousands of wine barrels which once came ashore here.

THE MARKETS AND FOODSHOPS

There has been a fish market on the same site for over a thousand years; today it's housed in and around the beautiful neo-Gothic Pescheria. Next to this are the fruit and vegetable stalls, brimming with seasonal produce at much lower prices than elsewhere in the city. The market *campi* and the streets behind here were where the original traders and merchants lived, and there are echoes of all this in the names—Ruga de' Orefici (Goldsmiths' Row), Ruga Speziali (Spicemakers Street) and Riva dell'Olio (Oil Quay) Today, they're lined with butchers' shops offering beautifully prepared meat, bakers

selling traditional breads and biscuits, *alimentari* (general food stores), purveyors of fresh pasta, dried fruit and beans, cheese, teas, coffees and spices, making the area perfect for food souvenirs.

SAN GIACOMO DI RIALTO AND THE GOBBO DI RIALTO
🕐 Mon–Sat 7–12, 3–6 🎟 Free

The little church of San Giacomo, on the San Polo side of the bridge, is said to be Venice's oldest, founded, according to legend, on the same day as the city itself; 26 March 421. It dates from the 12th century, and retains its ancient Greek cross ground plan and portico, while the clock above the church is famous for its inaccuracy—and has been since its installation in the 15th century. Opposite the church is a statue of a kneeling figure supporting a staircase leading to a small column. This is the Gobbo di Rialto, the Rialto Hunchback, which during the Middle Ages marked the end of a route between the Piazza and the Rialto. Condemned wrongdoers could escape prison by running the course, naked, in a fixed time.

BACKGROUND

The Rialto was one of the earliest parts of the lagoon to be settled and the word 'Rialto' is a corruption of Rivo Altus, the high bank, an area higher than anywhere else and thus less likely to flood. Settlements grew up on the marshy islets here and drainage was started, freeing space for the expanding city centre. By the 10th and 11th centuries the Rialto was the site of Venice's commercial heart, and in 1097 the market was permanently established here. A pontoon of boats linked the two banks in the 12th century and in the 13th the first of five wooden bridges was built across the canal. From the increasingly grand buildings on the Rialto, Venetian merchants controlled trade between Europe and the Far East, while Europe's major banks and international trading companies set up offices. In 1499 news of Portuguese explorer Vasco da Gama's voyage round the Cape of Good Hope to India reached the Rialto, the stock market crashed, and the good times were over as the merchants realized that Venice's overland monopoly to the East would cease. The Rialto's international role gradually declined, though, along with the Piazza, it remains the spiritual heart of the city to many Venetians today.

DON'T MISS
● Stroll along the *fondamente* on either side of bridge for a great photo opportunity.
● Browse in the market, particularly the fish, fruit and vegetable stalls.
● Pop into San Giacomo church.

TIPS
● The fish market is closed on Mondays.
● Rialto shops are excellent for food specialities to take home.
● The clothes and shoe shops round here carry good, mid-range stock.
● To see the Rialto at its best come very early as the market is opening, but before the mass of tourists arrive.

Barges filled with produce head for the Rialto markets (top)

Riva degli Schiavoni

This broad quayside with its procession of *palazzi*, historic hotels, stalls and cafés, has some of the best views in Venice, and is an ideal place for an evening stroll.

The distinctive Danieli is one of Venice's top hotels

Stained-glass window in the Danieli Hotel

The Ponte della Paglia is a good place to get that shot of the Bridge of Sighs

BASICS

✚ 62 J10 • Riva degli Schiavoni, San Marco

🚤 San Zaccaria

🍴 Wide choice

TIPS

● Have a drink in the Danieli to see the interior.

● It makes sense to come to the Riva early or late, as this is an area that's heaving with daytrippers throughout the day.

● Many *vaporetto* lines leave from the San Zaccaria stops on the Riva; check numbers and directions carefully if you're catching a boat here.

Bust at the foot of the staircase inside the Danieli Hotel (above far right)

SEEING RIVA DEGLI SCHIAVONI

The wide waterfront of the Riva degli Schiavoni stretches beside the Bacino di San Marco from the Palazzo Ducale to the Rio Ca' di Dio, crossing several canals along the way. The promenade continues all the way to Sant'Elena, changing its name as you head east to become the Riva Ca' di Dio, the Riva di San Biagio and the Riva dei Sette Martiri. The eastern end is very quiet, and this is the section to pause for a drink and take in the superb views. Nearer the Palazzo Ducale, crowds can be so thick you have to queue to cross the bridges, while the souvenir stalls block the panorama across to San Giorgio Maggiore. Stroll in whichever direction appeals, bearing in mind the west end is at its best early or late in the day.

HIGHLIGHTS

PONTE DELLA PAGLIA

The Ponte della Paglia, *the* place for that obligatory shot of the Ponte degli Sospiri (▷ 116), was built in 1360, and enlarged in 1847. It name probably derives from the straw *(paglia)* which was delivered here as bedding for the prisoners. It is made of Istrian stone, and on the outside of the pillar at the top of the treads there's a charming shrine, dating from 1580, with a carving of the Virgin (1583), known as the Madonna dei Gondolieri. On either side of the bridge, this stretch of the Riva is crammed with souvenir stalls; if you're into kitsch and cheap goods, this has to be one of the best selections in all Venice.

SANTA MARIA DELLA VISITAZIONE (LA PIETÀ)

The 18th-century church of Santa Maria della Visitazione (▷ 152) is best known for its associations with Antonio Vivaldi (1678–1741), Venice's most popular composer.

GRAND HOTEL DANIELI

Few hotels in the world are better known than the Danieli, named after its first proprietor, Dal Niel. The building was once the Palazzo Dandolo and dates from the 15th century, an era when the Republic

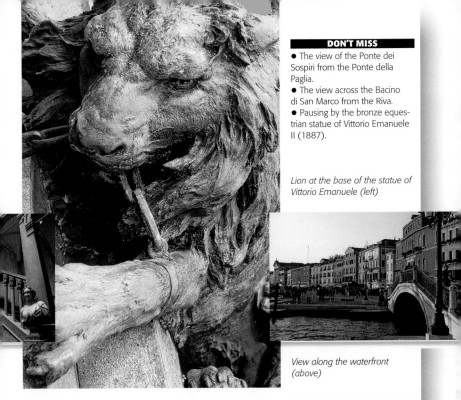

DON'T MISS
- The view of the Ponte dei Sospiri from the Ponte della Paglia.
- The view across the Bacino di San Marco from the Riva.
- Pausing by the bronze equestrian statue of Vittorio Emanuele II (1887).

Lion at the base of the statue of Vittorio Emanuele (left)

View along the waterfront (above)

was encouraging the aristocrats to erect *palazzi* that would demonstrate Venice's ever-growing power and wealth. Its lovely ochre façade is typical of the period, with pointed Gothic windows and arches on all floors. In the 16th century it was the French embassy and by the fall of the Republic it had changed hands many times, finally being divided into flats occupied by several families. It was first rented in 1822 by Dal Niel, who turned it into an hotel. The interior retains many of the original features, cunningly combined with décor of an overwhelming opulence, which makes full use of the richest of furnishings, fabrics and lighting. In 1948 an annexe was constructed to the west. The *calle* running down the east side of the hotel is Calle delle Rasse, its name a link with the Riva's Slav history. Rasse derives from *rascia*, a woollen fabric from Raska in Croatia, which was used to cover the *felze* (cabins) on gondolas.

BACKGROUND

The Riva degli Schiavoni gets its name from the Italian word for Slav, *schiavone*, which, in Venice, was synonymous with slave. In the early days of the city's history slave trafficking was common, and most of the slaves were Slavs from the Dalmatian coast. By the 11th century the Slavs themselves were Christians and no longer fair game for slave traders, and over the years the Riva became the base for merchants from the east coast of the Adriatic who traded with Venice. The quayside they used has one of the city's most glorious locations, and it was targeted by the Senate in the 18th century for a makeover. Between 1780 and 1782 the architect Tommaso Temanza was responsible for widening what had been a typically narrow *fondamenta* into today's broad promenade, paved with Istrian stone. The Riva has had many illustrious visitors. As early as 1362 the poet Petrarch lived here, but it was the 19th century that saw an influx of famous foreigners. Henry James stayed at No. 4161, and Charles Dickens, Marcel Proust, John Ruskin and Richard Wagner all stayed at the Danieli hotel. The Riva today is still among the classiest addresses in the city, with an array of top-end hotels.

A SPOONFUL OF SALT

Salt, that vital commodity essential for health and food preservation, was the catalyst that kick-started the Venetian economy and underpinned it for centuries to come. Salt was *'il vero fondamento del nostro stato'*, the true foundation of our state, with a mark-up hovering around 80 per cent and a monopoly on all trade throughout the Adriatic and the inland towns. The Romans' main salt-making centre was Comacchio, a coastal town south of the lagoon, but the Venetians established their own salt works by 523 and in 923 destroyed Comacchio, burning the citadel and massacring the inhabitants. Venice then concentrated on trading salt, which they bought up and shipped through the city. Within a few years, no salt could move on a ship in the Adriatic unless it was a Venetian ship bound to or from Venice.

Detail of a ceiling painting by Antonio Torri and Pietro Ricchi (1674) in the church of Sant'Alvise

Santi Apostoli's campanile rises above its square

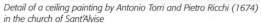

THE SIGHTS

SANT'ALVISE

➕ 58 F5 • Campo Sant'Alvise, Cannaregio ☎ 041 524 4664
🕐 Mon–Sat 10–5, Sun 1–5. Closed Sun in Jul and Aug, Easter, 15 Aug
💰 Chorus Pass (for all churches in Chorus group) €8; single ticket €2.50
🚤 Sant'Alvise
www.chorusvenezia.org

Sant'Alvise, dedicated to St. Louis, stands near the northern edge of Cannaregio in a low-key residential area. It was founded in 1388 by the noblewoman Antonia Venier, to whom Sant'Alvise had appeared in a dream, and stands isolated on its own island, accessible only from the south across the *rio* of the same name. The exterior façade is pure Gothic, with a flat brick surface divided by brick pilasters and broken only by an *oeil-de-bouef* (ox-eye shaped) window and Istrian stone doorway. Inside, little remains of the original, single-nave, basilical form. Above the entrance, Venice's first example of a hanging choir was added in the 15th century for the nuns from the adjoining convent to use for attending Mass. There were other alterations, including a charming *trompe l'oeil* ceiling in the 17th century, and in the 18th the church acquired its main treasures, three stunning canvases by Giambattista Tiepolo (1696–1770). These show scenes from Christ's passion; *The Crowning with Thorns* and the *Flagellation* in the nave, and *Christ's Ascent to Calvary* in the chancel. Under the hanging choir are the eight tempera panels known as the 'Baby Carpaccios', naively charming biblical scenes which English writer John Ruskin attributed to Vittore Carpaccio as a young child—they certainly date from around the time of the painter's childhood (1470), but are now attributed to Lazzaro Bastiani or a follower of his.

SANTI APOSTOLI

➕ 59 G8 • Campo Santi Apostoli, Cannaregio ☎ 041 523 8297
🕐 Mon–Sat 7.30–11.30, 5–7, Sun 8.30–12, 4.15–6.30 💰 Free 🚤 Ca' d'Oro

The church of Santi Apostoli lies at the eastern end of the Strada Nova, at the crossroads between the main route to the railway station and the narrow streets leading north to the Fondamente Nuove. A church was first founded here in the 9th century and today's incorporates some parts of this early building, but dates principally from 1575, with later additions. Santi Apostoli's interior appearance is pure 18th century, only the Cappella Corner remains discernibly 16th century. It was probably designed by Mauro Codussi (1440–1504) and has a splendid altarpiece, the *Communion of St. Lucy*, by Giambattista Tiepolo. Caterina Cornaro (▷ 32), Queen of Cyprus, was once buried here. Santi Apostoli's campanile, finished in 1672, is one of the tallest in Venice. An old story relates how an elderly sacristan fell from the top but, miraculously, was caught by the minute hand which, slowly turning, eventually deposited him safely on the parapet.

SAN BARNABA

➕ 60 D10 • Campo San Barnaba, Dorsoduro 2771 ☎ 041 270 2464
🕐 Mon–Sat 9.30–12.30 💰 Free 🚤 Ca' Rezzonico

It's easy to hurry past the church of San Barnaba, the focal point of a waterside *campo* on the route between the Accademia (▷ 94–100) and Campo Santa Margherita (▷ 80). This is an ancient foundation, from the 9th century, and is the third church to be built on the site. It dates from 1749, and architecturally, is a re-

working of the Gesuati (▷ 101), with a classical façade punctuated with Corinthian columns and topped by a triangular pediment. Inside, the single nave has three side altars and a series of frescoes from the school of Tiepolo. The square brick campanile was built in the year 1000 and is one of the oldest in Venice. The 18th-century inhabitants of the neighbourhood were known as Barnabotti and included many impoverished noblemen, drawn here by cheap rents. Foreign visitors wrote home about the sight of silk-clad beggars—the nobility were forbidden to work but obliged to wear silk, creating some interesting sartorial sights. San Barnaba has starred in two Hollywood movies; Katharine Hepburn fell into the adjoining canal in the classic *Summertime* (1955) and, years later, the church masqueraded as a library in *Indiana Jones and the Last Crusade* (1989), in which Harrison Ford encountered most of the rat population of Venice.

SAN CASSIANO

➕ 59 F8 • Campo San Cassiano, San Polo ☎ 041 721 408 🕐 Apr–end Sep daily 10–12, 5.30–7; Oct–end Mar daily 10–12, 4.30–6 💰 Free 🚤 San Stae, Rialto

If you're wandering round the Rialto markets, make a detour to the church of San Cassiano. It's dedicated to an early martyr who was hacked to death by some particularly nasty children, a fate which destined him to become the patron saint of schoolteachers. His martyrdom is depicted in a painting opposite the altar. Tintoretto fans should seek out the church; it contains three major paintings by the artist. The barn-like exterior of San Cassiano is pretty dull, though it does have a pleasing 13th-century campanile. The interior, with its

The Risen Christ, *a 17th-century painting in San Cassiano*

ceiling panel by Constantino Cedini, a Tiepolo fan, and a mass of heavy decoration, makes up for this. The Tintorettos are in the chancel. Note the *Crucifixion* (1565–68), with its startlingly low viewpoint, which makes you feel as if you're looking at the scene while lying on the grass. The other two paintings show the *Resurrection* and the *Descent into Limbo*; both have been heavily restored.

SANT'ELENA

➕ 63 Q13 • Campo Chiesa, Castello ☎ 041 205 155 🕐 Mon–Sat 5–7, Sun 9–12.30 🎫 Free 🚢 Sant'Elena

Until the 19th century, Sant'Elena was a separate island as the city ended at the site of the Biennale (▷ 76). The occupying Austrians needed space to house and exercise their troops, and they reclaimed land from the lagoon and connected this new quarter to the city by bridges. It was later given over to apartment blocks, leaving the original island of Sant'Elena as the home of a naval college, Venice's football ground and an ancient church. The original church was founded here in the second half of the 12th century to house the body of Sant'Elena (c257–336), mother of the Roman emperor Constantine. First an Augustinian monastery, it was ceded by Pope Gregory II to the Benedictines in the 1430s, who rebuilt the church in the Gothic style. The doorway, moved here from Sant'Aponal near the Rialto in 1929, has a lovely lunette showing Vittore Cappello, a Venetian admiral who died fighting the Turks in 1467, kneeling before the Virgin. Sant'Elena lies in a chapel to the right of the entrance, though this is a moot point, as the Aracoeli church in Rome also claims to house the saint's body.

SAN FRANCESCO DELLA VIGNA

The superb Palladian church of San Francesco della Vigna in the northeast of Castello is one of Venice's best-kept secrets.

BASICS
➕ 62 K9 • Campo di San Francesco, Castello 2786
☎ 041 520 6102
🕐 Daily 8–12.30, 3–7
🎫 Free
🚢 Ospedale, Celestina

RATINGS			
Cultural interest	●	●	● ●
Value for money	●	●	● ●
Walkability	●	●	● ●

The font in San Francisco della Vigna (above)

It's a bit of a hike through a shabby area of Venice near the old gas works to reach San Francesco della Vigna, a church standing in one of the most historic areas of the city. It was here, according to legend, that an angel appeared to St. Mark and told him that the lagoon islands were to be his final home. Later, the area was planted with vines, and when the Franciscans were given the land in 1253 they commemorated this in the name of their church.

THE CHURCH

Their first structure was demolished in the late 15th century and in 1534 work began on a new building, masterminded by Sansovino (1486–1570), a Renaissance architect from Tuscany. Some 30 years later, in 1568, Andrea Palladio was brought in to design the façade, a monumental stunner in pure white Istrian stone that's the first of his trademark superimposed temple fronts. It follows the design of Greek temples and is worth a few minutes' study to appreciate the perfect proportions of each element. Inside, there are further treats among the rational, humanistic design, with its broad nave and side chapels, dreamed up by the scholar monk Francesco Zorzi. As a Franciscan, he held to the tenets of modesty and restraint, a notion that disappears in the side chapels, decorated by the families who paid for them. To the left of the chancel is the Cappella Giustiniani, whose walls are adorned with marvellous sculptured reliefs by the Lombardo family. Off here, a door leads to the Cappella Santa, with a serene *Madonna and Child* by Giovanni Bellini (1430–1516). From here, you can access the peaceful cloisters. Back in the church, head for the right transept where you'll find a *Madonna and Child Enthroned* (c1460) by the Greek Antonio da Negroponte, a synthesis of Renaissance style and Gothic imagery that shows the Virgin surrounded by fruit and flowers. Elsewhere there are two Veronese canvases; the *Holy Family with Saints* (c1551) in the fifth chapel on the left was his first commissioned work in Venice.

SAN GIACOMO DELL'ORIO

The church of San Giacomo dell'Orio, with its fascinating mix of architectural and decorative styles, is the focus of a quintessentially Venetian *campo* and neighbourhood.

San Giacomo dell'Orio was founded in the 9th century and rebuilt in 1225, when the square *campanile* was added. This rebuild incorporated some very old columns, a couple of which were brought from Constantinople on ships returning from the Fourth Crusade in 1204 and may well be Roman in origin. You can see these behind the pulpit and the right transept; the latter column is a solid mass of age-old green marble with an Ionic capital. The builders followed a Veneto-Byzantine plan, where the central apse is surrounded by arches delineating the side areas. Two hundred year later this all looked a bit old hat, and renovations at this time added a three-nave transept and an apse, making the whole church a mix of Byzantine and Gothic. At the same time, San Giacomo acquired its beautiful ship's keel roof, while later Renaissance additions provided the icing on the cake in the shape of sculpture, wood and gilding. Like that of so many old Venetian churches, the façade faces the water rather than its *campo*.

THE PAINTINGS
San Giacomo's biggest pictorial treasure is the cycle of paintings by Palma il Giovane (1548–1628) in the side chapel known as the Old Sacristy. These were commissioned in 1581, hot on the heels of the resolutions of the Council of Trent, which emphasized the central role of the Eucharist as both sacrifice and sacrament. From now on, artists would concentrate on a variety of scenes incorporating Christ's supreme sacrifice, rather than on the traditional, simpler, theme of the Last Supper. Palma's cycle shows episodes from both the Old and New Testaments, and includes subjects ranging from the *Fall of Manna* (bread from heaven to Moses' wandering people in the desert) to a candle-lit *Paschal Lamb*, which alludes to the altar table and its daily Sacrifice. The pictures radiate light and faith and, in their time, were the perfect means of communication between the church's teachings and the faithful. Back in the main church there are two further splendid works by Palma in the Chapel of the Holy Sacrament, a *Via Crucis* and *The Burial of Christ*. A far older image hangs in front of the main altar in the shape of a *Crucifix* (1350) by Paolo Veneziano (c1290–1362), while the altar is dominated by a glowing *Virgin and Saints* (1546) by Lorenzo Lotto.

RATINGS
Cultural interest	● ● ●
Historic interest	● ● ● ●

BASICS
✚ 58 E8 • Campo San Giacomo dell'Orio, Santa Croce 1456
☎ 041 524 0672
🕐 Mon–Sat 10–5, Sun 1–5. Closed Sun in Jul and Aug, Easter, 15 Aug
🎟 Chorus Pass (for all churches in Chorus group) €8; single ticket €2.50
🚤 Riva di Biasio, San Stae
🎧 Guided tours organized by Chorus (tel 041 275 0462); information sheets and audioguides
www.chorusvenezia.org

Solid architectural form and airy space give rhythm to the interior design of San Giacomo dell'Orio (top and above)

St. Lucia now shares a church with St. Geremia

The church of San Giobbe is dedicated to St. Job

San Giorgio degli Greci serves Venice's Greek community

SAN GEREMIA E LUCIA

✚ 58 E7 • Campo San Geremia, Cannaregio 🕐 Mon–Fri 8.30–12, 3.30–6.30, Sun 9.30–12, 5.30–6.30 🎟 Free 🚤 San Marcuola, Ferrovia

Until the mid-19th century San Geremia could count this church his own, but since the destruction of the church of Santa Lucia, to make way for the railway station, he's had to share it with St. Lucia, whose mummified corpse is preserved in the church. This is a big, plain 18th-century building, dominated by a dome, whose austere grey-and-white interior is high and echoing. Despite this lack of inherent appeal, it's a great deal busier than many Venetian churches, due to a constant stream of devotees of the martyred St. Lucia. She was put to death in Syracuse in 304, after which her body went to Constantinople, from where she was brought home in triumph by the Venetians after the Fourth Crusade in 1204. Such was her modesty that, when praised by a would-be suitor for the beauty of her eyes, she promptly plucked them out, hence her role as patron of the shortsighted. There's a remarkable devotional painting of the saint holding her eyes—looking horribly like fried eggs—on a plate, or you can inspect her glass-encased, mummified corpse, decently covered by a red robe with just her little mummified feet sticking out.

SAN GIOBBE

✚ 58 C6 • Campo San Giobbe, Cannaregio ☎ 041 524 1889 🕐 Mon–Sat 10–12, 3–6 🎟 Free 🚤 Ponte Tre Archi

For something with a distinctly Florentine taste, head for the church of San Giobbe, dedicated to an Old Testament figure, Job, who has been raised to sainthood. This is a Renaissance

church, rational and airy in design and spirit, and it's the only place in Venice where you can see the terracotta work of the Florentine della Robbia family. San Giobbe was built around 1463 to commemorate the visit of San Bernardino of Siena, a fiery preacher and evangelist.

The lovely Renaissance doorway and chancel are the work of Pietro Lombardo (1435–1515). The Lombardo family were also responsible for the sculpture in the sanctuary and on the arch between it and the nave. Doge Cristoforo Moro (in office 1462–71), who paid for the construction of the church, is buried beneath the chancel floor, his tomb decorated with yet more Lombardo work. You'll find the della Robbia tiles and roundels in the Cappella Martini (second on left).

SAN GIORGIO DEGLI GRECI

✚ 62 K10 • Fondamenta dei Greci, Castello 3412 ☎ 041 523 9569 🕐 Wed–Mon 9–11, 2.30–4.30 🎟 Free 🚤 San Zaccaria

Greeks first came to Venice in the 11th century, and their numbers increased hugely after the fall of Constantinople to the Turks in 1453. In the heady atmosphere of the Renaissance they were particularly welcome as scholars, artists, scribes and publishers, while the goods shipped in by Greek merchants sold well throughout Venice. They became the largest ethnic group after Jewish people, their presence greatly enriching the cultural life of the city. The community was soon confident enough to apply for its own church in which to celebrate mass according to the Orthodox rites, and in 1470 permission came for the establishment of a church, college and Scuola.

In 1526 the Greeks purchased land and commissioned Sante Lombardo to design a church, most of which was constructed between 1539 and 1561. The cupola and splendidly leaning campanile were added later. A century later, in 1678, Baldassare Longhena designed the Collegio Flanghini and the Scuola di San Nicolò dei Greci; the college now houses the important Hellenic Centre for Byzantine and Post-Byzantine Studies and the Greek archives (www.istitutoellenico.org), while the Scuola is home to the Museo dei Dipinti Sacri Bizantini (Museum of Greek Sacred Paintings; tel 041 522 6581; daily 9–5). The interior of the church is Greek Orthodox in style, with a *matroneo* (women's gallery) and *iconostasis*, a solid, richly ornamented screen blocking off the main altar from the body of the church and behind which most of the celebration of the mass takes place. Some of the icons (sacred paintings) date from the 12th century, but many are 16th-century examples by Michael Danaskinàs, a friend and contemporary of Domenikos Theotokopoulos, another Greek artist living in Venice, and better known as El Greco. There are more icons, as well as other religious objects, in the adjacent museum. Most date from the 15th to 18th centuries and form one of Europe's most important icon collections. Their artistic interest lies in the definite divide between those that remain purely Greek in both composition and symbolism, and those which strive to synthesize Eastern and Western styles, a process that was to be triumphantly completed by El Greco.

SAN GIORGIO MAGGIORE

See pages 130–131.

THE SIGHTS

RATINGS

Cultural interest	● ● ● ○
Historic interest	● ● ● ○

BASICS

➕ 62 K10 • Campo San Giovanni in Bragora, Castello 2464
☎ 041 520 5906
🕐 Mon–Sat 9–11, 3.30–5.30
🎫 Free
🚉 Arsenale

The Baptism of Christ by Conegliano above the high altar (top)

The 15th-century font in which Vivaldi was baptized (below)

SAN GIOVANNI IN BRAGORA

The historic church of San Giovanni in Bragora is set in a quiet and spacious square with strong Vivaldi connections.

Popular legend puts the foundation of San Giovanni in Bragora in the early 8th century, making it one of the oldest churches in the lagoon, though there's no proof for this whatsoever, as the earliest written records of its existence date from 1090. The curious name is shrouded in mystery and explanations ranging from a derivation of the dialect word *brago*, meaning mud, through *bragolare*, to fish, to *agora*, the Greek word for an important public square. The patron saint is St. John the Baptist, whose body the Venetians claimed to have brought to Venice from the East. Construction started on the present church in 1475, making it one of the last Gothic churches in the city—it was built around the same time as the Renaissance San Michele (▷ 152). The interior does show some drift towards Renaissance architecture, which you can see best by comparing the Gothic nave with the chancel. There was once a choir in the nave, which was demolished in the 18th century; look for the slightly raised floor under the last span of the nave to see where it once stood.

THE PAINTINGS
The Gothic interior houses three splendid pictures. Over the high altar there's a *Baptism of Christ* (1492) by Cima da Conegliano, a calm, perfectly balanced scene with a landscape background that's reminiscent of the countryside around the artist's home town of Conegliano, which also figures in the scene. Cima is also responsible for the painting to the right of the sacristy door, depicting *St. Helen and St. Constantine* (1501). On the left of the sacristy door is a 1498 *Resurrection* by Alvise Vivarini, where the figure of Christ is based on a classical statue of Apollo, still to be seen in the Museo Archeologico.

THE VIVALDI CONNECTION
Vivaldi's music is inexorably entwined with Venice, and his life with this church. He was born in one of the houses on the *campo* and baptized in the ornate red marble font, which started life as the capital of a Gothic column. On the wall to the right of the font are copies of the original baptismal registration, dated 6 May 1678. There's a plaque on the outside wall recording that the *Prete Rosso* (Red Priest) was baptized in San Giovanni. Vivaldi is often known by this nickname, which refers either to his red hair or the red cassock he often wore.

Tullio Lombardo's marble relief of the Coronation of the Virgin in the church of San Giovanni Crisostomo

Symbols of the Four Evangelists in San Giovanni Decollato

SAN GIOVANNI CRISOSTOMO

➕ 59 H8 • Fondamenta San Giovanni Crisostomo, Cannaregio ☎ 041 522 7155 🕐 Mon–Sat 8.30–12. 3.30–5, Sun 3.30–5.30 💶 Free 🚤 Rialto

If you want to see an example of Renaissance architecture at its intimate best, head for San Giovanni Crisostomo—literally, St. John the Golden-Tongued—a few minutes' walk north from the Rialto. Its patron was the Archbishop of Constantinople, where churches followed a Greek cross floor plan, so it's fitting that its architect, Renaissance master Mauro Codussi (1440–1504), should have based his design on this layout. Inside there are two fine paintings. On the right-hand altar is Giovanni Bellini's outstanding last work, painted in 1513 when the artist was over 80, showing *Saints Jerome, Christopher and Louis of Toulouse*. It's awash with atmospheric colour, which owes much to the then upcoming Giorgione (c1478–1510), a perfect example of an old master learning right to the end of his career. On the high altar hangs *Saints John the Baptist, Liberale, Mary Magdalen and Catherine* by Sebastiano del Piombo, painted in 1509. There's an added bonus in the marble relief of the *Coronation of the Virgin* by Tullio Lombardo (c1455–1532).

SAN GIOVANNI DECOLLATO

➕ 58 E7 • Campo San Giovanni Decollato, Santa Croce ☎ 041 524 0672 🕐 Mon–Sat 10–12 💶 Free 🚤 San Biagio

Venetians refer to this church, dedicated to the decapitated St. John, by its dialect name of San Zan Degolà. Its origins are ancient indeed, probably as early as the 7th to 8th centuries, when an oratory was erected on an island in the small group that made up Santa Croce. In 1007, the Venier family built a parish church on the site, which was restored, but not much altered, by the Pesaros in 1213. With its triple-naved basilical interior and keel-vaulted ceiling, it's a perfect example of a Veneto-Byzantine church where little has changed over the centuries. Slender Greek marble columns, typically 11th-century, separate the central nave from the aisles, and even the brick floor is contemporary—warm colours and soft light were designed to help contemplation. Once abandoned, the church was restored between 1983 and 1994 after the parishioners of nearby San Giacomo dell'Orio organized a protest at its dilapidated state. San Giovanni's chief treasures are its misty Veneto-Byzantine frescoes, rare in Venice, where many early ones have been victims of humidity. Those on the right-hand wall are the oldest, haunting images of *The Annunciation* and *St. Helena and Four Saints* dating from the 11th century. In the chapel to the right of the high altar is a superb 14th-century depiction of *St. Michael the Archangel,* showing the saint triumphant over Satan, while the ceiling frescoes, dating from the 13th and 15th centuries, show the *Symbols of the Four Evangelists* and *Christ Among the Evangelists*. This evocative early art is the perfect backdrop for the Orthodox rites held here; San Giovanni has recently become Venice's Russian church.

SAN GIOVANNI ELEMOSINARIO

➕ 59 G8 • Ruga Vecchia, San Polo 480 ☎ 041 275 0462 🕐 Mon–Sat 10–5 Sun 1–5. Closed Sun in Jul and Aug, Easter, 15 Aug 🎟 Chorus Pass (for all churches in Chorus group) €8; single ticket €2.50 🚤 San Silvestro, Rialto www.chorusvenezia.org

It's easy to miss the entrance to the church of San Giovanni Elemosinario, tucked between the shops on the Ruga Vecchia near the Rialto. The church is so old it was traditionally under the protection of the doge, who attended Mass here weekly. The disastrous Rialto fire of 1514 totally destroyed the first building (1071) and the design for the replacement was entrusted to Antonio Abbondi (active 1505–9), known as Scarpagnino, who was also involved in the reconstruction of the market area. This explains its integration into the surrounding buildings that left the area in front as an open space, which was rented out by the clergy to stallholders and provided useful income. The work was finished by 1531 and resulted in a small church on a Greek cross plan with a vaulted, domed roof and plain, classical interior architectural features, which provided a good setting for the numerous works of art. The highlight is a superb painting by Titian of the church's patron, *St. John the Almsgiver* (1545), over the main altar, but don't miss the Cappella Corrieri on the right, where you'll find one of Pordenone's finest pictures, showing *Saints Catherine, Sebastian and Roch* (c1530–35).

Back in the church, the organ shutters are the work of Titian's son, Marco Vecelli, and the central dome was decorated by Pordenone, with a depiction of *God the Father in Glory*.

Look out for the piece of 12th-century sculptural relief in the left aisle, which shows a gentle ox reverently licking the Christ Child's face.

San Giorgio Maggiore

One of Palladio's greatest churches provides the perfect backdrop to the Bacino di San Marco; few other buildings could look as right as San Giorgio does from the Piazzetta. The best city views in Venice are from its campanile.

The cloisters of the San Giorgio Maggiore complex

The Palladian façade of San Giorgio Maggiore

The campanile gives some of the best views over Venice

One of the four Evangelist statues on the church

SEEING SAN GIORGIO MAGGIORE

The open waters of St. Mark's Basin frame the great Palladian church of San Giorgio Maggiore. Visiting here takes a bit of planning; although just a short hop across the water from San Marco, it's served by only one *vaporetto*, No. 82, leaving at 10-minute intervals from San Zaccaria. Start at the church before taking the elevator up the campanile for wonderful views over the city and the lagoon—a great way to get a bird's-eye view and, if you're new to Venice, your bearings. If you want to visit the monastery, home to the Cini Foundation, you'll need to come at the weekend, as during the week the complex is only open to groups.

HIGHLIGHTS

THE CHURCH
San Giorgio Maggiore presents the final solution to the great Renaissance architectural puzzle: how to impose classical design onto a building that has no classical precedent. Andrea Palladio (1508–80) solved this by uniting two temple fronts on the façade, the giant Composite columns of the nave rising above the Corinthian columns marking the height of the lower aisles, an arrangement echoed in the luminous interior and emphasized by the use of white marble and stucco. This is a triumphantly light and airy building, full of soaring space from the high windows inspired by Roman bath design. The choir is hung with two fine pictures by Tintoretto, *The Fall of Manna* and *The Last Supper* (1592–94). Just off the choir to the right, the Cappella dei Morti contains what may well be Tintoretto's last work, a haunting *Deposition* (1594). The superb wooden choir stalls, carved with scenes from the life of St. Benedict, date from the 1590s.

THE MONASTERY
Adjoining the church is the monastery complex, one of Venice's great delights and now home to the Fondazione Cini (tel 041 520 5558; 041 524 0119 for tour bookings, guided tours Sat–Sun, www.cini.it). Two cloisters lie at its heart: the Cloister of the Bay Trees, planned by Giovanni Buora between 1520 and 1540, and the Cloister of the Cypresses, designed in 1579 by Palladio. Around these har-

monious spaces lie a dormitory designed by Buora, a double stairway and library by Baldassare Longhena and Palladio's magnificent refectory, reached through two ante-rooms. The buildings are surrounded by beautiful, verdant gardens, with an outdoor theatre, the Teatro Verde, tucked away in one corner.

Detail on one of the church's exterior columns (above)

The Stoning of St. Stephen, *by Tintoretto (left)*

BACKGROUND

The island site of San Giorgio may have been inhabited in Roman times, and certainly became the site of a church as early as AD790. In 982 the Benedictines arrived, adding a monastery to the church; both were destroyed by an earthquake in 1223. The monastery was rebuilt in 1443, but it wasn't until 1565 that Palladio was commissioned to design a new church. Building was slow; the church was finally completed in 1610, and a new campanile finished in 1791. During Renaissance times, the monastery had close links with its sister house in Florence, and it was to San Giorgio that Cosimo de' Medici, head of the powerful banking family that controlled the city, fled when he was banished from Florence in 1433. He brought with him the architect Michelozzo, whose designs had immense influence on Venetian civic architecture. The monastery complex was again augmented, by a cloister and refectory, both designed by Palladio, in 1561. After the fall of the Republic in 1797, Napoleon dissolved the monastery and declared the island a 'free port'. In 1951 the monastery and island were acquired by Count Vittorio Cini, who established the Fondazione Cini in memory of his son, Giorgio, who had been killed in an air accident. New buildings were erected and major restoration carried out. The internationally renowned Foundation organizes conferences and stages exhibitions, concerts, dance and occasional opera.

MORE TO SEE

THE CAMPANILE
Take the elevator up the campanile for the best vantage point in Venice. From the top, both city and lagoon are spread before you. There's no better place to appreciate the lie of the city, the lagoon islands and the open sea beyond.

Santi Giovanni e Paolo

Dubbed the 'Pantheon of Venice', this vast brick Dominican preaching church is the final resting place for many doges. Its surrounding *campo* has one of Venice's finest statues.

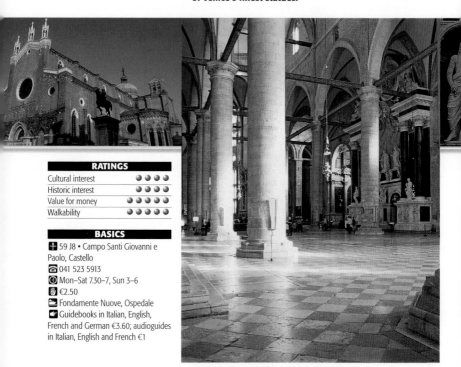

RATINGS

Cultural interest	● ● ● ○
Historic interest	● ● ● ○
Value for money	● ● ● ● ●
Walkability	● ● ● ● ○

BASICS

✚ 59 J8 • Campo Santi Giovanni e Paolo, Castello

☎ 041 523 5913

🕐 Mon–Sat 7.30–7, Sun 3–6

💶 €2.50

🚤 Fondamente Nuove, Ospedale

📘 Guidebooks in Italian, English, French and German €3.60; audioguides in Italian, English and French €1

Detail of the figure on the tomb of Doge Michele Steno (top)

The imposing Gothic façade of the church (above left)

The spacious nave was designed to accommodate the crowds that flocked to this preaching church (above right)

SEEING SANTI GIOVANNI E PAOLO

Northern Castello is home to the Gothic church of Santi Giovanni e Paolo, known in the Venetian dialect as San Zanipolo. Its monumental tombs of doges and heroes are one of its main artistic draws. Outside lies one of the city's most spacious squares, complete with a splendid equestrian statue and the magnificent façade of what was once one of the grandest of all Venice's *scuole*. Tackle the church first, then head straight for a table outside Rosa Salva, a bar renowned for its excellent coffee, from where you can admire the Colleoni monument and take in the everyday life of this busy *campo*. Choose a sunny day to come as the interior of the church can be very dark if it's gloomy outside.

HIGHLIGHTS

THE BUILDING

Santi Giovanni e Paolo is a huge church. Its size is typical of all churches constructed by the mendicant orders, who needed space to accommodate as many people as possible, and tended to construct their churches on the fringes of the central areas. In Venice, this meant away from San Marco. The church is built of red brick with stone ornamentation, and is among the most ambitious expressions in Venice of Gothic architecture, complete with a soaring façade and five-bay rear apse at the east. The main doorway, flanked by the tomb of Doge Tiepolo, who donated the land for the church, is surrounded by Byzantine reliefs and marble columns from an abandoned church on Torcello (▷ 174), and has traces of a Renaissance approach in its design. The Cappella di Sant'Orsola (closed), between the apse and the door to the right transept, is the burial place of Gentile (1429–1507) and Giovanni Bellini (1430–1516), two of Venice's finest painters. Inside, no choir impedes the view down the vast and shadowy interior, a single spatial unit punctuated by simple columns. This is offset by the multitude of wall tombs and monuments, among them those of some 25 doges, and works by artists such as Giovanni Bellini, Lorenzo Lotto and Veronese.

The tomb of Pietro Moncenigo is one of the church's highlights (below left)

View of Santi Giovanni e Paolo from the Campanile in San Marco (below right)

THE MOCENIGO MONUMENTS

The west wall is devoted entirely to the glorification of the Mocenigo dynasty, one of Venice's most prominent families. They secured the services of the Lombardo family, the city's best sculptors, and all three—Pietro, Tullio and Antonio—have works here. The superb tomb on the left of the entrance commemorates Doge Pietro Mocenigo, whose sarcophagus, decorated with episodes from the his life, is supported by warriors representing the three Ages of Man and crowned with a statue of Mocenigo himself. The reliefs depict the labours of Hercules, and the Latin inscription suggests that his enemies' money paid for it all. The central monument, around the door, commemorates Alvise Mocenigo, and that on the right, Giovanni.

SAINTS VINCENT FERRER, CHRISTOPHER AND SEBASTIAN (GIOVANNI BELLINI)

The second altar on the right displays Giovanni Bellini's beautiful polyptych *Saints Vincent Ferrer, Christopher and Sebastian*. Painted in 1465, it's among the artist's earlier works, but already shows the innovative handling of light that characterizes his work. St. Vincent, the central figure and a Dominican himself, was a fiery preacher and supporter of the early Spanish Inquisition. On the left, St. Christopher crosses the river carrying the Christ Child, while St. Sebastian, liberally punctured by the arrows of his martyrdom, is on the right. The panels above the saints show the annunciation on either side of a *Pietà*, and the *predella* panels—the little narrative scenes below the saints—depict miracles performed by St. Vincent.

BACKGROUND

The Dominicans are an order of mendicant monks, founded in Italy during the 13th century. It was a time of religious revival and the order, along with the Franciscans, lived and worked among the common people. Dominicans arrived in Venice in 1224, living a refugee-like existence in tents near the Arsenale. In 1234 Doge Giacomo Tiepolo was inspired by a dream to donate an area of marshy ground on the north side of the city to the Dominicans for a permanent home. The first church was founded in 1246, and demolished in 1333 to make way for the present church. Construction was complete by 1390, and the church was finally consecrated in 1430. It now serves the surrounding area.

MORE TO SEE

● Morosini monument in the church
● Vendramin monument in the church
● Nicolò Marcello monument in the church
● Corner monument in the church
● Ceiling paintings by Veronese in the Cappella del Rosario
● *St. Antonius Pierozzi Giving Alms to the Poor* by Lorenzo Lotto in the church
● Powerful equestrian statue of the mercenary Bartolomeo Colleoni (▷ 80) by Andrea Verrocchio (1435–88), opposite the entrance.
● Superlative Renaissance façade of the Scuola Grande di San Marco (▷ 80), completed in 1495, with stunning marble *trompe l'oeil* panels by the Lombardo family.

San Marco

San Marco is one of the world's most beautiful architectural complexes. Its huge open space is dominated by an exotic Veneto-Byzantine basilica, the embodiment of Venice's role as the medieval bridge between East and West.

The panoramic view from the Campanile towards San Polo

St. Theodore atop his column in the Piazza

Sitting in the Piazza San Marco and enjoying the scene

BASICS

✚ 61 H10 • San Marco, 30124 Venezia
🚤 San Marco (Vallaresso), San Zaccaria

The Basilica

✚ 61 H10 • Piazza San Marco, San Marco
☎ 041 522 5205
🕐 May–end Sep Mon–Sat 9.45–5.30, Sun 2–4; Oct–end Apr Mon–Sat 9.45–4.30, Sun 2–4; also Pala d'Oro, Tesoro, Gallery and Museum
💶 Basilica free; Pala d'Oro €1.50; Tesoro €2; Gallery and Museum €3
🚤 San Marco (Vallaresso), San Zaccaria
📖 Electa guide at bookstalls in major museums, postcards, general guides and religious souvenirs at basilica
🎫 Tours available through various travel agencies; must be booked in advance; further details in the *Leo Bussola* information booklet (▷ 298)

The Campanile dominates the Basilica di San Marco (right)

SEEING SAN MARCO

The Piazza San Marco is a showcase for some of the finest Byzantine, Gothic and Renaissance architecture in Venice. Dominated by the glittering bulk of the Basilica di San Marco and its soaring Campanile, and flanked by the Palazzo Ducale (▷ 112–117), it's home to compelling buildings and museums, trendy shops and a clutch of historic cafés. The Piazza is best seen in deep midwinter, daybreak or at dead of night, and a summer daytime visit may prove something of an endurance test, but it nevertheless remains an unmissable sight. The best approach is by foot from the west end of the Piazza; *vaporetto* No. 1 will drop you at Vallaresso/San Marco, just a couple of minutes' walk. Take time to look around the Piazza with its arcades and the Torre dell'Orologio, before going up the Campanile for the great cityscape and an overview of the Piazza. Then head for the interior of the Basilica, being sure to ascend to the loggia before you enter the church itself—once inside, you can't backtrack. After this, stroll through the Piazzetta down to the water's edge to take in the panorama over the Bacino di San Marco to San Giorgio Maggiore (▷ 130–131) and the mouth of the Grand Canal, before settling at a café table for an unforgettable, if pricey, drink in one of the world's greatest urban settings. For a plan of the area see the map on page 305.

HIGHLIGHTS

THE BASILICA

Eleventh-century Venice still looked culturally east to Byzantium, and this explains the decision to construct a church that is completely oriental in style. San Marco, with its centralized Greek-cross plan and multiple domes, is modelled on two basilicas in Constantinople, and the interior, with its raised choir and gold-ground mosaics, also owes much to the east. The north façade (fronting the Piazzetta dei Leoncini) was among the last areas to be completed, and is pierced with the Porta dei Fiori, built in the 13th century and incorporating an 8th-century Byzantine relief (in the first arch) of the Twelve Apostles. The main façade has five arched entrances and was considerably

DON'T MISS IN THE BASILICA

- Quadriga (bronze horses)
- Loggia overlooking the Piazza
- Upper level of interior from galleries
- Entrance and atrium mosaics
- Interior
- Cupola mosaics
- Pala d'Oro
- Madonna Nicopeia

The Lion of St. Mark and St. Theodore tower over the Piazzetta

SANSOVINO'S BIG MISTAKE

In 1537, Jacopo Sansovino was appointed architect for the city library, to be constructed in the Piazzetta to house the state collection of Latin and Greek manuscripts and precious books. Successful and visionary, he was the obvious choice , and he designed a groundbreaking building that combined Roman High Renaissance ideas with the Venetian love of ornament, creating a building described by Palladio as 'the richest and most ornate since antiquity'. Things went badly wrong when the barrel vaulting of the ceiling collapsed shortly after its construction. Sansovino was thrown in jail, and only released on the pleadings of his friend, the painter Titian. He was forced to redesign the vault and pay for the repairs out of his own pocket, losing his position as Venice's favourite architect to the up and coming Palladio.

changed between the 11th and 15th centuries by the addition of marble columns and carved stonework in the Gothic style. The Sant'Alippio doorway, on the left, is the only one on the façade to preserve its 13th-century mosaic, which shows both the earliest known representation of St. Mark and that of the Basilica itself. The central door is adorned with Romanesque carvings dating from the 13th century. Considered to be the exterior's greatest treasures, these show the earth, the seas and animals on the underside, with the virtues and beatitudes on the outer face and the zodiac and labours of the months on the inner face. The outer arch shows Christ and the Prophets and dates from around 1260.

Behind the arches of the façade lies the narthex (atrium), a transitional space between the light of day and the semi-darkness of the interior that's totally Byzantine in conception. From here, steep steps rise to the gallery, where you'll find yourself at eye-level with the mosaics in the interior. This level gives access out onto the Loggia, once used by the doge as a vantage point during religious and civic festivals. You'll share the view with replicas of the famous bronze horses, the Quadriga, whose originals are inside. These marvellously evocative creatures were looted from Constantinople in 1204. They were probably made for the Hippodrome there in the 3rd century, but could be as much as 500 years older, and are the only four-horse chariot group to survive from antiquity. Apart from a brief spell in Paris

The Last Judgement *by Lattanzio Querena (1836) on the Basilica's main portal (left)*

The Piazza San Marco, wth the Campanile and Basilica di San Marco in the background (below)

TIPS

● Don't start your Venetian sightseeing in San Marco; it's so overwhelming that it makes sense to save it till you've got a handle on the rest of the city.
● Remember the Basilica is a church, so cover your arms and shoulders when visiting; miniskirts and skimpy shorts are also unsuitable.
● If you have time, attend a service in the Basilica and see it in its real role as a functioning church.
● The queue to enter the Basilica starts to build around 9.15 and the wait can be as long as an hour, so come early or late in the afternoon when the daytrippers have gone.
● You'll have to move steadily through the Basilica, so read up on what you'll see before you go.
● Try and visit the Piazza at night, when you'll see it without crowds.
● Choose a clear day to go up the Campanile; heat or mist will obscure visibility.

during the Napoleonic years, the horses have stood at San Marco for 800 years, as much a symbol of Venice as the winged lion of St. Mark.

Descending the stairs, you enter the Basilica proper, where the first impression is of dully glittering darkness, illuminated by shafts of light as the mosaics are struck by slanting sunbeams. The walls and domes are entirely covered with over 4,000sq m (43,055sq ft) of these mosaics, executed over six centuries and telling stories from the Bible. The finest are the early Veneto-Byzantine examples, which include the *Pentecost* dome over the nave, the central dome, at the crossing, showing the *Ascension*, and *Christ Emmanuel*, above the main altar. Old as it looks, the huge *Christ Pantocrator* above the apse is in fact a faithful 16th-century copy of the 11th-century original. Mosaics changed after the 15th century and the later examples are in a more painterly style, as craftsmen followed cartoons by contemporary artists, thus introducing perspective and relief. Both Titian and Tintoretto had a hand in these.

The focal point of the interior, with its undulating 12th-century marble floor, is the iconostasis, a carved marble screen that's Byzantine and hides the chancel and high altar. The remains of St. Mark lie beneath the altar, which is backed by the Pala d'Oro, a 14th-century opulent gold altarpiece. It's covered with over 3,000 precious stones and decorated with 80 enamel plaques, many from Constantinople and dating from the 10th to 12th centuries, and was made by a

Sienese master in 1342. To the left is the Chapel of the Madonna Nicopeia, a much-revered 12th-century Byzantine icon, and there's more Byzantine work in the Tesoro (Treasury). The 12th-century incense censer in the shape of a domed church and two 11th-century icons of the Archangel Michael are worth looking for here.

THE CAMPANILE

✉ Piazza San Marco, San Marco ☎ 041 522 4064 🕐 Apr–end Jun, Sep, Oct daily 9–7; Jul, Aug daily 9–9; Nov–end Mar daily 9.30–4.15. Sometimes closed for maintenance from Sun after 6 Jan till end of Jan 💶 €6 🚤 San Marco (Vallaresso), San Zaccaria 📖 Leaflet available

The Campanile (Bell-tower), the great punctuation point on the Venetian skyline, stands almost opposite the Basilica entrance at the east end of the Piazza; at 99m (325ft) it's the city's tallest building.

The original structure, dating from the early 10th century, functioned as a combined bell-tower and lighthouse—the harbour occupied what is now the Piazzetta. Over the centuries it was constantly modified, the most extensive alterations being made by Bartolomeo Bon between 1511 and 1514, when the spire and gilded angel were added. Today's Campanile is less than 100 years old; on 14 July 1902 at 9.52am disaster struck, when the entire tower, weakened over the centuries, subsided into a tidy heap of bricks and debris. No other building was damaged and the only casualty was the custodian's cat. It was rebuilt *Com'era, dov'era* (Like it was, where it was) in 1912, Sansovino's little Loggetta (1537–1549) at the foot of the tower being pieced together from its fragments found in the rubble.

THE PIAZZA AND THE PIAZZETTA

Emerging from the narrow surrounding streets, the sheer scale of the Piazza is breathtaking. At the east end of its wide expanse rears the Basilica di San Marco, with the Palazzo Ducale, overlooking the Piazzetta, to the south. Arcaded buildings run down the long sides of the Piazza; these are the Procuratie Vecchie to the north, and the Procuratie Nuove opposite. They housed the offices of the Procuratie, the officials who ran the government offices, oversaw the upkeep of the Basilica and supervised its finances. The original Procuratie Vecchie was built in the 12th century, and first rebuilt in 1500 by Mauro Codussi, the work being completed by Bartolomeo Bon and Sansovino in 1512. Scamozzi and Sansovino were responsible for the Procuratie Nuove; built from 1582 to 1640, its design echoes the older buildings. After the fall of Venice in 1797, the two wings were linked by another arcaded building, the Ala Napoleonica, now home to the Museo Correr (▷ 108–109).

The Piazzetta runs down to the water's edge and is flanked by the Palazzo Ducale to the west (left) and the Biblioteca Nazionale Marciana (▷ 109) and the Zecca (Mint), designed by Sansovino between 1527 and 1537, to the right. Its two granite columns are topped by a winged lion, symbol of Venice, and St. Theodore, the city's first patron saint, complete with his symbolic crocodile. Both statues and columns were brought back from Tyre (in modern-day Lebanon) in 1170, and the space between them was declared a public execution area; many modern Venetians refuse to walk between the two. The Zecca, erected between 1537 and 1545, was moved here from its 9th-century home on the Rialto. It was Sansovino's first

Decorative carving on the portal of the Basilica (above left)

The Basilica's distinctive domes (above middle)

Looking over Caffè Quadri from the Campanile (above right)

The upper portion of the Campanile (below)

View towards Murano from the Campanile (far left)

big commission and the first building in the city to be built entirely of stone, rather than having a wooden frame with a stone façade. On the other side of the Basilica, the tiny space fronted by marble lions is known as the Piazzetta dei Leoncini.

TORRE DELL'OROLOGIO

San Marco's clock tower was built between 1496 and 1506, and Mauro Codussi was responsible for the overall design. Its legend runs *Horas non numero nisi serenas* (I number only peaceful hours) and the exterior stone dial shows the 24 hours in Roman numerals, with the interior face showing the signs of the zodiac and phases of the moon. It's topped by two bronze 'moors', so-called for their dark patina, which were cast in the Arsenale in 1497.

BACKGROUND

Originally a marshy island known as the Morso, the area of the Piazza San Marco stands at one of the lowest points in Venice, and until the 9th century was an orchard for the nearby convent of San Zaccaria (▷ 160). There were two churches here, dedi-

cated to San Teodoro—the city's first patron—and San Geminiano, and a lighthouse, the precursor of the Campanile. In 829 the first Basilica was built to house the remains of St. Mark, brought to Venice from Alexandria. This was replaced in 976 by a bigger sanctuary, and a hundred years later work began on the present Basilica, built between 1063 and 1094 and the third to occupy this site. In the 12th century Doge Sebastiano Ziani transformed the area in front of the Basilica into a public space, whose general shape remains today. The buildings, with the exception of the Basilica and the Campanile, date mainly from the period of urban renewal at the end of the 15th century. This continued for over a hundred years, and saw the construction of the Procuratie, the Zecca (Mint), the Libreria Sansoviniana and the Loggetta at the foot of the Campanile. Napoleon's occupation in the early 19th century signalled the destruction of San Geminiano to make way for the Ala Napoleonica, which links the two Procuratie at the west end of the Piazza. The whole area still floods easily, and 2004 saw the start of an ambitious scheme to raise the *fondamenta* and install a state-of-the-art drainage and pumping system on the water side of the Piazzetta.

The stone and gilded face of the Torre dell'Orologio's clock (far left)

The Byzantine Basilica di San Marco, Venice's most famous building (below)

The unfinished façade of the church of San Marcuola

Santa Maria del Giglio is richly decorated with sculpture

Flight of Angels by Sebastiano Ricci in Santa Maria dei Carmini

SAN MARCUOLA

✠ 58 E7 • Campo San Marcuola, Cannaregio ☎ 041 713 872 🕐 Mon–Sat 10–12, 5–7, Sun 8–1, 4.30–8 💷 Free 🚤 San Marcuola

You'll notice San Marcuola, one of the city's few churches lacking the usual grand marble façade, looming up next to the *vaporetto* stop of the same name. The builders never got round to putting on the stone facings, and you can still see the sockets and ledges on the brickwork which would have supported the marble. It's an interesting example of what lies behind every grandiose façade. This rather pedestrian church, whose name is a Venetian corruption of St. Ermagora and St. Fortunato, was designed by Giorgio Massari (1687–1766) and built between 1728 and 1736; the interior has statues of the church's patron saints and an early Tintoretto interpretation of the *Last Supper*. There's a ghost story connected with the church, which tells of a priest who proclaimed his total disbelief in ghosts from the pulpit. That night every corpse buried in the church rose up and beat the unfortunate cleric.

SANTA MARIA DEI CARMINI

✠ 60 D10 • Campo dei Carmini, Dorsoduro 2617 ☎ 041 270 2464 🕐 Mon–Sat 2.30–5.30 💷 Free 🚤 San Basilio, Ca' Rezzonico

Most visitors associate the Carmini with Tiepolo (1696–1770), whose dizzying work decorates the Scuola of the same name. Santa Maria, now a parish church, was built originally as the Venetian heart of the Carmelite order—a statue of the Virgin of Carmelo perches on top of its campanile. The building is a wonderful mixture of styles, with a Renaissance façade fronting a predominantly Gothic interior, laid out on a basilica plan and dating from the 14th century. Twelve ancient columns support each side of the soaring vault 97m (318ft) high, drawing the eye to the 14th-century Gothic apse. Large and very ordinary baroque paintings cover most of the interior walls, but there are a couple of gems, notably Cima da Conegliano's *Adoration of the Shepherds* (1509) in the right nave and Lorenzo Lotto's *St. George and the Dragon* (1529) on the left-hand side of the nave—look closely at the meticulously detailed landscape, complete with the tiny figures of St. George and the Dragon, considered by the art historian Bernard Berenson (1865–1959) to be one of the most beautiful in all Italian art. On your way out, pause to take in the lovely Gothic side door embedded with Byzantine stonework fragments.

SANTA MARIA DELLA FAVA

✠ 61 H9 • Campo Rubbi, San Marco ☎ 041 522 4601 🕐 Mon–Sat 8.30–12, 4.30–6.30, Sun 8.30–12 💷 Free 🚤 Rialto

The church of Santa Maria della Fava (Our Lady of the Bean) takes its name from a special cake traditionally eaten on All Souls' Day (1 November) and produced by a local baker. The church dates from the 18th century and contains two wonderfully contrasting paintings by two great 18th-century artists. Above the first altar on the right hangs Giambattista Tiepolo's early *Education of the Virgin*, a touching composition imbued with light and colour. In contrast you'll find Giambattista Piazzetta's *Madonna and Child with St. Philip Neri* (on the left), a far more sombre picture, redolent of the gravitas of the Counter-Reformation. The statues lining the nave are by Torretto (c1694–1774), best known, perhaps, as the master of Canova.

SANTA MARIA DEL GIGLIO

✠ 61 F10 • Campo Santa Maria del Giglio, San Marco 2542 ☎ 041 275 0462 🕐 Mon–Sat 10–5, Sun 1–5. Closed Sun in Jul and Aug, Easter, 15 Aug 💷 Chorus Pass (for all churches in Chorus group) €8; single ticket €2.50 🚤 Giglio www.chorusvenezia.org

Santa Maria del Giglio, founded in the ninth century by the Jubanico family, is also known as Santa Maria Zobenigo, a name derived from its first patrons. The church was rebuilt in the 1680s by the Barbaro family, and few other Venetian façades are such an in-your-face case of self-aggrandizement. Pause to marvel at the total lack of religious symbolism among the crowded statues and reliefs, all extolling the virtues and triumphs of the Barbaros. The family, in fact, had a much greater opinion of themselves than that held by their fellow citizens. Admiral Antonio Barbaro, who paid for much of the church's rebuilding, was actually dismissed from the fleet for incompetence. He is one of the five heroic statues on the façade; the others represent his brothers. Above them hover the allegorical figures of Venice, Virtue, Wisdom, Honour and Fame and below are relief maps of the places associated with the clan's glorious triumphs. Inside there's a profusion of mainly undistinguished religious art, though some relief is available in the shape of two Evangelists by Tintoretto (1518–94) behind the altar, and there's a disputed Rubens—the only work by the master in Venice—in a side chapel.

SANTA MARIA FORMOSA

The Renaissance church of Santa Maria Formosa stands in a rambling and lovely *campo* in Castello.

The irregular space of the Campo Santa Maria Formosa (▷ 80) is edged with fine *palazzi*, but dominated by the church itself, the first of eight sanctuaries founded on the lagoon in the 7th century by St. Magno, Bishop of Oderzo. The Virgin appeared to him as a buxom and shapely matron—*formosa*—and instructed him to follow a white cloud and build a church wherever it settled. St. Magno built a now-vanished church, which was replaced in the 11th century by a typically Byzantine Greek-cross plan structure. Once a year, it was visited by the doge in commemoration of the rescue by the parishioners of some young women who had been abducted. For reasons lost in time, a straw hat was traditionally presented to the doge to commemorate his visit.

THE CHURCH
The present church of Santa Maria Formosa was the first in Venice to be revamped according to Renaissance ideals, an architectural *tour de force* given the retention of the original Byzantine plan. It was designed by Mauro Codussi in 1492, when the earlier church was beginning to show signs of deterioration. The church has two façades, one on the canal (1542) and one on the *campo* (1604), both added after Codussi's death; the campanile is baroque. The canalside frontage was financed by the Cappello family, though the little relief of a mortar to the right of the door is much later. This commemorates the destruction of the dome in 1916 by an Austrian incendiary bomb; it was rebuilt in 1921. The interior has a Renaissance Latin-cross plan superimposed on the Greek, giving an overwhelming impression of space and balance. The three naves are almost the same length as the barrel-vaulted side chapels, which they intersect at domed cross vaults, producing an interior where the space is as central to the architecture as the solid stone—a key aspect of Renaissance design.

Two paintings are worth tracking down. One, in the first chapel on the south (right) side, is a triptych (1473) by Bartolomeo Vivarini showing the *Madonna della Misericordia*— the Virgin sheltering the faithful beneath her cloak; it was paid for by parishioners, and some of the kneeling figures are believed to be portraits of the donors. The other, near the main altar, is Palma il Vecchio's *Santa Barbara* (1522–24), an early martyr put to death by her own father.

RATINGS
Cultural interest	● ● ●
Historic interest	● ● ●
Value for money	● ● ● ●

BASICS
✚ 61 J9 • Campo Santa Maria Formosa, Castello 5263
☎ 041 523 4645
🕐 Mon–Sat 10–5, Sun 1–5. Closed Sun in Jul and Aug, Easter, 15 Aug
🎫 Chorus Pass (for all churches in Chorus group) €8; single ticket €2.50
🚤 San Zaccaria
www.chorusvenezia.org

Santa Barbara and Saints *by Palma il Vecchio (above)*

Gargoyle on the façade (below)

Santa Maria Gloriosa dei Frari

●

Venice's second largest church and the power-base of the Franciscans.

The Triptych *by Giovanni Bellini (1488), in the sacristy*

Pyramidal monument to Antonio Canova

Wooden beams emphasize the height of the Gothic ceiling

RATINGS	
Cultural interest	●●●●○
Historic interest	●●●●○
Photo stops	●●●○○
Value for money	●●●●○

BASICS

✚ 58 E9 • Campo dei Frari, San Polo 3072

☎ 041 522 2637

🕐 Mon–Sat 9–6, Sun 1–6. Closed Easter, 15 Aug

🎟 Chorus Pass (for all churches in Chorus group) €8,; single ticket €2.50

🚤 San Tomà

📖 Information sheets in Italian, English, French and German

🎧 Guided tours organized by Chorus (tel 041 275 0462); information sheets and audioguides in Italian, English, French and German

www.chorusvenezia.org
Superb site in English and Italian giving comprehenisve information about the architecture and art of all the churches in the Chorus group.

www.basilicadeifrari.it
Italian and English site with full information on the history, art and architecture of the church.

Relief of Doge Francesco Dandolo's tomb (top)

Wooden stalls of the Gothic-Renaissance coro *(choir, right)*

SEEING SANTA MARIA GLORIOSA DEI FRARI

The great Gothic church of Santa Maria Gloriosa dei Frari is one of the city's most compelling, rich in history and the burial place of the famous. Like Santi Giovanni e Paolo (▷ 132–133), it is built of brick, its plain exterior relieved by the stone detail round the entrances and windows and a few pieces of sculpture. Inside, it is huge, its size almost overwhelming the profusion of monuments, paintings and decoration. Rather than wandering about, it's best to make a methodical tour, starting at the right, just inside the main (west) entrance. The highlights below follow this route in an anti-clockwise direction. To see it all thoroughly you should allow an hour to 90 minutes.

HIGHLIGHTS

MAUSOLEO TIZIANO

The monument to the great artist Titian is distinguished by its size rather than its artistic merit, and was erected in the mid-19th century to designs by pupils of the sculptor Antonio Canova (1757–1822), who is buried opposite. A riot of figures and ornament, including a stone replica of the great Assumption painting further down the church, the monument was erected as a gift from Ferdinand I of Austria, also ruler of the Veneto. Titian died during the major plague outbreak of 1576, and was one of the handful of victims to be properly buried in the city, rather than hastily interred on a lagoon island, a measure of the huge fame he had achieved in his own city.

SACRESTIA AND THE MADONNA AND CHILD

The sacristy lies off the right transept of the church and contains one of the most beautiful of all Venetian paintings, Giovanni Bellini's triptych of the *Madonna and Child with Saints Nicholas, Peter, Mark and Benedict* (1488). It was commissioned for the sacristy by Niccolò, Marco and Benedetto Pesaro in memory of their father Pietro, hence the inclusion of these four saints. It's a ravishing picture, imbued with soft light and warm colour, but it's also a technical masterpiece, with a staggering command of perspective and architectural detail, heightened by the painting's relationship to its original gold frame.

● Wrap up warmly if you're visiting during winter; the church is not heated.
● Look out for details of the concerts held in the magnificent setting of the Frari.
● If you're in Venice between Christmas and the end of January don't miss the *presepio* (crib) here; one of the city's most charming, it comes complete with sound and light effects, running water and moving figures.

CAPPELLA DI SAN GIOVANNI BATTISTA

This chapel, to the right of the high altar, contains Venice's only sculpture by the Florentine master Donatello (1386–1466). The attenuated, expressive wooden figure of the prophet, in polychrome and gilded wood, was commissioned by Florentine merchants in 1438 from their fellow countryman, working at that time in Padua.

THE HIGH ALTAR AND THE ASSUMPTION

Titian's great *Assumption* over the high altar dominates the church. It was painted between 1516 and 1518 and attracted attention for its radical composition. No previous altarpiece had departed from vertical composition, the norm being gentle, static figures grouped around a central focus. Titian divided his painting into horizontal zones and filled every figure with energy and movement. To balance this, individual figures are used to stress the vertical within each group and so complement the thrusting height of the surrounding architecture.

THE CORO

The simplicity of the Frari's interior makes the perfect foil for the sumptuousness of the *coro* (monks' choir), one of the most ornate pieces of woodcarving in the city. It dates from 1468 and is the work of Mauro Cozzi, who oversaw the incredible carving and superb intarsia (mosaic woodwork) decoration.

THE MADONNA DI CA' PESARO

Another magnificent Titian hangs on the left-hand aisle. The *Madonna di Ca' Pesaro* was painted in 1526, eight years after the *Assumption*, and shows the Virgin with saints and members of the Pesaro family, the donors. Once more, Titian breaks ground compositionally, this time moving the figure of the Virgin—normally firmly at the centre—to

Santa Maria Gloriosa dei Frari (left)) ranks after San Marco as the most important Veneto-Gothic structure in Venice

Statue of Jacopo Negretti, also known as Palma il Giovane (above)

the right, and bisecting the picture with two massive columns. The painting was commissioned by Bishop Pesaro, who is buried in the tomb to the right, and refers to his expedition against the Turks in 1502, hence the turbaned figure on the left. The Virgin is said to be modelled on Titian's wife, Celia, who died in childbirth.

CANOVA MONUMENT

It's impossible to miss the vast white pyramid in the left aisle, an over-the-top marble monument to the sculptor Canova. It was designed by the sculptor himself as a mausoleum for Titian and completed by his pupils in 1827. Mourning figures approach a half-open door, a trick copied from Roman tombs, but first prize has to go to the wonderfully soporific and deeply unintimidating lion.

BACKGROUND

The Franciscans—*frari* in dialect—first came to Venice around 1222, and were granted a plot of land in 1250. Work started on their first church on the site in the 1270s, but almost as soon as it was complete (1338) a larger one was needed to accommodate the crowds that flocked to hear the friars preach. Wealthy local families contributed enough money to enable the construction of a virtually new church, together with a new campanile, and work started in 1340. The bell-tower, the second highest in the city, was finished in 1396, but it was not until the 1430s that the church, together with the adjoining cloisters, chapter-house and convent (now housing the Archivio di Stato (▷ 69) was complete. The convent was suppressed under Napoleon, but the church remained in the care of the Franciscans, who today still administer to the needs of the surrounding parish.

TOMBS

The Frari has some superb tombs of members of prominent Venetian families. Highlights are the spectacularly bad-taste monument to Doge Giovanni Pesaro (1669), complete with Moors, rotting corpses and two griffins; the serene Renaissance tomb of Doge Niccolò Tron (1473); and that of Doge Francesco Foscari, who died, a few days after his son's execution for treason, in 1457, after 34 years as doge. The composer Claudio Monteverdi (1567–1643) is buried in the third chapel to the left of the high altar.

Santa Maria dei Miracoli

The little canalside church of Santa Maria dei Miracoli, with its exuberant marble-clad façade, is Venice's most exquisite example of Renaissance architecture.

From left to right: The Madonna and Child *adorn the exterior of the church; the church's single nave is light and airy; marble statue of the Madonna; the elegant exterior of the church*

BASICS

✚ 59 H8 • Campo Santa Maria Nova, Cannaregio 6075
☎ 041 275 0462
🕐 Mon–Sat 9–6, Sun 1–6. Closed Easter, 15 Aug
🎫 Chorus Pass (for all churches in Chorus group) €8; single ticket €2.50
🚤 Ca' d'Oro, Rialto
ℹ Guided tours organized by Chorus (tel 041 275 0462); information sheets and audioguides in Italian, English, French and German
www.chorusvenezia.org
Superb site in English and Italian giving comprehensive information about the architecture and art of all the churches in the Chorus group.

SEEING SANTA MARIA DEI MIRACOLI

The exterior of Santa Maria is as lovely as the interior, so spend time walking around the church before you go in. The bridge overlooking the left-hand side is a good vantage point to admire the design. Inside, take your time, and if you have a Chorus Pass, be sure to pick up an audioguide, an excellent introduction to the church. Your visit will take anything from 10 minutes to half an hour or so.

HIGHLIGHTS

THE EXTERIOR

Santa Maria dei Miracoli is one of the few Venetian churches wholly visible from the outside. The north side runs along a canal and the other three walls rise up from the pavement. For this reason, the designer, Pietro Lombardo (1435–1515), gave as much emphasis to the sides and rear as to the façade, decorating all four walls with columns, pilasters and inlaid polychrome marble. Unlike most classically based Renaissance buildings, the columns are Corinthian at the lower level—you'll notice that their capitals are ornately carved, while the next level are much plainer. These are Ionic, normally used at ground level. It's a small point, but indicative of the subtleties employed throughout the design, hardly noticeable details which contribute to the overall harmony of the church. Notice also the number of pillars down the side, far more than necessary, but making the church appear longer and its site not as cramped as the reality. Look, too, at the canalside wall, where the water reflects the columns, giving a quite deliberate illusion that the whole structure is rising from the water. All the walls are faced with different coloured marble and adorned with crosses, circles and octagons in darker contrasting stone. Tradition says some of these were surplus marbles from the decoration of San Marco itself.

THE INTERIOR

The interior has a single nave with a barrel-vaulted roof. At the west end is the raised nuns' choir, once reached by a private corridor that ran from the adjoining convent, supported by square carved columns.

The main altar and apse, approached up a flight of steps topped by a delicately carved balustrade, still display the miraculous Madonna for whom the church was built. The entire interior is faced with multi-coloured marble and contains some of the richest and most intricate and delicate carving to be found in Venice, seen at its best when the sun streams in, illuminating the rose, white, gold and silver-grey marbles. The altar steps and balustrade leading to the raised choir are beautifully carved with half-size figures of saints and an Annunciation, thought to be by Tullio Lombardo (c1455–1532), Pietro's son. All three family members worked on the rest of the carving, seen at its best at the base of the pillars in the choir and the columns below the nuns' choir at the back of the church. The ceiling of the choir is carved and decorated with 16th-century panels by the school of Titian, representing St. Francis, St. Clare and the Virgin, and the vault was decorated in 1528 with paintings of the Prophets by Pier Maria Pennacchi.

Ceiling detail in Santa Maria dei Miracoli (above)

Elegantly spaced pillars line the canal façade of the church (below)

BACKGROUND

In 1408 the Amadi family commissioned a *Virgin and Child* from the artist Nicolò di Pietro, which they placed in a street shrine. The Virgin soon became the object of popular adoration, credited with miraculous powers, which included reviving a man who had spent nearly an hour under the waters of Giudecca Canal. In time, a wooden chapel was built to house the Virgin, which was later extended as a church, lavishly funded by devout families. The commission was given to the Lombardo family, Renaissance stoneworkers who fused design, decoration and sculpture into a unique whole, and produced a homogeneous building covered both inside and out with polychrome marbles, put together with a great sensitivity to texture and colour. Work started in 1481 and the entire building was finished by 1489. Apart from the painted ceiling panels, installed in 1528, the church has remained untouched since it was built, though the adjoining convent was almost totally destroyed in 1810. This little gem is one of the most popular wedding churches in Venice.

Santa Maria della Salute

The silhouette of Santa Maria della Salute, one of Venice's landmark buildings, dominates the mouth of the Grand Canal. It's a superb example of Venetian baroque architecture.

The church is faced with dazzling white Istrian stone

Baldassare Longhena's great Salute church is a key feature on the Venetian skyline

Looking up into the Salute's great dome

RATINGS	
Cultural interest	● ● ●
Historic interest	● ● ● ●
Photo stops	● ● ● ●

BASICS

✠ 61 G11 • Campo della Salute, Dorsoduro
☎ 041 522 5558
🕐 Church: Apr–end Sep daily 9–12, 3–6.30; Oct–end Mar daily 9–12, 3–5.30. Sacristy: Mon–Sat 10–11.30, 3–5, Sun 3–5
💶 Church free; sacristy €1.50
🚤 Salute

SEEING SANTA MARIA DELLA SALUTE

Santa Maria della Salute is the city's most important 17th-century church. Its gleaming white bulk looms over the San Marco entrance to the Grand Canal. Approach it through the labyrinthine streets of Dorsoduro or catch the No. 1 to Salute.

HIGHLIGHTS

THE EXTERIOR

Revolutionary in design, the huge, domed, octagonal construction combined prevailing trends and influences in a totally new fashion, creating a building where traditional Veneto-Byzantine architectural elements go hand in hand with new baroque ideas. Baldassare Longhena designed it in 1631 and the plan owes much to Palladio. From the quayside, a flight of steps leads up to the Palladian façade, distinguished from the other seven sides by huge half-columns and the classically inspired main doorway. The main dome is buttressed by circular volutes, or *orecchioni*, 'little ears', while behind it, the smaller domes and twin campaniles echo the Byzantine style of earlier buildings. Over 120 statues decorate the niches and pinnacles.

THE INTERIOR

In contrast to the exterior exuberance, the interior is austere, with six chapels clustered around the central space and the cupola, supported by eight enormous pillars, rising high overhead. This layout is loaded with Marian symbolism, and the shape of the church refers to the eight-pointed Marian star, the dome represents the Virgin's crown, and the central plan is a symbol of the womb. The inscription *Unde origo inde salus* (from the Origins came Salvation) in the middle of the beautiful marble floor is a reference to the story of Venice's foundation under the Virgin's protection, while the encircling roses allude to the rosary, the Virgin's own prayer. Another dome rises over the choir, and the high altar, also designed by Longhena, portrays the Virgin and Child rescuing Venice from the plague, while a serene Byzantine icon forms the focal point. Flemish artist Justin le Court (1627–79) was responsible for the sculpture, and Francesco Morosini brought the Byzantine painting back to Venice in 1672.

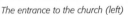

SALUTE

On 21 November is the feast of the Salute, when Venetians still come to give thanks for good health. A week before the feast, a pontoon bridge is constructed over the Canal Grande, to give direct access to the church, and citizens cross it to hear Mass, light candles and meet their friends.

The entrance to the church (left)

One of the circular volutes or orecchioni (above)

The magnificent polychrome marble floor (below)

THE PAINTINGS

With the exception of an early Titian, the *Descent of the Holy Spirit* (1555), on the third altar on the left, the finest pictures are in the sacristy, whose entrance is to the left of the high altar. Here are no fewer than eight Titians, brought here from the suppressed church of San Spirito in 1656. The earliest (1510) commemorates the end of an earlier plague and shows *St. Mark Enthroned between Saints Cosmas, Damian, Roch and Sebastian*; St. Roch is invoked against infectious diseases and Cosmas and Damian were both doctors. The powerful ceiling panels show *Cain and Abel*, *David and Goliath* and the *Sacrifice of Abraham* and were painted between 1542 and 1544. Look for a tranquil *Madonna* by Palma il Vecchio (c1480–1528) and Tintoretto's superb *Marriage Feast at Cana* (1561), which contains a supposed self-portrait—the artist is the first Apostle on the left.

BACKGROUND

The 1629 outbreak of plague killed over 45,000 people, a third of the city's population, in 12 months. In October 1630 the Senate vowed to build a church in honour of the Virgin if she would save the city; within weeks the pestilence retreated, probably due as much to the onset of winter as divine intervention. The Senate held a competition to find an architect worthy of the commission, and it was awarded to Baldassare Longhena. Buildings were razed to free up space and over a million wooden piles were driven into the subsoil to support the foundations. Work started on 1 April 1631 and was completed in 1681, a year before the architect's death. The church was dedicated to the Madonna della Salute, the Virgin of both 'health' and 'salvation'. The feast of the Salute remains an important day for all Venetians (see panel).

The church of San Maurizio now houses a museum, including a superb collection of musical instruments

Flowers decorate the graves on Ísola di San Michele

SANTA MARIA DELLA VISITAZIONE

➕ 62 K10 • Riva degli Schiavoni, Castello ☎ 041 523 1096 ⏱ Open for concerts only. Piccolo Museo de la Pietà Mon, Wed 11–4 🚏 San Zaccaria

The white façade of Santa Maria della Visitazione, also known as La Pietà, punctuates the eastern stretch of the Riva degli Schiavoni (▷ 122–123). It is linked with the Venetian composer, Antonio Vivaldi, who was first violin master, and later choirmaster at the adjoining orphanage. He wrote many of his finest pieces to be performed by the orphanage musicians, so renowned for their musical prowess that often parents tried to pass their children off as orphans to get them into the orchestra or choir. The church's rebuilding started in 1745, and Vivaldi probably advised the architect, Giorgio Massari (1687–1766), for few other churches have such fine acoustics. From its completion in 1760, it was as much a concert hall as a church, and today it has a season that runs throughout the summer months. Inside, La Pietà is a dazzle of white and gold, with a dizzying Tiepolo ceiling panel, The Glory of Paradise, above the nave, and another by the same artist over the high altar. There's a small Vivaldi museum—the Piccolo Museo de la Pietà—behind the church; walk down the calle to No. 3701 if you're interested.

SAN MAURIZIO

➕ 60 F10 • Campo San Maurizio, San Marco ☎ 041 241 1840 ⏱ Daily 9.30–8.30 🎟 Free 🚏 Giglio

Rebuilt in the early 19th century and hardly used in the 20th, San Maurizio found a new role in 2004 when it opened as a Vivaldi exhibition centre. The Greek-cross interior is now home to a series of exhibits of the life and times of Venice's most popular 18th-century composer, with excellent information panels in English and Italian. The chief draw is the fine collection of old musical instruments, whose sound provides the music that's a constant backdrop to your visit. You can buy CDs, tapes and DVDs relating to the composer and book concert tickets for events at La Pietà and the ex-church of San Vidal, another popular concert venue just off Campo Santo Stefano.

SAN MICHELE

➕ 59 K5 • Isola di San Michele ☎ 041 729 2811 ⏱ Apr–end Sep daily 7.30–6; Oct–end Mar daily 7.30–4; 25 Dec, 1 Jan 7.30–noon 🎟 Free 🚏 Cimitero

It's a short hop on the vaporetto to Venice's wonderfully atmospheric cemetery island. Most of Ísola di San Michele is covered by the cemetery, where Venetians are buried in tiers of stone coffin drawers or rest under an assortment of monuments. The cemetery was established in 1807 during the Napoleonic era when city burials

were forbidden, but bodies only lie here for 10 years or so before being removed to ossuaries on other lagoon islands. This overcrowding is the reason behind the extension to the cemetery, destined for completion in the next few years. Non-Catholics are better served spatially, and romantically overgrown areas still house the graves of long-forgotten foreign consuls and sea captains. Here, too, are the graves of composer Igor Stravinsky, impresario Serge Diaghilev and American writer Ezra Pound. To enter the cemetery you will pass through the cloisters of Mauro Codussi's beautiful church of San Michele in Isola, designed in 1469 and the first Venetian building that's truly Renaissance in spirit and design. In his use of Istrian stone for facing this church, Codussi changed the face of Venice forever, and every gleaming white Venetian façade is a monument to his ideas.

SAN MOISÈ

➕ 61 G10 • Campo San Moisè, San Marco 1456 ☎ 041 528 5840 ⏱ Mon–Sat 9.30–12.30 🎟 Free 🚏 San Marco (Vallaresso)

Walking from San Marco to the Accademia you'll pass the church of San Moisè, an over-the-top baroque extravaganza that's a hot contender for the award for the worst building in Venice. Take it in as a glorious example of the fact that lavish does not equal lovely. It's named after Moses, another illustration of the Venetian tendency to canonize Old Testament figures, a habit borrowed from the Byzantines. The 1668 façade is a riot of flora and fauna, including a very strange looking camel. The high altar by Arrigo Meyring, dating from around 1670, shows not only Moses receiving the

Angels adorn the interior (above) and the exterior (bottom left) of the church of San Moisé

The striking Corinthian porch of San Nicolò da Tolentino

tablets of the law on Mount Sinai, but the mountain itself. San Moisè is home to one of the city's fine 18th-century organs, and there are occasional recitals.

SAN NICOLÒ DEI MENDICOLI

See page 154.

SAN NICOLÒ DA TOLENTINO

58 D8 • Campo dei Tolentini, Santa Croce 265 ☎ 041 522 2160 Daily 9–12, 4–6 Free Piazzale Roma

The church of San Nicolò da Tolentino stands tucked away near Piazzale Roma, well off the beaten track, though fans of lavish baroque decoration should make a point of seeing it. It was built for the Theatine Order, established in Rome in the early 16th century, whose members fled north to Venice after the sack of Rome in 1527. They first settled in Dorsoduro, but moved to the present site in Santa Croce in 1590, commissioning Vicenzo Scamozzi to design a church and convent in 1591. There was a major fallout between the order and the architect, resulting in an unfinished façade when the church was consecrated in 1601. This was remedied between 1706 and 1714 when the massive classical Greek-Roman temple front was designed by Andrea Tirali. Restrained and sober, it's the perfect introduction for the decorative blast that greets you inside. San Nicolò is wedding cake baroque at its most exuberant, its interior swarming with *putti*, white stucco, coloured marble, gilding and frescoes. The paintings are mostly by non-Venetians, though the high altar and choir are the work of Baldassare Longhena. First prize in the decorative stakes goes to the tomb of Doge Francesco Morosini, which shows the great man reclining in ecstatic delight, while angels pull aside the surrounding drapes. The modern building on the left of the side of the church is the entrance to Venice's architectural faculty, one of the most prestigious in Italy, now housed in the ex-convent buildings.

SAN PANTALON

58 D9 • Campo San Pantalon, San Polo ☎ 041 523 5893 Sun–Fri 3.30–7, Sat 4.30–7 Free San Tomà

To see one of the most mind-boggling ceilings you'll ever come across, head for the church of San Pantalon, set on the fringes of the university district near Campo Santa Margherita. The saint, court physician to the Emperor Galerius in the 4th century, converted to Christianity and was put to death for his faith by Diocletian. As a doctor, Pantalon was well respected in plague-ridden Venice, and there was a church dedicated to him on the same site as early as the 11th century. This was demolished in the 17th century and rebuilt between 1668 and 1686 by Francesco Comino. The church contains some fine paintings, notably Veronese's last great work, *St. Pantalon Healing the Sick* (1587), and a serene *Coronation of the Virgin* (1444) by Antonio Vivarini in the Cappella del Sacro Chiodo, a side chapel where a nail from Christ's Cross was venerated. The church's chief draw, however, is the astounding ceiling, the world's largest area of painted canvas. It's the work of the little-known Gian Antonio Fumiani, who worked on the canvases telling the story of *The Miracles and Martyrdom of San Pantalon* between 1680 and 1704. The 60 panels were invisibly joined to make one entire, vertiginously foreshortened whole, where whirling saints are drawn up past mighty architecture to the golden light of heaven. Fumiani fell off the scaffold to his death during the final stages of its assembly.

SAN PIETRO DI CASTELLO

63 P10 • Campo San Pietro di Castello, Castello 70 ☎ 041 523 8950 Mon–Sat 9–6, Sun 1–6. Closed Easter, 15 Aug Chorus Pass (for all churches in Chorus group) €8; single ticket €2.50 Giardini www.chorusvenezia.org

At the far eastern end of Castello stands the island of San Pietro, reached by two long bridges. Its church, also San Pietro, is one of oldest foundations in Venice and, until 1807, it was the city's cathedral. It stands in isolation, overlooking a 'church green' with a wonderfully drunken Gothic campanile beside it. The still stately, but ramshackle old *palazzo* to the right of the church was once the Bishop's Palace. The present church was designed by Palladio (1508–80), but the façade was only completed in 1596, resulting in a somewhat watered down interpretation of his original concept. The interior is high and bare, with the atmosphere of a humble parish church. Look for St. Peter's Throne in the right-hand aisle, a carved marble seat from Antioch that incorporates an Arabic funerary stele inscribed with verses from the Koran. The splendidly baroque high altar was designed by Baldassare Longhena in 1649 as a setting for the funerary urn of San Lorenzo Giustiniani, the first patriarch of Venice. The tiny Lando chapel, off the left aisle, contains a lovely Roman mosaic of black and white tesserae, with a wonderfully rendered polychrome mosaic bowl of fruit in the central tondo.

SAN NICOLÒ DEI MENDICOLI

The 13th-century Veneto-Byzantine church of San Nicolò dei Mendicoli is one of the oldest churches in Venice.

This most ancient church was founded, like the cathedral in Torcello (▷ 176), in the 7th century, possibly by a group of Paduans fleeing the Lombard invasions. The original church was dedicated to San Niceta, a Serbian martyr, but was replaced in the 12th century by the present building. It is one of the city's oldest churches, and has miraculously retained its original plan, with a partition screening the nave from the altar area. In the 15th century the portico was added to the front. Designed as a shelter for beggars and mendicants, it's one of only two remaining in Venice—the other fronts San Giacomo in the Rialto (▷ 121). The interior was reworked in the 16th century, and the church served as the parish church for this working-class area through to the 19th century. By 1900 its congregation had fallen away, and San Nicolò was closed between 1903 and 1924 for the first of a series of prolonged repairs. The next restoration took place from 1972 to 1977 by the British-based Venice in Peril fund, which re-roofed the church, raised and restored the floor, and conserved much of the interior decoration. The exterior featured in Nicolas Roeg's 1970s movie *Don't Look Now*, starring Donald Sutherland and Julie Christie.

THE CHURCH AND CAMPO
The interior of the church, much more than the sum of its parts, is a wonderful muddle of architectural elements, panelling, wooden sculpture, and bits and pieces. It epitomizes the long history of the building and gives an impression of comfortable charm. The basic plan is that of a 12th-century basilica, with two rows of 12th-century columns topped by 14th-century capitals. Above these, on either side of the nave, are gilded statues of the Apostles, and there's a fine 15th-century statue of the church's patron, St. Nicolas, above the high altar. Today this is separated from the nave by a pierced screen, topped with a Crucifixion, that echoes the original iconostasis. The ceiling has painted 16th-century panels depicting scenes from the life of St. Nicolas. Outside, the ensemble of campanile, *campo*, *fondamenta* and bridges is a typical Veneto-Byzantine urban scheme. The bell-tower is 12th century, there's an ancient column topped by the lion of St. Mark, and a flagpole, once used by the Nicolotti, a working-class faction constantly at loggerheads with the Castellani from eastern Venice, who were based in this area.

TIP

● This corner of Dorsoduro also contains the churches of Angelo Raffaele (▷ 69) and San Sebastiano (▷ 157), within a 5-minute walk

RATINGS

Cultural interest	●●●○
Historic interest	●●●○
Value for money	●●●●○

BASICS

✚ 310 B10 • Campo San Nicolò dei Mendicoli, Dorsoduro 1907
☎ 041 275 0382
🕐 Mon–Sat 10–12, 4–6, Sun 4–6
💶 €1 entry to church
🚤 San Basilio, Ca' Rezzonico
ℹ Information leaflets in Italian, English and French
🎫 Postcards

Detail of the ceiling tondo (top)

The church stands on a quiet canalside campo *in Dorsoduro (above)*

SAN POLO

The historic church of San Polo, whose origins are rooted in the 9th century, occupies Venice's second-largest square.

The *sestiere* of San Polo, the Venetian version of San Paolo (St. Paul), gets its name from this church, an ancient foundation dating from the 9th century. It was built facing the canal, away from the *campo*, though later buildings have blocked its water façade and entrance. The original Byzantine church was heavily altered in the 14th and 15th centuries with Gothic elements such as the side portal, the rose window and the wooden ceiling. In 1804 there were more alterations in an attempt to impose a neoclassical look; some of these were removed in the 1930s, but the interior remains a rather unsatisfactory jumble. The campanile, detached from the church across the *salizzada*, has suffered less since its construction in 1362; look out for the pair of stone lions at the base. Inside, paintings include a *Last Supper* by Tintoretto (1518–94) to the left of the entrance as you go in, and the *Marriage of the Virgin* by Veronese (1528–85) in the left apse chapel.

VIA CRUCIS

San Polo's main draw is the brilliant cycle of paintings by Giandomenico Tiepolo (1727–1804) in the Oratory of the Crucifix, which occupies the former narthex of the main church, now inaccessible from outside. Giandomenico was the son of the more famous Giambattista (1696–1770), who is represented in San Polo by a painting showing the *Virgin Appearing to St. John of Nepomuk* on an altar in the left aisle of the main church. Giandomenico was only 20 when he painted the *Via Crucis*, the 14 episodes from Christ's journey to Calvary, and the cycle is one of the rare examples of his work not stylistically dictated by his father, with whom he mostly collaborated. Here are none of the radiantly colour-filled, light-drenched works normally associated with the Tiepolos, but a series of surprisingly realistic paintings, with the emphasis firmly on everyday life and normal people. These are far darker paintings, whose characters are sharp portraits of contemporary Venetian society in the decades that preceded the fall of the Republic. To the left of the entrance Christ is shown carrying his cross in the hours before his death; to the right, the story continues immediately beside the door, while the paintings further down show St. Vincent Ferrer, St. Helena and St. Philip Neri. The ceiling panels show *Angels in Glory* and the *Resurrection*.

Exterior of San Polo (top)

Giandomenico Tiepolo's Via Crucis *(Way of the Cross) (above)*

The Annunciation *in the church of San Rocco*

San Salvador has a plain exterior but two superb Titians

Relief on the exterior wall of San Silvestro

SAN ROCCO

➕ 58 D9 • Campo di San Rocco, San Polo ☎ 041 523 4864 🕐 Apr–end Oct daily 7.30 or 8–12.30, 3–5.30; Nov–end Mar daily 8–12.30, 2–4 🎫 Free 🚤 San Tomà

If you haven't already overdosed on paintings by Tintoretto (1518–94) in the adjoining Scuola Grande di San Rocco (▷ 164–167), it's worth going into the church of San Rocco to see the artists's take on the life of St. Roch. The church stands at right angles to the Scuola and makes a good architectural contrast. It was designed by Bartolomeo Bon and built between 1489 and 1508; its appearance seems much later as the interior was extensively altered in the 18th century. There are paintings by Tintoretto and his school throughout the church; the major panels are those in the chancel, which show scenes from St. Roch's life. Be warned, the iconology is confusing to say the least and the pictures are hard to see whatever time of day you visit. Luckily, the lower ones, by far the easiest to see, are the best. They show *St. Roch Curing the Plague Victims* on the right, and *St. Roch Healing the Animals* opposite.

SAN SALVADOR

➕ 60 G9 • Campo San Salvador, San Marco 4826 ☎ 041 523 6717 🕐 Mon–Fri 3–7 🎫 Free 🚤 Rialto

The luminous interior of San Salvador is a Tuscan symphony in cool grey and white. The design spans well over 30 years and Giorgio Spavento (died 1509), Tullio Lombardo (c1455–1532) and Sansovino (1486–1570) were all involved in the planning. The 17th-century façade is nothing special, it's the interior that fires the imagination. The key to the design is three interlocking Greek crosses which pay homage to San Marco and Byzantium while simultaneously giving the church the basilical length required by religious orders. There's some fine Veneto-Tuscan sculpture, including Sansovino's monument to Doge Francesco Venier on the right wall. Further down is the tomb of Caterina Cornaro, who was briefly the Queen of Cyprus (▷ 32). Caterina, who died in 1510, was a helpless pawn in the diplomatic dealings that led to Venice's annexation of the island after the death of her Cypriot husband.

San Salvador has two paintings by Titian (c1478–1576). *The Annunciation* at the end of the right-hand aisle is clearly autographed, *Tizianus, fecit, fecit*—did someone doubt it, or was it just a reminder to his fans of his genius? His other painting, *The Transfiguration*, hangs over the high altar, screening a magnificent silver reredos.

SAN SILVESTRO

➕ 61 G9 • Campo San Silvestro, San Marco ☎ 041 523 8090 🕐 Mon–Sat 7.30–11.30, 4–6 🎫 Free 🚤 San Silvestro

You will walk past the church of San Silvestro if you approach the Rialto from the *vaporetto* stop of the same name. A big, plain building, tucked away off the main streets, San Silvestro was completely rebuilt in the neoclassical style between 1837 and 1843. There's little to admire in the interior with the exception of a stunningly simple *Baptism of Christ* by Tintoretto (1518–94), featuring Christ standing in what appears to be a mountain stream, over the first altar on the right.

Across from the church is the Palazzo Velier (1022), where the artist Giorgione died in 1510.

SAN STAE

➕ 58 F7 • Campo San Stae, Santa Croce 1981 ☎ 041 275 0462 🕐 Mon–Sat 10–5; Sun 1–5. Closed Sun in Jul and Aug, Easter, 15 Aug 🎫 Chorus Pass (for all churches in Chorus group) €8; single ticket €2.50 🚤 San Stae www.chorusvenezia.org

San Stae is the Venetian version of Sant'Eustachio, a martyr who converted after seeing a vision of the crucified Christ between a stag's antlers. The church has as dramatic a setting as you could wish for, on its own *campo* right on the Grand Canal. It was built in 1678 on the site of a Veneto-Byzantine church, but the façade, the sort of late baroque design where every gesticulating saint seems to be battling in some divine gale, postdates the church and was added in 1709 by Domenico Rossi.

Things are less turbulent inside, where there's the gleam of startling white *marmorino* (marble veneer) all around the single-nave, barrel-vaulted interior. In 1722, a legacy enabled the church to ask all the leading artists of the day to produce a painting of an apostle of their choice for San Stae; the results are still here, an anthology of the last burst of pictorial creativity before the end of the Republic. The finest paintings are Giambattista Tiepolo's *Martyrdom of St. Bartholomew* (left wall), a horribly realistic rendering of the saint being flayed alive, painted in 1722 when the artist was 26; *The Liberation of St. Peter* (right wall) by Sebastiano Ricci (c1659–1734); and Giambattista Piazzetta's startlingly thought-provoking *Martyrdom of St. James the Great* (1717) showing the saint as a confused old man, also on the left. The church is often used for concerts and exhibitions.

SAN SEBASTIANO

This Dorsoduro church is brilliantly and lavishly decorated by the late Renaissance genius, Veronese.

A church and monastery, dedicated to the Virgin, were first founded here in the 14th century, and rebuilt, with St. Sebastian as an additional patron, after a plague outbreak in 1464. In 1505, this was demolished and a new church, designed by Scarpagnino (1505–49), erected. In 1555 Veronese started work on the internal decoration of the church, completed in two bursts, from 1555 to 1559 and 1565 to 1570. The church was closed in 1810 and reopened in 1856. During the 1980s and 1990s the interior was restored.

THE DECORATIVE SCHEME

San Sebastiano's prior commissioned Paolo Caliari, a fellow native from Verona, also known as Veronese, while the artist was in his 20s, and the iconography of the cycle of paintings is probably the prelate's inspiration. It brought together the church's two patrons, the Virgin and St. Sebastian, using scenes from their lives and New and Old Testament incidents to illustrate the triumph of faith over heresy, and thus of the Resurrection over sin and its consequences, plague and death.

Veronese first painted the ceiling of the sacristy with a *Coronation of the Virgin* and the *Four Evangelists* in 1556, moving on to the body of the church the following year. The three great ceiling panels over the nave depict scenes of the *Life of Esther*, surrounded by sumptuous painted architectural illusionism. Veronese then worked on to the monks' choir, running around the back and side walls of the church, the organ panels and surrounding decoration, between 1558 and 1559. In 1565 he returned to the church, completing the work around the high altar, which portrays the *Martyrdom of St. Sebastian* set against an imaginary Rome, in 1570.

San Sebastiano's decoration is a *tour de force*, full of visual tricks, dizzying perspectives and foreshortenings, and glowing with rich, jewel-like tones, a reminder of the artist's fascination with theatre design. Veronese's genius lies not only in his technical ability, but also in his gift to portray figures that are modelled on real people and scenes that appear as contemporary events, but are yet removed from the everyday world by the clear, transparent tones and unearthly light. *The Virgin and Child* above the high altar is also by Veronese, while there's a Titian, *St. Nicholas* (1563), on the left wall of the first chapel on the right. Veronese is buried in the chapel to the left of the chancel.

Many of the architectural details of San Sebastiano are, in fact, trompe l'oeil paintings (top)

Veronese is buried beneath his bust (above) near the organ

RATINGS

Cultural interest	● ● ●
Historic interest	● ● ●
Value for money	● ● ● ●

BASICS

✚ 60 F10 • Campo Santo Stefano, San Marco 2774

☎ 041 522 5061

🕐 Mon–Sat 10–5, Sun 1–5. Closed Sun in Jul and Aug, Easter, 15 Aug

🎫 Chorus Pass (for all churches in Chorus group) €8; single ticket €2.50

🚤 Accademia, San Samuele

🎧 Guided tours organized by Chorus (tel 041 275 0462); information sheets and audioguides in Italian, English, Frenchand German

www.chorusvenezia.org

The quiet beauty of Santo Stefano belies its bloody past (above)
Beautiful decorative detail on the arches along the nave (below)

SANTO STEFANO

The historic church of Santo Stefano, overlooking its lovely *campo*, is among the finest examples of Venetian high Gothic.

Santo Stefano stands at the north end of the *campo* of the same name (▷ 81). It's the only church in Venice to be built directly over a canal—you can see it passing under the apse if you stand on the first bridge in the *calle* leading towards San Marco. This Augustinian church, founded in the 13th century and rebuilt in the 14th and 15th centuries, had to be re-consecrated no fewer than six times because of repeated murders within its walls.

You enter through a magnificent Gothic doorway, decorated with carved stone ropework, leaves and vegetation, and surmounted by a typically Gothic arch and side pinnacles. Inside, the superb ship's keel roof immediately catches the eye, as do the diamond-patterned red-and-white brickwork, painted intarsi and parade of marble columns separating nave and aisles. As in so many Venetian churches, these are often hung with rich brocade, a reminder of Venice's ancient Byzantine links—a common practice in eastern churches. The bronze plaque in the middle of the nave floor marks the tomb of Doge Francesco Morosini (in office 1688–94). He is best known for blowing up the Parthenon in Athens, but was also responsible for looting the lions that now stand outside the gates of the Arsenale (▷ 69). Look out, too, for the lovely Lombardo monument to Giacomo Surian (1493), a physician from Rimini, to the left of the door. The baptistery contains Pietro Canova's monument to Giovanni Falier (1808).

THE SACRISTY PAINTINGS

Santo Stefano's best paintings are in the sacristy at the bottom of the right aisle; among them are four shadowy late works by Tintoretto (1518–94), which include the *Agony in the Garden*, the *Washing of the Disciples Feet* and the *Last Supper*. The composition of all three is typical of Tintoretto's highly theatrical late style—note the lack of a central balance and the astonishing perspective. These paintings are all illuminated by brilliant shafts of light against dark and brooding backgrounds.

San Trovaso is dedicated to saints Gervasio and Protasio

The interior of San Zulian contains a fine ceiling painting by Palma il Giovane, among other works by the artist

THE SIGHTS

SAN TROVASO

✚ 60 D11 • Campo San Trovaso, Dorsoduro 1098 ☎ 041 522 2133 🕐 Mon–Fri 8–11, 3–6, Sat 8–11, 3–7, Sun 8.30–1 🎫 Free 🚤 Accademia, Zattere

The present San Trovaso, built between 1584 and 1657, is the fourth church on this site. Its puzzling name is another example of Venetian mangling of two distinct saints' names, in this case the martyrs St. Gervasio and St. Protasio. The church is remarkable for its two virtually identical façades, one at each end, and is clearly influenced by the design of the Palladian church of Zitelle on the Giudecca (▷ 104). According to the story, San Trovaso stood on the boundary between the two areas controlled by the rival gangs of the Nicolotti and the Castellani. Two entrances meant that each faction could arrive at religious ceremonies in style without the danger of confronting each other. The main draw in the spacious, but rather bland, interior are the paintings. Works by Tintoretto (1518–94) and his son, Domenico (c1560–1635), are scattered around—the *Last Supper* in the left transept and the *Temptation of St. Anthony* in the chapel to the left of the high altar are by the master. On the side wall there's a charming contrast to the latter in the shape of an International Gothic gold-ground picture of *St. Chrisogonus* (c1450) by Michele Giambono. The Renaissance is represented by the marble reliefs in the Clary Chapel in the right transept. These show a procession of angels, some playing musical instruments, while the others hold the symbols of the Passion.

SAN ZACCARIA

See page 160.

SAN ZULIAN

✚ 61 H9 • Campo San Zulian, San Marco 605 ☎ 041 523 5383 🕐 Mon–Sat 8.30–12, Sun 5–8 🎫 Free 🚤 San Zaccaria, Rialto

The streets making up the Mercerie are more associated with conspicuous consumerism in most people's minds than with religion, and the church of San Zulian (San Giuliano), set right in this busy thoroughfare, is the exception that proves the rule. It's one of only two Venetian churches you can walk right around (the other is Angelo Raffaele, ▷ 69), and is a monument to the wealth of one man, Tommaso Rangone, who paid for its construction in the 1550s. He had no qualms about reminding worshippers who paid and there's a large monument to him right in the middle of Sansovino's harmonious façade. Rangone made his fortune from a treatment for syphilis—a scourge in this maritime city—and prided himself on his scholarship. The interior has a ceiling painting by Palma il Giovane (1548–1628), and there's a late Veronese *Pietà* over the first altar on the right.

SCALZI, CHIESA DEGLI

✚ 58 D7 • Fondamenta degli Scalzi, Cannaregio ☎ 041 715 115 🕐 Daily 7–11.50, 4–6.50 🎫 Free 🚤 Ferrovia

Properly known as Santa Maria di Nazaretta, the Scalzi is so-called after its owners, the Carmelitani Scalzi, the barefoot Carmelites who in fact wear the sandals worn by many religious orders. They arrived in Venice in 1633 and 12 years later purchased land for a church, whose funding was hotly contested by the patrician class. Gerolamo Cavazza put up 70,000 ducats, most of which went on the façade, designed by Giuseppe Sardi. The church was consecrated in 1680. It was

noted for its Tiepolo ceiling, destroyed in 1915 by an Austrian bomb destined for the nearby station, though even without this, the interior remains a riot of multicoloured baroque excess. Venice's last doge, Lodovico Manin, is buried in the second chapel on the left.

SCUOLA GRANDE DEI CARMINI

See page 161.

SCUOLA GRANDE DI SAN GIOVANNI EVANGELISTA

✚ 58 E8 • Calle della Scuole, San Polo 2454 ☎ 041 718 8234 🕐 Telephone to arrange visit 🎫 Donation (€5) 🚤 San Tomà, Piazzale Roma

San Giovanni Evangelista was one of the six *Scuola Grande*, Venice's super players on the charitable guild field. In medieval times it was the guardian of a relic of the True Cross, which made it among the richest of the guilds, with funds enough to commission the great *Miracle of the True Cross* cycle (▷ 98) that now hangs in the Accademia. Its headquarters, among the city's most beautiful Renaissance complexes, stand down a narrow *calle*, close to the Frari (▷ 144–147). The building was designed by Mauro Codussi in 1454 and stands on the right of a tiny *campo*, approached through a magnificent archway, designed by Pietro Lombardo (1481). This entrance arch, with its delicate carving and classical lines, is surmounted by an eagle, the symbol of St. John the Evangelist. The *scuola* itself has a superb double stairway leading to the Albergo, the main committee room, which is hung with paintings depicting episodes from the life of St. John. Concerts are held regularly in the *scuola*, though the church itself has been closed for many years.

Giovanni Bellini's celebrated Madonna and Child with Saints *(above)*
San Zaccaria *is a mix of architectural styles (left)*

SAN ZACCARIA

The lovely church of San Zaccaria is a beguiling blend of Gothic and Renaissance architecture, with paintings spanning the development of Venetian painting.

San Zaccaria, dedicated to the father of John the Baptist, who is said to be buried in the church, is the only Venetian church with an ambulatory and a crypt. It's set on Campo San Zaccaria (▷ 81), not far from San Marco, and had strong medieval links with the basilica—the doge came here annually for Easter Mass. The first Byzantine church was founded here in the 9th century and altered in the 10th, before receiving another overhaul between 1170 and 1174, when the campanile was added. The 14th century saw yet another update, this time in the Gothic style, but no sooner was the work complete than the Benedictines, who owned it, decided on a complete rebuild. Work started in 1458 and continued for over a century, resulting in a building that incorporates both Gothic and Renaissance styles. You can see this best in the façade, the work of Antonio Gambello (c1460–1537) and Mauro Codussi (c1440–1504): Gothic as far as door level, and firmly Renaissance in the upper portion. To the right of this, the brick façade of the older church is still visible behind a little garden.

THE TREASURES
Inside, you'll notice the rib-vaulted ambulatory at once, an elegant ring of elliptical cupolas around the high altar, lit by long windows, the only ones in Venice so reminiscent of northern European Gothic. Looking around, the church is filled with 17th- and 18th-century paintings of distinctly variable quality. Standing artistically apart from the majority is Giovanni Bellini's luminously stunning *Madonna and Child with Saints* in the second chapel on the left. Painted in 1505, it's one of the city's great paintings, perfectly set in a contemporary frame whose design echoes the architectural elements of the work. It's worth visiting the Chapels of St. Athanasius and St. Tarasius in the right aisle. St. Tarasius' chapel was once part of the original church and houses three ornate *ancone*—wonderfully hieratic pictures in sumptuous gold Gothic frames—by Antonio Vivarini (c1415–76/84) and Giovanni d'Alemagna (died 1450). This chapel also gives access to the permanently waterlogged crypt, burial place of eight early doges.

RATINGS

Cultural interest	●●●○
Good for kids	●●●○
Historic interest	●●●○

BASICS

✚ 61 J10 • Campo San Zaccaria, Castello 4693
☎ 041 522 1257
🕐 Mon–Sat 10–12, 4–6, Sun 11–12, 4–6
🎫 Free; €1.50 to chapels of St. Tarasius and Athanasius, sacristy and crypt
🚤 San Zaccaria

THE PRICE OF COLOUR
Venetian Renaissance artists relied on natural pigments, brought in from all over Europe and beyond. Browns and greys were easily obtainable—brown umber from Umbria, burnt Siena from Tuscany, Naples yellow from the slopes of Vesuvius. It was the reds, blues and golds that pushed the price of paintings up. In the 16th century Venice was the world's most important trading centre for red paints, made from the South American cochineal insect. The heavenly azure of the Virgin's robe is painted with ultramarine, an intense blue pigment obtained from the mineral lapis lazuli and worth more than its weight in gold.

The façade of the scuola *is adorned with busts and statues (above)
The main door leads into an elegant vestibule (below)*

SCUOLA GRANDE DEI CARMINI

**This uniquely preserved *scuola* retains its 18th-century
appearance and is home to dazzling works by
Giambattista Tiepolo.**

Of Venice's remaining charitable confraternity buildings the Scuola
Grande dei Carmini was the only one to escape the maraudings of
Napoleon's troops, and is the only surviving *scuola* that still retains its
18th-century appearance. Tucked away just off beguiling Campo
Santa Margherita, in the *sestiere* of Dorsoduro, this Carmelite stronghold has some flamboyant interior decoration, as well as a series of
nine superb Tiepolo panels, enough to convert even the most anti-
baroque art lover. For a dizzying blast of *trompe-l'oeil* perspective this
is the place to come.

THE SCUOLA
The Carmelites, founded in Palestine in 1235 as a women's order, are
a religious confraternity especially devoted to the Virgin Mary. This is
their Venetian headquarters from which they practise their charitable
works, attending services in the nearby church of Santa Maria dei
Carmini (▷ 142). They moved here in 1667 and commissioned
Baldassare Longhena (1598–1682), designer of the Salute
(▷ 150–151), to convert the existing building. He added the perfectly symmetrical façade, and planned the interior, which, like that
of all *scuole*, includes a *salone* and *albergo;* meeting rooms for the
members of the confraternity. In 1739 the Carmelites employed the
artist Giambattista Tiepolo to decorate the upper hall containing the
Salone, a task that occupied him until 1749. Access to this upper
chamber is via a wonderfully ornate double staircase, all gilded stucco
and well-fed *putti*, and the hall itself is dominated by Tiepolo's
panels. Don't even attempt to understand the iconography—
loosely based around the Carmelite emblem, the scapular—but
just enjoy the swirling figures, the startling colours, the audacious
off-centre composition and the mind-blowing accomplishment of
the *trompe-l'oeil* perspective. The archive room next door contains a *Judith and Holofernes* by Giambattista Piazzetta
(1683–1754), while the ground floor has 18th-century
chiaroscuro (light and shade) works.

SCUOLA DI SAN GIORGIO DEGLI SCHIAVONI

This intimate little building contains one of the most accurately observed and charming of all picture cycles, full of vivid detail.

The Slavs, inhabitants of the Dalmatian (modern Croatia) coast on the Adriatic, first came to Venice as slaves but, by the 15th century, were sufficiently established as merchants and sailors to set up a *scuola* to protect their interests. Around 1500 a purpose-built *scuola* was created and in 1502 Vittore Carpaccio was commissioned to decorate the walls of the upper meeting chamber with episodes from the lives of Dalmatia's three patrons, St. George, St. Tryphon and St. Jerome. The work was completed between 1507 and 1509, and the paintings were subsequently moved to the ground floor when the building was enlarged in 1551. They are still here today, the only one of Carpaccio's cycles to remain in the *scuola* for which it was painted.

THE PAINTINGS

The Carpaccio cycles occupies the upper part of the walls of the *scuola's* ground-floor hall, a dimly lit, wood-panelled chamber that's entered straight from the street. The narrative starts on the left-hand wall with the story of *St. George and the Dragon*, with the saint thrusting his lance into the creature's throat while the princess, surrounded by half-dismembered corpses, looks on. In the next picture, the *Triumph of St. George*, the dragon is finished off and the entire town converted to Christianity, with baptisms taking place in the next panel, *St. George Baptizing the Gentiles*. St. Tryphon, an obscure saint from Asia Minor, appears next, exorcizing a devil from the Roman Emperor's daughter—the demon appearing as a remarkably innocuous looking basilisk. The following two pictures show the *Agony in the Garden* and the *Calling of St. Matthew*, and the right-hand wall has three episodes from the *Life of St. Jerome*, an early father of the church, who, as we see in the first panel, earned a lion's undying devotion when he removed a thorn from its paw. The second picture shows the funeral of the saint, complete with the lion mourning in the background, while the third shows *St. Augustine in his Study* at the moment he had a vision of Jerome's death. This last is among Venice's best-loved paintings, a meticulously observed and recorded depiction of a 16th-century study that includes one of the most appealing little dogs ever painted.

RATINGS

Cultural interest	● ● ● ● ●
Good for kids	● ● ●
Historic interest	● ● ●
Value for money	● ● ● ●

BASICS

🗺 62 K9 • Fondamenta dei Furlani, Castello 3259A

☎ 041 522 8828

🕐 Apr–end Oct Tue–Sat 9.30–12.30, 3.30–6.30; Nov–end Mar Tue–Sat 10–12.30, 3–6, Sun 10–12.30. Closed 1 May, 15 Aug, 21 Nov

💶 €3

🚏 Arsenale, San Zaccaria

📄 Leaflet in Italian, English and French

TIP

● Allow time for your eyes to accustom to the dim light, and take time to pick out the wealth of detail in the paintings.

The Scuola di San Giorgio degli Schiavoni (above) lies tucked away in a little alley

Taking time to decipher the iconography of Carpaccio's paintings in the scuola (left)

Scuola Grande di San Rocco

Powerful masterworks by Tintoretto fill the richest of all Venice's *scuole*.

Tintoretto's Glory of St. Roch on the central ceiling panel in the Sala dell'Albergo

Decorative column on the exterior of the Scuola

Frescoes in the chapter house, by Tintoretto

RATINGS	
Cultural interest	●●●●●
Historic interest	●●●●○
Value for money	●●●●●

BASICS

✚ 58 D9 • Campo San Rocco, San Polo 3052
☎ 041 523 4864
🕐 28 Mar–2 Nov daily 9–5.30; 3 Nov–27 Mar daily 10–4. Closed Easter
🎫 €5.50, under 26 €4
🚤 San Tomà
📖 Leaflet and floor plan in Italian, English, French and German. Several guidebooks in Italian, English, French, German and Spanish. All illustrated but with differing levels of information. Prices €4.50–€15
🎧 Italian, French and English €5
www.scuolagrandesanrocco.it

Houses line the canal behind the Scuola (right)

SEEING THE SCUOLA GRANDE DI SAN ROCCO

Tintoretto's powerful picture cycle in the Scuola Grande di San Rocco is a series of 54 staggering paintings, produced by the artist in three bursts of creativity over a period of 23 years. This colossal achievement covers the walls and ceilings of the sumptuous headquarters of the richest of the 15th-century *scuole*, dedicated to San Rocco (St. Roch). The Scuola has three magnificent halls, the Ground Floor Hall being linked to the Great Upper Hall and the adjoining Albergo, both on the first floor, by a splendid and monumental staircase. Start your visit upstairs in the Albergo, the first to be decorated, then spend time in the Great Upper Hall before moving downstairs. You should allow 1 to 2 hours for a thorough visit.

HIGHLIGHTS

CRUCIFIXION (SALA DELL'ALBERGO)

The *Crucifixion*, painted in 1565, is a powerful synthesis of narrative and passionate devotion, described by English writer John Ruskin (1819–1900) as 'beyond all analysis and above all praise'. This is one of the greatest paintings in the world, packed with detail and drama, and bathed in light. The composition is extraordinary, the figure of the crucified Christ dominating and forming the central axis from which radiating diagonals spread out to encompass the other elements of the narrative. Within this tight compositional frame, the scene is packed with diverse activity, the figures full of movement and the natural and architectural details further pulling the scene together. Tintoretto originally envisioned many of the figures as nudes, and only added clothing and decoration as the work progressed.

ADORATION OF THE SHEPHERDS (GREAT UPPER HALL)

This New Testament scene is a perfect example of just what sets Tintoretto apart from other artists of his day. His work defies conventional contemporary ideas of perspective, colour, form and light and always pursues a compositional scheme that heightens the inherent drama of the scene. Thus the Virgin and Child are here placed on the higher level of a two-floor stable, whose poverty is accentuated.

Tintoretto's Crucifixion *of 1565 (above left and far right) Steps leading up to the Scuola (below)*

There's no gentle light, no ordered calm, as in traditional Bethlehem scenes, but a livid sky and a tumbledown building where the very roof is collapsing through the rafters.

THE LAST SUPPER (GREAT UPPER HALL)

The Last Supper was a popular subject with Tintoretto, who departed, in almost all his versions, from the horizontal table with the Apostles on either side of the central figure of Christ. Here, the table is a diagonal arrowing up from the right hand, with Christ leaning forward towards his followers. There's a strong sense of darkness that forebodes the tragedy to come, emphasized by the servants in the kitchen area, who go about their work oblivious to the drama about to unfold. We, the spectators, are drawn into the scene by the linking figures on the steps that act as a lead into the heart of the painting.

THE ANNUNCIATION (GROUND FLOOR HALL)

The ground floor paintings were the last to be executed. In *The Annunciation*, the angel, a whirling mass of wings and drapery that's attended by a swarm of accompanying cherubs, crashes into the Virgin's chamber. She draws back in astonishment and fear, while the mass of shattered beams and the broken brickwork of the outside walls seem to stand for the spiritual chaos that will be swept aside by the coming of the Redeemer.

FLIGHT INTO EGYPT (GROUND FLOOR HALL)

Tintoretto was born in the foothills of the Dolomites to the north of Venice and it's tempting to believe that he used his memories of his birthplace as the background for this picture, one of the few in San

The richly carved and decorated Renaissance façade of the Scuola (left)

Rocco where landscape plays a major part. The figures of the Virgin and Child and St. Joseph may be fleeing danger, but they are surrounded by the beauty of God's creation, a promise that good will prevail against evil. This is a fine painting in which to take in the artist's late style; its fluid brushwork, off-centre composition and dramatic light give an edge that was centuries ahead of its time.

BACKGROUND

St. Roch (1295–1327) was born in France but spent much of his life in Italy working with the plague-stricken. Soon after his death he became patron of plague sufferers, and was particularly revered in Venice, where his body was brought in 1485, becoming one of the city's co-patrons in 1576. The Scuola was founded in 1478 and, in 1515, Bartolomeo Bon started work on the Scuola building. During the years before its completion in 1549, other architects were involved in the design, but its interior decoration is almost entirely by Tintoretto, who worked here in three bursts. In 1564 he won the commission by presenting a finished canvas rather than a sketch and volunteering to do the work for nothing more than the cost of his materials. Tintoretto completed the first phase, the Albergo, between 1564 and 1567, going on to decorate the Great Upper Hall between from 1575 to 1581 and working on the Ground Floor Hall from 1583 to 1587. The Scuola is still the seat of the Archbrotherhood of St. Roch, the only confraternity to have been spared dissolution under Napoleon. Today, it has about 350 members of both sexes, who meet annually in Council and continue to function as an active charity.

GALLERY GUIDE

Albergo
Scenes from the Passion of Christ and the Crucifixion on the walls.
Allegories of the seasons, guilds and Virtues on the ceiling.

Great Upper Hall
Scenes from the Old and New Testaments on walls and ceiling. Panel paintings on easels by Tintoretto (1518–94), Titian (1478–1576), Giorgione (1476/8–1510), Giovanni Bellini (1430–1516) and Tiepolo (1696–1770).
Seventeenth-century carved wooden stalls by Francesco Pianta; many are caricatures of trades including a Painter, said to be Tintoretto complete with brushes.

Staircase
Two large canvases painted by Antonio Zanchi (1631–1722) and Pietro Negri to commemorate the end on the 1630 plague.

Ground Floor Hall
Scenes from the New Testament.

Squero di San Trovaso, one of Venice's gondola-building yards

The Fondamente Zattere has the air of a sunny promenade with fine views across to La Giudecca

SQUERO DI SAN TROVASO

✚ 60 D11 • Rio San Trovaso, Dorsoduro 🚢 Zattere

Venice had over 10,000 gondolas in the 16th century; today there are only a few hundred, built in a handful of specialist boatyards, called *squeri*. One of the most famous, and easiest to see, is the Squero di San Trovaso, on the waterfront of the Rio San Trovaso, just behind the Zattere. Construction sheds and workshops are set back from the *rio*, and there's generally always activity of some sort, as gondolas are overhauled and repaired.

Venice's gondolas developed in a unique fashion to meet the conditions of the city and lagoon, with shallow keels and perfect manoeuvrability, ideal for the narrow city *rii*. Being asymmetrical along the central line gives them a slight list to the right, which compensates for the weight of the gondolier, who rows in the Venetian fashion, standing. Eight types of wood are used in the construction: oak, elm, fir, larch, lime, walnut, cherry and mahogany, with beech for the oars. These rest in the *forcola*, a sensuously carved rowlock, whose shape allows the oar to be used in eight different positions. The bow is decorated with the *ferro*, whose six front-facing prongs traditionally represent the six *sestieri* of Venice. Gondolas have been painted black since 1562, when laws were passed forbidding excessive ornamentation, and the traditional cabin, the *felze*, was abolished in the 19th century. Modern water conditions take a tremendous toll on the boats, which suffer particularly from the backwash of motorboats, and they need to be cleaned and overhauled as often as once

a month. To get a real insight into the beauty of the craft and the expertise of the gondolier, take a *traghetto* across the Grand Canal and watch the oarsmen.

TEATRO LA FENICE

✚ 61 F10 • Campo San Fantin, San Marco 1965 ☎ 041 786 611 ⊙ Guided visits only, bookable in advance in person or by tel, fax or internet 💷 €6 🚢 Giglio www.teatrolafenice.it

Fenice is the Italian word for phoenix, and in true phoenix tradition, Venice's opera house, designed by Giannantonio Selva in 1792, rose from the ashes of the disastrous fire of 1996 to reopen for the 2004–5 season. Fire has struck the building more than once, notably in 1836, when it had to be virtually rebuilt. Following this, it became one of Italy's foremost opera houses, staging the premières of both *Rigoletto* and *La Traviata*, and functioning as a focus point for protests against the Austrian occupation. Audiences were known to bombard the stage with bouquets in the national colours of red, green and white and to shout repeatedly 'Viva Verdi', the composer's name being an acronym for Vittorio Emanuele, Re d'Italia (Vittorio Emanuele, King of Italy). The

1996 conflagration is shrouded in mystery, occurring when the nearest canal, which would have provided water for the pumps, was undergoing periodic cleaning and was thus dry. The reconstruction dragged on for years, but it's generally agreed it was worth the wait. The new theatre is a stunner, a beautiful reconstruction of the glittering gilt and stucco auditorium, marble-clad foyer and glistening chandeliers that includes state-of-the-art systems and equipment. Book well in advance for performances or join one of the regular tours.

ZATTERE

✚ 60 D11 • Zattere, Dorsoduro 🚢 Zattere, San Basilio

The Zattere is the name given to the string of *fondamente* overlooking the Canale della Giudecca on the southern side of Dorsoduro. It runs from the Punta della Dogana, in the east, to the Stazione Marittima in the west, and gets its name from the quayside's original function as an unloading point for bulky goods, which were floated in on rafts known as *zattere*. Much of this cargo landed up at the huge Magazzini del Sale (salt warehouses) near the Dogana, now used as boathouses and occasional exhibition space. Further west are the churches of the Gesuati (▷ 101) and Santa Maria della Visitazione (▷ 152). The Zattere's chief charms are its sunny, sheltered position and wide pavement (sidewalk), making it one of the city's most popular places for the *passeggiata*, the popular late afternoon stroll. There are benches, restaurants and cafés, and some of Venice's best ice-cream, at Nico's.

A golden phoenix surmounts La Fenice's sign

Farther Afield

The Venetian lagoon is a watery expanse of 34 islands, wetlands, fish farms, dunes and mudflats. The main inhabited islands are Murano, Burano and Torcello, with the long strip of the Lido forming a barrier against the open sea. If you have time, there are others to explore: rural Sant'Erasmo, tranquil San Francesco and the Armenian stronghold of San Lazzaro.

MAJOR SIGHTS

THE SIGHTS

BURANO AND MAZZORBO

These adjacent islands in the northern lagoon have a long tradition of fishing and lace-making.

BURANO

Burano was one of the first places in the lagoon to be settled, and even after the decline of nearby Torcello (▷ 174), it continued to prosper as a fishing community. With the men away on the boats, lace-making became the traditional occupation for the women, and gossamer-fine Burano lace was renowned all over Europe. Both traditions continue today, on a smaller scale, and Burano retains a sense of individuality and an atmosphere that's very different from that of Venice. Much of this is due to the almost impossible picturesqueness of the place, where the *rii* are still busy with boats, nets are hung out for mending and drying, and the *fondamente* are lined with vividly painted houses, a practice said to have originated to help the fishermen distinguish their own houses on the way home.

Walk from the *vaporetto pontile* towards Via Galuppi, the main street, and you'll pass houses in a rainbow of colours to find restaurants specializing in the freshest of fresh fish, and a wealth of lace shops. Much of the lace is now imported and machine-made, but some women still produce the real thing. You can trace the history of Burano lace in the Museo del Merletto (tel 041 730 034; Apr–end Oct Wed–Mon 10–5; Nov–end Mar Wed–Mon 10–4; €4). It stands on the *campo* at the end of Via Galuppi, named for Baldassare Galuppi, Burano's most famous son, a 17th-century composer who set many of Carlo Goldoni's plays to music. On the other side of the square is the church of San Martino (daily 8–12, 3–7; free), with a drunkenly tilting campanile and a fine *Crucifixion* by Tiepolo (1696–1770).

MAZZORBO

Mazzorbo was first settled in the 10th century and is linked to Burano by a wooden bridge, which has stupendous views across the lagoon to Venice. Walk across it from Burano and find yourself in yet another different world, one of small farms, pine trees and winding pathways. These lead to the 14th-century Gothic church of Santa Caterina, once the focal point of a thriving medieval community. Nothing remains of the early *palazzi*, which were dismantled by their owners, their stones shipped across to booming Venice. Between the bridge and the *vaporetto* stop there's a charming park, great for a picnic, and a good place for kids to run around and let off steam.

RATINGS	
Good for kids	●●●●●
Historic interest	●●●●
Photo stops	●●●●●
Specialist shopping	●●●●

BASICS
🚩 304 • Ísola di Burano
🚢 Burano (LN)
🎫 Included in some tours. See page 297 for details of the Musei delle Isole pass

TIPS
• Come to Burano on the ACTV service (▷ 50) rather than by expensive excursion boat—you'll have longer and will be able to go at your own pace.
• The trip from Murano to Burano takes 35 minutes.
• Combine Burano with Torcello for a day's outing.

You will find lace for sale all over Burano (above)

THE LIDO

The Lido is an island bulwark between the Adriatic and the lagoon, with hotels, beaches and outdoor pursuits.

The island of the Lido is essentially a long, narrow, sandbank. To the north, across the Porto di Lido, lies the mainland at Punta Sabbioni; to the south, the Porto di Malamocco, the busiest of the lagoon entrances, divides the Lido from the island of Pellestrina. Once a sparsely inhabited island of dunes and pinewoods, the Lido today combines its role as a residential suburb with that of seaside resort and overspill hotel area for Venice . It was 'discovered' by mid-19th-century Romantic writers, including Lord Byron and Robert Browning, and opened up as a resort in Edwardian times when the cult of the seaside first emerged. The grandiose hotels constructed for the leisured rich still survive (▷ 21).

WHAT TO DO AND SEE

If you're in Venice with children, or feel like a change, the Lido makes a pleasant respite. A 10-minute boat trip from the city will bring you to a different world, where cars, buses and supermarkets are the back-drop to lazy beach days. You could visit the ancient church of San Nicolò, founded in the 10th century. It was here that the Doge came on Ascension Day after the celebration of the city's marriage to the sea (▷ 221). The Lido is rich in art nouveau—a style known as Liberty in Italy—and art deco buildings. Look out for the Hungaria Palace and the Villa Monplaisir (No. 14) on the Gran Viale, the main boulevard that links the lagoon with the sea, and don't miss the Hotel Excelsior, a neo-Moorish fantasy, complete with minaret. You can visit these on your way to the Lido's main attractions—the beaches, tennis courts, golf course and walking and cycling opportunities. If you need some exercise and a respite from stony streets, this is the place to come.

A DAY ON THE BEACH

Great strides have been made in improving the water quality of the Adriatic, making a beach day a more attractive prospect than it once was. All the grand hotels have their own *stabilimenti* (private beach establishments), with loungers, sunshades, changing cabins and restaurants; other privately run *stabilimenti*, much patronized by Venetians who come here on summer afternoons, offer similar facilities at lower prices. The *comune*, the local council, has free beaches, both on the Lido and the nearby island of Pellestrina.

RATINGS	
Good for kids	●●●●○
Outdoor pursuits	●●●●○
Photo stops	●●●○○
Value for money	●●●●○

BASICS
Tourist Information Office
✚ 304 • Gran Viale Santa Maria
Elisabetta 6a, Lido di Venezia
☎ 041 526 5721
🕐 Jun–end Sep daily 9.30–4
🚤 Lido

Walkway on the Lido beach overlooking the open Adriatic Sea (top)

Liberty-style decoration on the Hungaria Palace Hotel (above)

Murano

The lagoon island of Murano is a miniature Venice, and has been the historic heart of Venetian glass production for over 800 years, reaching its peak between the 5th and 16th centuries.

Glassmaker at work on the Riva Longa

Golden mosaic of the Madonna (above left), one of the highlights in the 12th-century church of Santa Maria e Donato (above right)

RATINGS				
Cultural interest	● ● ●			
Good for kids	● ● ● ●			
Photo stops	● ● ● ●			
Specialist shopping	● ● ● ● ●			

BASICS

➕ 318 • Ìsola di Murano
🚤 Colonna, Faro, Navagero, Museo, Venier
🛍 Wide choice

The Barovier cup (top)

Exquisite Murano glassware by Stefano Toso (below)

SEEING MURANO

It's a 10-minute trip across the lagoon to Murano, a self-contained community with its own Grand Canal, fine churches, *palazzi* and glass-blowing industry. There are numerous privately run excursions from the city, but for good value and flexibility make the trip independently via the ACTV services (▷ 50). Allow two to three hours for a thorough visit. It's quite feasible, given an early start, to combine a visit to Murano with a trip to the northern islands of Burano and Torcello; study the *vaporetto* timetable with care as onward connections run half-hourly only.

HIGHLIGHTS

THE GLASS FACTORIES

Away from the kitsch on offer in the shops along the Fondamenta dei Vetrai, superb glass is still produced on Murano. Venetian glass is made by the blowing and flamework process, whereby glass is repeatedly heated, stretched and blown to build up gradually the finished piece. The workers perform as a team, led by the chief blower, the *maestro* (master). Each workman's individual skills are an integral part of the process and each member of the team has a specific and highly specialized role. The work is intense, concentrated and very hot. For this reason, the most serious production houses are not open to the public, but plenty of others are (see Tips panel opposite).

MUSEO DEL VETRO

✉ Fondamenta Giustinian 8 ☎ 041 739 586; www.museiciviciveneziani.it
🕐 Apr–end Oct Thu–Tue 10–5; Nov–end Mar Thu–Tue 10–4 💶 €4, Rolling Venice card holders €2.50 🚤 Museo
Italy's only glass museum is housed in the beautiful *palazzo* that was the former residence of the Bishop of Torcello. It traces the history of glass-making on Murano via a series of displays of glass right through from Roman times to the present day, with sections on the actual manufacturing process. One of the earliest of the ornate pieces is the 15th-century Barovier marriage cup, while other rooms are devoted to Venetian mirrors—a monopoly for centuries—and mind-blowing examples of 18th- and 19th-century polychrome glass chandeliers. Look

out for the examples of the different speciality glass for which Venice was famed: *milfiori* (thousand flowers), a technique where strands of coloured and transparent glass are fused; *stellaria*, where plain glass is shot with copper crystals; and *vetro latino*, with its porcelain-like finish. Note, too, the beautiful collections of *perle*, the intricate and delicate glass beads used all over the world as a form of currency.

SANTA MARIA E DONATO AND SAN PIETRO MARTIRE

✉ Campo San Donato 🕐 Apr–end Sep 9–12, 4–6.30; Oct–end Mar 9–12, 4–6 🎫 Free 🏛 Museo

Murano's greatest architectural treasure is the church of Santa Maria e Donato, a beautiful 12th-century basilica with a colonnaded exterior apse that's a classic of Veneto-Byzantine style. Inside, the mosaic marble paving, all geometric designs, flowers and animal motifs, dates from 1140 and is overlooked by a golden mosaic of the Madonna. The church of San Pietro has two superb pictures by Giovanni Bellini (1430–1516), *The Assumption* and a *Virgin and Child with Saints*.

BACKGROUND

Murano was a Roman settlement, and later, one of the first lagoon islands to be permanently inhabited, becoming a prosperous trading community by the 11th century. In 1291, the Senate decided to transfer all glass furnaces to the island to avoid the constant danger of fire within the city. This had the bonus of keeping all the *maestri* (master glass-workers) and their trade secrets safely in one place, protecting Venice's monopoly on glass. In the 14th century every mirror in Europe was made in Venice. So possessive was Venice of the manufacturing process that any worker leaving the island was proclaimed a traitor, and even today skills are passed on solely by apprenticeship with a master. The industry declined during the 19th century with the advent of industrial glass making, but has revived to become the main money-maker, with a profusion of small factories, many in the hands of families who have been involved in the business since the 13th century.

Mosaic floor in Santa Maria e Donato (above)

Decorative glassware (central strip above)

TIPS

● Bear in mind that the glass factories are closed on Saturday and Sunday.
● If you're buying, remember that the cheaper the glass, the less likely it is to have been made on Murano. All Murano glass is marked as such.
● The best production houses open to the public include Mazzega (▷ 195), where you can see demonstrations of chandelier production; CAM Vetri D'Arte, which specializes in mirrors and goblets; and Fratelli Barbini, one of the most innovative of all glass producers.

Torcello

●

The evocative rural backwater of Torcello, dreaming in the past, is Venice's most ancient settlement and the site of a superb basilica, the oldest building in the lagoon.

Mosaics (above and bottom) in Basilica di Santa Maria Assunta

Views over Torcello (above and opposite)

Inside the Basilica di Santa Maria Assunta

RATINGS	
Cultural interest	●●●●●
Good for kids	●●●●○
Historic interest	●●●●●
Walkability	●●●●○

BASICS
✚ 304 • Torcello
🚤 Torcello
🍴 Several bar/restaurants
🎫 Some souvenir stalls

MORE TO SEE
MUSEO DEL TORCELLO
🕐 Mar–end Oct Tue–Sun 10.30–6;
Nov–end Feb Tue–Sun 10–5
The museum houses a low-key display of archaeological finds from Torcello and the lagoon.

SEEING TORCELLO
From the landing stage a path runs beside Torcello's canal, crossed by the simple stone span of the Ponte del Diavolo (Devil's Bridge), to the main piazza. Around here everything there is to see is grouped. You will also find the so-called Trono di Attila, a primitive stone chair once used by the bishop.

HIGHLIGHTS
THE CHURCHES
The island has two wonderful churches—the Basilica di Santa Maria Assunta (open Mar–end Oct daily 10.30–6.30; Nov–end Feb daily 10–5) and the church of Santa Fosca. The basilica dates from 638 and is the oldest building in Venice. It was altered in the 9th and again in the 11th century, but has remained virtually unchanged since. The lofty interior, bare and cool, has some superb mosaics from the 9th to 12th centuries, on the vaults and walls. Wholly Byzantine in style, they represent *Christ and the Apostles* in the right-hand apsidal chapel, the *Virgin and Child* in the apse, and the finely detailed *Last Judgement* on the west rear wall. Next to the basilica is the beautiful 11th-century church of Santa Fosca, another Byzantine-influenced construction with a Greek-cross plan and an external colonnade. Behind the basilica is the campanile, whose steep, twisting ramps lead to a panorama of water, sky, mudflats and marsh.

BACKGROUND
Torcello was founded in the 5th century by Roman citizens fleeing successive waves of invading barbarians on the mainland. It was the first serious lagoon settlement and, by the 14th century, was home to a prosperous community, whose population numbered over 20,000. During the 1400s, when malaria was rife, the population fled to Venice, leaving the palaces to decay and the canals to silt up. Today, all that remains of past glories are a handful of scattered houses and restaurants, a hotel, a couple of bridges crossing a muddy canal, an 11th-century church and the great basilica of Santa Maria Assunta.

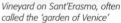
Vineyard on Sant'Erasmo, often called the 'garden of Venice'

Delicate wrought-iron work (middle) at the monastery on San Francesco del Deserto (right), supposedly founded by St. Francis

THE SIGHTS

SANT'ERASMO

⊞ 304 • Isola di Sant'Erasmo
🚢 Capannone, Chiesa, Punta Vela

Bigger than Venice itself, Sant'Erasmo is one of the lagoon's best-kept secrets. It lies northeast of the city, a long, flat, sparsely inhabited island where sandy paths criss-cross well-kept fields and tiny vineyards. Sant'Erasmo produces huge quantities of vegetables for the city markets, and produce marked 'San Rasmo' or 'nos-tranno' on market stalls will certainly have come from here. The major crop is artichokes, and the island produces some unique varieties, resulting in a long growing season—artichokes of various types are available in Venice practically year-round. The island is traversed by a single road, where rickety old unli-censed cars trundle up and down, there are no police here to worry about, and no doctor, chemist or school either. The island does have a tiny store at the main settlement, built around the church, and a couple of *trat-torie*. Its chief charm lies in its bucolic atmosphere and the beautiful countryside. Take *vaporetto* No. 13, alight at Capannone, and you can spend the whole day ambling through vineyards and past old farm-houses to the old Austrian stronghold of Forte Massimiliano, the perfect antidote to the stony streets of Venice.

SAN FRANCESCO DEL DESERTO

⊞ 304 • Isola di San Francesco del Deserto ☎ 041 528 6863; www.isola-sanfrancescodeldeserto.it ⊕ Tue–Sun 9–11, 3–5. Guided visits by Franciscan monk 🎫 Free but donation recommended 🚢 Access by taxi from Burano (to book tel 041 735 420, 041 730 001 or mobile 335 581 3731– Gianni Amadi & Figli)

Legend and truth intermingle to tell how, in 1220, St. Francis of Assisi returned to Italy from the Holy Land. On his way he stopped at a lagoon island near Venice, where he planted his staff in the ground. It grew into a tree, and swallows flew in to perch in it and sing to the holy man. The island is today known as San Francesco del Deserto, a cypress-clad oasis of peace near Burano (▷ 170) that's home to a thriving Franciscan monastery. The monks have been here since soon after the death of St. Francis, when the island's owner, Jacopo Michiel, bequeathed it to the Order. The present church, dating from the 15th century, is surrounded by two cloisters, a refectory, offices and monks' cells, and is approached by a tree-lined avenue. Cypresses, deciduous trees, orchards and vegetable gardens cover the rest of the island; there's no other place in the lagoon as tranquil. If you want to visit, you can negoti-ate a price with Burano's water taxi owner, who runs occasional group tours to the island. The monks also run retreats and workshops.

SAN LAZZARO DEGLI ARMENI

⊞ 304 • Isola di San Lazzaro degli Armeni ☎ 041 526 0104 ⊕ One guided tour daily 3.25–5.15 (coincides with *vaporetto* No. 20 from San Zaccaria at 3.10) 🎫 Adult €6; child (under 12) €3 🚢 San Lazzaro

Allow an afternoon to visit the Armenian monastery island of San Lazzaro, home to a small community of monks and one of the world's most important cen-tres of Armenian culture and learning. This tiny island was gifted by the Doge in 1717 to an Armenian abbot called Mekhitar, who had fled north up the Adriatic to escape the Turks in

the Peloponnese. Armenians had been in Venice since the 11th century, and with the establish-ment of the monastery, the Venetian Armenian community became the focus of Armenian Catholic culture throughout the world. It remains so today, and the monastery is supported and visited by Armenians from around the world.

The monastery tour takes in the immaculate cloister and the church, rebuilt after a fire in 1883, before heading upstairs to the museum and modern library, containing over 40,000 priceless books and manuscripts. The museum is a jumble of objects and bits and pieces, ranging from an Egyptian mummy to fine antique porcelain and paintings donated by Armenian benefac-tors. The old library was once the haunt of Lord Byron, who used to row across from Venice three times a week to wrestle with the Armenian language, said to be among the world's most fiendishly difficult. The monks are proud of the Byron connection, the fact that they were the only monastery in the city to be spared the Napoleonic axe, and their long association with Venice, still occasionally referred to here as La Serenissima.

VIGNOLE

⊞ 304 • Isola di Vignole
🚢 Vignole

Vignole, like Sant'Erasmo, is a market garden island, reached by *vaporetto* No. 13. It was once a popular summer resort for Venetians escaping the heat of the city, but, like its neighbour, is now dedicated to artichokes and asparagus rather than pleasure. It retains the ruins of a medieval chapel dedicated to Sant'Erosia, and is a popular weekend island with picnicking Venetians, who come here by boat.

This chapter gives information on things to do in Venice other than sightseeing. Shops and entertainment venues are shown on the maps at the beginning of each section.

What to Do

SHOPPING

Venice is filled with wonderful shops, many specializing in traditional Venetian products . Most stores, particularly those aimed at visitors, are open all day, operating an *orario continuato* from 9.30 or 10am until 7.30pm. Increasingly, some shops are open on Sundays, lifting their shutters around 11am and staying open till 7 or 7.30pm.

For locals, mornings are set aside for food shopping, and this is the time to visit the city's markets at the Rialto, along the Via Garibaldi, the Strada Nova and in many of the key neighbourhood *campi*—though there are no fish markets on Monday. Markets and food shops open around 8 or 8.30am, while other shops operate from 9.30 or 10am. Traditionally, shops have

There is an excellent selection of men's fashion shops in Venice

closed for lunch and the siesta, usually from 1 to 4pm, and this is still the case with food shops and smaller, family-run businesses.

In August many Venetians flee the big heat, with smaller businesses shutting for the traditional two-week break, revolving around Ferragosto, the public holiday on 15 August. Many shops also close on Monday morning, and food shops tend to close on Saturday afternoon; many of them are open on Sundays, as are *pasticcerie*, for whom Sunday is the busiest day of the week as people buy trays of cakes and pastries for Sunday lunch.

SHOPPING AREAS AND SHOPS

Pages 179–183 highlight what's where in the shopping line throughout the city and the islands. San Marco has the most stores, along with outlets for many of Italy's big-name designers, jewellers and leather producers. Across the Rialto Bridge, San Polo is noted for good-value clothes and leather stores. Some of Venice's real shopping jewels are tucked away in quiet corners, and these are the places to hunt out for special buys such as jewellery, antiques, beads, paper goods, textiles and accessories.

Most Venetian shops are small, with the accent firmly on personal service and individual design; if you're looking for malls and department stores you'll have to cross the causeway and head for Mestre, or better still, Padova (Padua).

SOUVENIRS

Traditional souvenirs are glass from Murano, lace from Burano, sumptuous textiles, glass beads, jewellery and marbled paper products. Mask shops sell a bewildering variety of Carnival masks, many made in the Far East. Locally produced masks fetch high prices, but make wonderful souvenirs, as do strings of beads, earrings and necklaces. Food souvenirs include pasta, rice and polenta, olive oil, dried *porcini* (mushrooms), vinegars and spices, or traditional food specialities such as Burano biscuits.

For the best in kitsch, head for the stalls along the Riva and near the Piazza San Marco, where you can pick up paintings of gondolas and sunset

scenes, gondoliers' shirts and hats, plastic gondolas, gondolas in snowstorms and a mind-boggling selection of some of the best of the worst glass trinkets and ornaments.

CREDIT CARDS AND SALES TAX

Credit cards are widely accepted in Venice, though not usually for amounts under €20. Food shops and markets

Handcrafted Italian shoes can be a work of art

remain the exception, and some shops, particularly family-run businesses, still offer a good discount for cash.

You should always get a *ricevuta fiscale* (official receipt), which will include the IVA (VAT) details, as Italian law requires all shopkeepers and restaurateurs to provide this. Receipts can be useful if you need proof of purchase for customs or to make an insurance claim.

The Duty Free scheme operates at many Venetian shops; this ensures a rebate of sales tax to visitors from outside the EU; ask at individual stores for details and the necessary paperwork.

San Marco and Castello

HOW TO GET THERE

📠 1 to Rialto, Sant'Angelo, Giglio, San Marco (Vallaresso), San Zaccaria, Arsenale, Giardini, Sant'Elena; 82 to Rialto, San Samuele, San Marco (Vallaresso), San Zaccaria, Giardini; 41, 42, 51, 52 to Celestia, Bacini, Sant'Elena

Crowds have been flocking since the 11th century to the shops of San Marco, particularly along the string of streets known as the Mercerie, which links the Piazza San Marco with the Rialto. Together with the *calli* running west of the Piazza towards the Accademia Bridge, this area, the most expensive in Venice, is home to many of the big Italian names, as well as shops selling Venetian goods, such as paper, glass and masks. Castello offers vibrant local stores with some of the city's best buys at low prices and a good range of artisan outlets.

Exquisite hand-printed Venetian paper makes a great souvenir

THE MERCERIE AND FREZZERIA

The *calli* known as the Mercerie are Venice's busiest shopping streets, where you'll find everything from fashion to shops specializing in just one item, such as Borsalino, in Calle dell'Ovo, with a great selection of hats; Fantoni Libri Arte, in Salizzada San Luca, which sells gorgeously illustrated books on art, architecture, design and the decorative arts; and Coin Beauty on Campo San Luca, which sells only cosmetics and beauty products.

The Frezzeria, whose streets wind their way from San Marco to the Fenice, is another good trawling ground; delights include

Antichità Marciana, a charming shop which specializes in hand-painted velvets and antique jewellery.

WEST OF PIAZZA SAN MARCO

Venice's densest concentration of big-name fashion outlets lies west of Piazza San Marco, in and around Calle Larga 22 Marzo. Here you'll find Prada, Valentino, Fendi, Versace, Armani and Laura Biagiotti, while Calle Vallaresso, cutting down to the Grand Canal just west of the Piazza, is home to Gucci, Bottega Veneta, Missoni and Ferré. Near the Accademia bridge, Campo Santo Stefano gives access to the streets running northeast towards the Rialto, home to the city's widest selection of paper product stores and some of the best of Venice's bead and jewellery shopping. Head for Paolo Olbi on Calle della Mandola for marbled paper, or hunt in the bead shops here for necklaces and single beads, which can be made up as jewellery on the spot. From Campo Santo Stefano too, a left turn brings you into Calle della Bottegha, home to some of Venice's finest antique stores, such as the Kleine Galerie, which specializes in maiolica, porcelain, and antique books and prints.

CASTELLO

Castello sprawls eastwards from the Rialto to the city's easternmost tip. The eastern zone is a vibrant, working-class area packed with everyday, local stores, and is worth exploring for

its food shops and inexpensive clothes and leather outlets. The Rialto end is home to classier shops, such as the jeweller Sigifredo Cipolato, on the Casselleria, who specializes in the famous ebony Moors' head brooches and earrings, and

Mask shops are big business, especially during Carnevale

Il Milione on Campo di Santa Marina, with its elegant Fortuny look-alike handmade lamps. Moving east, the streets around Campo Santa Maria Formosa have a good selection of bead and mask shops; Papier Mâché on Calle Lunga Santa Maria Formosa is noted for its contemporary masks.

WHERE TO EAT

CAVATAPPI
Campo della Guerra, San Marco 525
Tel 041 296 0252
Over 30 wines by the glass and nibbles including generously filled *panini* and *cicheti*.
🕐 Feb–end Dec Tue–Sat
9am–11pm, Sun 10–1

WHAT TO DO

The Rialto

HOW TO GET THERE
📧 1, 82 to Rialto

The streets on either side of the Rialto Bridge, and the bridge itself, are second only to the Piazza San Marco area for shopping. The east bank of the Grand Canal here is in San Marco and Castello; the west is in San Polo. The San Polo side is home to the Rialto Market, while the surrounding streets have some of the city's most interesting food shops, as well as medium-range clothing and leather stores. East of the bridge, itself lined with souvenir stalls and shops, there's a subtle difference; you'll find more expensive stores as the area segues into the Mercerie and its glittering shops.

THE MARKETS
There's been a morning produce market at the Rialto for over a

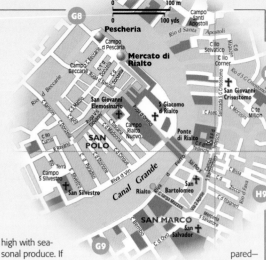

The streets of the Rialto are as busy as they were 800 years ago

thousand years, and the area still explodes into a riot of lively stalls daily from Monday to Saturday. Italian food markets are one of the country's most enjoyable shopping experiences and there are few whose position rivals that of the Rialto (▷ 120–121), where stallholders set up on the edge of the Grand Canal. For sheer interest, the Pescheria (fish market) is unrivalled, and from Tuesday to Saturday, you can see the myriad varieties of super fresh fish and crustaceans that form a vital part of the city's cuisine. Nearby, right on the water's edge, is the Campo della Pescaria, packed with rows of fruit and vegetable stalls, piled

high with seasonal produce. If you're buying, you'll find prices here lower than elsewhere in the city. Moving along the Ruga dei Orefici towards the bridge there are more stalls, aimed at the tourist, with leather bags, belts and purses, T-shirts and scarves, souvenirs, jewellery, beads and toys jostling for your attention.

THE EAST BANK
The hub of the Rialto's east bank is Campo San Bartolomeo, into which the main shopping streets of the Mercerie and Calle dei Fabbri lead via Via 2 Aprile, a wide stretch that's home to a state-of-the-art Benetton and old-established local shops such as Fabris, noted for linen, lace-work, scarves and gloves. The Riva del Ferro stretches beside the Canal and is linked with San Bartolomeo by Calle Larga Mazzini, where you'll find a branch of Golden Point, excellent for underwear, and Salizzada Pio X, where souvenir stalls sell soccer shirts, wooden toys, scarves, T-shirts and beads. Steps lead up onto the Rialto Bridge, where there are jewellery stores, as well as souvenir and leather shops; prices here are high and you'll do better looking elsewhere if you're seriously shopping.

THE WEST BANK
The cluster of streets around the Rialto market is a draw for food shoppers, and locals come from all over the city to patronize the *alimentari*, butchers, bakers and produce shops here. Meat is beautifully displayed and pre-

pared—pick up the makings of a picnic. Aliani, on the Ruga Rialto, is a traditional grocer selling meat and cheese from all over Italy, as well as prepared dishes. On the same street is El Forner de Canton, a wonderful bakery with a huge

Freshly caught fish being bought by a discerning shopper

selection of bread. Mingling with the food shops in the Ruga Rialto are leather and fashion stores; this area is a good place to buy shoes and mid-range fashion for both sexes.

WHERE TO EAT
ALLE BOTTE
Campo San Bartolomeo, San Marco 5482
Tel 041 520 9775
This tiny bar serves a mean spritz, wine by the glass and snacks such as seafood *cicheti* and bulging meat-filled *panini*. You can also enjoy a simple meal in the back room.
🕒 Sep–end Jul Mon–Tue, Fri–Sat 11–3, 6–11, Wed 10–3

San Polo, Santa Croce and Dorsoduro

HOW TO GET THERE

🚌 1 to Piazzale Roma, Riva di Biagio, San Stae, San Silvestro, San Tomà, Ca' Rezzonico, Accademia, Salute; 41, 42, 51, 52 to Santa Marta, Zattere

West of the Rialto, San Polo, Santa Croce and Dorsoduro contain some of Venice's most appealing shops. Galleries, jewellers and fashion outlets abound, and this is the place to venture into the quiet *calli* and *campi*. Follow the yellow street signs that guide you along the main route through this side of the Grand Canal and you'll find plenty of choice, or duck down side-streets for specialist shopping at better prices than around San Marco.

SAN POLO

From the Rialto, San Polo's main drag winds west towards the area's main square, Campo San

Masks of every shape and size fill the shops

Polo. This string of streets is lined with fashion, shoe and accessory shops. Look out for Manuela, just off the Ruga Ravano , which has classic shoes at keen prices, and Hibiscus (▷ 190) for accessories and clothes. Near here, on Campo San Aponal, check out Piaroa, with its Indian and South American clothes and home accessories. On Calle del Figher is Barbieri & Scomparin, where cosmetics and toiletries jostle shelves lined with pots and pans. This stretch of the through route leads into Campo San Polo; behind here is Laboratorio Arte & Costume, a second-hand shop crammed with fabulous clothing and hats. There's more outra-

geous fashion at Atelier Pietro Longhi, one of Venice's best Carnevale costume hirers, on the main route to the Frari, while at the bottom of the Frari bridge is L'Angolo d'Oro, a great artisan jeweller. Sabbie e Nebbie, on Calle dei Nomboli, is worth a visit for its contemporary Italian and Japanese ceramics.

SANTA CROCE

Santa Croce is university territory and Cartoleria Arte e Design, on Campiello Mosca, is popular with students for its great range of art supplies and papers. Near here, on Fondamenta dei Tolentini, is Mare di Carta, a wonderful bookshop devoted to all things nautical in Italian and English. Walking east through Santa Croce, Ceramiche la Margherita stocks affordable, hand-decorated ceramic plates and bowls, tucked away under Sottoportico della Siora Bettina. Artisan workshops are scattered throughout the area, and Dalla Veneziana, on Calle Pesaro, specializes in *tiraoro*, the traditional gold-leaf gilded frame technique.

DORSODURO

Dorsoduro is one of the city's prime residential areas. It is rich in art galleries, jewellers and bookstores, many on or near the main route through to the Accademia. Venice's best range of English-language titles can be found at Ca' Foscarini, the university bookshop on Campiello degli Squellini, which is also home to Arras, with its hand-woven textiles in silk, cotton and wool. On Campo Santa Margherita, you'll

find a huge range of keenly priced hardware and kitchen bits and pieces at Di Pol, while heading towards the Accademia, stop at Gualti, noted for its funky resin jewellery. Near here is an excellent and traditional mask shop, Ca' Macana,

Choose from a wide selection of books on Venice

on Calle delle Botteghe, while towards the Accademia is the Libreria Toletta (▷ 192). South from here you'll find lovely paper products at Il Pavone, while Cornici Trevisanello, on Campo San Vio, makes beautiful and intricate frames.

WHERE TO EAT

DA GINO
Calle Nuova Sant'Agnese, Dorsoduro 853A
Tel 041 528 5276
This friendly bar, right on the Accademia–Guggenheim route, serves one of the best selections of *tramezzini* and *panini* in town.
🕐 Sep–end Jul Mon–Sat 6am–8pm

WHAT TO DO

Cannaregio

HOW TO GET THERE
📇 1 to Ferrovia, San Marcuola, Ca'
d'Oro; 41, 42, 51, 52 to Ferrovia, Guglie,
Tre Archi, Sant'Alvise, Orto, Fondamente
Nuove

Cannaregio, spreading along
the top west corner of Venice,
is a *sestiere* of contrasts, amply
reflected in its shops. Its main
route runs from outside the
railway station east to the
Rialto, and includes the Strada
Nova, a wide shopping street
containing some of the city's
best value and locally popular
shops. Behind its bustle lies
another world, where three
parallel canals are lined with
quiet *fondamente*, home to
small shops and artisan workshops. Stick to the main route
for serious shopping, but if
you're exploring, keep an eye
open for some highly traditional and individualistic shops
along the back-lying *calli*.

*Display in one of the Jewish
stores in the Ghetto*

THE STRADA NOVA ROUTE
Heading east from the station
the first stretch of the route is the
Lista di Spagna, noted for some
wonderfully tacky souvenir stalls.
Across the Canale di Cannaregio,
you're in the Rio Terrà San
Leonardo, where it's worth looking out for Mic-Mac, a good
women's fashion store, and Rizzo
bakery, its shelves piled high with
breads, rolls and Venetian cakes
and biscuits. The street has a
morning market, with excellent
fruit, vegetable and fish stalls,
and street vendors offering
umbrellas and plastic leggings for
those unlucky enough to arrive
during an *aqua alta* (high tide).
Further along, you'll find one of

Venice's best
health food and
natural cosmetic
shops, Cibele, on Campiello
Anconetta. The *campiello* turns
into the Rio Terrà della
Maddalena, home to some
trendy fashion shops, among
them Mori e Bozzi (▷ 198), with
its super-cool shoes, and Prima
Visione, a cutting edge shop that
stocks clothes by Miss Sixty,
Indian Rose and Energy. Cross
another couple of bridges and
you're in the Strada Nova proper,
with one of Venice's largest and
best-stocked supermarkets, Billa
(▷ 193), on your left just after
the bridge. There are good mid-
range men's shops here, as well
as the food stores serving the
local people. Campo Santi
Apostoli leads south towards the
Rialto, and it's this last stretch
that's the place to head for a
browse in Coin (▷ 199),
Venice's only department store;
the children and baby store
Prénatal is right opposite.

BACKSTREET CANNAREGIO
The main shopping areas to the
north of the main route lie on
either side of the Rio di San
Felice, the canal that runs along
the west end of the Strada Nova.
To the west is the Ghetto, home
to fascinating Jewish stores and
bookshops, including Laboratorio
Blu, Venice's only children's
bookstore, which carries a good
range of English publications.
Behind here the three canals of
the Misericordia, Sensa and
Sant'Alvise are edged with *fondamente* whose shops serve the
local inhabitants; worth a browse
for the sheer fascination of

what's
on offer. East
of San Felice, behind
Santi Apostoli, a through route
heads north to the Fondamente
Nuove. Here are more food
shops, bottle shops, vegetable
stalls and bookshops. Look out
for the wonderfully eccentric

*The Strada Nova has an excel-
lent fruit and vegetable market*

fishing tackle and bait store on
Salizzada Luigi Borzato.

WHERE TO EAT
BAR AI MIRACOLI
Campo Santa Maria Nova, Cannaregio
6066A
Tel 041 523 6048
**Enjoy snacks and drinks inside
or at tables in the square.**
🕐 Daily 6am–11pm

LA PERLA
Rio Terrà dei Franceschi, Cannaregio
4615
Tel 041 528 5175
**Rated as about the best pizze-
ria in town, with excellent beer
on tap.**
🕐 Sep–end Jul Thu–Tue 12–2, 7–9.45

The Islands

🚤 41,42, DM to Murano; LN to Murano and Burano; 1, 82 to the Lido

Most visitors to Venice spend a day visiting the lagoon islands, two of which, Murano and Burano, have been famous for centuries for their highly specialized products. Murano has been the heart of the city's glass industry since 1291, when it was moved here from the main islands, while Burano was renowned for its exquisite lace. Both glass and lace are on offer in vast quantities; if you want to buy, it's well worth doing some research before you shop. The resort-cum-residential island of the Lido has plenty of shops, so if you're having a day on the beach it might be worth factoring in a half hour or so to browse on your way back to the *vaporetto*.

Burano's lace is renowned throughout the world

MURANO

Murano has scores of glass shops and showrooms, many offering cheap imported glass, which, if you're really prepared to hunt among the junk, could make inexpensive gifts. The real thing is a totally different ball game; this is glass for serious collectors looking for a future heirloom piece, and prices reflect this. The serious production houses are not open to the public, so if you want to see glass-blowing, head for one of the bigger showrooms; Mazzega (▷ 195), on Fondamenta da Mula, or Formia (▷ 234), just before the Ponte Vivarini are both good choices. Some outstanding producers who admit a limited number of visitors to their factories include Fratelli Barbini (tel 041 739 777), which specializes in mirrors, and Elite Murano (tel 041 736 168), which makes truly beautiful goblets and reproductions of antique Venetian glass. Call ahead for an appointment if you're interested. Three major glass houses, Barovier e Toso, Carlo Moretti and Venini, share a showroom, Murano Collezioni, on Fondamenta Manin. Murano also has some small producers of innovative glass jewellery in striking designs—beads, earrings and necklaces that are a far cry from the garish products aimed at the mass market. Davide Penso (▷ 196) is among the best of these.

BURANO

Lace stalls and shops abound on Burano, but much of the lace, like Murano glass, is brought in from the Far East and can be found almost anywhere in Europe. Genuine Burano lace is on offer in a handful of shops, which often have lacemakers demonstrating their skills in the showrooms; Emilia (▷ 197) is among the best. Prices for real lace are extremely high, reflecting the expertise and long hours required for its production; the work imposes a huge strain on the eyesight. Less pricey are Burano's famous biscuits, deliciously crisp, thick cookies delicately flavoured with vanilla and citrus, which make an excellent gift.

THE LIDO

If you're keen on street markets, head for the Lido on a Tuesday morning, when the lagoon-facing waterfront of the Riviera Benedetto Marcello erupts into a weekly market, from 8.30am to around midday. Get

Murano glassware makes excellent souvenirs or mementoes

off the *vaporetto* and follow the local women to this lively strip of temporary commerce, where there's everything on offer from fruit and vegetables, cheese and meats, to clothes, household linen, hardware, plants and flowers, shoes and bags. Prices are competitive and low, and it's virtually guaranteed you'll be one of the very few foreigners there.

BUSA ALLA TORRE
Murano
See page 261.

AL GATTO NERO
Burano
See page 259.

WHAT TO DO

C   D   E   F

4

Canale delle Sacche

Canale delle Navi

Sant'Alvise

SACCA DI
S ALVISE

Rio d'Riformati

Fond d'Riformati

Fond d'Sacca S Girolamo

C llo d'Cantier

C llarga d'Penitenti

Fond Contarini

C Cee Nuove

C d'Forner

R S
Girolamo

ACCA DI S
GIROLAMO

Fond C Coletti

Rio di San Girolamo

Fond S Girolamo

C terà Farini

C Cee Nuove

Rio d'Sensa

C Rotonda

C Capitello

Sant'Alvise

5

Tre
Archi

C d'Forner

C tintoria

C d'Pegola

Fond d'capuccine

Campo
S d'Alvise

C Lorredan

Campo
S Giobbe

PONTE D
TRE ARCHI

Fond d'Battello

Rio d'Raffaello

C d'Chiovere
d'Girolamo

Rio d'Misericordia

Fond d'Ormesini

Rio d'Sensa

San Giobbe

C llo d'
Pazienza

Fond d'Cannaregio

Canale d'Cannaregio

Fond Savorgnan

CANNAREGIO

Campo
Ghetto
Nuovo

Cantina
ad Canton

6

C te
Cendon

C d'a corti

IL
GHETTO

Panificio
Volpe

Campo
Ghetto Nuovo

C d'ormesini

C dell'Aseo

C llo
Lombardo

Mori &
Bozzi

Parco di
Savorgnàn

Guglie

PONTE
D'GUGLIE

Rio Terra S Leonardo

Campo
S Leonardo

C llo
dell'Anconetta

7

C Carmelitani

C bril della dei Cavalli

Rio Terà Lista d'Spagna

Canal Grande

Rivi di Biasio

Scalzi

Ferrovia

STAZIONE FERROVIARIA
SANTA LUCIA

PONTE
DEGLI SCALZI

Fond Crotta

Campo
S Simeon
Grande

Riva d'Biasio

Campo
S Simeon
Profeta

Museo
di Storia
Naturale

San Giovanni
Decollato

Campo
S Stae

San Stae

Museo del
Tessuto e
del Costume

Palazzo
Mocenigo

San
Marcuola
Campo
S Marcuola

San Marcuola

TAZIONE
ROVIARIA
MERCI

Ferrovia

C llo d'
Comare

Ramo
Chiovereto

San Giacomo
dell'Orio

Campo San
Giacomo
dell'Orio

Campo
S M Mater
Domini

8

Giardino
Papadopoli

Campo d'Lana

Scuola Grande di
San Giovanni
Evangelista

Laberintho

Balocoloc

SAN POLO

San Nicolò
da Tolentino

Campo di
S Agostin

Campo d'
Tolentino

Archivio
di Stato

Santa Maria
Gloriosa dei
Frari

Campo
dei Frari

Gilberto
Penzo

San Polo

Campo
San Polo

ColorCasa

9

San
Rocco

Scuola Grande
di San Rocco

Ideauomo

Tragicomica

Museo Casa
Carlo Goldoni

C   D   E   F

Tonolo

San
Pantalon

G

4

5

5

6

K

L

Cimitero

Cimitero

Ísola di
San Michele

6

7

8

9

185

Madonna dell'Orto

C llo
Piave

QUARTIERE
GRIMANI

Madonna
dell'Orto

Sacca della
Misericordia

Canale delle Fondamenta Nuove

Canale d'Misericordia

Fondamente
Nuove

Gesuiti

Campo
del Gesuiti

Gianni
Basso

Campo
S Marziale

Ca'
Pesaro

Canal
Grande

Ca' d'Oro

Campo
S Felice

Ca' d'Oro

Santi Apostoli

Campo
Santi
Apostoli

Rio di Santa Apostoli

Campo
S Canzian

Cpl S
Cresetta

Campo
S Maria
dei Miracoli

Santa Maria
dei Miracoli

Campo
S Maria Nova

Santa Maria
dei Miracoli

Campiello
Widman

Pescheria

Campo
di Pescaria

Campo
Beccarie

Mercato di Rialto

Drogheria
Mascari

Casa del
Parmigiano

Macelleria Rialto
Chinellato e Dinon

San Giovanni
Elemosinario

San Cassiano

Campo
S Cassiano

Campo
Rialto
Nuovo

La Cantina

Francis
Model

Hibiscus

Campo
S Aponal

Campo
S Silvestro

San
Silvestro

PONTE
DI RIALTO

San Giovanni
Crisostomo

Ballarin

Coin

Vivaldi
Store

Buosi

San
Marina

Rosa
Salva

Santi Giovanni
e Paolo

Campo Santi
Giovanni
e Paolo

Santi Giovanni
e Paolo

Campo di
S Marina

Rialto

Riva di Vin

Calzature
Casella

Bata

La Perla

Italo
Mariani

Domus

Golden
Point

Diesel

Calzoleria

San
Salvador

Furla

Al Duca di Aosta

Sergio
Rossi

Santa Maria
della Fava

Campo
S Antonio S Lio

Campo
Santa Maria
Formosa

Santa Maria
Formosa

Fondazione
Querini
Stampalia

Mistero

Canal Grande

G

H

J

San Silvestro
Campo S Silvestro
San Silvestro
Rialto
G
Riva d vin
Rio d Fontego
Calzature Casella
Buosi
H
Campo S Lio
C Spezier
Bissa
Rio d Spezier
C d Fava
Rocca
C d Stagneri
Mercerie e salizzeria
C Ballotte
Salizz S Lio
C M Nuovo
C d Paradiso
J
Rio d Tette
Campo Santa Maria Formosa
C larga S Lore
Borgoloco S Lore
9
La Perla
Bata
Italo Mariani
San Salvador
Golden Point
Furla
Al Duca di Aosta
Santa Maria della Fava
C C d Fava
Santa Maria Formosa
C te d Paradiso
C Arca
Rio d Tera
Domus
Sergio Rossi
Diesel
Calzoleria La Parigina
San Zulian
Marchini
Fondazione Querini Stampalia
C d Pozzo Roverso
Mistero
C d Pre
Campo S Benedetto
Lellabella
Italosport
Paul & Shark
Bevilacqua
Libreria Studium
Campo S Filippo e Giacomo
C Figher
Campo S Provolo
Campo S Zaccaria
Anticlea Antiquaria
Campo S Zaccaria
Pot Pourri
Testolini
SAN MARCO
Rolando Segalin
Studio Genninger
Caffè Quadri
Museo Diocesano d'Arte Sacra
PONTE DEI SOSPIRI
PONTE DEL VIN
Ottica Urbani
Museo Correr
Pauly
Piazza San Marco
Caffè Florian
Piazzetta San Marco
Palazzo Ducale
PONTE DELLA PAGLIA
Riva degli Schiavoni
San Zaccaria
Venetia Studium
Camiceria San Marco
Teatro La Fenice
Bottega Veneta
Giardini ex Reali
APT
San Marco
Bevilacqua
Santa Maria del Giglio
Giglio
Vallaresso
11
Grande
Salute
C Abbazia
Santa Maria della Salute
Campo d Salute
Fond Dogana alla Salute
Dogana di Mare
Punta della Dogana
Fond Zattere ai Saloni
Bacino
Campo S Giorgio
San Giorgio
San Giorgio Maggiore
12
Campo Nani e Barbaro
Fond S Giovanni
Canale della Grazia
Zitelle
Fond d zitelle
13
QUARTIERE CAMPO DI MARTE
Fond d Croce
Fond d Croce
C d Gran
C dell'Adio Madona
R d Squero
C d Garibaldo
C Campielo
C llo Ospizio
C Esterna
C d Fonderia
C larga d Cooperativa
14

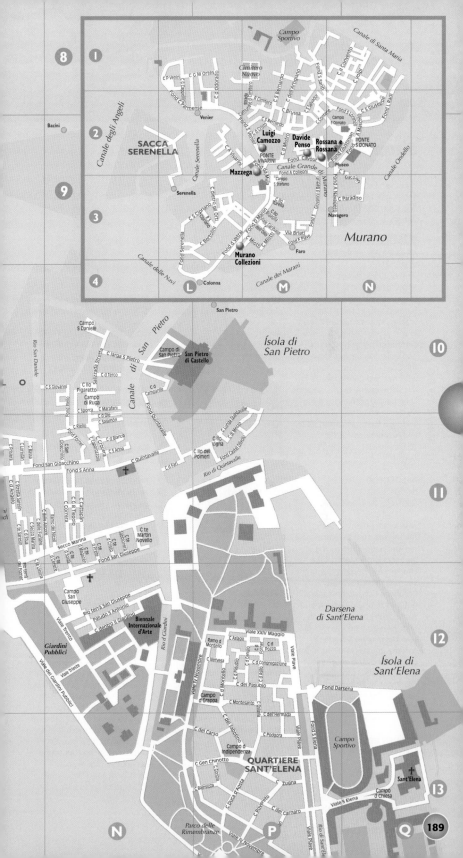

Shopping Directory

This selection of shops, arranged by theme, includes some of Venice's top fashion stores and specialist food stores, plus shops selling gifts, glass, jewellery and paper and leather goods.
See pages 184–189 for shopping locator maps.
See page 200 for chain store chart.
See page 288 for clothing sizes.

See pages 184–189 for shopping locator maps.
See page 200 for chain store chart.
See page 288 for clothing sizes.

ACCESSORIES AND MASKS

ARABESQUE BARBIERI
Map 188 K9
Ponte dei Greci, Castello 3403
Tel 041 522 8177
Elegant little Arabesque Barbieri sells nothing but scarves, stoles and pashminas in silk, wool, cashmere and a wonderful range of colours and styles; all tracked down by the English-speaking owner, who has excellent contacts in the silk-weaving towns around Lake Garda. Scarves for dressing up, keeping you warm and adding a touch of individuality and luxury to any outfit.
🕐 Mon–Sat 10–1, 3.30–7.30 🚤 San Zaccaria

BALOCOLOC
Map 184 F8
Calle Longa, Santa Croce 2134
Tel 041 524 0551
www.balacoloc.com
All the hats sold here are original and handmade by the owner, Silvana Martin, who changes her designs to suit the season. There are lovely brimmed hats, doge-like knitted hats in bright designs and some pretty berets. You can take your time and have a real rummage while Silvana sits making up her creations in the background. The shop also stocks costumes for the Carnevale at better prices than some of the more well-known shops.
🕐 Mon–Sat 9–7.30 🚤 San Silvestro

GOLDEN POINT
Map 185 G9
Mercerie, San Marco 4944
Tel 041 241 3687
www.goldenlady.it
This outlet for Golden Lady hosiery has tights (panty hose), stockings, socks and underwear in a huge range of styles and designs. Although more expensive than major UK outlets the quality and value are excellent. You will also find branches in Piazza San Marco and Marco Polo Airport.
🕐 Mon–Sat 10–7, Sun 10.30–6.30 🚤 Rialto

Mask designs are rooted in Venetian history

HIBISCUS
Map 185 G9
Ruga Rialto, San Polo 1060–61
Tel 041 520 8889
A rainbow of hot Indian colours shines in the great selection of ethnically inspired scarves, jackets, bags and jewellery in this tempting store, a wonderful, if expensive, contrast to the vast number of cheap glass and mask shops in this area. The clothes are well cut and comfortable, and the stock changes continually.
🕐 Mon–Sat 9.30–7.30, Sun 11–7 🚤 San Silvestro

LELLABELLA
Map 187 F9
Calle della Mandola, San Marco 3718
Tel 041 522 5152
Lellabella has everything the keen knitter could need, from 2- and 4-ply to the most luxurious angora, cashmere and silks. Quirky yarns with fur trim, spangles and lurex thread are also on offer, along with embroidery silks, knitting needles and patterns.
🕐 Daily 9.30–7.30, closed Sun Jul–Aug 🚤 Sant'Angelo

MONDONOVO
Map 186 D10
Rio Terrà Canal, Dorsoduro 3063
Tel 041 528 7344
Venice's most famous *mascheraio* has been setting an example to other mask makers for decades with its enormous variety of traditional and modern masks, handmade on the premises from papier-mâché and beautifully gilded and painted.
🕐 Mon–Sat 9.30–6.30 🚤 Ca' Rezzonico

OTTICA URBANI
Map 187 G10
Frezzeria, San Marco 1280
Tel 041 522 4140
www.otticaurbani.com
If you're looking for a pair of glasses without a designer label attached to them but still stylish, Ottica Urbani has its own range which includes a pair designed by Le Corbusier and some styles that fold up into a smart little box. Excellent value, and it can turn round orders in a day or so.
🕐 Mon–Sat 9.30–1.30, 3.30–7.30 🚤 San Marco (Vallaresso)

LA PERLA
Map 185 G9
Campo San Salvador, San Marco 4828
Tel 041 522 6459
www.laperla.com
If Venice is the most romantic city in the world, make sure you are wearing the most romantic lingerie. The name speaks for itself: exquisite pieces made from the most sumptuous materials. Some night- and swimwear are also available, and the staff are helpful and discreet.
🕐 Mon–Sat 10–7.30 🚤 Rialto

RISUOLA TUTTO DI GIOVANNI DITTURA
Map 186 E11
Calle Nuova Sant'Agnese, Dorsoduro 871
Tel 041 523 1163
One of Dorsoduro's last traditional neighbourhood shoe stores specializes in *friulani*—jewel-bright velvet and silk slippers with bicycle-tyre soles. Prices for these truly Venetian souvenirs are astonishingly cheap (from €15) for the quality. They also sell wellies and waders during the months of *acqua alta* (high water).
🕐 Mon–Sat 9–7.30, Sun 10–6
🚤 Accademia

TRAGICOMICA
Map 186 E9
Calle dei Nomboli, San Polo 2800
Tel 041 721 102
www.tragicomica.it
Superb handmade masks, created by an artist trained at Venice's Accademia delle Belle Arti, echo the 18th-century heyday of Carnevale. Look out for Harlequins, Columbines and pantaloons, the plague doctor and some imaginative mythological masks.
🕐 Mon–Sat 10–7 🚤 San Tomà

BOOKS, STATIONERY AND GIFTS

APT
Map 187 H10
Palazzetto Selva, Giardinetti Reali, San Marco 2
Tel 041 529 8711

You can pick up tourist information and book tickets at this branch of the tourist information service, but its chief draw is the excellent selection of guidebooks, maps, picture books of Venice, videos, tapes, CDs and DVDs, plus foreign-language reading matter and better-than-average souvenirs.
🕐 Daily 10–6 🚤 San Marco (Vallaresso)

BAC ART STUDIO
Map 186 E11
San Vio, Dorsoduro 862
Tel 041 522 8171
www.bacart.com
For some stunning photos of Venice to take home and prove

Browsing at a pavement (sidewalk) stall outside a bookshop

to people that it really does look dreamlike, Bac Art Studio has an impressive range. There are also framed prints of original art, as well as stationery and calendars.
🕐 Mon–Sat 9–1, 2.30–6
🚤 Accademia

DOMUS
Map 185 G9
Calle dei Fabbri, San Marco 4746
Tel 041 522 6259
This store sells everything for the home and kitchen—all with a truly Italian style. Choose from china and glass, kitchen gadgets and storage jars and a great range of Italian essentials such as coffee makers, ice-

cream makers, electric cheese graters and juicers.
🕐 Mon–Sat 9.30–7.30, closed lunch 1–2 Mon and Sat 🚤 Rialto

EBRÛ
Map 186 F10
Campo Santo Stefano, San Marco 3471
Tel 041 523 8830
www.albertovallese-ebru.com
Alberto Vallese was a front-runner in the reinvention of beautiful paper marbling in Venice, and his products are still the best—dozens of shapes and sizes of notebooks, folders, photo frames, boxes and albums come in a choice of marbled or stamped paper in a huge variety of colours. Superb value for top-quality products.
🕐 Mon–Sat 10–1.30, 2.30–7.30, Sun 11–6 🚤 Accademia

GIANNI BASSO
Map 185 H7
Calle del Fumo, Cannaregio 5306
Tel 041 523 4681
Going into Gianni Basso's *stampatore* will take you back in time. The huge old printing presses are still in action, making business cards for people all over the world. Gianni has resisted change—he doesn't have a fax or website and takes order by post only. He also sells beautiful lithographs of Venice then and now.
🕐 Mon–Fri 8.30–12.30, 2.30–6.30, Sat 8.30–12.30 🕐 Fondamente Nuove

GILBERTO PENZO
Map 184 E9
Calle Seconda dei Saoneri, San Polo 2681
Tel 041 719 372
www.veniceboats.com
Gilberto's slavishly academic yet still practical approach to re-creating Venetian boats in miniature, including gondolas, is respected the world over. His crowded workshop is fascinating and you can buy models of classic Venetian vessels of all sizes, including inexpensive kits to build yourself when you get home.
🕐 Mon–Sat 10–1, 4–7.30 🚤 San Tomà

LEGATORIA PIAZZESI
Map 187 F10
Campiello Feltrina, San Marco 2511
Tel 041 522 1202
The last remaining paper shop in Venice uses its block and marbled papers for book-binding, photo frames, waste-paper baskets and lots more. It's not cheap, but you can buy single sheets, lovely enough to frame.
⊙ Mon–Sat 10–1, 4–7.30 🚤 Santa Maria del Giglio

LIBRERIA STUDIUM
Map 187 H10
Calle Canonica, San Marco 337C
Tel 041 522 2382
In addition to its wide selection of works on Venice, travel books and English-language paperbacks, this shop stocks the ultimate Venetian street index: *Calli, Campielli e Canali* (published by Edizioni Helvetia) a street-map guide that shows every *sestiere* number—you need never be lost again. Fittingly, for a shop just behind San Marco, the back room is crammed with religious works, icons and prayer books.
⊙ Mon–Sat 9–7.30, Sun 10–2 🚤 San Zaccaria

LIBRERIA TOLETTA E TOLETTA STUDIO
Map 186 D11
Calle Toletta, Dorsoduro 1214
Tel 041 523 2034
The Libreria is an excellent bookshop with a huge range of coffee-table books on Venice, guidebooks, Italian classics, art and cookery books—and they're all offered with a 20 to 40 per cent discount. Across the *calle*, the Studio has more art books, posters, T-shirts and small gifts suitable for souvenirs.
⊙ Mon–Sat 9.30–1, 3–7.30; also Oct–May Sun 3.30–7.30 🚤 Ca' Rezzonico

LIVIO DE MARCHI
Map 186 E10
Salizzada San Samuele, San Marco 3157A
Tel 041 528 5694
Wooden sculpture for the 21st century is showcased here, with immensely tactile carvings of everything from crumpled jeans and creased shirts to books, paintbrushes and tableware. It's expensive, unique and beautiful.
⊙ Mon–Fri 9–12.30, 1.30–6; Sat by appointment 🚤 San Samuele

RIGATTIERI
Map 186 F10
Calle dei Frati, San Marco 3535–36
Tel 041 277 1223

Libreria Studium is a bookworm's delight

This place stocks the best of Italian ceramics. Decorative plates, vases and umbrella stands, pyramids of fruit and vegetables, elegant pieced-work baskets and tureens are all for sale, along with tiny and affordable take-home gifts.
⊙ Mon–Sat 9–1, 3–8 🚤 Sant'Angelo

SPAZIO LEGNO
Map 186 F13
Fondamenta San Giacomo, Giudecca 213B
Tel 041 277 5505
Saverior Pastor, master *marangon* (oar-maker) specializes in carving the elaborate walnut *forcole*, gondola rowlocks. Each is unique to a

particular gondolier, and the sinuous lines have made these pieces *objets d'art* in their own right. If your budget won't stretch this far, the workshop sells bookmarks and postcards.
⊙ Mon–Fri 8.30–12.30, 1.30–5.30 🚤 Redentore

TESTOLINI
Map 187 G10
Fondamenta Orseolo, San Marco 1744–8
Tel 041 522 9265
Venice's top stationer has a huge range of goods with Italian style, well worth a browse for quirky folders, briefcases, files and thousands of pens and papers. Art supplies, incuding the excellent value Venezia watercolours, are on offer in the annexe down the street, and Testolini also sells computers and accessories.
⊙ Mon–Sat 9–7 🚤 San Marco (Vallaresso), Rialto

VIVALDI STORE
Map 185 H8
Fontego dei Tedeschi, San Marco 5537
Tel 041 522 1343
You'll find every example of 18th-century Venetian music in this stylish store, with the accent on the city's most popular composer, Antonio Vivaldi. CDs and tapes are the main draw, but you will also find sheet-music and scores, T-shirts, videos and other music-orientated souvenirs such as mouse mats, mugs, trays and table mats.
⊙ Daily 10–7 🚤 Rialto

FOOD AND DRINK
BALLARIN
Map 185 H8
Salizzada San Giovanni Crisostomo, Cannaregio 5794
Tel 041 528 5273
This excellent *pasticceria* has a superb range of cakes and pastries, to sample with a cup of coffee or take-away. It also makes delicious chocolates and sweets—look out for the chocolate-coated orange peel,

WHAT TO DO

WHAT TO DO

SUPERMARKETS IN VENICE

If you're catering for yourself, or just want to pick up picnic supplies or a drink, it may be easier to head for a supermarket rather than struggle with non-English speakers in a traditional *alimentari* (general food store). Venice's supermarkets are hard to spot; the list below covers most city areas.

BILLA
Zattere
Dorsoduro 1491,
tel 041 5226187
Strada Nova
Cannaregio 3659,
tel 041 523 8046

Cannaregio
Fondamenta Contarini,
Cannaregio 3027,
tel 041 524 4786
Lido
Gran Viale, tel 041 526 2898

CO-OP
Santa Croce
Campo San Giacomo
dell'Orio, Santa Croce 1493,
tel 041 275 0218
Santa Croce
Fondamenta Santa Chiara
(Piazzale Roma),
tel 041 527 6639
Castello
Calle del Pistor, Castello
5989, tel 041 522 3415

Giudecca
Campiello Ferrando,
Giudecca, tel 041 528 7625
Murano
Riva Longa 27, Murano,
tel 041 527461

SMA
Dorsoduro
Campo Santa Margherita,
Dorsoduro 3112,
tel 041 522 6934

SU VE (SUPERMARCATO VENEZIANO)
Castello
Calle del Mondo Novo,
Castello 5811,
tel 041 522 9138

candied fruit and fresh cream chocolate truffles.
🕐 Mon–Sat 7.30–7.30, Sun 8–7
🚤 Rialto

LA CANTINA
Map 185 F8
Ruga Rialto (also known as Ruga Vecchio San Giovanni), San Polo 970A
Tel 041 523 5042
Even though it's more expensive than other wine shops in the outlying areas, you can get your empty bottled refilled from €2.50 per litre of red wine. A bottle of *prosecco* costs around €5. Credit cards not accepted.
🕐 Mon–Sat 9–1.20, 4–8 🚤 San Silvestro

CANTINA AD CANTON
Map 184 F6
Fondamenta degli Ormesini, Cannaregio 2678
Tel 041 713 129
This is a no-frills wineshop, where refills start at €1.90 per litre for something quite drinkable, such as Merlot, Tocai or Pinto Grigio. The location means cheaper prices, with a good bottle of *prosecco* for around €4. No credit cards accepted.
🕐 Mon–Sat 9.30–1, 4.30–8; Occasionally open Sun 🚤 Madonna dell'Orto

Shopping for food in the Rialto is a pleasurable experience

CASA DEL PARMIGIANO
Map 185 G8
Erberia, San Polo 214–15
Tel 041 520 6525
www.aliani-casadelparmigiano.it
A stone's throw from the main Rialto markets, this little family-run shop sells superb cheese, *salumeria* (delicatessen) from all over Italy and light-as-a-feather homemade fresh pasta. Locals consider this one of the best shops in Venice, so be prepared to queue. A number of cheeses and salamis are vacuum-packed, ideal for taking home.
🕐 Tue–Sat 8–1, 5–7.30, Mon 8–1
🚤 Rialto

DAI FRADEI
Piazza Baldassare Galuppi 380, Burano
Tel 041 735 630
Buranese biscuits are a traditional Venetian treat, and this well-stocked shop sells the whole range, all produced on the island. Browse the shelves, a cornucopia of pasta of all sorts, wines and liqueurs, and sample before you buy. Dai Fradei also produces its own excellent ice-cream in imaginative flavours—the pink grapefruit is truly refreshing on a hot day.
🕐 Daily 9–6.30 🚤 Burano

DROGHERIA MASCARI
Map 185 G8
Ruga Spezieri, San Polo 381–2
Tel 041 522 9762
www.imascari.com
On the 'street of spice merchants', this wonderful shop, crammed with interesting foods, spices, dried fruit and nuts, teas, coffees and sweets, also has nicely wrapped packets of dried mushrooms, jars of truffles, balsamic vinegar and beautiful biscuits. It's a great place to track down that take-home foodie souvenir, or even buy a jar of Frank Cooper's Oxford marmalade.
🕐 Mon–Tue, Thu–Sat 8–1, 4–7.30, Wed 8–1 🚤 Rialto

GOBBETTI
Map 186 D10
Rio Terrà Canal, Dorsoduro 3108B
Tel 041 528 9014

It's easy to miss Gobbetti's entrance, just past the Ponte dei Pugni. This is the home of the best chocolate mousse cake in town, and a number of other superb sweet creations. There are miniature examples of all the big cakes, so you can sample the full range—try the fruit mousses or the cream tarts, delicately flavoured with green tea or lime.

🕐 Mon–Sat 8.30–1.30, 3–7.30, Sun 8.30–1.30 🚢 Ca' Rezzonico

MACELLERIA RIALTO CHINELLATO E DINON
Map 185 G8
Calle Cesare Battisti, San Polo 92–93
Tel 041 522 2188

This excellent butcher has high-quality beef, veal and pork, but its real speciality is the beautifully boned and dressed pheasant, quail and guinea fowl, all ready to pop in the oven. You'll also find a great range of *svizzere* (interesting hamburgers) and *polpette* (meatballs), ideal for easy cooking.

🕐 Mon–Sat 7–1.30 🚢 Rialto

MARCHINI
Map 187 H9
Calle Spadaria, San Marco 676
Tel 041 522 9109
www.golosessi.com, www.fantasy-chocolate.com

Many Venetians rate this as the best *pasticceria*, and the selection of exquisitely decorated cakes, pastries and confectionary, all made with the highest-quality ingredients, takes most visitors' breath away. Pop in for a sugary mouthful, or buy a tray to take away—making sure to include a couple of *baute veneziane*, chocolates in the form of carnival masks. They make to order.

🕐 Wed–Mon 9–8 🚢 San Marco

MERCATO DI RIALTO
Map 185 G8
Ruga dei Orefici, San Polo

Traders have been selling their fruit, vegetables and other produce here for a thousand years. While much is shipped from the mainland, the colour, plumpness and taste of the goods is still far superior to what we're used to in supermarkets back home. Look out for the truly local produce from Sant'Erasmo, labelled 'San Rasmo' or 'nostranni'. No credit cards accepted.

🕐 Mon–Sat 8–1 🚢 Rialto

You'll be spoiled for choice at Pantagruelica

PANIFICIO VOLPE
Map 184 E6
Calle del Ghetto Vecchio, Cannaregio 1143
Tel 041 715 178

Panificio Volpe specializes in traditional unleavened Jewish bread and delicious pastries and confections, in a city not particularly renowned for its bread. This is one of the few really good Venetian bakeries, and its reputation is such that you'll have to get there really early if you want to see what's on offer. No credit cards accepted.

🕐 Mon–Sat 7–1.15, 4.30–7.30 🚢 Guglie

PANTAGRUELICA
Map 186 D10
Campo San Barnaba, Dorsoduro 2844
Tel 041 523 6766

Pantagruelica is arguably the finest food shop in Venice, offering the best produce from all over Italy, lovingly tracked down by the enthusiastic owner, who is happy to spend time talking about the food producers he patronizes. The emphasis is on quality, so expect to find organic produce heavily featured. It's highly recommended for its cheese, *salumeria*, oils, dried goods and fresh truffles in season.

🕐 Mon–Sat 9–8 🚢 Ca' Rezzonico

PESCHERIA
Map 185 G8
Fondamenta dell'Olio, San Polo

A visit to a fish market may not at first sight appeal to everyone, but the produce, atmosphere and location, right on the Grand Canal, make this one special. There are some real characters amongst the fishmongers, but it's the strange fish, inky squid and still-scuttling crabs that are the real stars. If you're buying, all stall holders will gut, slice and prepare your purchases for you, so all you have to do is put them straight into the pan. No credit cards accepted.

🕐 Tue–Sat 8–1 🚢 Rialto

ROSA SALVA
Map 185 J8
Campo Santi Giovanni e Paolo, Castello 6779
Tel 041 522 7949

This is a great place for those who need to stop for a sugar rush. Rosa Salva sells a huge range of cakes, chocolates and sweets; some for on-the-spot consumption and some to take home. The staff are very friendly, many Venetians rate their coffee the best in town, and prices are very reasonable at the bar. No credit cards accepted.

🕐 Mon–Sat 7.30–8.20, Sun 8.30–8.20 🚢 Ospedale

TONOLO
Map 186 D9
Calle San Pantalon, Dorsoduro 3764
Tel 041 523 7209
Tonolo is a great place for a quick cappuccino and brioche if you're en route from the Accademia to the Frari. Choose from light-as-air pastries and superb cakes to eat in or take away, or order ahead for special occasions. It makes excellent *fritelle* (doughnuts) during Carnevale and biscuit horsemen for St. Martin's Day in November.
🕒 Tue–Sat 7.45am–8.15pm 🚤 San Tomà

VIA IL MERCATO DI GARIBALDI
Map 188 M11
Via Giuseppe Garibaldi, Castello
This small but atmospheric market, just outside the north gates of the Via Garibaldi (gardens), sells fish, *salumeria* (cooked and cured meats), fruit and vegetables. If you are visiting the Museo Storico Navale or the Biennale, it is worth taking a look and enjoying a relatively tourist-free experience; if you're buying, prices are among the city's lowest.
🕒 Mon–Sat 8–1 🚤 Arsenale

VINARIA NAVE DE ORO
Map 186 D9
Campo Santa Margherita, Dorsoduro 3664
Tel 041 522 2693
Fill up your plastic water bottles or even a huge flask at this wine shop, popular with students. The staff are very friendly and willing to describe the wines on offer. It's a great place to find out about the latest evening offerings in the ever-buzzing Campo Santa Margherita. No credit cards accepted. There are other branches at Castello 5786B (Calle del Mondo Nuovo) and Cannaregio 1370 (Rio Terrà San Leonardo).
🕒 Tue–Sat 8.30–12.20 4.30–7.30, Mon 4.30–7.30 🚤 Ca' Rezzonico

VINO… E VINI
Map 188 K9
Fondamenta di Furlani, Castello 3301
Tel 041 521 0184
If you are unsure which kind of wines you should be taking home, ask the staff at Vino… e Vini. You'll get a detailed response and will come out of the shop with enough knowledge to impress your friends back home. You can get a Mionetto *prosecco* (considered the best) from €10. You can also fill up plastic bottles here from €4 and buy gourmet specialitites.
🕒 Mon–Sat 9–1, 5.30–8.30 🚤 San Zaccaria, Arsenale

Murano glassware can be both functional and beautiful

GLASS
LUIGI CAMOZZO
Map 189 M2 (inset)
Fondamenta Venier 3, Murano
Tel 041 736 875
Luigi Camozzo is one of Murano's true maestri, renowned for his engraving. His pieces are heavily textured, the glass incised and etched to resemble stone and marble. The shapes are simple and his pieces are true works of art; he also runs courses in glass engraving.
🕒 Mon–Fri 11–1.30, 2.30–6
🚤 Murano Venier

MAZZEGA
Map 189 M2 (inset)
Fondamenta da Mula 147, Murano
Tel 041 736 888
www.mazzega.it
This highly-regarded, old-established glass manufacturer produces excellent Venetian glass of all types. Visit on a weekday to see the demonstrations of chandelier production and glass sculpture.
🕒 Daily 9–4 🚤 Museo or Venier

MURANO COLLEZIONI
Map 189 L3 (inset)
Fondamenta Manin 1D, Murano
Tel 041 736 272
If you're looking seriously for modern glass, it's well worth a visit to browse the huge range and compare styles and prices. This outlet is run by three big names in the glass industry—Borovier e Toso, Carlo Moretti and Venini.
🕒 Daily 10.30–5.30, closed Sun Nov–Apr 🚤 Colonna

PAULY
Map 187 H10
Calle Larga San Marco, San Marco 4391A
Tel 041 520 9899
www.paulyglassfactory.com
Pauly is one of the best city-centre outlets for Murano glass, with the accent on modern design, clean lines and vivid colours. It also sells glass jewellery and some traditional pieces.
🕒 Mon–Fri 9.30–6, Sat–Sun 10–6
🚤 San Marco (Vallaresso)

ROSSANA E ROSSANA
Map 189 M2 (inset)
Riva Lunga 11, Murano
Tel 041 527 4076
www.ro-e-ro.com
This glassmaker produces some high quality, decorative pieces which combine centuries of tradition with graceful and clean modern and classical lines and many of the best Muranese techniques.
🕒 Daily 10–6 (5 in winter)
🚤 Murano Venier

WHAT TO DO

STUDIO GENNINGER
Map 187 G10
Calle dei Barcaroli, San Marco 1845
Tel 041 522 5565
Leslie Ann Genninger is grudgingly considered one of the master beadmakers in Venice—not bad for an American, and an American woman at that. She follows the rules in making her beads, but creates something altogether different.
🕐 Mon–Sat 10.30–6.30 🚢 San Marco (Vallaresso)

SUSANNA & MARINA SENT
Map 186 F11
Campo San Vio, Dorsoduro 669
Tel 041 520 8136
For a more contemporary take on Murano glass, Marina and Susanna Sent have funky vases, plates and jewellery that won't break the bank. They also have very interesting *lattimo* (milk glass) pebbles in a variety of hues that would look great just about anywhere.
🕐 Daily 10–6, closed Nov and Jan, Dec closed Sun and Tue, other days 11–6 🚢 Accademia

---

JEWELLERY

ANTICHITÀ
Map 186 E11
Calle Toletta, Dorsoduro 1195
Tel 041 522 3159
Beautiful antique beads and other jewellery, and a fine selection of small antiques, fabrics and lace. Choose your beads and have them made up on the spot.
🕐 Mon–Sat 10–1, 3.30–7.30 🚢 Accademia

ANTICLEA ANTIQUARIATO
Map 187 J10
Calle San Provolo, Castello 4719A
Tel 041 528 6946
This tiny treasure house overflows with cabinets and drawers full of antique beads, and is hung with quirky antiques. You can buy ready-made pieces or wait while they fashion beads of your choice into earrings, bracelets and necklaces.
🕐 Daily 10–7.15 🚢 San Zaccaria

ANTIQUARIATO OGGETISTICA CLAUDIA CANESTRELLI
Map 186 F11
Campiello Barbaro, Dorsoduro 364A
Tel 041 522 7072
Tucked away on one of Dorsoduro's prettiest *campi* is Claudia's little shop, selling old prints, lamps and ornaments, though the chief draw are the exquisite 18th-century style earrings which she makes. Each pair is different, but most incorporate pearl drops, tiny emeralds and rubies and lustre beads, at surprisingly good prices. She gives a 10 per cent discount for cash.
🕐 Daily 10–12.30, 3–6 🚢 Salute

Venice has a fine tradition of handmade jewellery

ANTIQUUS
Map 186 F10
Calle delle Botteghe, San Marco 3131
Tel 041 520 6395
If you'd like to pick up an antique piece, Antiquus has a beautiful collection of gold and silver jewellery from other eras, including lovely brooches and earrings in the shape of Moors' heads, and fish pendants. It also sells paintings, furniture and silver.
🕐 Tue–Sun 10–12, 3.30–7.30, Mon 3.30–7.30 🚢 Sant'Angelo

DAVIDE PENSO
Map 189 M2 (inset)
Fondamenta Rivalonga 48, Murano
Tel 041 527 4634
www.davidepenso.com
Davide Penso was among the first of the Murano glassmakers to produce innovative, immensely wearable glass jewellery with a modern twist. Since 1997 he has launched four different collections of necklaces, earrings and bracelets using old techniques and incorporating gold and tinted glass in a totally new way. He also produces traditional *millefiore* beads made up into earrings and necklaces at very good prices.
🕐 May–Sep daily 10–1.30, 2.30–6; Oct–Apr daily 9–1, 2.30–5 🚢 Murano Venier

ETHNOS
Map 186 F10
Campo Santo Stefano, San Marco 2958
Tel 041 528 9988
This is a great place to pick up more modern takes on Venetian glass beads. The prices are very reasonable and for those who believe in the power of stones, the chunky rose quartz and amethyst necklaces are sure to unleash some positive energy. Bright handbags and scarves are also sold.
🕐 Tue–Sat 10–1, 4–7.30, Mon 4–7.30 🚢 San Samuele, Sant'Angelo

LABERINTHO
Map 184 F8
Calle del Scaleter, San Polo 2236
Laberintho, up a very narrow *calle*, is a great find. The young designers work on site making unique and inspired pieces featuring inlaid stones set into rings, earrings and necklaces. Prices are not too high, considering the originality and craftsmanship of the jewellery.
🕐 Tue–Sat 9.30–1, 2.30–7 🚢 San Tomà

PERLE E DINTORNI
Map 187 F10
Calle della Mandola (Della Cortesia), San Marco 3740
Tel 041 520 5068
It's easy to spend hours in this shop, choosing beads for a necklace. However, the staff are on hand to help you combine colours and effects which a novice would never have dreamed of. There is also ready-made jewellery in a range of prices.
🕐 Mon–Sat 9.30–7.30, Sun noon–7
🚤 Sant'Angelo

LACE, LINENS AND FABRICS
ANNELIE
Map 186 D10
Calle Lunga Santa Barbara, Dorsoduro 2748
Tel 041 520 3277
If you can't get to Burano, this shop has some lovely antique lace inlays. It also sells authentic little lace-trimmed tablecloths, sheets and bedclothes at affordable prices, along with very special baby clothes and dreamy nightwear.
🕐 Mon–Sat 9.30–12.30, 4–7.30
🚤 Ca' Rezzonico

BEVILACQUA
Map 187 H10, 187 F10
Fondamenta della Canonica, San Marco 337B and Campo Santa Maria del Giglio, San Marco 2520
Tel 041 528 7581 and 041 241 0662
www.luigi-bevilacqua.com
The big Italian fashion houses, like Dolce & Gabbana, come to Bevilacqua for their traditionally made Venetian brocades, velvets, taffetas and damasks, still produced on 17th-century looms. The curtain ties, swags and key tassels make wonderful souvenirs.
🕐 Mon–Fri 9.30–7, Sat 10–4.30
🚤 San Zaccaria, Santa Maria del Giglio

COLORCASA
Map 184 F9
Campo San Polo, San Polo 1989–91
Tel 041 523 6071
This shop is crammed with some of the most sumptuous decorating fabrics you can imagine—silks, brocades and figured velvets are for sale by the length or made up into cushions, drapes and bags. Silk key tassels and curtain swags are equally tempting, and ColorCasa stocks wonderfully warm *trapunti* (quilted bedcovers) in vivid fabrics.
🕐 Mon–Sat 9.30–1, 3–7.30 🚤 San Tomà

EMILIA
Piazza Baldassare Galuppi 205, Burano
Tel 041 735 299
The pick of Burano's lace outlets has some exquisite examples of real Burano lace, used to trim table linen, bedcovers, underwear and

Bevilacqua's old 17th-century looms are still in action

handkerchiefs. Prices are high, with a small mat retailing at around €120. The shop also organizes demonstrations of lace-making, so it's worth popping in to see the work in progress.
🕐 Daily 9–6.30 🚤 Burano

GAGGIO
Map 186 F10
Calle delle Botteghe, San Marco 3441–51
Tel 041 522 8574
www.gaggio.it
Sumptuous hand-printed silk velvets and lush fabrics are used for wall-hangings and cushions and incorporated into bags, hats and scarves,

renowned among dressmakers and designers. It's obviously expensive, but off-cuts or small lengths are available—expect to pay around €150 a metre.
🕐 Mon–Fri 10.30–1, 4–7, Sat 10.30–1. Closed Sun 🚤 San Samuele

TROIS
Map 186 F10
Campo San Maurizio, San Marco 2666
Tel 041 522 2905
This is the only place in Venice where you can still buy original Fortuny fabrics, and at better prices than in the UK and US. It also stocks small antiques and specializes in beadwork.
🕐 Mon–Sat 10–1, 5–7.30 🚤 Santa Maria del Giglio

VENETIA STUDIUM
Map 187 G10
Calle Larga XXII Marzo, San Marco 2403; Calle delle Ostreghe, San Marco 2428; Merceria San Zulian, San Marco 723
Tel 041 522 9281, 041 520 0505, 041 522 9859
Fortuny-style pleated silk and figured velvet scarves, pillows and bags in a huge range of heavenly tones are available at this far-from-cheap and very tempting Venetian speciality store. They also make Fortuny-style lamps and have branches throughout the city.
🕐 Mon–Sat 9.30–7.40, Sun 10.30–6
🚤 San Marco (Vallaresso)

LEATHER GOODS AND SHOES
BATA
Map 185 H9
Mercerie, San Marco 4979A
Tel 041 522 9766
www.bata.it
Deep in San Marco's busy, sprawling Mercerie district, this modern, stylish Italian emporium offers quality leather items, from shoes to smart, understated jackets. There is also an excellent women's section with lots of accessories. Staff are attentive and there are plenty of places to sit down and take a breather.
🕐 Mon–Sat 9.30–7.30, Sun 10.30–7
🚤 Rialto

BOTTEGA VENETA
Map 187 G10
Calle Vallaresso, San Marco 1337
Tel 041 522 8489
www.bottegaveneta.com
An elegant shop, famed throughout the world for its superior leather goods. This is an opportunity to get your hands on the new lines while staying in the Veneto region or to indulge yourself with a belt, bag or wallet in super-soft leather. A great place to buy classic gifts that are practical and enduring.
◉ Mon–Sat 10–7.30, Sun 11–7
🚤 San Marco (Vallaresso)

CALZATURE CASELLA
Map 185 G9
Campo San Salvador, San Marco 5048
Tel 041 522 8848
In the world of shoes, this is a Venetian institution. It's particularly popular with Japanese visitors, who come for its quality. The emphasis is on classic styles, although the occasional twist on the old appears each season.
◉ Mon–Sat 10–7 🚤 Rialto

CALZOLERIA LA PARIGINA
Map 187 H9
Merceria San Zulian, San Marco 727
Tel 041 523 1555
Funky footwear fills this attractive outlet in the Mercerie shopping district. Leading brands represented include Clarks, Camper and Timberland. Lesser-known makes such as Husky, John Lobb and Vicini are well worth checking out. Another branch is located near the Scala di Bovolo at San Marco 4336.
◉ Mon–Sat 9.30–7.30, Sun 11–1, 1.30–6.30 🚤 San Marco

FRANCIS MODEL
Map 185 G8
Ruga Rialto/del Ravano, San Polo 773A
Tel 041 521 2889
Tired of the mass-produced, generic designer goods on sale around the San Marco shopping district? This atmospheric shop, which has been in business for over 40 years, might be right up your *calle*. Family *artigiani* produce wonderful handbags, briefcases and elegant portfolios, though, naturally, limited edition, high-quality, hand-crafted goods come at a price.
◉ Mon–Sat 9.30–7.30, Sun 10–6
🚤 Rialto

FURLA
Map 185 G9
Mercerie del Capitello, San Marco 4954
Tel 041 523 0611
Unusual leather bags for women are the lifeblood of this alluring shop. Exotic colours and designs give the goods a unique, vibrant

Hand-crafted designer handbags from Francis Model

character. There is also a good selection of gloves, belts and other accessories for women.
◉ Mon–Sat 9.30–7.30, Sun 10.30–7
🚤 Rialto

ITALO MARIANI
Map 185 G9
Calle del Teatro, San Marco 4775
Tel 041 523 5580
This shop, popular with locals, carries an excellent range of stylish Italian shoes, boots, bags and briefcases at sensible prices—and they're even better if you hit the January sales.
◉ Mon–Sat 9.30–1, 3–7.30, Sun 10.30–6.30, but closed Sun Nov–Apr
🚤 Rialto

MORI & BOZZI
Map 184 F6
Rio Terrà Maddalena, Cannaregio 2367
Tel 041 715 261
Visit this friendly shop down the Strada Nova if you like your shoe styles a little different from the norm – and cutting edge at that. There are many unusual shapes by trendy names, and budget shoppers can take their pick of designer copies.
◉ Daily 9.30–12.30, 3.30–7.30
🚤 San Marcuola

ROLANDO SEGALIN
Map 187 G9
Calle dei Fuseri, San Marco 4365
Tel 041 522 2115
Since its foundation over 50 years ago, this quirky little store has been creating made-to-order shoes and carrying out repairs. To see what Venetian style can be all about, take your time window-shopping even if you don't buy.
◉ Mon–Fri 10–12.30, 3.30–7.30, Sat 10–12.30 🚤 Rialto

SERGIO ROSSI
Map 187 H9
Mercerie San Zulian, San Marco 705
Tel 041 241 3615
www.sergiorossi.com
If it's leather shoes you're after, this is the place to gauge the latest trends, with the help of the exceptionally friendly and welcoming staff. Men's and women's ranges are extensive and should cater for most tastes.
◉ Mon–Thu 10–1, 2–7, Fri and Sat 10–7, Sun 2–6.30 🚤 San Marco

MEN'S FASHION
BUOSI
Map 185 G9
Campo San Bartolomeo, San Marco 5382
Tel 041 520 8567
Discerning Venetian professionals come here for fine tailoring and ready-to-wear clothes by Italy's top men's designers. Everything here is classical and high quality, from fine lawn and cotton shirts

through cashmere and lambswool sweaters to suits and overcoats for both winter and summer. Alterations are done in two to three days.
🕐 Mon–Sat 9–7.30, Sun 10–7
🚉 Rialto

CAMICERIA SAN MARCO
Map 187 G10
Calle Valleresso, San Marco 1340
Tel 041 522 1432
This wonderful shop specializes in all manner of shirts. Top-name brands are well represented, and there's a good range of accessories, including ties. If you fancy something original, then choose from the colourful array of natural fibre fabrics, or have a shirt, pyjamas or bathrobe tailored for you.
🕐 Mon–Sat 9.30–7, closed Sun
🚉 San Marco (Vallaresso)

AL DUCA DI AOSTA
Map 185 H9
Mercerie, San Marco 4922–46
Tel 041 522 0733
This is the place to get popular, classic and smart men's clothes beloved of Italian men, including the latest wares by Burini, Kiton and Fay. International labels with a conservative twist, such as Burberry, are also available.
🕐 Mon–Sat 10–7.30, Sun 11–1, 2–4.30
🚉 Rialto

IDEAUOMO
Map 186 E9
Campo San Tomà, San Polo 2817
Tel 041 520 5030
Family-run Ideauomo is very popular with local men, who value its well-tailored, classic clothes. It sells everything from suits and overcoats to casual wear and sweaters, changing the stock regularly. Prices are good and alterations will be ready in two to three days.
🕐 Mon–Sat 10–5.30
🚉 San Tomà

La Fenice Atelier specializes in embroidered linen and lingerie

ITALOSPORT
Map 187 G10
Campo Manin, San Marco 4254
Tel 041 520 0696
The superb selection of quality sportswear includes fashionista-friendly labels such as Di Kappa and Fila. Pick up the latest official Juve, Milan, Roma, Venezia and Internazionale *calcio* (football) kits here.
🕐 Mon–Sat 9.15–7.30, closed Sun
🚉 Rialto, Sant'Angelo

PAUL & SHARK
Map 187 H9
Mercerie, San Marco 4844
Tel 041 523 7733
Paul & Shark is one of Italy's big names for casual

menswear, and you'll find an excellent choice of smart, laid-back classic clothing here. It is particularly noted for well-tailored, comfortable trousers (pants) and sports clothes.
🕐 Mon–Sat 10–7.30, Sun 11–7
🚉 Rialto

WOMEN'S FASHION
COIN
Map 185 H8
Salizzada San Giovanni Grisostomo, Cannaregio 5787
Tel 041 520 3581
Coin, one of Italy's best department store chains, has everything a woman could possibly want in the shape of separates, suits, coats, jackets and accessories at great prices, and also sells homewares and linen. The staff win the prize for being among the most engaging shop assistants in Venice. Visit Coin Beauty at Campo Santa Luca for endless beauty bargains.
🕐 Mon–Sat 9.30–7.30, Sun 11–7.30
🚉 Rialto

DIESEL
Map 185 G9
Calle dei Fabbri, San Marco 4664
Tel 041 241 1937
Diesel offers cutting edge, club-wise fashion that's made its mark all over Europe. There's a huge range and lower prices here in the Veneto, its base, than you'll find back home.
🕐 Mon–Sat 10–7.30, Sun 11–7
🚉 Rialto

LA FENICE ATELIER
Map 186 F10
Calle dei Frati, San Marco 3537
Tel 041 523 0578
If you're looking for beautiful lingerie and table linen, this is a good place to start. Cristina Linassi has nightgowns and dressing gowns in gossamer fine cotton and smooth linens, all exquisitely finished with lace or embroidery, while table linens come in rich damasks.
🕐 Daily 10.30–7.30
🚉 Sant'Angelo

WHAT TO DO

LAURA CROVATO
Map 186 F10
Calle delle Botteghe, San Marco 2995
Tel 041 520 4170
This is basically a second-hand shop, although by the prices and, admittedly, the quality of the stock, you'd never know it. You can still pick up some unusual bits and pieces, particularly costume jewellery and bags.
🕐 Mon 3.30–7.30, Tue–Sat 11–1, 3.30–7.30 🚤 Sant'Angelo

MANEKI – NEKO
Map 186 F10
Campo Sant'Angelo, San Marco 3820
Tel 041 520 3340
Crisp cottons and linens are used here to make beautiful, easy-to-wear shirts and blouses, ranging from strictly tailored classic designs to casual, ideal for dressing up or down. It also stocks pretty nightgowns and bathrobes. Everything is designed and made by the owner, who has been supplying well-heeled Venetians for over 20 years.
🕐 Mon–Sat 10–7.30, Sun 11–7 🚤 Sant'Angelo

MISTERO
Map 187 J9
Ruga Giuffa, Castello 4755
Tel 041 522 7797

Mistero has three shops next to one another: one sells items for the home, another sells young fashion and the third ladies' clothes (including bigger sizes). The ladies' shop—Atelier—has amazing tops, trousers (pants), dresses and scarves imported from India, with a huge selection of colours to chose from.
🕐 Mon–Sat 9.30–12.30, 3.30–7.30, Jun–Aug also Sun 10.30–7.30 🚤 San Zaccaria

POT POURRI
Map 187 G10
Ramo dei Fuseri, San Marco 1811A
Tel 041 241 0990
www.potpourri.it/

A stylish hat to set off your designer clothes

The layout of this shop is just like a house, with clothes strewn on seats and hangers on the backs of doors. The luxuriously feminine clothes are beautifully made and women of most ages will find them very wearable. Visit their website before you come and arrange a 10 per cent discount.
🕐 Mon–Sat 10–1, 3.30–7.30 🚤 San Marco (Vallaresso)

SER ANGIU
Map 186 E11
San Vio, Dorsoduro 868
Tel 041 523 1149
This is perhaps one of the only clothes shops in Venice where you get a lot for your money by rummaging along the crowded rails and through the boxes piled high with goodies—you'll find a wide range of discounted designer clothes and brilliant pieces from labels you've never heard of. The stock is updated weekly and the staff is friendly and eager to help.
🕐 Wed–Sat 2–8pm 🚤 Accademia

CHAIN STORES

Venice is a great place for shopping. This chart tells you what to expect in many of the stores throughout the city. Call the contact number to find your nearest branch or visit the website.

NAME	TYPE OF GOODS	TEL NO	WEBSITE
Benetton	Womenswear	041 526 6275	www.benetton.com
Calzedonia	Womenswear	041 524 0636	www.calzedonia.it
Coin	Department store	041 520 3581	www.gruppocoin.it
Coin Beauty	Cosmetics and toiletries	041 520 3581	www.gruppocoin.it
Diesel	Clothing and accessories	041 241 1937	www.diesel.com
Foot Locker	Shoes and sportswear	041 522 0803	www.footlocker-europe.com
Frette	Household goods	041 522 4914	www.frette.it
Golden Point	Womenswear	041 241 3687	www.goldenlady.it
La Perla	Womenswear	041 522 6459	www.laperla.com
Luisa Spagnoli	Womenswear	041 523 4378	www.luisaspagnoli.it
Mandarina Duck	Accessories	041 522 3325	www.mandarinaduck.it
Mondadori	Books, music, DVDs	041 522 4533	www.mondadori.it
Prenatal	For children	041 522 1593	www.prenatal.it
Stefanel	Womenswear	041 241 0089	www.stefanel.it

WHAT TO DO

ENTERTAINMENT

Venice draws heavily on its musical legacy to provide visitors with unique opportunities to enjoy Venetian music in unforgettable settings. An evening at the opera or a concert of 18th-century music is one of the best ways to enjoy the city's beautiful buildings.

CINEMA

The 12 days of the Venice Film Festival are, sadly, atypical as far as movie-going in Venice is concerned, as this major culture fest only highlights the lack of cinema here. The Festival apart, the only year-round cinema is the Giorgione Movie d'Essai (▷ 209). From July to September you can catch mainstream popular films at the open-air screenings in Campo San Polo, while

Inside the Ateneo Veneto, Campo San Fantin

the Videoteca Pasinetti (▷ 210), runs short film seasons. Check the local press for screening details.

CLASSICAL MUSIC, OPERA AND BALLET

The Fenice orchestra divides its energies between opera, classical music and ballet, and its time between the Fenice and the Teatro Malibran (▷ 211). The opera season runs from November to June, but classical concerts are performed throughout the year in the churches and *scuole*. Most musical events take place in churches. The dance season theoretically matches that of the opera, but there's normally

little on offer and the summer dance schedule organized during the Biennale (▷ 221–222) generally has more exciting live dance performances.

MUSIC IN CHURCHES AND SCUOLE

Concerts of 18th-century music in churches and *scuole* are a big draw. Standards of performance vary, but the venues are magical, often enhanced by musicians playing in 18th-century costume. The main venues are the churches of La Pietà and the Frari and the *scuole* of San Giovanni Evangelista, San Rocco and San Teodoro (▷ 208–209). The ex-church of San Vidal also stages regular performances.

THEATRE

Venice's main theatres are the Teatro Goldoni and the Teatro Malibran (▷ 211). Both offer a varied schedule of plays, and the Malibran also acts as a concert and dance venue. The Goldoni is strong on Venetian classics, but is also noted for contemporary productions. Smaller, more avant-garde city theatres include the Teatro Fondamenta Nove, which also offers dance and film, the Teatrino Groggia, and the Teatro da l'Avogaria (▷ 211), an experimental theatre. The season runs from November to June, when the Biennale takes over. Note that performances are in Italian.

WHAT'S ON

For concerts, theatre and opera, there are comprehensive day-by-day listings in the *Leo Bussola*, an information-packed listings guide obtainable free from the

tourist information offices. Performance is also listed in the *Venezia News* (€2.20), a monthly bilingual listings magazine, and the two local daily papers, *Il Gazzettino* and *La Nuova Venezia*; all are available from newsstands. Posters also advertise cultural events, and the staff at the tourist office in the Giardini ex-Reali (▷ 104) has full listings and will also book tickets for some venues.

Inaugural concert at the reopening of Teatro La Fenice

TICKETS

For performances at the Fenice, Goldoni and Malibran, book in advance, either at the venues or via the theatres' websites. Otherwise, tickets can be bought at the box offices just before the performances. VeLa sells performance tickets at the *vaporetto* stops at Piazzale Roma, the Rialto, Ferrovia, San Zaccaria and the Rialto. The APT office at the Giardini ex-Reali also books and sells tickets, and many hotels will provide tickets for classical music concerts.

SMOKING

Smoking is prohibited in all public places.

C D E F

4

Canale delle Sacche

Canale delle Nav[i]

SACCA DI
S ALVISE

Sant Alvise

Teatrino
Groggia

5

SACCA DI S
GIROLAMO

Fond d Sacca S Girolamo

C llo d Cantier

C llo d Colonne

Fond C Coletti

Rio d Riformati

Fond d Riformati

Fond Contarini

Sant'Alvise

Campo
S Alvise

Tre
Archi

Fond S Girolamo

Rio d S Girolamo

Rio d San Girolamo

C d Capuccine

Fond d Capuccine

R S
Girolamo

Rio d Sensa

Fond d Sensa

C Tintoria

C d Chiovere
Rio d S Girolamo

Fond d Battello
Rio d Battello

C d Magazen

Curiola

Rio d Sensa

San Giobbe

PONTE D
TRE ARCHI

C Bosello

Canale di Cannaregio
Fond d Cannaregio

Fond Savorgnan

C d Ghetto Vecchio

C d Forno

Fond d Ormesini
Rio d Misericordia

Rio d Sensa

Campo
S Globbe

C llo d
Pazienza

C d Misericordia

C d te
Cendon

C te d i tori

C Riello

IL
GHETTO

CANNAREGIO

Campo
Ghetto
Nuovo

C d Farnese

C d Ormesini

C d Case Nuove

C llo
dell'Anconetta

C llo
Lombardo

Quadrifoglio

6

Parco di
Savorgnàn

Guglie

Salizz S Geremia

PONTE
D GUGLIE

Rio Terra S Leonardo

Campo S
Leonardo

San
Marcuola

Campo
S Marcuola

San Marcuola

7

STAZIONE FERROVIARIA
SANTA LUCIA

Scalzi

Rio Terra Lista d Spagna

Fond d Scalzi

PONTE
DEGLI SCALZI

Canal Grande

Campo
S Simeòn
Grande

Campo
S Simeòn
Profeta

Riva d Biasio

Rivi di Biasio

Rio d Biasio

Museo
di Storia
Naturale

San Stae

Campo
S Stae

San Stae

Ferrovia

San Giovanni
Decollato

Videoteca
Pasinetti

Museo del
Tessuto e
del Costume

Palazzo
Mocenigo

Ferrovia

Fond S Simeòn Piccolo

C llo d
Comare

Ruga Vecchia

Ruga Bella

San Giacomo
dell'Orio

Campo San
Giacomo
dell'Orio

Bagolo

Easy Bar

Campo
S M Mater
Domini

8

Giardino
Papadopoli

Campo d Lana

Rio d S Zuane

Scuola Grande di
San Giovanni
Evangelista

Campo
S Agostin

SAN POL[O]

San Nicolò
da Tolentino

Campo di
Tolentini

Rio Terrà Tomà

Archivio
di Stato

Santa Maria
Gloriosa dei Frari

San
Rocco

Campo
dei Frari

Campo
San Polo

Arena di
Campo San Polo

San Polo

9

Scuola
Grande di
San Rocco

San
Pantalon

Museo Casa
Carlo Goldoni

202

C D E

ENTERTAINMENT LOCATOR

CLASSICAL AND CHURCH MUSIC

ATENEO VENETO
Map 205 G10
Campo San Fantin, San Marco 1897
Tel 041 522 4459
www.ateneoveneto.org
Occasional classical concerts are held at this cultural institute, right next to the Fenice in the maze of streets between the Rialto and Piazza San Marco. You are more likely to hear Chopin and Debussy than the Venetian favourite Vivaldi in the fresco-filled Aula Magna hall. No credit cards accepted.
🕐 Telephone for latest details
💶 Often free: telephone for latest details 🚉 Rialto, San Marco

CHIESA DI SAN GIACOMETTO
Map 203 G8
Campo di San Giacometto, San Polo
Tel 041 426 6559
www.prgroup.it
This intimate church of San Giacomo di Rialto, affectionately known as San Giacometto, near the Rialto markets is considered by many to be the oldest in Venice—the original building was erected in the 5th century. Frequent concerts by the Ensemble Antonio Vivaldi and other guest orchestras are held in one of the most evocative Venetian church interiors. No credit cards accepted.
🕐 Telephone for latest details
💶 €15.50–€18.50 🚉 Rialto, San Silvestro

EX-CHIESA DI SAN VIDAL
Map 204 E10
Campo San Vidal, San Marco 2862B
Tel 041 277 0561
www.interpretiveneziani.com
Chamber music by the likes of Bazzini, Bach, Schubert and Vivaldi is played year-round against the backdrop of Gaspari, Tirali and Carpaccio's 17th-century church interiors. No credit cards accepted.
🕐 Telephone for latest details
💶 €17–€22 🚉 Accademia

FONDAZIONE CINI
Map 205 J12
Isola San Giorgio Maggiore
Tel 041 524 0119
www.cini.it
The Giorgio Cini foundation was inaugurated in 1951 and is based on the tranquil island of San Giorgio Maggiore. Amongst its many cultural initiatives are concerts and recitals; in summer, some of these take place in the outdoor Teatro Verde (▷ 211). No credit cards accepted.
🕐 Telephone for latest details
💶 Telephone for latest details
🚉 San Giorgio

The Ateneo Veneto, one of Venice's oldest institutions

FONDAZIONE QUERINI STAMPALIA
Map 205 J9
Campiello Querini Stampalia, Castello 5252
Tel 041 271 1411
www.querinistampalia.it
This cultural institution organizes a diverse selection of artistic events, with regular Friday and Saturday classical concerts held in the opulent surroundings of a 15th-century *palazzo salone*. No credit cards accepted.
🕐 Fri–Sat 5 and 8.30pm 💶 €4 –€6, (including museum and exhibition admission) 🚉 Rialto, San Zaccaria

SANTA MARIA FORMOSA
Map 205 J9
Campo Santa Maria Formosa, Castello 2542
Tel 041 984 2542
www.collegiumducale.com
The curvaceous 15th-century church of Santa Maria Formosa lies in the Castello *sestiere* and plays host to the Collegium Ducale orchestra. As well as Venetian baroque chamber music, there is a good smattering of operatic pieces, from Albinoni to Rossini. No credit cards accepted.
🕐 Telephone for latest details
💶 €20–€25 🚉 San Zaccaria

SANTA MARIA GLORIOSA DEI FRARI
Map 202 E9
Campo dei Frari, San Polo
Tel 041 522 2637
www.chorusvenezia.org,
www.basilicadeifrari.it
The cavernous interior of the Frari church is the setting for quality concerts of sacred music. There are regular concert series in the spring and autumn, sometimes featuring orchestral ensembles, other times organ recitals. No credit cards accepted.
🕐 Telephone for latest details
💶 €8–€12, sometimes free; telephone for latest details 🚉 San Tomà

SANTA MARIA DELLA SALUTE
Map 205 G11
Campo della Salute, Dorsoduro 1
Tel 041 522 5558
The wonderful Salute church in Dorsoduro is the venue for a variety of classical organ music, heard at its most thunderous in the echoing acoustics of the soaring interior. As well as performances by the lead organist of the Basilica, guest performers also appear as part of Sunday Mass at 11am every week. No credit cards accepted.
🕐 Telephone for latest details 💶 Free
🚉 Salute

SANTA MARIA DELLA VISITAZIONE (LA PIETÀ)

Map 206 J10
Riva degli Schiavoni, San Marco 3701
Tel 041 522 6405
www.vivaldi.it

The celebrated Venetian composer Vivaldi (1678–1741) had many different roles in his lifelong relationship with La Pietà: from violin teacher to Master of Concerts. Today, the church celebrates his music and other renowned composers, including Handel and Baldassare Galuppi with concerts performed by three ensembles under the umbrella title of the Centro di Co-ordinamento Culturale; the 12-strong string orchestra, I Virtuosi di Venezia, and two female groups, Le Venexiane and Le Putte di Vivaldi, all of whom perform in 18th-century costume. No credit cards accepted.
🕐 Telephone for latest details
🎫 €13–€26 🚤 San Zaccaria

SCUOLA GRANDE DI SAN GIOVANNI EVANGELISTA

Map 202 E8
Campiello della Scuola, San Polo 2454
Tel 041 718 2347
www.orchestradivenezia.com

Classical and popular tunes by Vivaldi and other composers are played at this *scuola*, which was founded in the 13th century. Period costumes worn by the dancers who perform to the music add to these evocative events. No credit cards accepted.
🕐 Telephone for latest details
🎫 €21–€31 🚤 San Tomà

SCUOLA GRANDE DI SAN ROCCO

Map 202 D9
Campo San Rocco, Santa Croce
Tel 041 523 4864
www.sanroccofestival.com

This famous confraternity has a rich musical tradition stretching back over 500 years, and its magnificent interior is the splendid backdrop to regular baroque music concerts performed on period instruments,

featuring works by Monteverdi (1567–1643), long associated with the Scuola, and Giovanni Gabrieli (c1553/4–1612), who was organist here for 27 years. No credit cards accepted.
🕐 Telephone for latest details
🕐 Telephone for latest details 🚤 San Tomà

SCUOLA GRANDE DI SAN TEODORO

Map 203 G9
Salizada San Teodoro, San Marco 4810
Tel 041 521 0294
www.imusicineveziani.com

Baroque and operatic concerts are performed at this magnificent building from May to November. Vivaldi's *Le Quattro*

Live music ranges from classical and jazz to modern and hip

Stagioni (Four Seasons) features often, as does music from Mozart, Donizetti and Verdi. The orchestra and singers dress in 18th-century costume. No credit cards accepted.
🕐 Contact for latest details
🎫 €21–€31 🚤 Rialto

CINEMA

ARENA DI CAMPO SAN POLO

Map 202 E9
Campo San Polo, San Polo
Tel 041 524 1320
www.comune.venezia.it/cinema

For six weeks from late July to early September this large *campo* is transformed into an open-air cinema, attracting

18TH-CENTURY MUSIC IN 18TH-CENTURY SETTINGS

The music of Antonio Vivaldi (1678–1741) and his contemporaries, often performed by players in 18th-century costume, is a big hit with many visitors; it's sublime music in a sublime setting. You can track it down at the following venues:
La Pietà: performed by Virtuosi di Venezia, Le Veneziane, Le Putte di Vivaldi
San Giacometto: performed by Ensemble Antonio Vivaldi
San Vidal: performed by Interpreti Veneziani
Santa Maria Formosa: performed by Collegium Ducale
Scuola di San Teodoro: performed by I Musici Veneziani
Scuola Grande di San Giovanni Evangelista: performed by Orchestra di Venezia
Scuola Grande di San Rocco: performed by Accademia di San Rocco

audiences of up to 1,000 people. The backdrop of flickering colours across crumbling Venetian buildings adds to the drama and is sometimes more captivating than the films, generally repeats of first-run favourites from the previous season, showcased here. Films are usually dubbed into Italian. No credit cards accepted.
🕐 Telephone for latest details
🎫 €5.50–€7.50 🚤 San Silvestro, San Tomà

GIORGIONE MOVIE D'ESSAI

Map 203 G7
Rio Terrà dei Franceschi, Cannaregio 4612
Tel 041 522 6298
www.comune.venezia.it/cinema

A good selection of art-house films is shown at this two-screen Cannaregio theatre, halfway down Rio Terrà on Rialto side. Hollywood films are often dubbed into Italian,

WHAT TO DO

but shown in English on Tuesdays from October to May. Childrens' films are shown at 3pm on Saturdays and Sundays. No credit cards accepted and advance reservations are recommended, or turn up 30 minutes before a show.

📞 Telephone for latest details
✋ €4–€7 🚇 Ca d'Oro

PALAZZO DEL CINEMA
Map 207 off N13
Lungomare Marconi 90, Lido di Venezia
Tel 041 521 8711
www.labiennale.org

This is the home of the annual Venice Film Festival held in late August/early September. Although the main screen auditorium is huge (over 1,000 capacity), tickets get snapped up for the premières. The venue also hosts fashion shows and other events.

📞 Telephone for latest details
✋ Season tickets €50–€150; individual screenings €5–€15 🚇 Lido

VIDEOTECA PASINETTI
Map 202 E7
Palazzo Mocenigo, Santa Croce 1991
Tel 041 524 1320
www.comune.venezia.it/cinema

The small screen at the Videoteca Pasinetti is a valuable resource for lovers of the film industry and its history. Although functioning primarily as a resource centre and archive, it runs occasional film seasons, showing movies, videos, TV documentaries and newsreels from its vast collection of Venice-related film. No credit cards accepted.

📞 Telephone for latest details
✋ €3–€5 🚇 San Stae

CONTEMPORARY LIVE MUSIC
BAGOLO
Map 202 E8
Campo San Giacomo dell'Orio, Santa Croce 1584
Tel 0347 366506

Oriental lanterns, clean architectural lines and bright colours characterize this contemporary bar, popular with

Venetians and students. Live jazz pulls a loyal crowd each Thursday. It serves some great snacks and has a decent choice of *grappa* and German beers.

📞 Tue–Sun 6.30–11pm 🚇 San Stae

EASY BAR
Map 202 F8
Campo Santa Maria Mater Domini, Santa Croce 2119
Tel 041 524 0321

Beams, bricks, stylish hi-tech touches and an adventurous menu give this bar and music venue a contemporary feel. On Wednesday nights and during the Carnival shenanigans, Easy Bar hosts live rock and jazz

Live entertainment, Venetian-style, at Giorgione

bands—the action often takes place outside in the *campo*.

📞 Fri–Wed 7am–10pm 🚇 San Stae

GIORGIONE
Map 206 M11
Via Giuseppe Garibaldi, Castello 1533
Tel 041 522 8727

Venetians flock to this trattoria-cum-pizzeria for the quality food, Friulian wines and Venetian folk music. The owner, Lucio Bisutto, is one of the art's leading exponents and frequently performs his all-singing and a little dancing 'fisherman's tales from the osterie'.

📞 Thu–Tue 8pm–11pm 🚇 Giardini

MELOGRANO
Map 206 L11
Riva VII Martiri, Castello 1643
Tel 041 241 4196

On Saturday nights local jazz bands appear at this popular bar near the Giardini. It's also a great place to try *cicheti* and some decent tipples, away from the crowds.

📞 Tue–Sun 8am–1am 🚇 Giardini

QUADRIFOGLIO
Map 202 F6
Campiello dell'Anconeta, Cannaregio 1974–5

This bar near the station showcases live local bands every Friday evening. There's also the chance to munch on the excellent *taglieri* (meats and cheese slices) and *panini*, sip a cocktail and watch the nightly *passeggiata* on the Strada Nova. No credit cards accepted.

📞 Daily 8am–2am 🚇 San Marcuola

SUZIE CAFÉ
Map 204 C11
Campo San Basilio, Dorsoduro 1527A–B
Tel 041 522 7502

Popular with literature and philosophy students in the day, this friendly bar transforms itself into a swinging bar at night. On Friday nights, live jazz, reggae or funk bands perform. During the summer, a host of other home-grown bands appears at weekends. No credit cards accepted.

📞 Telephone for latest details
🚇 Zattere

TORINO@NOTTE
Map 205 G9
Campo San Luca, San Marco 4597
Tel 041 522 3914
www.torinonotte.tv

Live jazz, beer, spritz and toasted sandwiches make up the staple diet of the fun-loving crowd here. The action spills out onto the *campo* during the summer and at carnival time.

📞 Tue–Sat 7pm–1am 🚇 Rialto

ZENEVIA
Map 203 H9
Campo Santa Maria Formosa,
Cannaregio 5548
Tel 041 520 6266
This bar is popular for its inti-
mate nooks inside and its
seating outside on Campo
Santa Maria Formosa. Giant
spritz and glasses of Guinness
are consumed by an up-for-it
crowd who come for the live
jazz, blues and rock sounds
each Thursday.
🕐 Wed–Mon 9pm–2am 🚤 Zattere,
Rialto

DANCE, BALLET AND OPERA
TEATRO LA FENICE
Map 205 F10
Campo San Fantin, San Marco 1965
Tel 041 786 2424
www.teatrolafenice.it
Venice's beautifully rebuilt,
world-famous opera house
(▷ 168), ravaged by a catastrophic fire in 1996, opened
for business once more for the
2004–2005 winter season. The
theatre, whose interior is
among the most dramatic
venues in the world, is primarily an opera house, but also
stages ballet and occasional
concerts.
🕐 Guided visits, bookable in advance
in person or by telephone or internet.
Details not yet finalized 🎫 Tickets
around €40 🚤 Santa Maria del Giglio

TEATRO FONDAMENTE NUOVE
Map 203 H6
Fondamente Nuove, Cannaregio 5013
Tel 041 522 4498
Venice's premier avant-garde
venue, wonderfully set on the
northern lagoon in remote
Cannaregio, was founded in
1993 in an old joiners' shop. It
stages contemporary dance
and organizes performances,
film festivals, workshops and
exhibitions as part of its innovative Art and Technology
project, which explores the
relationship between artistic
creativity and technology.
🕐 Telephone for latest details
💶 €5–€10 🚤 Fondamente Nuove

TEATRO GOLDONI
Map 203 G9
Calle Goldoni, San Marco 4650B
Tel 041 240 2011
This famous and beautiful
theatre, named for the
Venetian playwright Carlo
Goldoni (1707–93) stages
plays from the 18th to 20th
centuries, using big contemporary names and leading Italian
directors. As well as its regular
theatrical productions, the
Goldoni puts on poetry readings, youth theatre and the
occasional musical performance.
🕐 Telephone for latest details
💶 €19–€21 🚤 Rialto

*The quality of musical perform-
ances in Venice is very high*

TEATRO MALIBRAN
Map 203 H8
Calle dei Milion, Cannaregio 5873
Tel 041 786 603; box office 041 899
909 090
A theatre has stood on this site
since 1677, and the Teatro
Malibran was Venice's most
élite performance venue
throughout the 18th century;
this wonderful building reopened in 2002 after extensive
renovation. Formerly known as
the Teatro di San Giovanni, it is
now named after Maria Garcia
Malibran, a famous 19th-cen-
tury singer who performed
here free of charge, and stages
well-known operas such as *La
Traviata* and more modern

works, as well as classical con-
certs and ballet productions.
🕐 Telephone for latest details 💶 €35
🚤 Rialto

TEATRO VERDE
Map 206 J13
Isola di San Giorgio Maggiore
Tel 041 528 990
www.cini.it
This open-air theatre is set in
wonderful parkland on the
island of San Giorgio Maggiore.
It was inaugurated in 1954 and
renovated in the late 1990s.
Since its reopening in 1999, it
has concentrated on staging
contemporary dance produc-
tions during the summer
months.
🕐 Telephone for latest details
💶 Telephone for latest details
🚤 San Giorgio

THEATRE
TEATRO DA L'AVOGARIA
Map 204 C10
Corte Zappa, Dorsoduro 1617
Tel 041 520 6130
This experimental theatre was
founded in 1969 by the internationally renowned director
Giovanni Poli. Since his death
in 1979 it has continued to
stage works by little-known
15th- to 19th-century play-
wrights.
🕐 Telephone for latest details 💶 Entry
by voluntary donation 🚤 San Basilio

TEATRINO GROGGIA
Map 202 E5
Calle del Capitello, Cannaregio 3161
Tel 041 524 4665
www.comune.venezia.it/teatrinogroggia
This small and very intimate
venue in far-flung Sant'Alvise is
renowned for its modern and
contemporary theatre productions and concerts. As well as
showcasing plays by emerging
Italian writers, it also puts on
the occasional productions in
English. The music ranges from
traditional American folk to
minimal avant-garde. No credit
cards accepted.
🕐 Telephone for latest details
💶 €2.75–€5.50 🚤 Sant'Alvise

WHAT TO DO

NIGHTLIFE

Nightlife in Venice is decidedly low key. Late-night possibilities are really limited to bars and live-music cafés, where you can hear jazz, blues or reggae, with an occasional Latino or rock session. The main party areas are Campo Santa Margherita in Dorsoduro, the heart of student nightlife, and Fondamenta della Misericordia in Cannaregio, where a string of waterfront bars and tiny clubs transforms the whole quayside into one long nightspot. If you really can't live without some serious clubbing, it's best to head for Mestre, a short bus or train ride across the causeway, or, in summer, the throbbing house and techno scene at the resort of Lido di Jesolo.

In Venice itself, late-night bars generally get going around 10.30–11pm and will stay open until around 2am, with later hours at the weekends, particularly those popular with students. Dress code is relaxed, so wear what you like, remembering that Venetian

Enjoying the nighttime scene in Campo Santa Margherita

bars can get very hot and crowded. Most places do not charge an entry fee, so you can hear live music for just the cost of your drink; details of what's on are listed in the monthly listings magazine, *Venezia News,* available at newsstands, and in the free *Venezia da Vivere* leaflet that you'll find in some bars and restaurants.

If you're heading across the causeway for some serious mainland clubbing at Mestre or Jesolo, bear in mind that although most venues open at 11pm, nothing much gets going until 1am and will rock on till dawn. If you're going to Mestre, take the bus from Piazzale Roma (2, 3, 4 or 6); in

summer, the nicest way to get to Jesolo is to take the No. 12 or 14 *vaporetto* from San Zaccaria to Punta Sabbioni, from where regular buses connect with Jesolo. Return boats run thoughout the night, though you may have to change at the Lido. All mainland clubs charge an admission fee, which ranges from €10–€15, and usually includes one drink.

GAY AND LESBIAN VENICE

Venice's gay scene is very low-key, with no bars or clubs that are specifically gay, though opportunities can be found on the almost exclusively gay Alberoni Beach on the Lido, and at Il Muro (The Wall), by the Giardinetti Reali on the St. Mark's Basin side of the Piazza San Marco.

There's more action in Padova (Padua), a 20-minute train ride away on the mainland, but Venice itself is a small town, with all the drawbacks that implies for gay locals and visitors. For evening eating, drinking and relaxation, it's best to head for Campo Santa Margherita, with its plethora of bars and cafés; Fondamenta della Misericordia in Cannaregio is also worth exploring.

For more information, pick up a copy of *Babilonia,* a monthly gay magazine which has listings for the whole of Italy, or log onto www.arcigay.it, the official site of Italy's foremost gay and lesbian network. ArciGay has a local branch in Mestre,

which sponsors festivals and activities, and offers counselling.

● ArciGay Dedalo
Scuola Pellico, Via Coasta 38A, Mestre; tel 041 538 4151.
🕙 Tue, Thu 9pm–11pm; telephone enquiries Mon 7pm–9pm, Thu 9pm–11pm.

Bacaro Jazz is a great place for informal jazz and good food

BARS AND PUBS

BACARO JAZZ
Salizzada del Fontego dei Tedeschi, San Marco 5546
Tel 041 528 5249
The fabulous Cuban *barista* (barman) here does his utmost to make you feel welcome, and more importantly mixes a mean mojito. Expect plenty of jazz and *gondolieri* enjoying themselves. There is good food, too.
🕙 Thu–Tue 11am–2am 🚤 Rialto

CAFÉ DEI FRARI
Fondamenta dei Frari, San Polo 3564
Tel 041 524 1877
This is a great place for an aperitif, especially if you want to dine nearby. Many

Venetians start their night with the house spritz or a glass of *prosecco*.
🕐 Mon–Sat 9–9, Sun 5–9pm 🚊 San Tomà

IL CAFFÈ
Campo Santa Margherita, Dorsoduro 2963
Tel 041 528 7998
Campo Santa Margherita is one of Venice's loveliest spots, and Il Caffè is a superb place to sit with a drink in hand and enjoy it all. The coffee is great, the *piadine* (thin, flat bread sandwiches) plentiful and the staff are young, bright and cheery. This becomes one of the lively square's focal points in the evening. No credit cards accepted.
🕐 Daily 7.30am–2am
🚊 Ca' Rezzonico

LA CANTINA
Campo San Felice, Cannaregio 3689
Tel 041 522 8258
There are a number of bars on the Strada Nova but this is by far the best. It serves beer *alla spina* (on tap) and reasonable wines, and is a good place to pop into if you're passing.
🕐 Tue–Sat 11am–11pm 🚊 Ca d'Oro

CANTINA DO MORI
Calle do Mori, San Polo 429
Tel 041 522 5401
The house spritz here is one of the most drinkable you'll get and the *cicheti* (or tapas) are the perfect accompaniment.
🕐 Mon–Sat 8.30–8.30 🚊 Rialto, San Silvestro

LA COLUMBINA
Campinello del Pegoloto, Cannaregio 1828
Tel 041 275 0622
Those who prefer to eat later will like the opening hours and daily-changing menu of Tuscan and Venetian food here, but La Columbina is more of a wine bar than a restaurant. It's a comfortable place with good, reasonably priced wines.
🕐 Daily 6.30pm–2am 🚊 San Marcuola

GREEN PUB
Campo Santa Margherita, Dorsoduro 3053A
Tel 041 520 5976
The name, as with many Venetian establishments, describes it accurately. The location, one of Venice's most vibrant areas by night, is what makes it so popular.
🕐 Fri–Wed 7.30am–2am 🚊 San Tomà

HAIG'S BAR
Campo Santa Maria del Giglio, San Marco 5277
Tel 041 528 9456
Haig's is an American-style piano bar, popular with visiting Americans and young locals— and those locals who wish

There are bars to suit all moods and tastes in Venice

they were younger! It serves very good but slightly pricey Venetian fare.
🕐 Daily 11.30–3, 7–2 🚊 Santa Maria del Giglio

IGUANA
Fondamenta della Misericordia, Cannaregio 2515
Tel 041 713 561
This Mexican bar/restaurant draws a crowd seeking sangria and song. Happy hour is from 6 to 7.30pm, but it's best to come later when the staff have warmed up. The burritos and fajitas are good too.
🕐 Tue–Sun 8am–2am 🚊 Madonna dell'Orto

INISHARK
Calle del Mondo Novo, Castello 5787
Tel 041 717 999
Inishark serves Guinness and shows soccer on wide-screen TV. Owners Alberto and Maria extend a warm welcome and are consistently entertaining.
🕐 Daily 5pm–1am 🚊 Rialto

L'OLANDESE VOLANTE
Campo San Lio, Castello 5658
Tel 041 528 9349
With outside seating, this is a great place to meet during the warmer months, especially during university term.
🕐 Mon–Fri 10am–1am, Sat 10am–2am, Sun 5pm–2am 🚊 Rialto

OSTERIA AGLI ORMESINI DA ALDO
Fondamenta degli Ormesini, San Marco 2710
Tel 041 715 834
There's a good selection of bottled beers, and board games for those who become competitive after a couple. Stay until the end and watch Aldo exercise his Alsatian dog.
🕐 Mon–Sat 8pm–2am 🚊 San Marcuola

PARADISO PERDUTO
Fondamenta della Misericordia, Cannaregio 2640
Tel 041 720 581
The atmosphere at this renowned nightspot makes up for the fairly average food. Cheap wine and eclectic music attract a diverse, alternative crowd. Its legendary all-night themed parties have ruffled many locals' feathers over the years.
🕐 Tue–Sun 7.45pm–midnight 🚊 Madonna dell'Orto

VINO VINO
Calle delle Veste, San Marco 2007A
Tel 041 2417688
This lovely little wine bar also serves food, and the crowd is as diverse as the wine list. It's not really a place to ask for a beer.
🕐 Wed–Mon 10.30am–midnight 🚊 San Marco

VITAE
Calle Sant'Antonio, San Marco 4118
Tel 041 520 5205
For a beer, spritz or a Cuba libre, join the upwardly mobile in this trendy designer bar. Staff can be a little over-exuberant, and like to put their favourite tracks on repeat, but the atmosphere is convivial.
🕐 Mon–Sat 9pm–1am 🚤 Rialto

CASANOVA
Lista di Spagna, Cannaregio 158A
Tel 041 275 0199
Near the station, this internet café-cum-disco, Venice's only real nightclub, attracts a diverse crowd: students, tourists and the gay and lesbian scene. In the early evening it shows live football *partite* (matches) on the Tele+ network. No credit cards accepted.
🕐 Wed–Sat 6pm–3am 💶 €8
🚤 Ferrovia

CASINÒ MUNICIPALE DI VENEZIA AND VENICE CASINO CA' NOGHERA
Ca' Vendramin Calergi
Palazzo Vendramin Calergi, Calle Larga Vendramin, Cannaregio 2040
Tel 041 529 7111
Ca' Noghera, Via Pagliaga 2, near Mestre
Tel 041529 7111
www.casinovenezia.it
If you want to place a bet in the opulent surroundings of a *palazzo* on the Grand Canal, Ca' Vendramin is the place to come, though the the Casinò at Ca' Noghera near Mestre is both busier, flashier and more popular. Both offer table games such as roulette, baccarat and blackjack and banks of slot-machines and electronic games. You'll be expected to wear a jacket and tie at the Ca' Vendramin Calergi.
🕐 Casinò Municipale slot machines daily 11am–3am, tables daily 2.45pm–2.45am; Venice Casino Mon–Fri, Sun 10am–4am, Sat 10am–5am 💶 €5 entry or €10 for

entry, including complimentary €10 token 🚤 San Marcuola or private boat (Navetta Casinò) from Piazzale Roma every 10 min; ACTV 4 or shuttle service from Piazzale Roma

FLORIDITA
Via Garibaldi, Castello 68
Tel 041 419 6963
Down in deepest Via Garibaldi, hot and steamy Floridita throbs to the sounds of salsa and merengue. Dancing is almost compulsory. No credit cards accepted.
🕐 Fri 9pm–4am 💶 €10 🚤 Arsenale

PICCOLO MONDO (EL SUK)
Calle Contarini Corfu, Dorsoduro 1056
Tel 041 520 0371

Go well dressed to the Casino, and take your passport

This is a small 'elegant and intimate' club with a dash of 1970s-style décor. It attracts a diverse crowd: from well-dressed Italians to student types from the nearby Università di Ca' Foscari. No credit cards accepted.
🕐 Daily 10pm–4am 💶 €10
🚤 Accademia

ROUND MIDNIGHT
Calle dei Pugli, Dorsoduro 3102
Tel 041 523 2056
Round Midnight is good bet if you can't get to Jesolo or the Lido for the dance clubs. This intimate club attracts all sorts for the mainstream house music. The drinks are a little

pricey. No credit cards accepted.
🕐 Mon–Sat 9pm–2am 💶 €8
🚤 Ca' Rezzonico

AREA CITY
Via Don Tosatto 9, Mestre
Tel 041 958 000, 0336 490 200
This club attracts the over 25s. The music policy is defined as house raffinata, or: less 'boom boom boom' and more 'la la la'! In this more-refined-than-usual club atmosphere, there's a very good restaurant too.
🕐 Fri–Sat 11.30pm–4am 💶 €12
🚤 ACTV bus 3 from Mestre

BLU ROOMS
Via della Industrie, 29 Zona Porto Industrie, Marghera
Tel 041 819 0377
Venice's nearest mainland dance club is housed in an impressive 1930s building, converted into a sophisticated-looking club with three sleek rooms and a diverse music policy. As well as 1990s house and commercial pop on Friday, there's also Latino music on Saturday. Other rooms play indie and chill-out music. No credit cards accepted.
🕐 Fri–Sat 9pm–4am 💶 €12 🚤 ACTV bus 2, 4, 6 from Piazzale Roma

MAGIC BUS
Via della Industrie, 118 Secondo Zona Industrie, Marcon
Tel 041 595 2151
www.magicbus.it
A multicoloured pop-art school bus greets you as you enter. Expect nights of electro-pop, ambient, techno and jungle, or the traditional Saturday night where rock, pop, funk and nu-metal is played. Look out for gigs by alternative Italian bands such as Articolo 31, famous DJs like Justin Robertson and legends like The Stranglers. No credit cards accepted.
🕐 Fri–Sat 10pm–4am 💶 €8 🚤 Take the Venice–Trieste motorway and exit at Marcon, then follow signs to II Zona Industriale

WHAT TO DO

SPORTS AND ACTIVITIES

At first glance, sporting opportunites would seem distinctly lacking in crowded, urban Venice, but those with energy to spare will find plenty to do. Most Venetians are more than happy to spend their leisure time simply enjoying the atmosphere and beauty of their superb surroundings, relaxing and doing nothing—the art of *dolce far niente*. But many are strong supporters of the city's two main spectator sports, soccer, the grand Italian passion, and rowing, Venice's own great obsession. At weekends, the streets of the Lido are filled with cyclists, and its quite usual to see joggers pounding the streets of Venice.

SOCCER

AC Venezia football team was founded in 1907 and has an enthusiastic and passionate local following. The club's fortunes fluctuate, and they are generally found in the second or third division, dreaming of the golden days of 1999,

You can learn sculling as well as traditional Venetian rowing

when they rose to the giddy heights of Series A. Home matches take place on Saturdays and Sundays between September and June, and visiting fans are herded straight off the trains onto special *vaporetti*, which take them directly to the stadium, on Sant'Elena in the far east of the city. Tickets cost between €18 and €45 and are on sale at the ground, at main ACTV and VeLa offices (▷ 54) or from two branches of the Banca Antoniana Popolare Veneta (Campo San Bartolomeo, San Marco 5400 and Strada Nuova, San Marco 5400). You can find out more by checking the team website www.veneziacalcio.it

ROWING

The main festivals all have a watery theme, and locals follow the fortunes of their rowing clubs eagerly, with young people participating at every level in preparation for the city's 120-plus annual regattas. Visitors can sign up for tuition, or rent boats to explore the lagoon under their own steam. Venetian rowing, *voga alla venetia*, is unique in that the rower stands up, facing the direction of travel.

There are various styles of rowing, the gondoliers' *voga ad un solo remo* (one-oar rowing) being the most famous and difficult. But with good tuition, it perfectly possible to learn the other types in a few lessons, and the satisfaction of mastering this elegant sport is immense.

OTHER ACTIVITIES

The early morning is the best time for jogging in Venice, where you can combine flat running through uncrowded streets with the bursts of energy needed to get you over the bridges at a good rate. Popular places include the wide *fondamenta* of the Zattere, along the Riva degli Schiavoni towards the Giardini Pubblici, or the quiet, tree-shaded green areas of Sant'Elena. Alternatively, you could hop on a boat and pound the well-paved roads and the beaches of the Lido.

If you feel the need for more strenuous activity, you can head out of town to the *terra firma*, the hills and some

splendid walking, or cross the lagoon to the Lido, with its beaches, bicycle rental, golf course, tennis courts and riding club, or join the early morning joggers along the Zattere or Riva—a magical time of day as the light strengthens and the city awakes.

Many Italians are passionate about their soccer

BASKETBALL
REYER VENEZIA AND APG BEARS
Via Vendramin 10, Mestre
Tel 041 534 5250
www.reyervenezia.it,
www.bears.shineline.it
Basketball is very popular in Italy; the Reyer club is one of the leading female clubs and the APG Bears the local men's team. If you are a sports fan, or just curious, games are played at the Palasport Taliercio on Sundays. No credit cards accepted.
🕐 Sun 6pm 🎟 Free admission usually
🚆 Train to Mestre and then bus No. 12 to Via Vendramin

CYCLING

ANNA GARBIN
Piazzale Santa Maria Elisabetta 2A, Lido di Venezia
Tel 041 276 0005

GIORGIO BARBIERI
Gran Viale 79A, Lido di Venezia
Tel 041 526 1490

NOLEGGIO LIDO ON BIKE
Gran Viale 21B, Lido di Venezia
Tel 041 526 8019
The 10km-long (6-mile) island of the Lido is perfect for cycling, with the option to take the ferry at Faro Rocchetta at the west end and continue your ride down the narrow island of Pellestrina. Several shops rent equipment; all require you to leave some form of ID, which they retain until you return the bicycle.
🕐 Mar–end Sep daily 8–8; Oct–Feb daily 9–1, 3–7 💶 €4 per hour for first 3 hours; €10 per day 🚤 Lido

GOLF

CIRCOLO GOLF VENEZIA
Strada Vecchia 1, Alberoni-Lido, Lido di Venezia
Tel 041 731 333
At the far end of the Lido is the excellent 18-hole, par 72, Alberoni golf course. Designed in 1928, it's considered one of Italy's top ten courses and has three practice courses, a club house, restaurant and equipment rental. Non-members will need to show proof of membership of their own club.
🕐 Apr–end Sep Tue–Sun 8–8; Oct–end Mar Tue–Sun 8.30–6 💶 Green fees: Tue–Fri €50, Sat–Sun €60 🚤 *Vaporetto* to Lido, then bus B to Alberoni

GYMS

EUTONIA CLUB
Calle Renier, Dorsoduro 3656
Tel 041 522 8618
www.eutonia.net
This gym near Campo Santa Margherita has excellent facilities and a small garden. Its numerous fitness courses and activities include step, spinning, yoga, belly dancing and even salsa and merengue classes.

🕐 Mon–Fri 10–10, Sat 10–1 💶 Annual enrolment €28, then 10 1-hour sessions €60; telephone for details of classes and prices for non-members 🚤 Ca' Rezzonico

PALESTRA CLUB DELFINO
Zattere, Dorsoduro 788A
Tel 041523 2763
www.palestraclubdelfino.com
State-of-the-art computerized technogym fitness rooms are on offer here, with a solarium and massage services for that essential post-exercise wind-down. You will need a fitness certificate signed by your doctor.
🕐 Mon–Fri 9–10, Sat 9–12 💶 €13.50 per day 🚤 Zattere

One of the holes at the excellent Circolo Golf Venezia

HORSEBACK RIDING

CENTRO IPPICO VENEZIANO
Ca'Bianca, Lido di Venezia
Tel 041 526 1820
A gentle ride through woods or a fast canter along the beach at Alberoni will give a real taste of the Lido island before it was developed, and make a change from an overdose of culture. This riding centre also offers expert tuition, either in one of its sand-and-grass exercise yards or under cover in the ring.
🕐 Telephone for times and prices 🚤 Lido

The rowing clubs listed below also have well-equipped gyms.

ROWING

CANOTTIERI GIUDECCA
Fondamenta Ponte Lungo, Giudecca 259
Tel 041 528 7409
You can learn to row the Venetian way in the quiet waters behind the Giudecca under the instruction of expert rowers, or take the tiller of a sailboat. No credit cards accepted.
🕐 Mon, Sun 2.30–7.30, Tue–Sat 9–12.30, 2.30–7.30; hours may vary in winter 💶 Enrolment €26; insurance €5; then €6 per lesson 🚤 Palanca

REALE SOCIETÀ CANOTTIERI BUCINTORO
Zattere, Dorsoduro 10, 15 and 261
Tel 041 522 2055, 041 520 5630, 041523 7933
www.bucintoro.org
Experienced rowers and novices are warmly welcomed by the famous Reale Societa Canottieri Bucintoro, based near La Punta della Dogana and the Salute church. Try your hand at *voga alla veneta* (Venetian rowing), *canotaggio* (regular rowing), canoeing, kayaking or sailing. Lessons are also available for children. No credit cards accepted.
🕐 Tue–Sat 9–5, Sun 9–1 💶 Enrolment €42, then €52 for 8 rowing lessons 🚤 Salute, Zattere

REMIERA CANOTTIERI CANNREGIO
Calle delle Cereria, Cannaregio 732
Tel 041 720 539
This friendly club, around the back of the station, will arrange *voga all veneta* courses for you with expert instructors. No credit cards accepted.
🕐 Mon–Sat 3–7, Sun 8.30–12.30 💶 Enrolment €26, membership €7 per month, lesson prices by arrangement 🚤 Tre Archi

SKYDIVING

AEROCLUB DI VENEZIA
Aeroporto G. Nicelli, San Nicolo
Tel 041 526 0808
www.skydivevenice.com
Fancy flying over the lagoon and looking down on San Marco? This club has 20 years' experience and has carried out over 25,000 jumps. One-off dives are available after a short, but thorough, introduction course. All equipment and qualified tuition is included. No credit cards accepted.
🕐 By appointment only 📞 Telephone for details about the latest courses 🚤 Vaporetto to Santa Maria Elisabetta (Lido), then bus A to San Nicolò

SOCCER

AC VENEZIA
Isola Sant' Elena
Tel 041 238 0711
www.veneziacalcio.it
The island of Sant'Elena, in eastern Castello, is home to the Stadio Penzo, the only league ground in Europe surrounded entirely by water. AC Venezia are a Serie B outfit, who rose to Serie A from 1998 to 2000. Their opponents arrive by train and are transferred to the ground on their own vaporetti for matches accompanied by flag-waving and singing. Tickets are available from the ground, ACTV and VeLa offices.
🕐 Sep–end Jun alternate Sun afternoons. Office open Mon–Fri 9–12.30, 2.30–7 💷 Curve (behind the goal) €10; Distinti (side of pitch) €20 🚤 Sant' Elena

SWIMMING

PISCINA COMUNALE SANT'ALVISE
Calle del Capitello, Cannaregio 3163
Tel 041 713 567
Venice's newest swimming pool is set in peaceful Cannaregio and offers lessons and swimming sessions; there's a warm mini-pool for smaller children. Note the opening hours for non-course swimming sessions, and remember you will have to

wear a swimming cap in the water and flip-flops to walk from the changing rooms to the pool. No credit cards accepted.
🕐 Mon, Wed, Fri 1–2.30. 9.30–10.15; Tue, Thu 3–4; Sat 5.45–7; Sun 10–12 💷 €4.50 per session 🚤 Sant'Alvise

PISCINA COMUNALE DI SACCA FISOLA
San Biagio–Sacca Fisola, Giudecca
Tel 041 528 5430
This municipal pool, set amid the modern council flats of the small island at the west end of the Giudecca, is for serious swimmers. The times given are for non-course swimming sessions, and remember you will

Supporting AC Venezia is a labour of love

have to wear a swimming cap in the water and flip-flops to walk from the changing rooms to the pool. No credit cards accepted.
🕐 Mon, Thu 10.30–12, 1–2.30; Tue, Fri 1–2.30, 6.30–7.15; Wed 3.45–5; Sat 3.45–5, 6.30–8; Sun 3–6 💷 €4.50 per session 🚤 Sacca Fisola

TENNIS

TENNIS CLUB CA' DEL MORO
Via Ferruccio Parri, 6 Lido, Lido di Venezia
Tel 041 770 965
Phone in advance to book one of the dozen or so clay, floodlit courts and to rent rackets, balls, line officials, umpire and ball boys at this fantastic club

on the Lido. A gym and pool are also available. No credit cards accepted.
🕐 Mon–Sat 8.30–8.30, Sun 8.30–8 💷 €9 per hour 🚤 Vaporetto to Lido, then bus B towards Alberoni

VENETIAN EXPERIENCES

VENICE EVENTS
Frezzeria, San Marco 1827
Tel 041 523 9979
www.veniceevents.com
You can have the wedding of your dreams expertly tailor-made by this friendly Anglo-Italian company which will organize everything from the paperwork and civil ceremony to the flowers, reception and that indispensable gondola journey. The service from this highly competent company is professional in the extreme, giving you a magic day to remember, arranged by a team that really understands every wedding is unique and special.
🕐 Mon–Fri 9–1, 3–6 💷 Tailor-made 🚤 San Marco (Vallaresso)

SQUERO CANALETTO
Rio dei Mendicanti, Cannaregio 6301
Tel 041 241 3963
www.squero.com
Thom Price, an American gondola-maker trained by a Venetian master and working in the traditional way, runs five-day workshops at his squero (gondola yard) to introduce small groups to the construction methods and history of the gondola down the centuries. Don't expect to learn how to build a gondola in a week, but do sign on for a deeper understanding of this beautiful, quintessentially Venetian craft.
🕐 Mon–Fri 9–4 (course hours) 💷 €575, telephone for details of discounts. Guided tours Tue and Fri at 10.30am, adults €25, children €5 🚤 Fondamente Nuove, Ospedale

HEALTH AND BEAUTY

Venice may not be the obvious place for pampering, but it could prove a real treat after days walking around the city. Venice's top spas (see below) have the advantage of being sited in the city's most sybaritic surroundings, well away from the crowded centre, where you can indulge yourself with the full range of treatments for face and body. If salt wind and spray have wreaked havoc with your hair, the city is well served with hairdressers to suit all tastes; appointments are often not necessary, but be warned that Italian hairdressers are all à la carte with regards to pricing, and every drop of conditioner or pat of mousse will be added to your bill.

For the ultimate well-being treatment, you could consider heading out of town to the peaceful, and still rural, Euganean Hills, where thermal springs provide healing waters at various spa resorts.

WHAT TO DO

CIPRIANA CASANOVA SPA
Giudecca 10
Tel 041 520 7744
www.hotelcipriani.it
The luxurious surroundings of the Cipriani hotel on La Giudecca are a wonderful place to enjoy some serious pampering at the Casanova Spa. Facial and body treatments, massage, manicures, pedicures and private training are all available, or you could book a full day's treatment, which includes use of the steam and sauna rooms. The Cipriani also has its own hairdressing salon, Puccio e Franco, which cuts and styles both men and women's hair, and offers facials and manicures.
🕐 Mon–Sat 10–7
💶 Full-day treatments from €450; other treatments from €60
🚤 Zitelle

HOTEL TERME MIRAMONTI
Piazza Roma 19, Montegrotto Terme, Padova
Tel 049 891 1755
www.relilax.com
Some of Italy's best-known thermal waters are found in the Euganean Hills, south of Padova (Padua) and an easy journey from Venice. The healing properties of the hot springs and mud have been recognized since Roman times, and the Miramonti is among the best of the spa hotels, offering a range of full beauty and therapeutic treatments

using both thermal waters and hot and cold mud. Set in rolling green surroundings, ideal for walking, the hotel has

A relaxing Jacuzzi—just the thing after a hard day's sightseeing

its own golf course and swimming pool.
🕐 1 March to mid-Jan; telephone or email for further details
💶 Full details on request
🚆 Train to Padua, then local service to Montegrotto; by car take A13 motorway towards Padua and exit at Padova Sud for Abano and Montegrotto

MARIE ROSE BEAUTY SALON
Hotel Gritti Palace
Campo Santa Maria del Giglio, San Marco 2467
Tel 041 794 611
www.starwood.com/grittipalace
For ultimate pampering in the beautiful surroundings of one of Venice's greatest hotels, book via the concierge for a

treatment in the Gritti's beauty salon, where facials, body treatments, manicures, pedicures and hairdressing are all available. It's on the ground floor.
🕐 Tue, Fri–Sat 9–12, 3.15–7.30; rest of week 9–6.30
💶 Manicure from €35; facial from €60; waxing from €25
🚤 Santa Maria del Giglio

SAN CLEMENTE BEAUTY AND WELLNESS CLUB
Isola di San Clemente 1, San Marco
Tel 041 244 5001
www.thi.it
Head across the lagoon on the private hotel launch from San Marco to the island of San Clemente, whose Beauty and Wellness Club offers a full range of beauty treatments, including massage, facials and body training. After your session, enjoy the hotel's swimming pool or stroll around the gardens.
🕐 Mon–Sat 9.30–7
💶 Manicure from €60; facial from €65

STEFANO E CLAUDIA
Riva del Vin, San Polo 1098B
Tel 041 520 1913
Join the city's most fashion-conscious women for a stylish Italian cut and blow-dry at Venice's smartest hairdressers, where a shampoo comes wth a view of the Grand Canal.
🕐 Tue–Sat 9–5
💶 Shampoo and blow-dry €30; full cut and blow-dry €65
🚤 San Silvestro

CHILDREN'S VENICE

Venice is not a children's city, and parents still at the stroller and toddler stage should think twice before tackling it encumbered with kids' paraphernalia. There are few attractions aimed specifically at children, but, equally, there are few more fascinating destinations for older kids. The actuality of the city—the boats, the daily life—will keep children enthralled and, as throughout Italy, locals will welcome them with open arms. Simply crossing bridges, taking the vaporetti and walking down streets without cars will be a major adventure. Aim to punctuate the sightseeing with boat rides, scoops of *gelati*—Venetians are master ice-cream makers—and trips to the beach or outer islands and your kids will get a lot out of a trip to Venice. Facilities such as children's menus or baby-changing tables don't really exist, but most children love pasta and pizza, all readily obtainable, and you can take a break from restaurant food by organizing a picnic.

ATTRACTIONS

LA LUNA NEL POZZO
Ex-Scuola Calvi, Fondamenta Sant'Iseppo, Castello 785
Tel 041 520 4616
Venice city council runs this place, which is aimed at local children up to the age of 14, but also welcomes visitors. There are plenty of games, toys and activities, and the centre organizes workshops where older children can try everything from painting and weaving to puppetry, mask-making and paper marbling. The Lilliput play area is for children under 6 accompanied by an adult.
🎟 Enrolment €7.70; then €7.70 per workshop, €1 per toy or game loan
🚤 Giardini

MUSEO STORICO NAVALE
Riva San Biagio, Castello 2148
Tel 041 520 0276
This museum is crammed with cannons, gondolas, parts of the ornate ceremonial Bucintoro vessels, uniforms and lots of military memorabilia. It is an impressive exhibition laid out over four floors, and shows you not only the history of maritime Venice, but the history of boats themselves (▷ 111).
🕐 Mon–Fri 8.45–1.30, Sat 8.45–1
🎟 €1.55 🚤 Arsenale

PUNTOLAGUNA
Campo Santo Stefano, San Marco 2949
Tel 041 529 3582
www.salve.it

Kids love Venice's Carnevale and take an active part

Puntolaguna is a state-of-the-art, multimedia space devoted to the ecology and safe-guarding of the lagoon. It runs workshops for children and there are videos and CD-ROMs to keep kids happy (▷ 119).
🕐 Mon–Fri 2.30–5.30 🎟 Free
🚤 Accademia

DAYTRIPS

SANT'ERASMO
Take your children across the water to rural Sant'Erasmo (▷ 176) for a day in the country. You can walk or cycle, take a picnic, or head for the little beach across the island from the *vaporetto* stop.
🚤 13

BURANO AND TORCELLO
Most children enjoy a day's outing to Burano and Torcello—a good long boat-trip, not much cultural sightseeing and they'll be fascinated by the eery atmosphere of Torcello. It makes another good outing with a picnic, and be sure to stop for an ice-cream on Burano on the way back.
🚤 LN to Burano, T to Torcello

THINGS TO DO

CLIMB A CAMPANILE
Children will love the bird's-eye view from the top of either the Campanile in the Piazza San Marco—from where they may be surprised there are no canals to be seen—or the one on the island of San Giorgio Maggiore, which gives a wonderful panorama of both city and lagoon.

GAMES IN THE CAMPO
Venetian kids play in their nearest *campo* and, after years of debate, the city council has once more given the OK to ball games. Local children are used to young strangers and will happily welcome a confident youngster into the fun—and all will practise the English they learn at school.

GLASS BLOWING
Murano is just 15 minutes away on the *vaporetto*, and makes a pleasant morning or afternoon trip. There are a number of foundries where

you can watch the beautiful and surreal art of glass blowing. Kids may not be so impressed with the end result, but watching the hot liquid turning into a fantastic shape is sure to amaze them. There's also a glass museum (▷ 172). 🚏 41, 42, DM

GO TO THE BEACH
Italian beaches are highly organized, commercial affairs and the beach at Lido is no exception, with many stretches privately run as *stabilimenti*, bathing establishments. Their hefty entrance fees will give you changing facilites, a lounger and umbrella, showers and toilets and access to their bars and restaurants. Locals head for the equally well-organized, but infinitely cheaper central area, at the bottom of the Gran Viale. Changing cabins, showers and bars are all available and you can rent pedalos when beach games pall. Many families take their own picnic. 🚏 51, 52 to Lido

THE GREAT DRAGON HUNT
St. George's Anglican Church, Campo San Vio, Dorsoduro
Tel 041 520 0571
email: st.george-venice@libero.it
Older children might enjoy this unique take on Venice, organized by the chaplaincy of the Anglican church in the city in aid of church funds. The hunt consists in tracking down and marking off 24 images of St. George and the Dragon, scattered all over the city. Route and transport instructions are given and each dragon has to be verified by answering one or two questions. The hunt criss-crosses Venice, introducing children (and their parents) to hidden corners they might otherwise miss; allow around 5 hours to complete the whole course.
🎫 All year, but telephone or email for further details 💶 €12 per questionnaire 🚏 Accademia

PARKS AND PLAYGROUNDS
Venice's tiny parks often have a few swings and a slide; the best, and biggest are in eastern Castello, where kids can let off steam in the surprisingly spacious gardens of the Giardini Pubblici and Sant'Elena. Take a picnic and make a meal of it.

GELATERIE
If all else fails, stop for a delicious scoop of ice-cream.

BOUTIQUE DEL GELATO
Salizzada San Lio, Castello 5727
Tel 041 522 3283
Be prepared to wait at this ever-busy, tiny *gelateria*, on the main drag from the Rialto

There's nothing like a scoop of ice-cream on a hot day

to Santa Maria Formosa, where locals head to find what they consider to be some of the best ice-cream in the city.
🎫 Feb–end Nov daily 10–8.30
💶 Cone €3–€4.50 🚏 Rialto

IL GELATONE
Rio Terrà Maddalena, Cannaregio 2063
Tel 041 720 631
This popular shop serves huge cones in a bewildering variety, including fresh fruit and yoghurt-based treats.
🎫 May–end Sep Mon 10.30–8, Tue–Sun 10.30–11; Oct to mid-Dec, mid-Jan to end Apr Mon 10.30–8, Tue–Sun 10.30–9. Closed mid-Dec to mid-Jan 💶 Cone €3–€5

IGLOO
Calle della Mandola, San Marco 4819
Tel 041 522 3003
This is a wonderful ice-cream shop where the creamy chocolate, vanilla and other traditional flavours vie with summertime fresh fruit tastes. Take a card and get your 10th ice free.
🎫 May–end Sep daily 10.30–9; Oct, Nov, Feb–end Apr daily 11.30–7.30. Closed Dec and Jan 💶 Cone €2.50–€5 🚏 Sant'Angelo

GELATERIA PAOLIN
Campo Santo Stefano, San Marco 296A
Tel 041 522 5576
The selection of ice cream here is endless and every choice fulfils its promise—what you'd expect from one of Venice's longest-established *gelaterie*. The old-fashioned varieties such as vanilla, chocolate, coffee, *stracciatella* (chocolate chip) and *nocciola* (hazelnut) are among the best in the city.
🎫 Late Jun–Aug daily 7.30am–11.30pm; closes 9.30pm rest of year 💶 Cone €3 🚏 San Samuele

GELATERIA SQUERO
Fondamenta Nani, Dorsoduro 989–90
Tel 041 241 3601
This relative new-comer on the *gelato* scene is giving nearby Nico a good run for its money with its super-light sorbets and mousses—a house speciality—and creamy ices.
🎫 Daily 11–8 💶 €3 🚏 Zattere

NICO
Zattere, Dorsoduro 958
Tel 041 522 5293
In the summer, Fondamenta Zattere is a perfect spot to sit and enjoy an ice-cream and look out over the shimmering water to Giudecca. The *gelati* and frozen yoghurt are beautifully made; try the *gianduitto* (chocolate and hazelnut with mounds of whipped cream), renowned throughout Venice. The café here serves a good selection of snacks and drinks.
🎫 Daily 8am–10pm 💶 Cone €2.50 🚏 Zattere

WHAT TO DO

FESTIVALS AND EVENTS

Venice's great festivals have long been an integral part of the city's life. The roots of many of today's festivals lie centuries deep, processions and celebrations commemorating key events in the city's history. Others are revivals or relatively modern.

WHAT'S ON WHERE

For practical details, look on the websites for the various events. The tourist offices have details, which are clearly listed in their publication *Leo Bussola* (▷ 298), and there are posters all over the city for big festivities such as the Redentore and the Regata Storica. These two, and the Vogalonga, will affect city transport, so check the posters at the *vaporetto* stops for details of curtailed services.

FEBRUARY/MARCH
CARNEVALE
10 days ending on Shrove Tuesday
Throughout city
www.carnivalofvenice.com,
www.comune.venezia.it/carnevale
Carnevale (▷ 21) is a stunningly successful modern take of Venice's pre-Lenten Carnival, revived in 1980. Events and entertainment are held all over the city every day; big days are the first Sunday and the Thursday before Shrove Tuesday.

SU E ZO PER I PONTI
4th Sunday of Lent
Tel 041 590 4717
Throughout city
www.suezoperiponti.org
The name means 'Up and Down the Bridges' and this fun trawl around Venice involves orienteering yourself between specific points throughout the city—with plenty of chances to pause for refreshment.
San Marco for start

APRIL
FESTA DI SAN MARCO
25 April
Bacino di San Marco
The feast day of St. Mark, Venice's patron saint, is celebrated by a morning Mass in the basilica and an afternoon gondola regatta between Sant'Elena and the Punta della Dogana at the entrance to the Grand Canal.
San Marco (Vallaresso), San Zaccaria

MAY
FESTA E REGATA DELLA SENSA
1st Sunday after the feast of the Ascension
Tel 041 529 8711, 041 274 7737
San Nicolò del Lido

The Festa e Regata della Sensa (Marriage to the Sea)

A re-enactment of the Marriage to the Sea (▷ 27) takes place off San Nicolò, when the mayor sails across St. Mark's Basin on a decorated boat to throw a laurel wreath into the sea, followed by a regatta.
Lido

VOGALONGA
1st Sunday after the feast of the Ascension
www.vogalonga.com
This is a 33km (20-mile) row from the Canale delle Giudecca through the lagoon and back down the Canale di Cannaregio and the Canal Grande to St. Mark's.
Canale di Cannaregio is the place to see boats re-enter city

COSTUME RENTAL
ATELIER PIETRO LONGHI
Rio Terà Frari, San Polo 2604B
Tel 041 714 478
Mon–Sat 10–1, 2.30–7.30
San Tomà

BALACOLOC
See page 190.

NICOLAO ATELIER
Rio Terà al Bagatin, Cannaregio 5565
Tel 041 520 7051
Mon–Fri by appointment only 9–1, 2–6
Rialto

JUNE
VENEZIA SUONA
Sunday closest to 21 June
Tel 041 275 0049
www.veneziasuona.it
Hundreds of bands and musicians play rock, jazz, folk and reggae from about 4pm in *campi* all over the city

FESTA DI SAN PIETRO
Week of 29 June
San Pietro di Castello
Venice's liveliest local festival celebrates the feast of St. Peter and is based around his church in Castello. Events include concerts, food stands, dancing and entertainment.
Giardini

JUNE/NOVEMBER
BIENNALE D'ARTE CONTEMPORANEA E ARCHITETTURA
Art (odd years) mid-June to Nov; architecture (even years) Sep–Oct
Tel 041 521 8711
Arsenale and Giardini Pubblici
www.labiennale.org
The Biennale, established in 1895, is one of Europe's most prestigious contemporary art festivals (▷ 21), drawing huge

WHAT TO DO

international crowds; its younger brother, the architectural Biennale, was founded in 1980 and is proving to be an equal crowd-puller.

📷 Arsenale, Giardini

JULY
FESTA DEL REDENTORE
3rd weekend in July
Bacino di San Marco, Canale della Giudecca

Venice's oldest continuously celebrated festival started in 1576 to give thanks for deliverance from plague (▷ 21). A pontoon bridge spans the Canale della Giudecca from near Salute to Redentore throughout the week, across which Venetians process to Il Redentore on La Giudecca.

AUGUST
FERRAGOSTO
15 August
Torcello

During the feast of the Assumption of the Virgin most Venetians leave the city for this bank holiday weekend and head for the beach. There's a concert on Torcello and the tourist office has details of other events.

📷 Torcello

MOSTRA INTERNAZIONLE D'ARTE CINEMATOGRAFICA
12 days, starting during the last week in August
Palazzo del Cinema, Lungomare Marconi, Lido
Tel 041 272 6501, 041 521 8878
www.labiennale.org

This high-profile, international Film Festival (▷ 21) has daily screenings and an increasing influx of big-name stars.

📷 Lido

SEPTEMBER
REGATA STORICA
1st Sunday in September
Canal Grande

A day's celebration of rowing kicks off with a spectacular historical procession down the Grand Canal of ornate boats rowed by locals in 16th-century costume (▷ 20). Four races follow, and the finishing line is at the Volta, the sharp curve on the Grand Canal, where the judges sit and the prizes are presented.

SAGRA DEL PESCE
3rd Sunday in September
Burano

Burano's big day sees outdoor stands selling fried fish and vast quantities of white wine. The festivities are followed by the last regatta of the season

📷 Burano

OCTOBER
SAGRA DEL MOSTA
1st weekend in October
Sant'Erasmo

Spectacular fireworks round off the Festa del Redentore

A wonderfully bucolic festival takes place on the farming island of Sant'Erasmo to celebrate the first pressing of the local wine. The sampling is accompanied by side-shows, foodstalls and the chance to see the locals letting their hair down.

📷 Sant'Erasmo

VENICE MARATHON
Last Sun in October
Tel 041 940 644
Finish at Riva dei Sette Martiri

This marathon run is from the Riviera del Brenta, on the mainland, across to Venice and through the city to finish in Castello. The Zattere is a good vantage point.

NOVEMBER
FESTA DI SAN MARTINO
11 November
Throughout city

The Festa di San Martino is Venice's answer to 'trick or treat', when swarms of children, armed with their mothers' pots and pans, dart around making a noise in praise of St. Martin, and earning treats to go and bang somewhere else. *Pasticcerie* sell horse-and-rider-shaped cakes, lavishly decorated with chocolate, icing and silver balls in honour of the feast.

FESTA DELLA MADONNA DELLA SALUTE
21 November
Santa Maria della Salute

This feast celebrates another plague deliverance (see Festa del Redentore) with a pontoon bridge across the Grand Canal from Campo Santa Maria del Giglio to just west of the church of the Salute. Locals process across to light candles and hear Mass, before sampling cakes and goodies on sale at stalls set up for the feast.

📷 Salute, Giglio

DECEMBER/JANUARY
LA BEFANA
Christmas, New Year and Epiphany
Throughout the city

The tourist board is making a real effort to make more of the traditionally low-key Christmas festivities, with Christmas markets at different venues, Christmas trees in the *campi* and lights twinkling down the main *calle*. Roasted chestnut stalls appear and 6 January sees the Regata delle Befane down the Grand Canal, a race with the rowers dressed as the Befana, the old woman who takes the place of Father Christmas in Italian life. Many churches have wonderfully ornate *presepi* (Christmas cribs), complete with sound-and-light effects, and often including moving figures and running water.

Venice is compact enough to explore on foot, and this section describes five walks that take in some of the most interesting parts of the city, plus a walk on the island of Murano. The start of the walks are marked on the inside front cover. This chapter also gives suggestions for excursions outside the city (see map on page 236).

Out and About

AROUND SAN MARCO

San Marco is the heart of Venice. This *sestiere* is much smaller than the others, but it's packed with narrow alleys, light-filled squares, magnificent patrician *palazzi*, churches, artisan workshops and mouth-watering stores. This walk winds its way through the maze and gives you an insight into the area's many facets.

THE WALK

Distance: 2.5km (1.5 miles)
Allow: 1.5–2 hours
Start: Ponte di Rialto
End: Rialto *vaporetto* stop (Riva del Ferro)

HOW TO GET THERE

Vaporetto: No. 1 or 82 to Rialto

With your back to the Rialto bridge, walk past the souvenir stalls and into Campo San Bartolomeo.

❶ This lively square was once part of the market, and it's still a popular rendezvous for Venetians. The church, remodelled in the 18th century, is used for temporary exhibitions. The bronze statue in the middle portrays Carlo Goldoni, Venice's most popular playwright.

Swing right along Via 2 Aprile, which widens out in front of the church of San Salvador (▷ 156). With the church on your left, continue along Calle dell'Ovo and turn left into Calle dei Fabbri, one of the city's major shopping streets. Take the first right, which leads into Campo San Luca.

❷ The marble plinth in the square supposedly marks the exact centre of the city, and the church is the burial place of the writer Pietro Aretino. He is said to have died of a laughter attack in 1556, brought on by an obscene remark about his sister.

Follow the crowds straight across the square and through to Campo Manin (▷ 77). Take the narrow *calle* halfway along the left-hand side of the *campo*, following the signs to the Palazzo Contarini del Bovolo and its famous stair (▷ 118). Backtrack into Campo Manin, turning left into the square, and cross the left-hand bridge, Ponte della Cortesia, to walk along Calle della Mandola. Take the first left, Calle

dei Assassini. This continues into Calle Verona, crosses a bridge and emerges into Campo San Fantin. The church of San Fantin faces the Teatro La Fenice (▷ 168) across the *campo*.

❸ San Fantin was founded in the 9th century; the present church, with its graceful domed apse, was built in the 16th century by Sansovino (1486–1570). San Fantin had its own *scuola*, devoted to comforting those condemned to death, which became the Ateneo Veneto (Academy of Letters and Sciences) in 1812.

Walk down the right side of the Fenice and turn left along the back of the theatre to cross a small bridge on your right to follow Fondamenta Santo Cristoforo for about 15m (50ft), then turn right over the bridge into Calle Caortorta, which leads into Campo Sant'Angelo (S. Anzolo, ▷ 79). On your left, across the canal, is the ex-Convento di Santo Stefano.

❹ The Convent was founded at the end of the 13th century by the Augustinians, who built the beautiful Gothic church (▷ 159). The convent buildings are now government offices, but you can walk round the Renaissance cloister.

Take the left-hand exit, over the bridge, from Campo Sant'Angelo and walk through to Campo Santo Stefano (▷ 81) and its church. Take Calle Spezier left out of Campo Santo Stefano (there's a *farmacia* on the corner of this narrow street), then walk through Campo San Maurizio.

❺ The present church of San Maurizio (▷ 152) was built in 1806, contrasting with the lovely Palazzo Bellavite opposite. This *campo* really comes to life during the antique markets that are held here at intervals throughout the year.

Keep going straight ahead through the *campo*, along Calle Zaguri, following the main route to San Marco. The next open space is the Campo Santa Maria Zobenigo, also known as Santa Maria del Giglio (▷ 142). Follow the route towards San Marco, walking along Calle Larga 22 Marzo and over the bridge towards the church of San Moisè (▷ 152–153). Continue past the church then turn left. You are now in the smart Frezzeria, where arrows (*frezze*) were once manufactured. Take the second right (Calle Salvadego) and walk through to the Bacino Orseolo.

❻ This is a 'dead-end' canal, and the nearest point to the Piazza San Marco reachable by gondola. Until 1869 only a narrow canal penetrated here and the congestion was immense, so the area was widened to allow more space for delivering passengers and turning gondolas. It's still among the busiest gondola stations.

From here, a right turn will lead you under the arcade of the Procuratie Vecchie and into the expanse of Piazza San Marco (▷ 139–140). Walk down the piazza and turn left under the Torre dell'Orologio and up the crowded Mercerie, taking the third right to San Zulian (▷ 158). Walk left down the side of the church and turn left opposite the Mondadori bookstore, taking the second right into the Mercerie San Zulian. Follow the yellow sign to the Rialto underneath the Sotoportego delle Acque to emerge onto the Mercerie. Walk on, across Via 2 Aprile and down to the Riva del Ferro.

❼ This is one of the few stretches of *fondamenta* beside the Grand Canal, and runs into the Riva del Carbon. The words 'ferro' and 'carbon' mean iron and charcoal; this quayside was once the unloading place for these materials.

OUT AND ABOUT

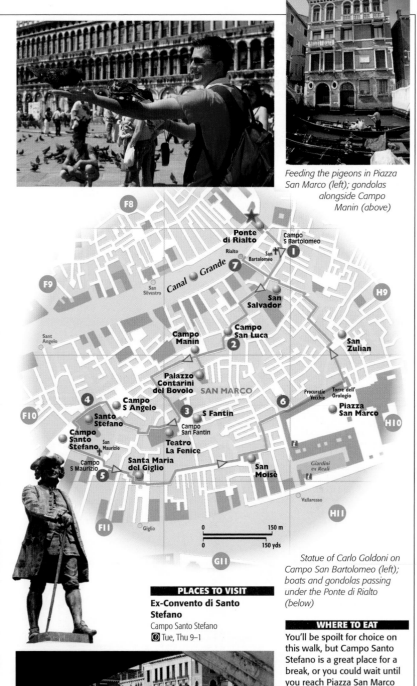

Feeding the pigeons in Piazza San Marco (left); gondolas alongside Campo Manin (above)

Statue of Carlo Goldoni on Campo San Bartolomeo (left); boats and gondolas passing under the Ponte di Rialto (below)

PLACES TO VISIT

Ex-Convento di Santo Stefano
Campo Santo Stefano
🕐 Tue, Thu 9–1

WHERE TO EAT

You'll be spoilt for choice on this walk, but Campo Santo Stefano is a great place for a break, or you could wait until you reach Piazza San Marco and splash out at Caffè Florian or Caffè Quadri (▷ 261).

WHEN TO GO

Morning, when the area is really bustling, is a good time for this walk, but be prepared for some of the narrower *calli* to be very crowded.

SAN MARCO TO THE ARSENALE AND CASTELLO

This walk takes you through Castello, a wonderfully varied *sestiere*, which includes some of the city's great churches and monuments. These contrast admirably with the everyday life of the local area, with its quiet residential streets, shops, markets and green spaces.

THE WALK

Distance: 3.2km (2 miles)	
Allow: 1.5–2 hours	
Start: San Zaccaria *vaporetto* stop	
End: Giardini *vaporetto* stop	

HOW TO GET THERE

Vaporetto: No. 1, 82, 41, 42, 51, 52 to San Zaccaria

With your back to the water, turn right and cross the Ponte del Vin, taking the second left turn (yellow sign to San Zaccaria) into Campo San Zaccaria (▷ 81), home to one of Venice's most interesting churches (▷ 160). Leave the *campo* in the left-hand corner along Salizzada San Provolo. This widens out into Campo Santi Filippo e Giacomo. Walk on to the next bridge. Just before this on the left is the entrance to the Museo Diocesano d'Arte Sacra (▷ 105). At the bridge, look left for a wonderful view of the Ponte di Sospiri.

❶ This is one of best, and least crowded, places to photograph the Bridge of Sighs, with the canal in the foreground and a glimpse of the Riva degli Schiavoni behind.

Walk on, bear right, then take the first right up Rama Va in Canonica, which crosses a busy street into Calle dell'Angelo. Cross the bridge at the end and turn right to walk briefly beside a canal, then turn left. Take the first right, then a left, and then a right onto Calle Ponte de la Guerra, which becomes Calle de la Banda. Cross another bridge to arrive in Campo Santa Maria Formosa (▷ 80). After visiting the church (▷ 143), head right down Calle Lunga Santa Maria Formosa, and take the third left (blue sign for Ospedale, yellow sign for Santi Giovanni e Paolo), up to cross a bridge. Continue up Calle Bressana to emerge into Campo Santi Giovanni e Paolo (▷ 80). To the left of the church's main door is the former Scuola Grande di San Marco, now Venice's main hospital.

❷ The façade was started by Pietro Lombardo and Giovanni Buora in 1487, and completed in 1495 by Mauro Codussi. Its chief glories are the *trompe-l'oeil* panels by Tullio and Antonio Lombardi, showing episodes from the life of St. Mark and his lion.

If you're not visiting the church, turn immediately right and head along Salizzada Santi Giovanni e Paolo. This straight stretch of alleyway changes names several times, but keeps its direction and will lead you to a T-junction and the Campiello Santa Giustina. Take the diagonally right turning ahead down Calle Zen, crossing the Rio di Santa Giustina.

❸ The Rio di Santa Giustina is one of Castello's main arteries, cutting through from the lagoon to the Bacino di San Marco. From the bridge, there's a fine view onto the lagoon and the cemetery island of San Michele.

Across the bridge, turn left, then right onto Calle San Francesco. Ahead looms the façade of the Franciscan church of San Francesco della Vigna (▷ 125). Turn right and cross the *campo* to pass under the colonnade. Cross the bridge and keep straight on, then bear left into Calle delle Gatte. Follow this to Campo delle Gatte and bear right through the square into Calle Riello. Take the first right onto Calle dei Furlani, which brings

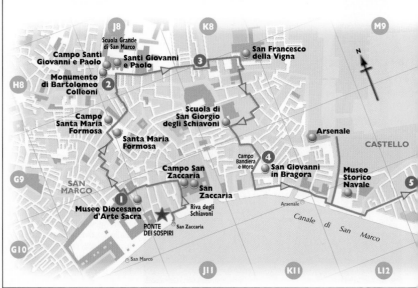

OUT AND ABOUT

you to the Scuola di San Giorgio degli Schiavoni (▷ 163). Turn left and walk beside the canal, then left at the next bridge into Salizzada San Antonin. At the bottom don't miss the tiny alley to the right, which leads into Campo Bandiera e Moro.

❹ This quiet square houses the church of San Giovanni in Bragora (▷ 128) and the lovely Palazzo Gritti-Badoer.

Cross the square diagonally right and down Calle de Dose to the Riva degli Schiavoni. Turn left and walk along the Riva, crossing two bridges to arrive at the Museo Storico Navale (▷ 111). From here you can detour along the right-hand side of the canal to the entrance to the Arsenale (▷ 69), retracing your steps to continue along the waterfront towards the heart of working-class Castello, based around vibrant Via Giuseppe Garibaldi.

❺ Via Giuseppe Garibaldi is the widest street in Venice. Look out for the plaque on the wall of a house on the right, which commemorates the explorers John and Sebastian Cabot, who once lived here.

Walk down past the market stalls and turn right into tree-lined Viale Garibaldi, which leads to the Giardini Pubblici (▷ 104), home to the Biennale (▷ 76) and a peaceful green spot to relax.

The pediment of the Arsenale (above); one of the stone lions at the entrance gate (right)

WHEN TO GO
Morning is a good time for this walk; churches and museums are open and the streets are at their liveliest with locals doing the daily shopping.

WHERE TO EAT
You could have a break in at one of the bars in Campo Santi Giovanni e Paolo, or wait until you reach Via Garibaldi. There are numerous down-to-earth bars and restaurants here, or you could pick up a picnic at the market stalls to eat along at the Giardini Pubblici.

Narrow calle in the Castello district (above); a modern mural decorates a wall in Castello (above right); view towards the Ponte dei Sospiri (right)

N9
San Pietro
P10

0   150 m
0   150 yds

P11

Biennale Internazionale d'Arte

Giardini Pubblici

Giardini

M12   N12

THROUGH DORSODURO

This walk takes you through the heart of Dorsoduro. En route you'll explore hidden corners, visit some of the city's most interesting churches and museums, and enjoy views that range from picturesque alleys to sweeping vistas encompassing some of Venice's great landmarks.

THE WALK

Distance: 3.7km (2.3 miles)
Allow: 2–2.5 hours
Start at: Ca' Rezzonico *vaporetto* stop
End at: Accademia *vaporetto* stop

HOW TO GET THERE

Vaporetto: No. 1 to Ca' Rezzonico

Alight at Ca' Rezzonico and walk down Calle Traghetto to Campo San Barnaba (▷ 79). Cross the square, walk past the vegetable boat and right over Ponte dei Pugni. Continue straight ahead down Rio Terrà Canal, bearing left to Campo Santa Margherita (▷ 80), the focal point of Dorsoduro. Turn right into the *campo*, then take the third turning left (yellow sign to Piazzale Roma/P.le Roma Ferrovia) off the square, and cross the canal. Over the bridge, turn left and follow the canal. Keep on this *fondamenta* as it passes the church of Angelo Raffaele on the other side of the canal, then turn right into Campiello Riello. Walk through to the next canal and turn left along Fondamenta Tron to reach San Nicolò dei Mendicoli (▷ 154) and its *campo*.

❶ This charming little square featured in Nicolas Roeg's cult 1970s movie *Don't Look Now*. Its earlier inhabitants were

fishermen and salt-pan workers, and it gave its name to one of two rival factions, the Nicolotti. The big building across the canal to the west was once a cotton mill; it's now part of the University.

Retrace your steps back through Campiello Riello and turn right over the first bridge. Turn left on the other side and walk along the Fondamenta de Pescheria to the church of Angelo Raffaele (▷ 69). Exiting the side door of the church, turn left and walk down the side of the church into the spacious Campo Angelo Raffaele (Campo de l'Anzolo Rafael), which leads into Campo San Sebastiano and Veronese's church of San Sebastiano (▷ 157). Cross the bridge in front of San Sebastiano and head down Calle Avogaria, which becomes Calle Lunga.

❷ This is a busy neighbourhood street, packed with little shops providing everyday necessities for locals, and interesting gift and antique shops, cafés and restaurants for visitors. Pause to admire the breads and pastries on offer, or pop into the wine shop where empty bottles are filled from giant casks.

Calle Lunga leads back to Campo San Barnaba, where you turn right under the *sotoportego* and follow this main route through Dorsoduro along Calle della Toletta to the Rio San Trovaso. Cross over Ponte delle Maravegie and turn right down the *fondamenta*, from where you'll see the façade of the church of San Trovaso (▷ 158) and the Squero di San Trovaso (▷ 168) across the water. At the bottom is the Fondamenta Zattere (▷ 168). Turn left and walk along beside the Canale della Giudecca until you come to the church of the Gesuati (▷ 101). Continue along the Zattere, cross a bridge and continue to pass the church of Spirito Santo.

❸ The church and convent of Spirito Santo were founded in 1483, though the present church dates from the 16th century. The convent was constantly rocked by scandal, the foundress being accused of squandering community funds to entertain her lover, the local priest.

Continue to the next bridge, cross it and turn left to walk beside the Rio de la Fornace, with the walls of the old Magazzini del Sale on your right.

OUT AND ABOUT

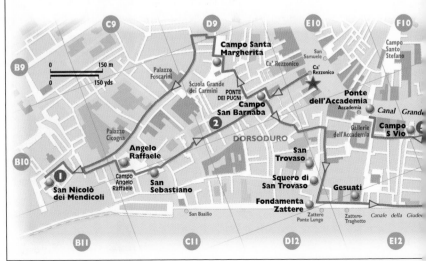

❹ This was where Venice's only raw material was stored. Salt was produced in salt pans near Chioggia. The warehouses, first built during the 14th century, could store up to 44,000 tons. Today, they're used as *cantiere* (boat sheds) and for exhibitions and events.

At the end of this street (T-junction), turn right and walk through a small *campo*, with the façade of the 15th-century ex-church of San Gregorio, a Benedictine foundation dating from the 9th century, ahead of you. Continue under the *sotoportego* (to the left), which once connected the church with its abbey, to cross the wooden bridge and reach the great church of Santa Maria della Salute (▷ 150–151).

After visiting the church, retrace your steps back to the T-junction and cross the bridge. Follow the street round to Campiello Barbaro, with its three acacia trees, across another bridge, and walk round to the Fondamenta Venier, where you'll find the entrance to the Collezione Peggy Guggenheim (▷ 92–93) on your right. Leaving the museum, turn right and follow the street along to emerge into Campo San Vio.

❺ This is one of only a handful of *campi* overlooking the Grand Canal and a good place to pause. The building on the right as you face the water is the Anglican church of St. George's; the first chaplain accompanied the English

Ambassador to Venice in 1604 and the present building has been in use since 1889.

Bear left and cross the bridge into the Piscina del Forner then Calle Nuova Sant'Agnese; walk along this, then turn right to the Ponte dell'Accademia (▷ 119).

House in Dorsoduro (right); detail of a ceiling painting in San Sebastiano (below)

Campo Santa Margherita (below and bottom); Dorsoduro's famous vegetable boat (below left)

WHEN TO GO

Try to avoid wet or windy weather as there's not much shelter in some areas and the Zattere can be very windy.

WHERE TO EAT

The Zattere makes a good stopping place; roughly halfway along the walk, it has a good choice of bars and cafés with outside tables and lovely views. Pick of the bunch is Al Chioschetto (Dorsoduro 1460A, Jun–Sep 7.30am-1am).

OUT AND ABOUT

Collezione Peggy Guggenheim

Giglio Salute Dogana di Mare

Santa Maria della Salute

Spirito Santo

G11

G12

N

❸ ❹

EXPLORING SAN POLO AND SANTA CROCE

The *sestiere* of San Polo contains the Rialto, the Frari and San Rocco. Santa Croce has its share of delights too, from grand *palazzi* and ancient churches to a clutch of the city's most characteristic squares. For all that, big sights aside, these quarters of the city are comparatively little visited. This walk explores the off-the-beaten-track corners of the area, with some delightful discoveries along the way.

THE WALK
Distance: 3km (1.8 miles)
Allow: 2 hours
Start at: San Rocco (nearest *vaporetto*: San Tomà)
End at: Frari (nearest *vaporetto*: San Tomà)

HOW TO GET THERE
Vaporetto: No. 1, 82 to San Tomà

With your back to the Scuola Grande di San Rocco (n164–167) and the church of San Rocco (n156) on your left, head right, then follow the curve of the street round the bulk of the Frari (n144–147) and into Campo dei Frari (n76–77). With the main door of the church behind you, cross the Ponte dei Frari, turn right along the canal, then left. Take a right turn at the supermarket and walk along to the T-junction, then turn left into Calle Saoneri. Cross a bridge and keep going until the street widens and you see the entrance to San Polo (n155) on your left. The wide expanse of Campo San Polo (n80–81) is at the far end of the church. Go under the Sotoportego de la Madonneta off the right-hand corner of Campo San Polo, and follow the yellow signs along to the Rialto. En route you'll walk past the de-consecrated church of Sant'Aponal.

❶ The *Crucifixion* and *Scenes from the Life of Christ* over the door of Sant'Aponal date from 1294; the church itself is an even older foundation, where Pope Alexander III is said to have taken refuge from Frederick Barbarossa's troops in 1177.

The route comes to a T-junction where the Ruga dei Orefici meets the Ruga degli Speziati.

❷ Both these names refer to the streets' medieval function when the Rialto area was the hub of the city's commerce and trade; Orefici gets its name

from the goldsmiths who once worked here, and Venice's ancient spice trade is commemorated in the word *speziati*.

Walk straight ahead into Campo Cesare Battisti.

❸ The buildings around the *campo* are the Fabbriche Vecchie and Fabbriche Nuove, built after the great fire of 1514. This broke out in midwinter and, as the surrounding canals were frozen, raged unchecked for a whole day, destroying the entire Rialto area with the exception of the campanile of the church of San Giovanni Elemosinario (▷ 129). Both blocks and the arcades of the Fabbriche were completed by 1550; Sansovino was responsible for the design of the Nuove. The buildings once housed trade, navigation and food supply administration; today, they're used as the city's law courts.

Turn left and walk along to the Rialto markets (▷ 120–121). Keeping the Pescheria and Grand Canal on your right, cross a bridge and continue along the Riva del Ogio (Riva dell'Olio) beside the water. At the end turn left and walk down Calle del Campanile into Campo San Cassiano.

❹ This square was the site of the world's first purpose-built opera house, which opened during the lifetime of the composer Monteverdi in 1636.

Leave the square in the righthand corner just past the church, walk over the canal and along to the junction with Calle Regina. Turn right, then first left into Calle del Ravano, over a bridge, then right again beside a canal; the entrance to the Ca' Pesaro, home to the Museo d'Arte Moderna (▷ 104–105) is at the bottom

on your right. Cross the canal and walk down Calle Pesaro, then turn right and emerge again on to the Grand Canal, overlooked by San Stae (▷ 156).

❺ The dazzling white baroque church of San Stae was built in 1709. To the left of it is the old Scuola dei Tiraoro e Battiloro, the headquarters of the goldsmiths' and silversmiths' guild, suppressed in 1876.

Turn left down Salizzada San Stae on the other side of the church and keep going till you see the entrance to the Museo del Tessuto, housed in the grandiose Palazzo Mocenigo (▷ 118), on your left. Past here, take the first turning right down Calle del Tentor, following the yellow signs to Piazzale Roma. After the second bridge turn left into Calle Larga to emerge into Campo San Giacomo dell'Orio (▷ 79), a charming square, always busy, that's a focal point for locals in this part of the city.

Walk across the *campo* keeping the church on your right, then take the right-hand bridge which leads via the Ruga Bella into Campo Nauzario Sauro. Turn left and walk through Campo dei Tedeschi, with its trees and benches, to the oddly shaped Campiello delle Stroppe. Keeping the open space on your left, walk down Calle del Cristo into the triangular canalside Campiello del Cristo. Cross the Ponte del Cristo, turn left and walk beside Rio Marin, across a bridge and right into Calle del'Ogio.

About 50m (55 yards) down, look right and you'll see the beautiful complex of the Scuola Grande di San Giovanni Evangelista (▷ 158), while ahead looms the mass of the Archivio di Stato (▷ 69). At the end of this narrow street, opposite the Archivio, turn left, then right over the bridge and you'll see the Campo dei Frari on the other side of the canal.

OUT AND ABOUT

WHEN TO GO
To catch the Rialto market, make this a morning walk, starting early if you plan to visit the churches and museums en route.

WHERE TO EAT
There are good cafés and bars for a stop in Campo San Giacomo dell'Orio. If hunger strikes before you reach the Campo, head for Alla Madonna near the Rialto (▷ 259).

OUT AND ABOUT

Shopping for fresh vegetables in the Rialto market (top right)

Painting of saints John the Baptist, Peter, Paul, Mark and Jerome in San Cassiano (above)

Adolfo Wildt sculpture in the Ca' Pesaro (right)

THROUGH THE BACKSTREETS OF CANNAREGIO

The quiet, spacious canals and sun-drenched *fondamente* of northern Cannaregio are some of the least known, and loveliest, parts of Venice. Modest houses and low-key *palazzi* line the canals, there's plenty of local life and the area is scatterd with a handful of superb and contrasting churches. This walk threads through narrow *calle*, along busy quaysides and across tree-shaded squares to show you the best of the *sestiere*, well away fom the crowds.

THE WALK

Distance:	4km (2.5 miles)
Allow:	2 hours
Start at:	Tre Archi *vaporetto* stop
End at:	Ca d'Oro *vaporetto* stop

HOW TO GET THERE

Vaporetto: No. 51, 52 to Tre Archi

Walk off the Tre Archi landing stage turn right down the Fondamenta di Cannaregio, passing the graceful Ponte dei Tre Archi on your right.

❶ This is the only bridge in Venice with more than a single span; it's name means 'three arches'. The Canale di Cannaregio is one of the three waterways in Venice to be classified as a *canale* (the others are the Canal Grande and the Giudecca); all the rest are *rii*.

Take the ninth turn-off to your left, ducking under a *sotoportego* into the Soto de Ghetto Vecchio. This widens out and passes through two small *campi* to a bridge over the Rio di Ghetto Nuovo, the canal that surrounds the Ghetto (▷ 102–103). Go over the bridge to the Campo

Ghetto Nuovo. Cross the *campo* diagonally right and take the bridge with the cast-iron balustrade over the Rio della Misericordia, turning left on the other side along the Fondamenta dei Ormesini.

❷ You are now well into an area that barely sees a tourist, with long, regular canals and *fondamente* lined with shops.

Take the first right up Calle Turlona and cross the bridge at the end. Turn right, continue straight ahead then turn left into Calle Capitello. This leads, via a bridge, to the little-known church of Sant'Alvise (▷ 124). Backtrack down Calle Capitello and turn left at the end into the Rio della Sensa.
    Walk left along the *fondamenta* and cross a bridge, then take the next turning left (blue sign to Fatebenefratelli) up Calle Loredan. This leads through to the third of the three parallel canals in this part of the *sestiere*, the Rio Madonna dell'Orto. Cross the bridge and turn right along the *fondamenta* to Madonna dell'Orto (▷ 106–107). With

the church behind you, bear left for a short distance and cross the bridge to the Palazzo Mastelli.

❸ The façade of this picturesque Byzantine-Gothic *palazzo* has a splendid relief of a man leading a heavily loaded camel. Legend says this refers to the builder of the house, an Eastern merchant who, having made his fortune, sent home for a beautiful wife. 'How will I find your house in such a vast and strange city?' wrote the girl, to which he replied 'Just look for a house with a reminder of home.' More prosaically, the camel probably refers to the trading links of the Mastelli family.

Walk through into the Campo dei Mori (▷ 78), and detour a few steps left to Tintoretto's house at No. 3399.

❹ This 15th-century house was occupied by the artist from 1574 until his death in 1594, when he lived here with his daughter, Marietta, also a painter.

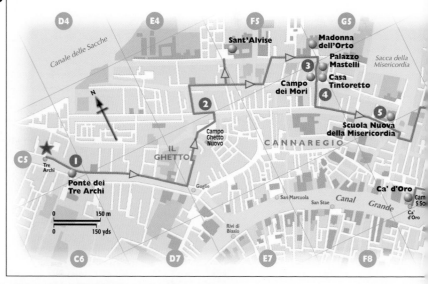

Cross the canal and continue down Calle Larga to the next canal. Turn left along the Fondamenta della Misericordia; the building on the left at the far end, dominating the Campo della Misericordia, is the defunct Scuola Nuova della Misericordia.

5 The *scuola* was designed by Sansovino in 1532 when the Misericordia became a Scuola Grande; it was never finished. The old *scuola*, across the Rio della Sensa to the north lies a short distance from Tintoretto's house and was used by the artist as a studio, where he worked on the *Paradiso* for the Palazzo Ducale (▷ 115–116).

Cross the bridge, turn right, then take the second bridge on the right and walk under two *soto-portegi* (arches) to emerge on the Calle Rachette and take a left turn. Walk on, cross another wide canal and head right along the Fondamenta Santa Caterina. This leads into the Campo dei Gesuiti (▷ 77), with the over-the-top marvels of the church (▷ 101) at the far end on the right.

With your back to the church and the *carabinieri* station on your left, cross the bridge and walk down Salizzada Seriman. Bear left into Salizzada Spezier, then right into Rio Terrà Santi Apostoli, passing the Co-op on the right. Turn right along Rio Terrà dei Francesci (past the cinema) and left onto Salizzada

Pistor; this will lead you down into the Campo Santi Apostoli.

Follow the yellow signs to the Rialto, turning left up the narrow Salizzada San Canciano immediately before the next bridge. This leads through Campo San Canciano into lovely Campo Santa Maria Nova, with its trees, benches and gossiping locals. The beautiful Renaissance church of Santa Maria dei Miracoli (▷ 148–149) stands at the far end. Turn right as you leave the church, cross a canal, then take the third turning left back onto Salizzada San Canciano. This leads to the main Rialto–Ferrovia route, so turn right and join the crowds through Santi Apostoli and along the Strada Nova. You'll pass pretty Campo Santa Sofia, fronting the Grand Canal, on your left. Take the narrow *calle* straight after the campo, which leads past the Ca' d'Oro (▷ 70–71), and on to the *vaporetto* stop.

WHEN TO GO

This is a good walk for either the morning or afternoon, though avoid the middle of the day when things will be very quiet and some churches are shut.

WHERE TO EAT

The cafés in and around Campo Santi Apostoli are a good place to pause and take a break. Alternatively, you could make a short detour to the Algiubagio (▷ 260) on the Fondamente Nuove near the Gesuiti , which is great for sandwiches, pizza and ice-cream, or stop off at the Osteria da Rioba (▷ 264–265) along Fondamenta della Misericordia.

Venice's second-largest sestiere has a very lived-in, local feel to it, with its quiet, peaceful streets and delightful old buildings, often strung with washing

AROUND MURANO

Murano and its glassworks are high on most visitors' list, but there's more to the island than crystal. This is an independant community with its own churches, housing, shops and way of life that's remarkably self-contained. This walk takes you through the heart of the island and gives glimpses of everyday Murano life from the main *fondamente*.

THE WALK

Distance:	2.5 km (1.5 miles)
Allow:	2 hours–half a day with visits
Start at:	Colonna *vaporetto* stop
End at:	Faro *vaporetto* stop

Take either the No. 42 from Piazzale Roma or the Fondamente Nuove or the DM from Piazzale Roma and disembark at Colonna. At the *pontile* turn right and walk up the Fondamente dei Vetrai. Cross the canal at the first bridge on the right to the showrooms exhibiting modern Murano glass.

❶ The exhibits here are by the glass firms of Barovier e Toso, Carlo Moretti and Venini, three of Murano's best-known and most innovative large-scale producers.

Continue along this side of the canal, lined with primarily Gothic structures.

❷ These were built as homes for the glassworks owners and doubled as warehouses for raw materials and workshops where the glass was blown.

Take the next bridge on your left back across the canal and walk along the Fondamente dei Vetrai to the church of San Pietro Martiri (▷ 173), one of Murano's only two functioning churches. Continue along the *fondamenta* (now Fondamenta da Mula), keeping an eye open for a narrow passage to your left just before the Ponte Vivarini, signed Formia.

❸ Formia is one of the best working *fornaci* (glass factories) to visit. Windows open into the busy workshops where teams of *maestri* and their helpers will be working flat out. Watch carefully and you'll be able to see how each member of the team has a very specific and skilled role in the the the manufacture of each finished piece (▷ 172).

Walk past the bridge to admire the Palazzo da Mula.

❹ This 15th-century Gothic *palazzo* was renovated in the 19th century, but still retains some lovely windows and Veneto-Byzantine motifs dating from the 12th and 13th centuries.

Cross the Ponte Vivarini and turn right along the Fondamenta Cavour, which becomes the Fondamenta Giustiniani at the canal junction.

❺ This is lined with glass shops, many selling cheap and unattractive foreign imports. If you want to buy, make sure the article comes from one of the main showrooms or boutiques and is guaranteed to be made on Murano.

Continue along the Fondamenta Giustiniani to the entrance to the Museo del Vetro (▷ 172–173). As you leave the museum turn left and walk along to the Campo San Donato and the superb basilica of Santa Maria e Donato (▷ 173).
    Cross the the bridge outside the back of the basilica and turn left to walk along the Fondamenta Sebastiano Santi, lined with modest canalside houses. Cross the next bridge on your left, turn left on the other

side, and walk back to the basilica entrance. With your back to the basilica entrance, take Calle San Donato and follow it along to a T-junction where you turn left onto Calle Conterie.

❻ The run-down buildings here date mainly from the 19th century, a time of huge expansion on Murano. During the 17th and 18th centuries Murano, as well as being Europe's main glass supplier, was also a popular resort with Venetian noblemen, who built country retreats surrounded by gardens on the island. During the late 1800s the gardens were built over and two inlets were filled to create new residential areas.

Follow Calle Conterie to emerge into Campo San Bernardo, a lovely, low-key *campo* with trees and benches, that gives a taste of Murano's true life away from the tourists. Turn left down Calle de Mistero and walk back down to hit the Fondamenta Cavour. Turn right across Ponte Vivarini, then right again and left over the next bridge across the Rio dei Vetrai. Turn right over the bridge and along the Fondamenta Daniel Manin, taking the third left into the wide Viale Garibaldi which leads across to the Faro *vaporetto* stop. Take the No. 41 or DM back to the city.

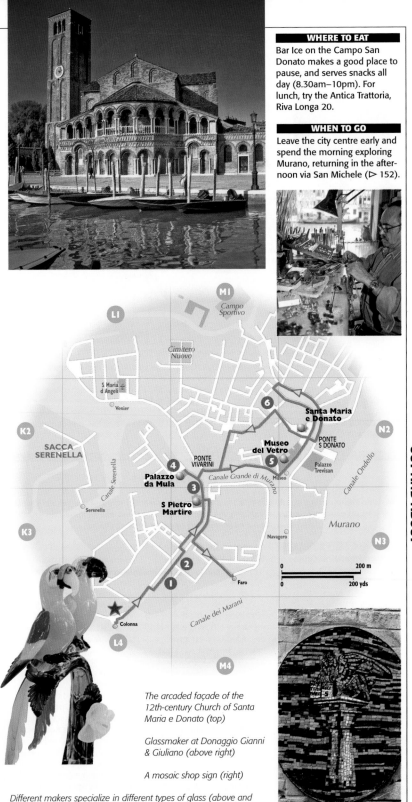

WHERE TO EAT

Bar Ice on the Campo San Donato makes a good place to pause, and serves snacks all day (8.30am–10pm). For lunch, try the Antica Trattoria, Riva Longa 20.

WHEN TO GO

Leave the city centre early and spend the morning exploring Murano, returning in the afternoon via San Michele (▷ 152).

Campo Sportivo

Cimitero Nuovo

S Maria d'Angeli

Venier

SACCA SERENELLA

Canale Serenella

Serenella

Santa Maria e Donato

Museo del Vetro

PONTE S DONATO

PONTE VIVARINI

Palazzo da Mula

Canale Grande di Murano

Museo

Palazzo Trevisan

S Pietro Martire

Navagero

Murano

Canale Ondello

Faro

Colonna

Canale dei Marani

0   200 m
0   200 yds

K2   K3   L1   M1   N2   N3   L4   M4

OUT AND ABOUT

The arcaded façade of the 12th-century Church of Santa Maria e Donato (top)

Glassmaker at Donaggio Gianni & Giuliano (above right)

A mosaic shop sign (right)

Different makers specialize in different types of glass (above and left) on Murano, so choose a factory whose products interest you

EXCURSIONS

The time may come when the watery pleasures of Venice begin to diminish and you need a change and a shot of something more modern. The region of the Veneto is rich in lovely cities, and the historic and thriving cities of Padua, Vicenza and Verona all lie within easy reach of Venice. Though all are popular, none of them is as crowded as Venice itself and an excursion will give a real taste of the Veneto, one of Italy's most dynamic regions. For a complete change of pace, you could combine boat and bus to explore the outer islands of the lagoon and the atmospheric old fishing town of Chioggia.

1. EXCURSION

PADOVA (PADUA)

Historic Padua, only a short train ride from Venice, is a university city and the Veneto's most important economic centre, combining art, monuments, churches and tempting shops, all scattered around a beguiling and compact historic district.

BASICS

Tourist Information Offices
Stazione Ferroviaria 36130
☎ 049 875 20 77
◷ Mon–Sat 9.15–7, Sun 9–noon
www.turismopadova.it

Galleria Pedrocchi 35130
☎ 049 876 79 27
◷ Mon–Sat 9–1.30, 3–7
www.turismopadova.it

HOW TO GET THERE

Padua is 32km (21 miles) west of Venice
By Train: All southwest trains from Venice on the Bologna line stop at Padua; journey time 25–35 minutes; tel 041 892 021 for information
By Bus: SITA buses from Piazzale Roma every 30 minutes: journey time 45 minutes; tel 049 820844 for information

CAPPELLA DEGLI SCROVEGNI

The chapel was built in 1300 by Enrico Scrovegni to atone for his father's usury—Scrovegni senior died screaming 'give me the keys of my strong box', and was nominated by Dante for a place in *Inferno*. Between 1303 and 1309 the walls were frescoed by Giotto with scenes from the life of Christ and the Virgin, set against a background of radiant blue. Visitors are limited to 25 at a time, but you can fill in the wait in the multimedia room, an excellent introduction to Giotto and his times.

MUSEI CIVICI EREMITANI

Occupying adjoining buildings to the Cappella degli Scrovegni, the Musei Civici Eremitani, Padua's main museum complex, focus on Venetian painting and sculpture from the early 14th to 19th centuries. The big local names in painting are all represented and include Giovanni Bellini, Titian, Tintoretto, Giorgione, Veronese and Tiepolo, and there are works by Flemish and Dutch artists. Sculptures date back to the 15th century, and the archaeological section is particularly strong in Roman sculpture, busts and statues from the surrounding area, as well as Egyptian, Greek and Etruscan antiquities. The Palazzo Zuckermann, across the road, houses the applied and decorative arts collections.

PALAZZO DELLA RAGIONE
The Palazzo della Ragione, medieval Padua's assembly hall and law courts, was built between 1218 and 1219. This vast building, altered repeatedly over the centuries, is remarkable today for the cycle of 15th-century astrological frescoes in the main hall, which also contains a huge wooden horse, constructed for a tournament in 1466. The ground floor has been home to food stalls for over 800 years, while the Piazza della Frutta and Piazza delle Erbe, on each side of the palace, host one of northern Italy's finest food and produce markets.

CAFFÈ PEDROCCHI
The splendidly eclectic Caffè Pedrocchi, built in the early 19th century, was once Padua's main intellectual salon; today, it doubles as a bar and restaurant. The upstairs rooms were restored and reopened in 1999, and present a succession of themed spaces whose decoration encompasses every style from Etruscan and Greek to Gothic and Renaissance—the Egyptian Room, with its starry ceiling and dog gods, is pick of the bunch.

BASILICA DI SANT'ANTONIO
The Basilica di Sant'Antonio, Il Santo, is one of Italy's main pilgrim shrines, packed with suppliants, who come to pray to this Portuguese-born patron of Italy. The Basilica was built between the mid-13th and 14th centuries and its treasures include marble bas-reliefs showing scenes from St. Anthony's life in the Cappella dell'Arca, which contains his tomb. Donatello (1386–1466) created the bronze panels on the high altar; he was also responsible for the superb equestrian bronze dominating the surrounding square, which shows the mercenary Erasmo de Narni, also known as Gattamelata (Honey Cat).

TIPS
● The PadovaCard is valid for 48 hours and gives free admission to all civic museums, free transport and reductions on other museums, guided tours, selected shops and accommodation. It costs €14 from tourist information offices.
● The train is by far the best way to get to Padua; you'll avoid most of the sprawling and unattractive outskirts and the station is an easy 15-minute walk from the historic heart of the city.

The Prato della Valle is adorned with statues of local dignitaries and surrounded by a canal

PLACES TO VISIT

Cappella degli Scrovegni
✚ 319 C1 • Piazza Eremitani 8
☎ Book at least 48 hours in advance (049 202 00 20) or book online; tickets to be collected 1 hour in advance
🕐 Daily 9–7. Closed 1 May, 16–18 Nov
💶 Adult €12; child (6–17) and students €5 (includes admission to Musei Eremitani)
www.cappelladegliscrovegni.it

Palazzo della Ragione
✚ 319 B2 • Piazza delle Erbe (entrance from Via VIII Febbraio)
☎ 049 820 50 06
🕐 Mar–Oct Tue–Sun 9–7, Nov–Feb Tue–Sun 10–6
💶 Adult €8; child (6–17) and students €4

Caffè Pedrocchi
✚ 319 B2 • Via VIII Febbraio 15 (entrance from Piazzetta Pedrocchi)
☎ 049 820 50 07
🕐 Tue–Sun 9.30–12.30, 3.30–6
💶 Adult €4; child (6–17) and students €2.50

Basilica di Sant'Antonio
✚ 319 C3 • Piazza del Santo
☎ 049 878 9722
🕐 Mon–Fri 6.20–7, Sat–Sun and holidays 6.30–7.45
💶 Free

OUT AND ABOUT

FROM THE LIDO TO CHIOGGIA VIA PELLESTRINA

This full-day excursion combines travel by land and water to take you to the ancient fishing port of Chioggia, a beguiling town, intersected with canals, which you can explore on foot.

BASICS

Tourist Information Office

San Francesco Fuori le Mura, Campo Marconi

☎ 041 550 0911

🕐 12 Jun–31 Aug Tue–Wed 9–1, Thu–Sat 9–1, 7.30–11.30, Sun 7.30–11.30pm; 1 Sep –11 Jun Tue–Wed 9–1, Thu–Sat 9–1, 3–6, Sun 3–6pm

HOW TO GET THERE

Co-ordinated bus and waterbus service

From Venice centre: *Vaporetto* No. 1, 51, 52, 61, 62 to the Lido, then

From the Lido: Bus 11 from Gran Viale Santa Maria Elisabetta to Pellestrina, then

From Pellestrina: Connecting *motonave* 11 to Chioggia

THE LIDO

Take the *vaporetto* from Venice to the Lido and disembark to cross the road, then walk down the Gran Viale Santa Maria Elisabetta. The No. 11 bus stop for Pellestrina and Chioggia is clearly marked 100m (110 yards) down on the right. The bus heads down the Lido (▷ 171) keeping to the sea side of the island, until swinging lagoonwards at the little settlement of Malamocco. From here, the island is relatively unspoiled, the apartment blocks and villas giving way to flower farms and fields of artichokes threaded with quiet canals. The furthest settlement is Alberoni, where the bus takes precedence to board the ferry for the shuttle across the Porto di Malamocco, the central sea access from the lagoon, to the long, sandy island of Pellestrina.

PELLESTRINA

Pellestrina is a superb contrast to the Lido, a sand-swept spit of land, dotted with tamarisk trees and great stands of bamboo, and bordered on the sea side by the massive *murazzi*, the walls against the sea erected by the Republic in the late 18th century. Its three settlements earn their living from fishing, both from the boats

you'll see moored on the lagoon side and from fish farming, whose nets and floating huts can be spotted on the calm lagoon waters.

At the village of Pellestrina the bus stops and passengers connect with the *motonave* for Chioggia, a 25-minute trip which passes the uninhabited end of the island before crossing the Porto di Chioggia to reach Chioggia itself.

A WALK ROUND CHIOGGIA

From the boat, head straight up Chioggia's main street, the Corso del Popolo, lined with arcaded buildings.

❶ This is one of the town's three parallel streets, each connected by straight *calli* and bridges which traverse the town's three canals. They make a grid pattern which reflects Chioggia's Roman past; the town was among the most ancient of the lagoon settlements.

Continue for 150m (165 yards) to the church of Sant'Andrea Apostolo and its adjoining campanile.

❷ The church was founded in the 11th and 12th centuries and rebuilt in 1743, when the façade was added.

Continue until you see the entrance to the Pescheria on your left.

❸ This was the town's original *granaio* (grainstore), built in 1328, where grain used for paying taxes to Venice was stored after Chioggia lost its independence during the Venetian Republic's struggle against the Genoese. It now houses the fish market (Tue–Sat 8–noon), where local fishermen sell fish straight off their boats; you'll see these moored in the canal on the other side of the market.

Continue down the Corso, past the charming pedimented police headquarters, to the Basilica di San Iacopo, an ornate baroque reconstruction dating from 1742 that's fronted by Chioggia's war memorial. Continue to the end of the Corso, and the Duomo of Santa Maria Assunta on the opposite side of the street.

❹ The square *campanile* dates from 1347 to 1350, while the present Duomo was designed by Baldassare Longhena in 1623, after a fire destroyed the original 12th-century cathedral. The three-naved interior is a symphony of white walls and cool grey Istrian stone pillars and columns, the whole dominated by the heavily carved pulpit, where two sinuous marble figures act as supports. The pictures include works by Palma il Giovane (1548–1628) and Giambattista Tiepolo (1696–1770).

Continue up and past the arch to visit the Museo Civico della Laguna Sud.

❺ The museum, housed in a 15th-century Franciscan convent, tells the story of Chioggia and the southern lagoon, with displays on the Roman era on the ground floor and a fascinating collection of boats and old fishing memorabilia on the upper floors. Look out for the models of traditional fishing methods and the exhibits on the construction of Chioggia's own fishing vessels, the *tartana* and *bragozzo*.

Leave the museum and swing right over the bridge to walk along the Canale della Vena, which runs parallel with the Corso.

❻ This canalside stroll is almost impossibly picturesque, with brightly painted fishing boats of all sizes on the water,

OUT AND ABOUT

tiny shops under the arcades, fruit and vegetable stalls and flapping washing in the adjoining courtyards all adding to the charm. The waterfront is the town's main food shopping street and thronged throughout the morning, while the narow *calli* leading off illustrate perfectly how the town has retained its medieval layout.

At the bottom of the canal turn right along Calle Santa Croce to reach the church of San Domenico.

❼ Standing on its own small island, the church of San Domenico was founded in the 13th century and reconstructed in the 18th-century. Its chief treasure is the 1520 *St. Paul*, the last picture painted by Vittore Carpaccio (c1460–1525). Don't miss the charming collection of ex-voto paintings, commissioned and presented by fishermen in thanksgiving for favours; one shows a sea rescue by helicopter.

Backtrack to the Canale della Vena and cross the elegant Ponte Vigo, guarded by four stone lions, to reach the bottom of the Corso and the *vaporetto*.

Sunset over the lagoon (above);
Buying tickets for the ferry
(right);
The Westin Excelsior hotel
(below);
Aerial view over the Lido
(bottom)

ACTIVITIES

One of the nicest ways to do this trip is to rent a bicycle on the Lido (▷ 216) and cycle all the way down the Lido and Pellestrina; you can take the bicycle on the boat. This gives you the freedom to stop at will, taking time to explore the settlements en route and perhaps have a swim as well. The Lido beaches (▷ 171) are mainly *stabilimenti*, bathing establishments where you pay, but there are free beaches on the western end of the Lido and more options on Pellestrina.

For the ultimate get-away-from-it-all beach day, alight at the request-only stop of Caroman on Pellestrina and find a secluded spot on the other side of the *murazzi*—you'll have to take a picnic with you. The quiet roads of the island are ideal for a leisurely stroll.

PLACES TO VISIT
Museo Civico della Laguna del Sud
See Tourist Information Office opposite
🎫 €2.50

Santa Maria Assunta (Duomo)
✉ Corso del Popolo
🕐 Oct–end May Mon–Sat 10.30–12, 3.30–6, Sun 8.30–1, 3.30–6; Jun–end Sep Mon–Sat 7.30–12, 3.30–6, Sun 8.30–1, 3.30–7

TIPS

● The journey time from the Lido to Chioggia is just over an hour, with twice-hourly departures. It's worth taking time to research when planning this trip to ensure the things you want to see in Chioggia are open.
● Check the timetable if you want to break the journey and spend time on Pellestrina.
● Pick up an English-language guide before you start your museum visit in Chioggia; there's no English labelling.

OUT AND ABOUT

VICENZA

Beautiful Vicenza, ringed with green hills, is a prime example of a prosperous Veneto town, with excellent facilities and an easy going lifestyle. Its artistic appeal lies in its superb *palazzi* and civic buildings, many of them the work of the great Andrea Palladio.

BASICS
Tourist Information Office
🏢 Piazza Matteotti 12
☎ 0444 320 854
🕐 Mon–Sat 9–1, 2.30–6
www.comune.vicenza.it

HOW TO GET THERE
Vicenza is 74km (47 miles) northwest of Venice
By Train: All northwest trains from Venice on the Verona line stop at Vicenza; journey time 55 minutes: tel 041 892 021 for information

All over the Western world, civic buildings and churches pay homage to Vicenza's architectural glories, the work of its most famous son, Andrea di Pietro della Gondola, also known as Palladio (1505–80). This pocket-sized city, a UNESCO World Heritage Site, contains some of his finest works, and with its laid-back atmosphere, smart shops, restaurants and green spaces it deserves to be one of the Veneto's must-sees. In 1404 Vicenza became a Venetian possession, adorned with Gothic palaces, but the big architectural makeover came in the 16th century when Palladio and his brilliant neo-classical style burst upon the scene. Though born in Padova (Padua), Palladio found his major patron, the humanist nobleman Trissino, in Vicenza and in the years between 1540 and 1580 utterly transformed the face of the city.

THE HISTORIC HEART
The heart of Vicenza is bisected by the Corso Palladio. It's lined with a stunning procession of grandiose mansions and *palazzi*, of which five were designed by Palladio. From the west end of the Corso and the Porta Castello, these are the Palazzo Thiene Bonin Longare (1562) on the left, the altered Palazzo Capra (1540–45) at No. 45, which retains its Palladian façade and doorway, and the Palazzo Thiene at

No. 47. This was probably first designed by Giulio Romano and later modified by Palladio. Palladio was also responsible for the Palazzo Pojana at No. 97, a superb double-block mansion which abuts the stupendous Palazzo Trissino, designed by Vicenzo Scamozzi (1552–1616), Palladio's most gifted pupil. At the far end of the Corso stands Casa Cogollo (1560–70), thought to have been Palladio's own house. The Corso opens into Piazza Matteotti, home to both the Teatro Olimpico and the Palazzo Chiericati (1550), one of Palladio's most triumphant buildings, now housing the Museo Civico.

South from here lies the Piazza dei Signori, the heart of the *centro storico*, dominated by Palladio's Basilica, started in 1549 and once the city's law courts and the architect's first reputation-making project, and his Loggia del Capitaniato. The double-tiered loggia of the Basilica encloses the earlier Gothic Palazzo della Ragione, which suffered from subsidence until Palladio's intervention. The huge and elegant complex next to the Loggia is the Monte di Pietà, Vicenza's 16th-century pawnshop. Behind the Basilica, the Piazza dell'Erbe sells fruit and vegetables as it has since medieval times. Scattered about central Vicenza, notably on Contrà Porti and Contrà Riale, are more Palladian palaces—Palazzo Barbaran (home to the Museo

Palladiano), Palazzo Colleoni Porto and Palazzo Iseppo Porto are the stars. Corso Fogazzero has a number of fine Gothic buildings and Palladio's superb Palazzo Valmarana-Braga (1566).

THE TEATRO OLIMPICO
The Teatro Olimpico, Europe's oldest indoor theatre, was designed by Palladio in 1579 and opened in 1585. The architect died before it was complete, though the astonishing trompe l'oeil permanent stage set of a classical city was inspired by his designs and executed after his death by Vicenzo Scamozzi. Five wood and stucco Renaissance street scenes radiate back from the front stage seemingly for several hundred metres. It's all illusion; the set is only 15m (40ft) deep and 2m (6.5ft) high. The auditorium is modelled on Greek and Roman theatres, with 13 semicircular wooden steps, which double as seating, rising in front of the stage. The theatre is still in use today.

THE MUSEUMS AND CHURCHES
Vicenza's main museum occupies the superb Palladian Palazzo Chiericati, and gives an overview of local painters, as well as a fine collection from further afield. This includes pictures by Giovanni Bellini (1430–1516), Tintoretto (1518–94), Veronese (1528–88) and Giambattista Tiepolo (1696–1770). The Venetian schools also figure strongly in the Palazzo Leoni Montanari, a superb baroque *palazzo* that contains 14 quirky genre paintings by Pietro Longhi (1702–85), as well as a large collection of Russian icons. Architecture fans should not miss the Museo Palladiano, in a palace designed by the

The Lion of St. Mark atop one of the columns in Piazza dei Signori

Vicenza stands in the gentle green Venetian plain (top); Villa Capra Valmarana 'La Rotonda' (above)

great man, and home to an internationally prestigious architectural institute.

Vicenza's churches are lower key; they include Santa Maria Nova, designed by Palladio in 1575; the Duomo, an ancient foundation that was restored after extensive damage in World War II; and the Gothic Franciscan San Lorenzo. Pick of the bunch is Santa Corona, a 13th-century Gothic church that houses a Palladio chapel and paintings by Giovanni Bellini and Veronese.

VILLAS AND GREEN SPACES

The hill on Vicenza's south-eastern edge is Monte Berico, an important plague shrine topped by a 17th-century basilica (Oct–end Apr 6–12.30, 2.30–6; May–end Sep 6–12.30, 2.30–7.30). Close by are two villas; Villa Valmarana, nicknamed 'Ai Nani' after the stone dwarfs on its wall, contains astounding frescoes by Tiepolo father and son. A few minutes from here is one of Palladio's most famous villas, the Villa Capra Valmarana, or the Rotonda. The Rotonda (1567) is the only Palladian villa built purely for pleasure and one of the most imitated; its four symmetrical façades have inspired countless other architects.

North of central Vicenza, across the River Bacchiglione, lies the Parco Querini, a lovely space with statues and cool green shade, while, to the south, the Parco Marzo is the perfect place to relax after all that sightseeing.

PLACES TO VISIT

Basilica Palladiana

✉ Piazza dei Signori
☎ 0444 323 681
🕐 Tue–Sun 10.30–1, 3–7
💶 €1

Teatro Olimpico

✉ Piazza Matteotti 11
☎ 0444 222 800
🕐 Sep–end May Tue–Sun 9–4.45; Jun–end Aug Tue–Sun 9–7
💶 Entry with Vicenza Card only €7; family ticket for parents and at least 1 child €12; reduced for EU citizens over 60 and students €4; child (under 14) free

Museo Civico (Pinacoteca)

✉ Palazzo Chiericati, Piazza Matteotti 37–39
☎ 0444 321 348
🕐 Sep–end Jun Tue–Sun 9–5; Jul–end Tue–Sun Aug 10–6
💶 Entry with Vicenza Card only €7; family ticket for parents and at least 1 child €12; reduced for EU citizens over 60 and students €4; child (under 14) free

Museo Palladiano

✉ Palazzo Barbaran da Porto, Contrà Porti 11
☎ 0444 323 014
🕐 Tue–Sun 10–6
💶 €3.50
www.cisapalladio.org

Santa Corona

✉ Contrà Santa Corona
☎ 0444 321 924
🕐 Mon 2–4pm, Tue–Sat 8.30–12, 3–5.30, Sun 3–5.30pm
💶 Free

Villa Capra Valmarana 'La Rotonda'

✉ Via Rotonda 29
☎ 0444 321 793
🕐 13 Mar–3 Nov gardens: Tue–Sun 10–12, 3–6; interior: Wed 10–12, 3–6. 4 Nov–16 Mar gardens: Tue–Sun 10–12, 2.30–5
💶 Gardens €5, interior €10

Villa Valmarana 'Ai Nani'

✉ Via dei Nani 2–8
☎ 0444 321 803
🕐 15 Mar–5 Nov Tue, Fri 3–6, Wed–Thu, Sat–Sun 10–12, 3–6
💶 €6

TIPS

● Visits to the Teatro Olimpico are only available by buying the full Vicenza Card combined ticket, valid for 3 days, from the tourist office and all partici-pating museums.
● The station is a 15-minute walk from the Vicenza's historic heart.
● The main *palazzi* are well signed.

OUT AND ABOUT

VERONA

Rose-red Verona, the setting for Shakespeare's *Romeo and Juliet*, is rich in Roman ruins, ancient churches, fine *palazzi* and monuments. One of northern Italy's most prosperous cities, with a thriving cultural life, it's an ideal place for a mix of sightseeing, excellent shopping and fine dining.

BASICS

Tourist Information Office

🔲 319 c2 • Via degli Alpini 9, off Piazza Brà

☎ 045 806 8680

🄲 Oct–end May Mon–Sat 9–6, Sun 9–1; Jun–end Sep daily 8–8

www.tourism.verona.it

HOW TO GET THERE

Verona is 124km (78 miles) northwest of Venice

By Train: Trains run regularly between Venice and Verona, with a journey time of 90 minutes (tel 041 892 021 for information).

OVERVIEW

Verona was founded by the Romans in 89BC, and it's history is unremarkable, a story of domination by exterior powers, ending with its annexation by Venice in 1402. Today it's among Italy's most prosperous provincial cities with a thriving economy, whose mainstays are manufacture, printing and pharmaceuticals. The city's historic core, still contained within massive 16th-century walls, has miraculously retained most of its Roman, medieval and Renaissance monuments, with the Piazza dell'Erbe still occupying the site of the Roman forum. The grid of streets round this area is within a loop of the River Adige, and it's here that virtually all the city's main monuments can be found.

PIAZZA BRÀ AND THE ARENA

Head first for Piazza Brà, a huge, irregular *piazza* fringed with cafés and dominated by one of the city's best-known monuments, the great Roman amphitheatre known as the Arena. Built in the 1st century AD, it's the third largest of the surviving Roman amphitheatres in Italy, an elliptical structure measuring 110m (456ft) by 139m (364ft) and capable of seating 25,000. In 1114 a serious earthquake destroyed all but four of the arches of the exterior arcade, but the interior is intact with steeply pitched tiers of pink marble seats and spectacular—if vertiginous—views from the top. Since 1913 it's been the venue for a popular summer opera season, with sets of gargantuan dimensions.

PIAZZA DELL'ERBE

Verona's focal square, the Piazza dell'Erbe, is connected with Piazza Brà by Via Mazzini, a pedestrianized thoroughfare that's home to the city's most tempting shops. At the far end, the Piazza, ringed by architecture spanning the centuries, is the scene of a lively daily food market. The finest buildings are at the northern end; the medieval Torre di Gardello, the beautifully frescoed late Renaissance Casa Mazzanti and the Palazzo Maffei, a highly decorated baroque palace. The tall buildings at the opposite end of the *piazza* once marked the edge of the Jewish ghetto.

PIAZZA DEI SIGNORI

The Piazza dei Signori is linked with the Piazza dell'Erbe by the bulk of the 12th-century Palazzo della Ragione and contains the elegant Loggia del Consiglio, built in the 15th century and marking the introduction of Renaissance architecture to Verona. A statue of the poet Dante (1265–1321) stands in the square, and, on its south side,

a gateway leads into the Mercato Vecchio, a superb courtyard with Romanesque arches and a splendid exterior Gothic staircase. From here you can climb the Torre de' Lamberti, built in the 12th century, and, at 83m (272ft), Verona's highest tower. Back on the Piazza dei Signori, the east exit leads to the Scaligeri tombs, extraordinary funerary monuments to the della Scala family, also known as the Scaligeri. By the 1200s this clan had emerged as Verona's most powerful family, boosting their fearsome reputation by naming themselves after dogs—the founder Mastino, 'the Mastiff', was followed by Cangrande, 'Big Dog' and Cansignorio, 'Lord Dog'. Their tombs show Cangrande, who died in 1329, mounted in all his power, while the canopied Gothic tombs of the others are enclosed in railings decorated with ladder motifs (della Scala means 'ladder').

CASA DI GIULIETTA

Verona's most popular tourist attraction, the Casa di Giulietta (Juliet's House), is besieged throughout its opening hours by hundreds of lovesick teenagers and foreign romantics, who adorn its walls with scribbled graffiti and notes beseeching Juliet's aid in affairs of the heart. The house has no connection with the Juliet story; the Montagu and Capulet families did exist, but they lived nearer Vicenza than Verona. The cult of Juliet was the inspiration of the Verona tourist board during the economically depressed 1920s. It's been a major draw ever since, and there's even a 'Juliet' club, complete with website. The house dates from the early 14th century and was probably originally an inn; the famous balcony, however, was erected by the city council in 1928.

OUT AND ABOUT

VERONA'S CHURCHES

Verona's main churches, with the exception of San Zeno, all lie in the *centro storico*. Near the river is the fine Gothic church of Sant'Anastasia and the Duomo (cathedral). Sant'Anastasia's interior is lovely, with beautiful pointed ceiling lunettes. The Romanesque Duomo's portico is flanked by lions and surmounted by *Christ in Glory*, and leads into a beautiful red-and-white stone apse. The side paintings include an *Assumption* by Titian (1487–1576).

If you cross the River Adige over the Ponte Garibaldi near the Duomo, you'll find yourself in 'Veronetta', with its two superb churches—15th-century San Giorgio in Braida and beautiful Santo Stefano, pieced together in the 12th century from earlier buildings. East lies the Teatro Romano, still used for a summer drama festival, while there are famous sunset views from the Castel San Pietro higher up the hill. West from here, along the river, stands San Zeno Maggiore, one of the loveliest of all Romanesque churches, founded in the 4th century and attaining its present form around 1398. A portal, topped by a 12th-century rose window, encloses superb 11th-century bronze doors that open into a lofty interior. The altarpiece is by Andrea Mantegna (1431–1506).

MUSEO CIVICO D'ARTE

Back in central Verona, you can cut southwest to reach the Scaligeri fortress known as the Castelvecchio, a splendid riverside structure which is home to the excellent Museo Civico d'Arte. The restored interior, all steel walkways and gleaming glass, is a labyrinth of passages, stairs and lofty rooms where the museum's collections are displayed. As well as sculpture and goldwork, there are works by big names here—look out for Mantegna's *Holy Family*, a serene *Madonna* by Giovanni Bellini (1430–1516), a *Nativity* by Tintoretto (1518–94) and *Santi Caterina e Veneranda* by Carpaccio (1460–1525).

PLACES TO VISIT

Arena
+ 319 b3 • Piazza Brà
☎ 045 800 3204
🕐 Tue–Sun 8.30–7.30, Mon 1.30–7.30 (subject to alteration during the opera season)
💶 €5

Torre de'Lamberti
+ 319 b2 • Cortile Mercato Vecchio
☎ 045 803 2726
🕐 Tue–Sun 9.30–7.30, Mon 1.30–7.30
💶 €3.50

Duomo
+ 319 b1 • Piazza del Duomo
☎ 045 592 813
🕐 Mar–end Oct Mon–Sat 10–5.30, Sun 1–6; Nov–end Feb Tue–Sat 10–4
💶 €2
www.veronatuttintorno.it/chiesevive

Casa di Giulietta
+ 319 c2 • Via Cappello 23
☎ 045 803 4303
🕐 Tue–Sun 8.30–7.30, Mon 1.30–7.30
💶 €4

Museo Civico d'Arte
+ 319 a3 • Corso Castelvecchio 2
☎ 045 806 2611
🕐 Tue–Sun 8.30–7.30, Mon 1.30–7.30
💶 €4

San Lorenzo
+ 319 b2 • Corso Cavour
☎ 045 592 813
🕐 Mar–end Oct Mon–Sat 10–6, Sun 1–6; Nov–end Feb Tue–Sat 10–4
💶 €2

Sant'Anastasia
+ 319 c1 • Piazza Santa Anastasia
☎ 045 592 813
🕐 Mar–end Oct Mon–Sat 9–6, Sun 1–6; Nov–end Feb Tue–Sat 10–4
💶 €1.50

Basilica di San Zeno
+ 319 off a3 • Piazza San Zeno
☎ 045 592 813
🕐 Mar–end Oct Mon–Sat 8.30–6, Sun 1–6; Nov–end Feb Tue–Sat 10–4
💶 €2

Stalls at the Piazza delle'Erbe (far left); Verona on the Adige river (top); the balcony at Juliet's House (middle); the 1st century arches of the Arena (above)

TIPS

● From outside the station, buses 11, 12, 13 (weekdays) and 91 and 92 (Sundays and holidays) leave from Marciapiedi A for Piazza Brà. Buy your ticket before you board from the machine at the stop or inside the station at the tobacconist.

● The VeronaCard gives free admission to all the main sites, museums and churches and all public transport within the city. It is available for either 1 or 3 days at €8 or €12 and is on sale at central museums, churches, galleries and tobacconists.

● Bicycles are available for rent from May–end Sep from: El Pedal Scaligero, Piazza Brà, tel 3335 367 770.

● Verona's famous opera season, with performances held in the Arena, runs from Jun to end August. More information at www.arena.it.

If time is short or you need a hand to unlock the hidden pleasures of Venice, there's plenty of choice on land or water to help you discover the city and the lagoon with local experts.

All forms of water related tours are popular, be it walking, taking a gondola ride or an excursion

BOAT TOURS

EXCURSIONS TO MURANO, BURANO AND TORCELLO
APT Venezia
Tel 041 529 8711
🕑 Apr–end Oct daily departures from Alilaguna pontile at the Giardinetti Reali at 9.30 and 2.30; Nov–end Mar departures from Alilaguna *pontile* at the Giardinetti Reali at 2. Minimum 4 people. Can be booked in advance at APT
💶 Adult €20; child (6–12) €10; under 6 free
Four-hour boat trip to the three northern lagoon islands with 35-minute stops at each.

GONDOLA SERENADE
APT Venezia
Tel 041 529 8711
🕑 Apr–end Oct daily 7.30pm; Nov–end Mar daily 3.30pm
💶 €35
A 40-minute gondola trip down quiet canals, which is accompanied by musicians and singers.

GRAND CANAL TOUR
APT Venezia
Tel 041 529 8711
🕑 Daily departures from the Alilaguna pontile at the Giardinetti Reali at 11.30. Minimum 4 people. Can be booked in advance at APT
💶 €30 (no reductions)
One-hour boat tour with commentary in Italian, English, French and German. Traverses the Grand Canal from the Giardinetti Reali to the station and returns via the Giudecca and San Giorgio Maggiore.

IL BURCHIELLO
Sita spa, Divisione Navigazione, Via Orlandini 3, Padova
Tel 0498 206 910
🕑 Mar–end Nov, departures on alternate days from either Venice (Stazione Marittima) or Padua, return by bus

💶 €62 per person (special rate €51 Jul–Aug) optional lunch €24
www.ilburchiello.it
Cruises along the Riviera del Brenta with stops at three important Palladian villas; Pisani, Barchessa Valmarana and Foscari Wildmann. Modern boats are used with catering facilities and commentary as you travel.

WALKING TOURS

VENICE ON FOOT
APT Venezia
Tel 041 529 8711
🕑 English daily 9.15; French daily 9.15; Spanish Tue–Thu, Sat–Sun 9.15; German Mon, Fri 9.15
💶 Adult €27; child (6–14) €19, Palazzo Ducale ticket €16
Two-hour walking tour around the main monuments of San Marco.

VENICE ON FOOT AND BY GONDOLA
APT Venezia
Tel 041 529 8711
🕑 English daily 3, French daily 3, Spanish Tue–Thu, Sat–Sun 3, German Mon, Fri 3
💶 €35
Combined city walking and gondola tours.

VENICE EVENTS
Frezzeria, San Marco 1827
Tel 041 523 9979
🕑 Daily 11.15, 4, 5.30 (depending on tour), contact office for details
💶 €30–€50 (depending on tour)
www.veniceevents.com
Anglo-Italian company offering themed tours of the city concentrating on history, art and architecture, as well as bespoke tours with the emphasis on anything from the museums and *scuole* to the lagoon and its wildlife.

AVVENTURE BELLISSIME
Calle dei Preti San Marco 2442A
Tel 041 520 8616
🕑 11 Mar–6 Nov
💶 €20–€40
www.tours-italy.com
A range of theme-based tours on foot in Venice, offering a host of options including Art and Architecture, Photography, Children's Venice and Specialist Shopping. Also boat trips around the lagoon and to the islands.

SPECIAL INTEREST

NATURAVENEZIA
Cooperativa Limosa, Via Toffoli 5, Venezia Marghera
Tel 041 932 003
🕑 By arrangemant
💶 Varies
www.limosa.it
Natural history excursions in Venice, the lagoon and the lagoon islands.

GIARDINI STORICI
Wigwam Club, Giardini Storici, Via Ca' Rossa 2B, Venezia Mestre
Tel 041 610 791 (booking essential)
🕑 Apr–end Nov
💶 Varies
www.giardini-venezia.it
Guided tours for small groups to visit private and historic gardens in Venice and the islands.

BESPOKE TOURS

ASSOCIAZIONE GUIDE TURISTICHE
Calle Cassellaria, Castello 5327
Tel 041 521 0762
🕑 Mon–Fri 9–6, Sat 9–1
💶 €200 for up to 30 people
Venice's official tourist guide co-operative offers excellent made-to-measure city tours in Italian, English, French, Spanish and German. Tours should be arranged in advance.

OUT AND ABOUT

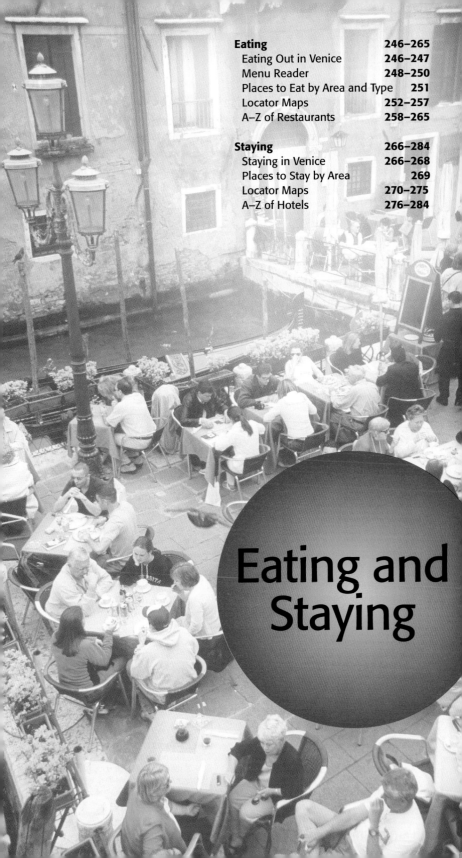

Eating and Staying

EATING OUT IN VENICE

Food in Venice can be glorious, but it can also be dire, so, if you want to eat well, steer away from places offering a *menù turistico* and be prepared to pay more than you might expect. Venetian cooking is based on fish, game and vegetables, with the accent on the fish and seafood. As everywhere in Italy, food is local and seasonal, and the year brings a delicious procession of specialities.

Dining alfresco (left); canalside restaurant in San Marco (middle); inside Caffè Quadri (right)

LA CUCINA VENEZIANA

One of the great joys of Venice are its *cicheti*, tiny tapas-style dishes of fish, seafood, vegetables and meat, that are eaten either at a *bacaro* (see opposite) or form part of the *antipasti* (starters) of a meal. Unlike much of Italy, the *antipasti* in Venice are an important part of eating, and can appear in such abundance you may have no room for much else. Don't worry, it's perfectly acceptable to finish with just a risotto or plate of pasta, or even move straight on to pudding.

Fish, eaten all year in Venice, reigns supreme, and it's worth wandering round the fish stalls of the Rialto market to see what will be on offer in the restaurants. Many of the crustaceans and smaller fish appear as *antipasti* or crisply fried in a *fritto misto* (mixed fried seafood), while larger fish are most commonly served freshly grilled (*alla griglia*), the skin crisp and salty, with a wedge of lemon. The main exception is *baccalà mantecato*, a creamy paste made with dried salt cod, olive oil and garlic.

Meat, on the whole, is not as popular; though chicken and veal escalopes are common. The great local meat dish is *fegato alla veneziana*, veal liver slow-cooked with onions, but Venetians also enjoy *polpette*, spicy little meatballs made of minced beef, pork and turkey.

Vegetables are eaten in huge amounts by Venetians, and most restaurants will have a more than adequate choice. The great local vegetable is a variety of *carciofi* (artichoke), grown on the island of Sant'Erasmo, producer of much of the best fresh produce in the Venetian markets. They are violet in colour, and the first young ones, known as *castrauri*, are thinly sliced and eaten raw in April; later, mature globes are boiled and eaten leaf by leaf, or have the leaves discarded,

leaving just the delicate choke. Another local vegetable is *radicchio di Treviso*, a long-leafed variety of the more familiar round red one. It appears from November to February and is always cooked, usually on the grill, a process that accentuates the contrast between the bitter leaves and sweet stalk. Vegetables also appear in soups and risotti—look out for *pasta e fagioli*, a bean and pasta broth, and *risotto di zucca*, a delicious golden rice dish made with pumpkin.

WHEN TO EAT

Hotels generally serve a buffet breakfast of fruit juice, cereal, yoghurt and cold meats and cheeses from around 8 to 9.30/10am. Locals often pop into a bar on their way to work for a cappuccino and a freshly baked *brioche* (sweet pastry). Late morning sees Venetians pouring into the bars and *bacari* for an *ombra*, a small glass of wine and a couple of *cicheti* (tiny snacks) before lunch. Both lunch and dinner operate in Venice on two different timescales—one for locals and one for tourists. *Trattorie* and *bacari* patronized by locals follow workers' rhythms, with lunch served from midday to about 2 and dinner from 6.30 to 9, while smarter restaurants follow Italian standard practice, with lunch from around 1 to 3 and dinner from 7.30 to 10. Eating earlier, like the locals, will probably prove cheaper, though there's no guarantee that smaller places will charge you the same price as their regular patrons.

WHERE TO EAT

Venice, like many Italian cities, has a confusing array of differently named eating places. A *ristorante* tends to be expensive, with polished service, immaculate tables and shining cutlery and glass. The *trattoria* is less formal, less expen-

EATING

sive, and often family-run. Such places may not have a printed menu, and the waiter will simply reel off a list of what's on offer; many speak enough English to help you choose. *Osterie* were originally pretty basic, and some still are, but the appellation has also been adopted by some very trendy establishments and can be synonymous with excellent food and rustic elegance. *Pizzerie* in Venice tend to open all day rather than just in the evenings; though be aware that wood-fired ovens are forbidden in the city due to the fire risk, and a Venetian pizza won't come near those served south of Rome. For fast, inexpensive food,

include small portions of the house specials—a great way to experience the best. Note that the price of fish on the menu is often quoted by weight, usually per 100g (*un etto*).

IL CONTO (THE BILL)

Most restaurants still charge for *pane e coperto* (cover charge), and may automatically bring bottled water with your order. Check the bill, and ask for a *ricevuta fiscale* (official receipt), which, by law, restaurants must provide. Normally, service is not included; if it is, it will appear as *servizio compreso*. Otherwise, 5 to to 10 per cent is the rule,

Cheese for sale (left); restaurant with a view in San Marco (middle); outside Caffè Florian at night (right)

your best bet is a *bacaro*, Venice's great contribution to Italian eating. *Bacari* serve wine and *cicheti*. Often hidden down side-streets, they are frequently very old, with blackened beams and a few rickety tables; some have long tables in a room behind the bar, where more substantial meals are served at lunchtime. Order a drink, and choose what you want to eat from the counter; the barman will keep a rough count of what you've had and you pay as you leave. Many close in the evenings, and few accept credit cards, but they are the best place to sample real Venetian cooking at excellent prices.

Venice's better restaurants lie in those parts of the city where there are still significant numbers of resident Venetians: northern Cannaregio, eastern Castello, Santa Croce, western Dorsoduro and the Giudecca. San Marco, on the whole, is overpriced; it's here that waiters lurk in doorways to persuade passing tourists to come in and eat—the wise visitor will realize this is the quickest route to mediocre food and rip-off prices.

WHAT TO EAT

A full Venetian meal is gargantuan—*antipasti*, a *primo* (first course) of soup, rice or pasta, a *secondo* (main course) of fish with vegetable *contorni* (side dishes), then *formaggi* (cheese) and *dolce* (pudding). Do as the locals do and pick and mix. *Antipasti* are so good that if the waiter suggests a selection and you overindulge, just skip the *primo* or *secondo*, or miss the *antipasti* and start with a *primo*. Few Venetians eat either cheese or pudding in restaurants, preferring to head for a *pasticceria* or choose a *gelato* if they want something sweet to round off the meal. Some of the city's best restaurants offer a *menù degustazione*, a tasting menu that will

depending on the restaurant and level of service. Most accept credit cards, though they cannot be used in *bacari* and most bars.

BARS AND CAFÉS

Sitting with a drink in a sunny *campo* or a bar will certainly double the price, and send it sky-high in the famous bars that ring the Piazza San Marco. Locals use bars for that essential shot of caffeine, the espresso—known simply as *un caffè*. They also drop in throughout the day for cold drinks, beer and snacks. Specialities of Venetian bars include rich, smooth *cioccolato* (hot chocolate), and Venice's own apéritif, the *spritz*, an alarmingly potent mix of white wine, Campari bitter or Aperol and soda, and *prosecco*, a light, dry, sparkling white wine from the Veneto. *Prosecco* is used to make the Bellini, a delicious summertime blend of white peach juice with sparkling wine, sampled at its best at Harry's Bar, its place of origin. Bars also serve sandwiches and rolls, the most typical being the *tramezzino*, a half-round of soft white bread, whose fillings include delicacies such as crabmeat, *bresaola* (cured dried meat) with cheese, or prawns with rocket and mayonnaise. Some bars and cafés also double as *gelaterie*, serving a fantastic range of ice-creams. As a rule of thumb, buy from those outlets marked *produzione propria* or *artigianale* to ensure you're getting the best freshly made, home-produced ices.

SMOKING

All restaurants in Italy are now non-smoking indoors, though you can smoke if you're eating at outside tables in warm weather. Some smaller establishments do, however, permit smoking and these are mentioned.

Venice is justly renowned for its fish and seafood. Although many restaurants provide English menus, to taste the best of Venetian cuisine, you may need to get away from tourist-orientated restaurants, so some Italian words may be useful—and a sense of adventure and willingness to try something new will add enormously to your eating experience. This menu reader includes key words to help you work out what's on offer, and help familiarize you with some of Venice's most famous dishes.

Rialto's fish market (left) sells a huge selection of seafood (middle); a kaleidoscope of pasta (right)

PIATTI (COURSES)
antipasto starter
cicheti starter served as tapas-style snack
contorni vegetable/side dishes
dolci pudding
formaggio cheese
menu à prezzo fisso fixed-price menu
panino filled roll
primo piatto first course
secondo piatto second/main course

PESCE (FISH) AND FRUTTI DI MARE (SEAFOOD)
acciughe anchovy
aragosta lobster
baccalà dried salt cod
branzino sea bass
calamari squid
canocie mantis shrimp
caparozzoli Venus clams
capelunghe razor-shell clams
capesante/canestrelli scallops
coda di rospe monkfish
cozze/peoci mussels
dentice dentex (like seabass)
dorate sea bream
fritto misto mixed fried fish
gamberi shrimp
granceola spider crab
granchio crab
merluzzo cod
moeche/moleche soft-shell crab
molloschi shellfish

ostriche oyster
pesce spada swordfish
polipi octopus
salmone salmon
sampietro John Dory
sarde sardines
scampi prawns
schie/cance baby prawns
seppie cuttlefish
sgombro mackerel
sogliola sole
tonno tuna
triglie mullet
trota trout
vongole clams

CARNE (MEAT)
agnello lamb
anatra duck
bistecca steak
braciola pork chop
cacciagione game
cavel/cavallo horse meat
cervo venison
cinghiale boar
coniglio rabbit
faraona guinea fowl
fegato liver
maiale pork
manzo beef
pancetta cured pork (similar to bacon)
pollo chicken
polpette spicy meatballs
prosciutto cotto cooked ham
prosciutto crudo Parma ham
salsiccia sausage
tacchino turkey

CONTORNI (VEGETABLES AND SIDE DISHES)
asparagi asparagus
carciofi artichokes
carote carrots
castrauri baby artichokes served raw
cavolfiore cauliflower
cavolo cabbage
ceci chickpeas
cetriolino gherkin
cetriolo cucumber
cicoria chicory
cipolla onion
fagioli dried beans (borlotti, canellini)
fagiolini green beans
fave broad beans
finocchio fennel
funghi mushrooms
insalata (verde/mista) green/mixed salad
insalatina baby salad leaves
latuga lettuce
melanzana aubergine
patate potatoes
peperone peppers
piselli peas
pomodori tomatoes
porri leeks
radicchio bitter red winter 'lettuce'
ruccola rocket (arugula)
sedano celery
spinaci spinach
verdure green leaf vegetables
zucca pumpkin
zucchini courgettes

EATING

SPECIALITÀ (LOCAL SPECIALITIES)

abbacchio roast lamb baked in a casserole, sometimes flavoured with anchovies

agnolotti crescent shaped pasta stuffed with chopped meat, spices, vegatables and cheese

anguille alla veneziana eels with tuna and lemon

baccalà alla vicentina dried cod poached in milk

fegato alla veneziana braised liver with onions

gnocchi dumplings usually made from potatoes

insalata di frutti di mare garnished seafood salad

osso buco tender beef or veal knuckle served with a strong sauce

pancetta herb-flavoured sliced pork

pasta e ceci pasta and chickpea soup

schie e polenta tiny shrimps with polenta

seppie in nero cuttlefish cooked in its own ink

stufato beef braised in white wine and vegatable

spaghetti all vongole veraci spaghetti with clams

trenette thin noodles served with pesto sauce and potatoes

vitello tonnato cold veal and tunafish sauce

Tomatoes on the vine (left); Venetian pastries (middle); fresh local fruit at the market (right)

baccalà mantecato dried cod creamed with oil and milk

bagna cauda hot sauce flavoured with anchovies for dipping vegatables

bigoli all buranese fat spaghetti in anchovy and onion sauce

bistecca alla fiorentina Florentine-style steak

bocconcini fried layered veal and ham

bollito misto meat platter

bovoleti baby snails cooked with parsley and garlic

bresaola air-dried spiced beef

brodetto classic mixed fish soup

broèto eel soup

cacciucco ali livornese seafood stew

calzone pizza dough rolled with the chefs choice, usually combining sausage, cheese and tomatoes, and baked

castradina lamb and cabbage stew

castrauri raw baby artichokes

cervello al burro nero calf brains in black-butter sauce

cima alla genovese rolled fillet of veal with eggs, mushrooms and sausages

costoletta alla milanese fried veal with breadcrumbs, sometimes with cheese

pasta e fagioli dried bean and pasta soup

pasticcio lasagne

piselli al prosciutto peas with strips of ham

pizzaiola tomato and oregano sauce, usually with beef

polenta maize meal, served as a *primo* or *contorno*

polenta de uccelli roasted small birds served with polenta

pollo alla cacciatore chicken with mushrooms and tomatoes cooked in wine

radicchio di Treviso al ferro long radicchio leaves cooked on the grill

ragù meat sauce

ravioli stuffed squares of pasta

risi e bisi risotto with peas

risi e luganega rice and pork sausages

risotto ai funghi mushroom risotto

risotto alla milanese rice with saffron and wine

risotto alla seppie cuttlefish black risotto

risotto del mare seafood risotto

risotto di radicchio risotto with radicchio

risotto di zucca pumpkin risotto

sarde in saor sweet-sour sardines

DOLCI (CAKES AND PUDDINGS)

bigne chocolate, coffee or liqueur cream filled profiteroles

bussolai, baicoli, esse hard, sweet biscuits from Burano flavoured with lemon and vanilla

cassatta alla siciliana sponge, sweet ricotta cheese, candied fruit and chocolate butter cream icing

fregolotta traditional Venetian plain cake flavoured with almonds

fritelle deep-fried sweet dough fritter

gelato ice-cream

macedonia fruit salad

semifreddo soft iced pudding flavoured with liqueur

tiramisù chocolate/coffee sponge and mascarpone pudding

zabaglione whipped egg, sugar and sweet wine froth, a traditional pick-me-up

zuccotto sponge cake soaked in liqueur with chocoalte, nuts and whipped cream

FRUTTA (FRUIT)

ananasso pineapple

arancia orange

banana banana

cedro lime

ciliege cherries

EATING

fico fig
fragole strawberries
lamponi raspberries
limone lemon
mela apple
melone melon
nespole loquats
pera pear
pesca peach
pesca noci nectarine
pompelmo grapefruit
susina plum
uve grapes

birra beer
birra alla spina draught beer (beer on tap)
caffè Americano weak coffee
caffè corretto coffee with a dash of *grappa* or brandy
caffè espresso coffee
caffè Hag decaffeinated coffee
caffè latte milky coffee
caffè macchiato strong coffee with a drop of milk
cappuccino milky coffee with froth

capperi capers
erbe aromatiche herbs
olio oil
pepe pepper
peperoncino chilli
pesto green sauce made from basil leaves, cheese, garlic, marjoram and pine nuts
prezzemolo parsley
rosmarino rosemary
sale salt
senape mustard
zucchero sugar

The ingredients to make trenette al pesto—*noodles with pesto (left); pastry shop (middle)*

LATTICINI E PASTICCERIA (DAIRY AND BAKERY)
bruschetta toasted bread with oil, garlic and tomatoes
burro butter
dolcelatte creamy blue cheese
focaccia oil-enriched dough left to rise slowly and usually topped with olive oil, and sometimes rosemary and onions
fontina smooth, dense cheese from northern Italy
gorgonzola strong blue-veined cheese
mozzarella fresh milk cheese
pane bread
panettone sweet yeast cake with dried fruit
panna heavy cream
parmigiano parmesan cheese
ricotta fresh milk cheese
toast toasted cheese and ham sandwich
tramezzino generously filled white bread sandwich
uove eggs

BEVANDE (DRINKS)
acqua minerale, frizzante/ naturale sparkling/flat mineral water
amaretto sweet almond-based drink
amaro bitter digestif
aperitivo before dinner apéritif
Bellini prosecco with fresh white peach juice

digestivo after dinner liqueur
frappé milkshake made with ice cream
frullato milkshake
ghiaccio ice
granita crushed ice covered in syrup (usually coffee)
prosecco sparkling white wine from the Veneto
sambuca aniseed-flavoured liqueur
secco, brut dry
spremuta di arancia freshly squeezed orange juice
spritz white wine, Campari bitter and soda
succo di arancia, pesca/pera/albicocchi orange/peach/pear/apricot juice
tè tea
tè al latte freddo tea with milk
tè al limone tea with lemon
vini della casa house wines
vini locali local wines
vini pregiati quality wines
vino bianco white wine
vino rosato rosé wine
vino rosso red wine
vino sfuso house wine (draught/on tap)

CONDIMENTI (SEASONINGS)
aceto vinegar
aglio garlic
basilico basil

IL CONTO (THE BILL)
coperto cover charge
IVA VAT value added tax
ricevuta fiscale official receipt
servizio compreso service included
servizio non compreso service not included

UTENSILI (UTENSILS)
bicchiere glass
bottiglia bottle
coltello knife
cucchiaio spoon
forchetta fork
piatto plate
tazza cup

METODI DI CUCINA (COOKING METHODS)
affumicato smoked
al ferro/al griglia grilled
al forno baked
arrosto roasted
al sangue rare
al vapore steamed
ben cotto well-done
bollito boiled
cotto cooked
crudo raw
fritto fried
frulatto whisked
passata sieved or creamed
ripieno stuffed
spiedini meat grilled over an open flame
stufato stewed
tostato toasted

EATING

As everywhere in Italy, locals in Venice firmly believe their own cuisine is unrivalled, and the concept of restaurants featuring cuisine from other parts of the world is alien. There are, accordingly, virtually no restaurants serving 'foreign' food, though more innovative establishments are experimenting with a lighter take on traditional Venetian cooking. The restaurants below are listed by area, and it's worth considering how long it will take you to get from your hotel to dinner after a long day's sightseeing—and perhaps choosing something local.

Fresh fruit display (left); the view from from Caffè Florian (middle); ice-cream (right)

CANNAREGIO

Al Bacco	Restaurant
Algiubagio	Bar and snacks
Al Mariner	*Bacaro*
Antica Mola	Restaurant
La Colonna	Restaurant
Da Alberto	*Bacaro*
Fiaschetteria Toscana	Restaurant
Gam Gam	Restaurant
Ostaria Boccadoro	Restaurant
Osteria al Bomba	*Bacaro*/restaurant
Osteria da Rioba	Restaurant
Vini da Gigio	Restaurant

CASTELLO

Al Covo	Restaurant
Al Mascaron	*Bacaro*/restaurant
Al Testiere	Restaurant
Al Vecio Penasa	Bar and snacks
Corte Sconta	Restaurant
Da Bruno	*Bacaro*/restaurant
Dal Pampo	Restaurant
Da Remigio	Restaurant
Da Sergio	Restaurant
Osteria Oliva Nera	Restaurant
Pizzeria 84	Pizzeria

DORSODURO

Ai Gondolieri	Restaurant
Al Bottegon	*Bacaro*
Casin dei Nobili	Pizzeria/restaurant
Codroma	*Bacaro*
L'Incontro	Restaurant
Locanda Montin	Restaurant

SANTA CROCE

Ae Oche	Pizzeria
Ai Postali	Bar and snacks
Al Vecio Fritolin	*Bacaro*/restaurant
Alla Zucca	Restaurant
Capitan Uncino	Restaurant
Il Refolo	Pizzeria
Ribo	Restaurant

SAN MARCO

Bistrot de Venise	Restaurant
Caffè Florian	Bar and snacks
Caffè Quadri	Bar/restaurant
Le Chat qui Rit	Restaurant
Do Forni	Restaurant
Harry's Bar	Bar/restaurant
Trattoria da Fiore	Restaurant
Vini da Arturo	Restaurant

SAN POLO

Alla Madonna	Restaurant
Al Ponte	Bar/restaurant
Antica Birreria la Corte	Bar/snacks/restaurant
Antica Osteria Ruga Rialto	*Bacaro*
Antiche Carampane	Restaurant
Da Fiore	Restaurant
Da Ignazio	Restaurant
Da Pinto	Restaurant
Da Renato	Restaurant
Il Giardino di Giada	Restaurant

THE ISLANDS

Al Gatto Nero	Restaurant
Alla Maddalena	Restaurant
Altanella	Restaurant
Busa alla Torre	Restaurant
Cipriani Restaurant	Restaurant
Harry's Dolci	Restaurant
Mistrà	Restaurant

EATING

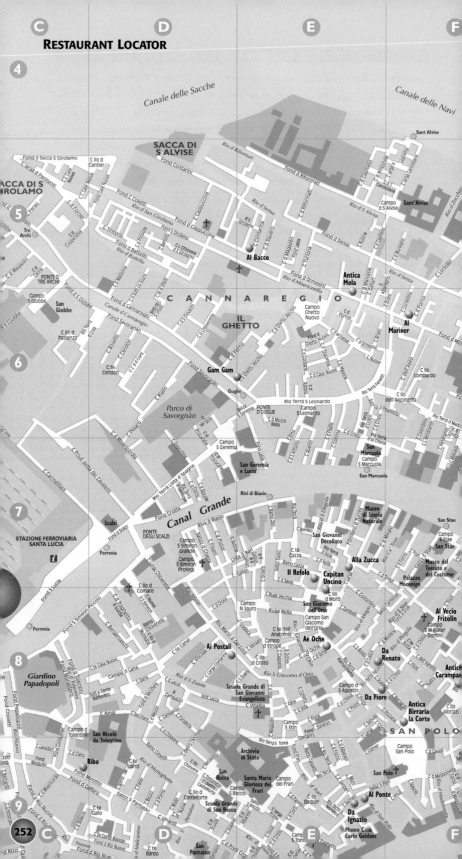

C   D   E   F

4

Canale delle Sacche   Canale delle Navi

Sant'Alvise

SACCA DI
S ALVISE

Fond d Sacca S Girolamo   C llo d
  C larga di Penitenti   Cantier
SACCA DI S
GIROLAMO   C de
Fond Contarini

Rio d Riformati

Fond d Riformati

Campo
S d Alvise

Sant'Alvise

5   Tre
Archi

Rio d San Girolamo
Fond d Coletti
Fond d Cappuccine

Fond d Girolamo
C Tintoria
Fond d Battello
Rio d Batello

Rio d Sensa

Fond d Sensa

Al Bacco

**Antica
Mola**

PONTE D
TRE ARCHI
Campo
S Giobbe   San
Giobbe

C A N N A R E G I O

**Al
Mariner**

6

Canale d Cannaregio
Fond d Cannaregio
Fond Savorgnan

IL
GHETTO

Campo
Ghetto Nuovo

C d
Ghetto Nuovo

Gam Gam

Guglie
PONTE
D'GUGLIE

Rio Terra S Leonardo

Campo
S Leonardo

C llo
dell'Anconetta

Parco di
Savorgnàn

Campo
S Geremia

San Geremia
e Lucia

San
Marcuola
Campo
S Marcuola

San Marcuola

7

Rio Terra Lista d Spagna
Fond Crotta

STAZIONE FERROVIARIA
SANTA LUCIA

Scalzi
PONTE
DEGLI SCALZI

Canal Grande

Rivi di Biasio

Riva d Biasio

Museo
di Storia
Naturale

San Stae

San Giovanni
Decollato

Campo
S Stae   San Stae

Ferrovia

Campo
S Simeon
Grande
Campo
S Simeon
Profeta

Alla Zucca

Museo del
Tessuto e
del Costume

Il Refolo

**Capitan
Uncino**

Palazzo
Mocenigo

Ferrovia

Fond S Lucia

C llo d
Comare

Ruga Vecchia

Ruga Bella

San Giacomo
dell'Orio

**Al Vecio
Fritolin**

8

Giardino
Papadopoli

Ai Postali

Campo San
Giacomo
dell'Orio

Ae Oche

**Da
Renato**

**Antica
Carampa**

Scuola Grande di
San Giovanni
Evangelista

Da Fiore

**Antica
Birraria
la Corte**

SAN POLO

Campo
San Polo

San Nicolò
da Tolentino

Ribo

Archivio
di Stato

San
Rocco

Santa Maria
Gloriosa dei
Frari

Campo
dei Frari

San Polo

Al Ponte

Scuola Grande
di San Rocco

**Da
Ignazio**

Museo Casa
Carlo Goldoni

San
Pantalon

G

4

5

6

K

L

Cimitero

Cimitero

Ísola di
San Michele

Madonna dell'Orto

QUARTIERE
GRIMANI

Madonna
dell'Orto

5

Osteria
Da Rioba

Sacca della
Misericordia

6

Canale delle Fondamenta Nuove

Gesuiti
Algiubagio

Fondamente
Nuove

Vini da Gigio

Campo
S Felice

Ca' d'Oro

Ca' d'Oro

Osteria
Al Bomba

La Colonna

Campiello
Wildman

7

Canal Grande

Ca'
Pesaro

San
Cassiano

Campo
S Cassiano

Il Giardino
di Giada

Campo
Beccarie

Da Pinto

Antica Osteria
Ruga Rialto

Fiaschetteria
Toscana

Alla Madonna

Campo
Rialto
Nuovo

PONTE
DI RIALTO

San
Silvestro

Campo
S Aponal

Campo
S Silvestro

San Silvestro

Rialto

Santi
Apostoli

Campo
Santi
Apostoli

Ostaria
Boccadoro

Da Alberto

Santa Maria
dei Miracoli

Da Sergio

Da
Bruno

Santa Maria
della Fava

Campo di
S Marina

Alle Testiere

Santa Maria
Formosa

Campo
Santa Maria
Formosa

Santi Giovanni
e Paolo

Campo Santi
Giovanni
e Paolo

8

Al Mascaron

9

Fondazione
Querini
Stampalia

253

Canal Grande

San
Salvador

San
Zulian

G

H

J

RESTAURANT LOCATOR

RESTAURANT LOCATOR

RESTAURANTS

AL BACCO

Map 252 E5
Fondamenta Capuzine, Cannaregio 3054
Tel 041 717 493

A fine evening is the time to head for this wonderfully typical *osteria* in the depths of Cannaregio, where you can eat in a charmingly old-fashioned panelled interior, or the pretty courtyard garden at the back. Seafood and fish are the keynotes here, simply and beautifully cooked. Expect plenty of locals exchanging banter with the ebullient owner and his staff.

🕐 Tue–Sun 12–3, 7–10
🍽 L €35, D €56, Wine €8
🚤 San Marcuola

AL BOTTEGON (CANTINONE GIÀ SCHIAVO)

Map 254 E11
Fondamenta Nani, Dorsoduro 992
Tel 041 523 0034

This wonderful *bacaro*, with its waterside setting and crowds spilling out onto the *fondamenta*, is a great place for

lunch and has one of the best wine cellars in the city. You can even buy wine, ready chilled, to take away. Three generations of the same family work here, cheerfully churning out delicious *cicheti* and bulging panini—a real Venetian institution.

🕐 Mon–Sat 8–2.30, 4–9.30

🍽 L €12, D €20, Wine €5
🚤 Zattere, Accademia

AL COVO

Map 256 K10
Campiello della Pescaria, Castello 3968
Tel 041 522 3812

They really know their fish at Al Covo, and it's best to rely on the waiter's guidance to enjoy the best of Venetian cooking—whatever ends up on your plate will be super-fresh and expertly cooked. The menu changes depending on the catch, but look out for *dorada* (bream) and *seppie nero con polenta* (squid cooked in its ink with polenta). This is a serious restaurant with a deservedly high reputation.

🕐 Fri–Tue 12–3, 6.30–10
🍽 L €60, D €90, Wine €9
🚤 Arsenale

AL GATTO NERO

Fondamenta della Giudecca 88, Burano
Tel 041 730 120
www.gattonero.com

Tucked away from the main drag on the lace island of Burano, this friendly trattoria faces the fish market across the canal. Expect fresh fish beautifully cooked, as well as some Buranese specials, such as the creamy *risotto alla buranella*—with seafood.

🕐 Tue–Sun 12–3, 7–9
🍽 L €40, D €60, Wine €7
🚤 LN

AI GONDOLIERI

Map 254 F11
Fondamenta Venier, Dorsoduro 366
Tel 041 528 6396
www.aigondolieri.com

The variety and quality of food and wine offered at this well-known gastronomic haven, one of Venice's finest restaurants, will surely please. The

accent is firmly on meat, with well-sourced, well-hung cuts beautifully cooked and served in elegant surroundings.

🕐 Wed–Mon 12–3, 7–10
🍽 L €60, D €90, Wine €12
🚤 Accademia

ALLA MADDALENA

Mazzorbo 7c, Mazzorbo
Tel 041 730 151

Get off the *vaporetto* at Mazzorbo and you'll find the Maddalena right opposite the *pontile*—a wonderful lagoon setting for this lunch-only restaurant. It's famous for its wild duck dishes during the shooting season, while at other times, seafood predominates on the menu. There's a waterside terrace and a quiet garden behind; make reservations for Sunday, when Venetian families flock here.

🕐 Fri–Wed 12.30–3. Closed 20 Dec–10 Jan
🍽 L €30, Wine €6
🚤 LN

ALLA MADONNA

Map 253 G8
Calle della Madonna, San Polo 594
Tel 041 522 3824 (no reservations)

If you ask any Venetian, this is one of the restaurants they will recommend, and the waiting locals outside hint at its popularity. It's a big bustling place, serving all the Venetian staples, with some run-of-the-mill dishes, such as *cotoletta alla Milanese*, you'll find all over Italy. The food is fairly simple but tasty, the service charming and the wine list small but well considered. However, you're not encouraged to linger over your meal.

🕐 Thu–Tue 12–3, 7–10
🍽 L €50, D €80, Wine €6
🚤 Rialto

AL MARINER
Map 252 F6
Fondamenta degli Ormesini,
Cannaregio 2676
Tel 041 720 036
The *barrista*, Caterina, is one of the reasons why you should come here. For a town short on exuberant characters and readily given warmth, Caterina

is a breath of fresh air. Local characters drift in and out for *ombre* (small alcoholic drinks), a quick chat and complimentary bowls of nibbles. The selection of *cicheti*, marinated, stewed and fried, is also worth experiencing. Decent pizzas are served in the evenings. No credit cards accepted. Smoking is permitted.
🕐 Mon–Sat 11–11
🍷 *Cicheti* for two €9. Wine/beer from €2 a glass
🚤 Sant'Alvise

AL MASCARON
Map 253 J9
Calle Lunga Santa Maria Formosa, Castello 5225
Tel 041 522 5995
Don't be put off by the paper tablecloths and having to share a table with locals—the food is worth it. There are no airs and graces about Al Mascaron, just great *cicheti* and an anything-goes atmosphere. It also has a menu for pasta, risotto and salads if you fancy something more substantial. No credit cards accepted.
🕐 Mon–Sat 11–3, 6.30pm–12.30am. Closed Sun, Christmas and New Year
🍷 *Cicheti* for two €12. Wine/beer from €1.50.
🚤 San Zaccaria

AE OCHE
Map 252 E8
Calle delle Oche, Santa Croce 1552A/B
Tel 041 524 1161
In a city where wood-burning ovens are forbidden, it's hard to find a really good pizza, but you won't be disappointed at Ae Oche. This little pizzeria has the most amusing staff and the pizzas are reassuringly good. There's a host of European beers to help wash it down.
🕐 Daily 12–2.30, 7–10
🍷 L €25, D €40, Wine €7
🚤 San Stae

AL PONTE
Map 252 E9
Ponte San Polo, San Polo 2741
Tel 041 523 7238
Affectionately known as La Patatina, after its famous chunky chips, this busy place offers bar snacks and table service. It's busy day and night with workers and students, serving straightforward Venetian fare, such as *polpette* (meat balls), seafood risotto and *fritto misto*. Eating at the bar is excellent value; you'll pay more for table service.
🕐 Mon–Sat 9.30–2.30, 5–10
🍷 L €15, D €35, Wine €5
🚤 San Tomà

AI POSTALI
Map 252 D8
Fondamenta Rio Marin O Garzotti, Santa Croce 821
Tel 041 715 156
This little café bar, next to a quietish canal, stays open late. You can sit with a cappuccino or a beer and listen to the animated banter of some of the locals who seem to constantly drift in and out. If you're peckish there are *antipasti, cicheti*, some *tramezzini* (generously filled sandwiches) and, of course, pasta, to keep the hunger pangs at bay. No credit cards accepted. Smoking is permitted.
🕐 Daily 11am–1am
🍷 Snacks €4
🚤 Riva di Biasio

ALLE TESTIERE
Map 253 H9
Calle del Mondo Nuovo, Castello 5801
Tel 041 522 7220
This tiny restaurant has a sky-high reputation for innovative and creative cooking, with local seafood and fish imaginatively cooked with spice and

herbs, a well-chosen cheeseboard and small, but excellent, wine list. There are two sittings nightly; choose the later one (9pm) for a more relaxed meal.
🕐 Tue–Sat 12–2, 7–10.30. Closed last week Dec, 2 weeks Jan, last week Jul, 3 weeks Aug
🍷 L €45, D €70, Wine €8
🚤 Rialto

AL VECIO FRITOLIN
Map 252 F8
Calle della Regina, Santa Croce 2262
Tel 041 522 2881
www.veciofritolin.it
Whatever was caught that morning will be beautifully marinated in a sweet and sour sauce, tossed in flour then fried or flame grilled at Al Vecio Fritolin. There's not a lot of choice here, but whatever is served is always delicious. Fried fish with polenta, and pasta with beans are the wholesome popular dishes. The fair selection of wines available will help the *cicheti* down. No credit cards accepted.
🕐 Tue–Sat 12–2.30, 7–10, and lunch on Sun
🍷 *Cicheti* for two €12. Wine/beer from €1.50
🚤 San Stae

AL VECIO PENASA
Map 255 J10
Calle delle Rasse, Castello 4585
Tel 041 523 7202
Just off the Riva degli Schiavoni and minutes away from Piazza San Marco, this busy bar is

ideal for a quick espresso and pastry at the bar for breakfast, or for toasted sandwiches at lunchtime. The staff maintain their good humour despite being run off their feet. No credit cards accepted. Smoking is permitted.

⏲ Daily 7am–11pm
🍴 Coffee €2, snack €4
🚤 San Zaccaria

ALLA ZUCCA
Map 252 E7
Ponte del Megio, Santa Croce 1762
Tel 041 524 1570
In Venice, as in all Italy, pity the vegetarians. But not at La Zucca (The Pumpkin), where

the mainly vegetarian cuisine is cooked with style and imagination. The dishes marry pumpkin, *zucchini* flowers and fennel with a huge array of cheeses, enthusing those who have no doubt had very limited choice elsewhere. It's great value for money and very popular, so book in advance.

⏲ Mon–Sat 12–2.30, 7–10.30. Closed Sun
🍴 L €55, D €85, Wine €8
🚤 San Stae

ALGIUBAGIO
Map 253 H7
Fondamente Nuove, Cannaregio 5039
Tel 041 523 6084
This café with a small terrace has a striking view of the watery graveyard, San Michele. Right on the *fondamenta*, much of its custom comes from locals and visitors awaiting *vaporetti*. Its three adjoining outlets do tasty pastries for breakfast and quick snacks and pizzas throughout the day. It also has a *gelateria* so, on a summer's evening, you can sit with an ice-cream on the edge of the *fondamente* and dangle your legs over the lagoon. No credit cards accepted. Smoking is permitted.

⏲ Wed–Mon 6.30–6.30
🍴 Pastries €1, cone €2.50
🚤 Fondamente Nove

ALTANELLA
Map 254 E13
Calle delle Erbe, Giudecca 268
Tel 041 522 7780
There's a nice feeling about the Altanella on the Giudecca, a long-established restaurant tucked down a *calle* with a waterside terrace and cosy interior. Service can be a little slow, but it's worth the wait for the unctuous *risotti* and wonderfully fresh fish. The wine list will have something for even the most choosy. No credit cards accepted.

⏲ Wed–Sun 12.30–2, 7.30–9. Closed 1–2 weeks in Aug
🍴 L €55, D €85, Wine €8
🚤 Palanca

ANTICA BIRRARIA LA CORTE
Map 252 F8
Campo San Polo, San Polo 2168
Tel 041 275 0570
This converted warehouse is

one of a small number of a new breed of Venetian eateries. The seating spills out into the evocative expanse of Campo San Polo, making it perfect for sunny days and balmy evenings. The inside is contemporary, with clean lines and chrome predominating. The food nods to all the Venetian and Italian classics—it's good quality and won't break the bank. You can snack or go the whole hog here.

⏲ Daily 11–3, 6–10
🍴 L €50, D €85, Wine €8
🚤 San Silvestro

ANTICA MOLA
Map 252 E5
Fondamenta degli Ormesini, Cannaregio 2800
Tel 041 717 492
On a beautiful night, try to get a table at Antica Mola. You can sit at the side of the canal or in the leafy garden at the back and take in the lively (but not by hectic San Marco standards) atmosphere of the Fondamenta degli Ormesini. The menu is limited as it relies upon the catch and what the chef fancies cooking that day.

⏲ Thu–Tue 10–2.30, 6.30–10
🍴 L €50, D €70, Wine €8
🚤 San Marcuola

ANTICA OSTERIA RUGA RIALTO
Map 253 G8
Ruga Rialto, San Polo 692, 30125 Venezia
Tel 041 521 1243
Old blends with contemporary and utility in this real find of a bar. The *cicheti* are among the best in town and are served by engaging, friendly staff who know their stuff. You can either stand at the bar and eat or take your seat in the wooden salon around the back. Old characters mix with artists, musicians and the odd visitor. It exhibits intriguing artwork and stages the occasional rock or jazz gig. No credit cards accepted. Smoking is permitted.

⏲ Daily 11–10
🍴 *Cicheti* or *tapas* for two €10. Wine/beer from €2
🚤 Rialto

ANTICHE CARAMPANE
Map 252 F8
Rio Terrà Carampane, San Polo 1911
Tel 041 524 0165
Not just another fish restaurant, the Carampane could be one of Venice's best-kept culinary secrets. The kitchen here shows a confident dedication to the history of Venetian cooking, but isn't afraid to use different ingredients and add a modern twist here and there. Let the experts choose your meal for you and enjoy the stories behind each dish.

⏲ Tue–Sat 12.30–3.30, 7.30–10
🍴 L €60, D €95, Wine €9
🚤 San Silvestro

EATING

BISTROT DE VENISE

Map 255 G9
Calle dei Fabbri, San Marco 4685
Tel 041 523 6651
www.bistrotdevenise.com
This restaurant is popular with local poets and artists who do readings and exhibit their

works here, as well as those visitors in the know, especially the French. The cooking can be variable, but good use is made of the freshest ingredients. The wine list boasts the richest pickings of the Veneto.
🕐 Daily 9am–1am
🍷 L €45, D €75, Wine €8
🚉 Rialto

BUSA ALLA TORRE

Map 257 M3 (inset)
Campo Santo Stefano 3, Murano
Tel 041 739 662
The ideal place for lunch after a morning at the glass foundries, Busa is a reliable fish restaurant, serving island dishes such as *spaghetti alla busara* (with onions and anchovies) and home-made pasta. In summer, you can sit outside table on the *campo*.
🕐 Daily 12–3.30
🍷 L €40, Wine €6
🚉 41, 42, DM

CAFFÈ FLORIAN

Map 255 H10
Piazza San Marco, San Marco 56–59
Tel 041 520 5641
www.caffeflorian.com
The sumptuous surroundings of Caffè Florian (▷ 76) have attracted well-heeled big names since 1720, and it still draws numerous visitors to the city who are willing to pay €7 for a cappuccino and a table in the Piazza San Marco. You can also indulge in light lunches, sandwiches and elegant afternoon tea, beautifully served by impeccably trained staff—a quintessentially Venetian experience.
🕐 Daily Mar–end Nov 10am–midnight.

Closed Wed rest of year
☕ Coffee €7, spritz €7
🚉 San Marco

CAFFÈ QUADRI

Map 255 H10
Piazza San Marco, San Marco 120–24
Tel 041 522 2105
www.quadrivenice.com
For something really special, book a table at the upstairs restaurant at Caffè Quadri (▷ 76), the great Piazza San Marco coffee house. The setting can't be bettered, and the surroundings, all neoclassical design, chandeliers and mirrors, are stunning. The food is good, too, with some Venetian staples served with a twist and vegetarian options—rare indeed in Venice. Alternatively, sit at one of the outside tables and enjoy the views of the Piazza.
🕐 Mar–end Nov daily 9–2.30. Closed Mon rest of year
☕ Coffee €7, spritz from €7
🚉 San Marco

CAPITAN UNCINO

Map 252 E7
Campo San Giacomo dell'Orio, Santa Croce 1501
Tel 041 721 901
If you're more interested in the wine list, but still want to sit down and eat, this trattoria is worth seeking out. The food—*risotto* or *fritto misto*—is perfectly designed to help a nice San Gimignano or Soave go down. The location, on one of the city's most unpretentious and charming *campi*, is an added attraction.
🕐 Thu–Tue 12–2.30, 7–10.30
🍷 L €60, D €85, Wine €8
🚉 San Stae

CASIN DEI NOBILI

Map 254 D10
Campo San Barnaba, Dorsoduro 2765
Tel 041 241 1841

Translated as 'little house of the noble people', this is a

great place to eat if you are a couple, but the wait for bigger groups might be frustrating. It's basically a pizzeria popular with students, and you'll be able to eat cheaply and well if you stick to the pizza menu. The waiters are happy to suggest alternatives from the usual range of Venetian-style *primi* and *secondi*. There's a nice garden for summer eating. No credit cards accepted.
🕐 Tue–Sun 12–2.30, 7–10
🍷 L €50, D €70, Wine €8
🚉 Ca' Rezzonico

LE CHAT QUI RIT

Map 255 G10
Calle Frezzeria, San Marco 1131
Tel 041 522 9086
If you are looking for something simple, this is an ideal place to stop for lunch, especially if you have children. They, and you, will be able to choose from the great range of hearty, filling and inexpensive dishes on offer at the self-service counter, ensuring everyone knows what they're eating—a major plus with picky young diners. A popular spot with visitors and locals, it can get a little hectic, but with the house wine on tap, you'll cope.
🕐 Sun–Fri 11–9.30
🍷 L €25, Wine from the tap €1.30 a glass
🚉 San Marco

CIPRIANI RESTAURANT

Map 255 H12
Hotel Cipriani, Giudecca 10
Tel 041 520 7744
www.hotelcipriani.com
If you book a table at the Cipriani Restaurant, its private launch will collect you from San Marco, then take you back again later. But the journey isn't the main reason for coming here—it's the exclusive location, the dining terraces, elegant interior and matchless regional Italian cuisine that have earned the Cipriani its reputation. The menu and wine list are very carefully thought out, the cooking and service superlative, making this an unforgettable experience.
🕐 Daily noon–11pm. Closed early Nov–early Apr
🍷 L €80, D €140, Wine €16
🚉 By way of the Cipriani's private launch, San Marco or 41, 42

CODROMA

Map 254 off C10
Ponte dei Socorso, Dorsoduro 2540
Tel 041 524 6789

That Codroma has been serving late-night *cicheti* for over a

hundred years and offers live jazz, serious credentials for local and visiting barflies. The *cicheti* are unbeatable and the house red is good. No credit cards accepted.

🕐 Mon–Sat 8am–2am, closed Sat in summer

🍴 *Cicheti* for two €10. Wine/beer from €2 a glass

🚊 Ca' Rezzonico

LA COLONNA

Map 253 H7
Campiello del Pestrin, Cannaregio 5329
Tel 041 522 9641

For a romantic but not necessarily expensive night out, this restaurant can offer that little bit more than most. It's small (just six tables), but you can still enjoy a bit of privacy. The food, like Osteria Oliva Nera (▷ 265), is inspired Venetian. Make sure you have room for a dessert, the perfect end to the evening.

🕐 Daily 12.30–2.30, 7.30–10. Closed 3 weeks in Aug, Mon in Jan

🍴 L €60, D €95, Wine €9

🚊 Fondamente Nuove

CORTE SCONTA

Map 256 K10
Calle del Pestrin, Castello 3886
Tel 041 522 7024

The understated décor belies the Corte Sconta's reputation as one of Venice's finest, and most famous, restaurants, where the ethos is firmly based on high quality and fresh fish—from lagoon to pan to plate. A procession of superbly imaginative *antipasti* is the highlight of any meal, followed by light fish dishes, home-made pasta and traditional puddings. Service is laidback, friendly and expert

and the wine list admirably matched with the cuisine. Booking is essential; ask for an outside table in summer.

🕐 Daily 12–3, 6–10. Closed early Jan–early Feb, mid-Jul to mid-Aug

🍴 L €60, D €90, Wine €9

🚊 Arsenale

DA ALBERTO

Map 253 H8
Calle Giacinto Gallina, Cannaregio 5401
Tel 041 523 8153

Perfect for lunch, this inexpensive but utterly authentic Venetian bar restaurant is run by three young men who,

despite their years, make it all seem so effortless. Their array of *cicheti* includes wonderful *sarde in saor* (sweet and sour sardines), *granseola* (spider crab) and *seppie in umido* (stewed cuttlefish). Booking recommended.

🕐 Mon–Sat 12–3, 7–10. Closed mid-Jul to mid-Aug

🍴 L €30, D €55, Wine €7

🚊 Fondamente Nuove

DA BRUNO

Map 253 H9
Calle del Paradiso, Castello 5731
Tel 041 522 1480

Whether it's a little *cicheti*, some roasted meat or a big plate of something fishy, Da Bruno caters for all tastes and appetites. This small but excellent restaurant features very reasonably priced dishes, which means you can try almost everything. If you're adventurous but your partner has a rather more conservative palette, you will both be pleased by what the menu—and indeed the wine list—has to offer.

🕐 Daily 12–3, 6.30–10

🍴 L €50, D €75, Wine €7

🚊 San Zaccaria

DA FIORE

Map 252 E8
Calle di Scaleter, San Polo 2202A
Tel 041 721 308

Perhaps better known for its fine cellar, Da Fiore is considered one of the top restaurants in Venice. However, dining here may not incur as much damage to the bank balance as some of the other 'top' restaurants. The food takes an international approach to Venetian cooking and uses international standards too. If you want to dine beside Venice's glitterati, book first.

🕐 Tue–Sat 12.30–2.30, 7.30–10.30

🍴 L €70, D €110, Wine €12

🚊 San Stae

DO FORNI

Map 255 H9
Calle dei Specchieri, San Marco 468
Tel 041 523 2148

The two dining rooms here offer completely different experiences. One is all starched tablecloths and Murano glass chandeliers, while the other is like an English pub, with wooden tables and exposed beams. The food is classic Italian with a twist; the scampi in champagne served with egg noodles is a perfect example of the house style.

🕐 Daily 12–3, 6–11

🍴 L €60, D €85, Wine €9

🚊 San Marco

DA IGNAZIO

Map 252 E9
Calle di Saoneri, San Polo 2749
Tel 041 523 4852

This friendly *trattoria* offers traditional Venetian cooking at good prices. It's ideal for children or small groups, the service is quick and the food regional Italian, with the fruits of the lagoon featuring heavily. In summer, the main draw is the shady courtyard.

🕐 Sun–Fri 12–3, 7–10

EATING

L €55, D €85, Wine €8
San Tomà

DAL PAMPO (OSTERIA SANT'ELENA)

Map 257 P13
Calle Generale Chinotto, Castello 24
Tel 041 520 8419

The sheer exuberance of the owner, Pampo himself, makes for a great evening out, as do the hearty cooking and robust wines. You may be the only visitors in the place but you're bound to feel at home.

Thu–Tue 12–2.30, 7.30–9. Closed Christmas and May and Aug
L €45, D €70, Wine €8
Sant'Elena

DA PINTO

Map 253 G8
Campo delle Becarie, San Polo 367
Tel 041 522 4599

If you wonder how some of the strange creatures you saw at the Pescheria taste, this little restaurant is a good place to

do some adventurous trying. Its famed for its *baccalà mantecato* (creamed salt cod). The wine list is mediocre, but the house wines are fine. You can sit inside or out, on the *campo*. No credit cards accepted.

Tue–Sun 7.30–2.30, 6–9.30
L €50, D €80, Wine €7
San Silvestro

DA REMIGIO

Map 256 K10
Salizzada dei Graci, Castello 3416
Tel 041 523 0089

Remigio's is a true local restaurant serving up excellent food at good prices. Enjoy the splendid *antipasti* and fish so fresh it's sticky. It gets very busy, so book first.

Mon 12.30–2.30, Wed– Sun 12.30–2.30, 7.30–10. Closed Christmas–end Jan, 2 weeks Jul and Aug
L €35, D €45, Wine €6
San Zaccaria

DA RENATO

Map 252 F8
Rio Terrà Secondo, San Polo 2245A
Tel 041 524 1922

The *gondolieri* who come here add a little bit of excitement to the fairly humble set-up, supping soups and stews alongside the other rather odd but entertaining selection of customers. You'll find some mouthwatering *cicheti* and a selection of delectable desserts. No credit cards accepted. Smoking is permitted.

Fri–Wed 11–3, 7–10
L €40, D €65, Wine €7
San Stae

DA SERGIO

Map 253 H9
Calle del Dose, Castello 5870A
Tel 041 528 5153

It's always good to seek out the places where the locals eat, as not only do they generally offer value for money, but they show you a whole new side to the place you're visiting. This no-frills café will feed you three courses for around €20. Its all good old-fashioned cooking, such as *risotto*, pasta and boiled meats. A few phrases of Italian may come in handy here, however. No credit cards accepted.

Daily 12–2.30, 7.30–10.30
L €26, D €40, Wine €7
San Zaccaria

FIASCHETTERIA TOSCANA

Map 253 G8
Salizzada San Giovanni Grisostomo, Cannaregio 5719
Tel 041 528 5281

One of Venice's finest restaurants in an old merchant's wine store, Fiaschetteria Toscana has shown consistent quality over the years. Enjoy classic Venetian dishes of seafood (of course), meat and game, all well prepared and beautifully presented. The extensive wine list includes robust Tuscan reds and whites, a contrast to the fresher wines from the Veneto and Friuli. The smooth, professional service makes eating here a real pleasure.

Wed–Sun 12.30–2.30, 7.30–10.30, Mon 12.30–2.30
L €65, D €105, Wine €9
Rialto

GAM GAM

Map 252 D6
Fondamenta Cannaregio, Cannaregio 1122
Tel 041 715 284

For some really authentic Venetian Jewish cuisine try Gam Gam (meaning 'more! more!'), the famous kosher restaurant in the Ghetto. After washing your hands in the fountain, you sit in pleasant, pastel surroundings and enjoy some excellent cholent, cous cous and bourekas. The wine list is kosher too, and includes Carmel and Golan.

Sun–Fri 12.30–10
L €45, D €75, Wine €9
Guglie

IL GIARDINO DI GIADA

Map 253 G8
Calle dei Botteri, San Polo 1659
Tel 041 721 673

This restaurant doesn't look like much from the outside, but inside it's a vision of pink tablecloths and flowers—and the food is top rate. There is a noticeable Chinese population round here, and this is just one

of the many fine Chinese restaurants that cater to both visitors and locals. It makes the most of being so near the fish market, it's inexpensive and a welcome break from pasta.

Daily 12–2.30, 7–10
L €40, D €70, Wine €7
Rialto

HARRY'S BAR

Map 255 H11
Calle Vallaresso, San Marco 1323
Tel 041 528 5777

If you are going to push the boat out in Venice, you'll get your money's worth at the world famous Harry's Bar. This

stylish and restrained restaurant has long been popular with visiting celebrities, including plentiful Americans, always a good barometer for quality and service. Harry's Bar is famous for its Bellinis (prosecco with white peach juice) and its carpaccio of beef (razor-thin slices of raw sirloin). Both are worth the hype.

Daily 9.30am–11pm
L €80, D €130, Wine €13
San Marco

HARRY'S DOLCI

Map 254 D12
Fondamenta San Biagio, Giudecca 773
Tel 041 522 4844

For summer dining, Harry's Dolci (Harry's Desserts) offers a little more than its counterpart at San Marco—and at more agreeable prices. It makes the most of its great location and fabulous views with a beautiful dining terrace right beside the water. Recommended are the pasta dishes, but make sure you leave room for the sublime puddings—the *tris di cioccolato*, a trio of chocolate concoctions, is stunningly good.

Wed–Sun 12–2.30, 8–10.30. Closed Nov–end Apr
L €80, D €110, Wine €12
Palanca

L'INCONTRO

Map 254 D10
Campo Santa Margherita, Dorsoduro 3062A
Tel 041 522 2404

The Sardinian fare served here gives a real insight into the range of Italy's regional cuisine. The sturdier flavours and vivid colours typify the Sardinian character and cooking, exemplified by the rabbit with myrtle and the wholesome *pane frattau* (paper-thin bread). There are some good wines from the south and the classic *seadas*: fat, sweet ravioli covered in hot honey.

Wed–Sun 12.30–2.30, 7.30–10.30, Tue 7.30pm–10.30pm
L €60, D €90, Wine €9
San Tomà

LOCANDA MONTIN

Map 254 D11
Fondamenta di Borgo, Dorsoduro 1147
Tel 041 522 7151

The Locanda, tucked away behind San Trovaso, has been a reliable choice for over fifty years. It has its ups and downs, but the cooking can still be top-notch and the service and atmosphere is traditionally Venetian. Straightforward Venetian specials and other dishes are perfectly presented, there's a fine wine list and good house wines, and a pretty garden for summer eating.

Thu–Mon 12–3, 7–10. Closed 2 weeks Jan and 2 weeks Aug
L €70, D €100, Wine €10
Accademia

MISTRÀ

Map 254 E14
Fondamenta San Giacomo, Giudecca 212/A
Tel 041 522 0743

Young and enthusiastic owners have converted part of an old warehouse overlooking the boatyards of the southern Giudecca into an airy and laid-back restaurant. Beautiful views over the lagoon are the backdrop to some competently cooked fresh fish and seafood. Off the beaten track, but well signed and packed with locals.

Wed–Sun 12–3, 7.30–10.30, Mon 12–3

L €25, D €35, Wine €12
Redentore

OSTARIA BOCCADORO

Map 253 H8
Campo Widman, Cannaregio 5405A
Tel 041 521 1021

Ostaria Boccadoro is where savvy, well-to-do Venetians come to eat. As with all good fish restaurants the menu changes daily, but expect the likes of polenta with shrimps, squid with inky pasta, tagliatelle with clams and scampi, or go for the raw fish dishes that feature heavily. The astute waiters pay you just enough attention and there is a good choice of wines from the Veneto and Friuli regions, plus some good Sardinian whites.

Tue–Sun 12–3, 7–10
L €45, D €75, Wine €18
Fondamente Nuove

OSTERIA AL BOMBA

Map 253 G7
Calle del Oca, Cannaregio 4297–98
Tel 041 520 5175
www.osteriaalbomba.it

This genuine neighbourhood *osteria* can be busy with gondoliers at lunchtimes, who take advantage of the good value and wide range of delicious *cicheti* that make up for the somewhat lack-lustre surroundings. Main dishes are mostly fish-based and there are vegetables cooked in a variety of ways, making it a

good vegetarian choice. No credit cards accepted.

Daily 10.30–2, 5.30–10.30
L €35, D €60, Wine €8
Ca' d'Oro

OSTERIA DA RIOBA

Map 253 F6
Fondamenta della Misericordia, Cannaregio 2553
Tel 041 524 4379

This restaurant is on the Misericordia, an area popular with the younger Venetian

EATING

crowd. The wooden tables and chairs may be a little too new to give it the feel of an authentic osteria, but all is forgiven when you sample the food, which includes perfectly timed fish *risotti* and the most tender stewed rabbit. There is a small

but well-chosen wine list, dominated by the Veneto, at honest prices.
🕐 Tue–Sun 10–2.30, 6–10
🍴 L €40, D €70, Wine €8
🚤 Madonna dell'Orto

OSTERIA OLIVA NERA
Map 256 K10
Calle della Madonna, Castello 3417–18
Tel 041 522 2170
Oliva Nera is one of a new breed challenging the old school of Venetian restaurateurs. Its menu, full of interesting quirks, yet executed confidently, shows that Venetian cooking can be given a contemporary edge. Delicious examples include scallops with wild mushrooms, octopus salad, and lamb cooked in thyme. The beautifully presented dessert menu includes *pannacotta* with wild fruits and a wonderfully rich mascarpone cheesecake. The uncomplicated décor and unpretentious staff make lunch or dinner here a refreshing change.
🕐 Fri–Tue 12–2.30, 6.30–10
🍴 L €50, D €85, Wine €9
🚤 San Zaccaria

PIZZERIA 84
Map 256 K9
Salizzada Santa Giustina, Castello 2907A
Tel 041 520 4198
This very basic pizzeria is run by an amiable, moustached Sardinian. It has no airs or graces, but serves pizza as good as you'll get in Venice, where fire restrictions prevent the use of wood-burning ovens. It's very popular so you

may have to hang about at the bar, or outside, until a table is free. Take the children to watch the skilful chef prepare your pizza before your very eyes. No credit cards accepted. Smoking is permitted.
🕐 Fri–Tue 5–9.30pm
🍴 D €18, Wine €6
🚤 Celestia

IL REFOLO
Map 252 E7
Campo del Piovan, Santa Croce 1459
Tel 041 524 0016
A charming and very trendy pizzeria, with tables set on one of Venice's prettiest *campi*, the 'Sea Breeze' serves excellent pizzas, creative salads and some good pasta dishes, dressed with the catch of the day. There's also nicely cooked veal and chicken for *secondi*. The house white and red are both very drinkable.
🕐 Tue–Sun 12–2.30, 7–10; closed lunch Tue
🍴 L €35, D €55, Wine €8
🚤 San Stae

RIBO
Map 252 D9
Fondamenta Minotto, Santa Croce 158
Tel 041 524 2486
Ribo is part of the Hotel Salieri and is a lovely spot for some al fresco dining in the summer, in the garden around the back. The food is simply great Venetian fish dishes, fresh and varied. The wine list is unpretentious, but pleasingly so. The light and airy dining room can accommodate large groups.
🕐 Thu–Tue 12–3, 7–10
🍴 L €55, D €85, Wine €8
🚤 Piazzale Roma

TRATTORIA DA FIORE
Map 254 F10
Calle delle Botteghe, San Marco 3461
Tel 041 523 5310
This friendly family-run trattoria serves fish cooked simply but to perfection. It would be easy to fill up on the antipasti of *baccalà* and *calamari* and not have room for further courses. There's a fairly basic wine list. No credit cards accepted.
🕐 Wed–Mon 12–3, 7–10
🍴 L €50, D €80, Wine €8
🚤 San Samuele

VINI DA ARTURO
Map 255 F10
Calle degli Assassini, San Marco 3656
Tel 041 528 6974
Tucked away near the Fenice theatre, this tiny restaurant is a well-kept secret among Venetians seeking a change from their traditionally fish-based menus. Here you'll find superb steaks, veal cutlets and escalopes, well-hung and cooked to perfection, which go down well after one of the imaginative salads served as *antipasti*. Desserts such as chocolate mousse and tiramisu are well above average and all made in-house. No credit cards accepted.
🕐 Mon–Sat 12.30–2.30, 7.30–10.30. Closed last 2 weeks in Feb and Aug
🍴 L €50, D €80, Wine from €9
🚤 Sant'Angelo

VINI DA GIGIO
Map 253 G7
Fondamenta San Felice, Cannaregio 3628A
Tel 041 528 5140
www.vinidagigio.com
This increasingly well-known restaurant is one of the best-value in Venice, recommended for its superlative fresh fish and meat and game. In season, try the *masorini alla buranella* (wild duck from Burano), and the superb and varied *antipasti*. The wines come from all over the world, and include an excellent range

served by the glass. Booking is essential and service can only be described as leisurely.
🕐 Tue–Sun 12–2.30, 7.30–10.30. Closed 3 weeks Jan–Feb, 3 weeks Aug–Sep
🍴 L €40, D €55, Wine €6
🚤 Ca' d'Oro

EATING

STAYING IN VENICE

Compared with its population, Venice has more tourist accommodation than any other Italian city. This ranges from the five-star luxury of some of the world's greatest hotels to the rather bland modern chain hotels and simple, low-key *pensioni*. Despite this, the city remains a seller's market, popular at all times of year, and this is reflected in the high prices of all its accommodation.

Look out for the famous Campari sign (right) on the Riviera Hotel on the Lido

WHERE TO STAY

There's little to be found in the way of special offers on any sort of room, and value for money is a relative concept. Given this, it's worth thinking hard about the location of your hotel, as this will make a huge difference to your enjoyment of the city.

San Marco has a large number of places to stay and is right in the heart of the action, but it's also constantly crowded and noisy, elements which could cost you sleep and might be hard to endure in the heat of summer. To the west, Cannaregio is a good bet for its range of relatively cheaper accommodation, particularly around the railway station, though again, this area can be extremely busy, as it's on the main route to San Marco for day-trippers. East of San Marco, Castello has much to offer; it's more remote, quieter and you'll pay far less for a room with a view than in the San Marco area. Across the Grand Canal, Santa Croce and San Polo have plenty of choice, particularly around the Rialto. Hotels here tend to be family-run, smallish places, with traditional Venetian-style rooms. Dorsoduro is another good choice, its quiet canals and residential streets providing peaceful nights, with the bonus of two major museums on the doorstep. For true peace and ultimate luxury, leave the city and head for the lagoon; two of Venice's most sybaritic hotels, the Cipriani and the San Clemente, are a boat-ride away from the razzmatazz of San Marco.

Wherever you choose, it's worth bearing in mind that this is a small city, so getting about from what seems a far-flung location may not prove too bothersome in reality—and the boats are half the fun. When choosing, think about your arrival, remembering you'll have to carry your luggage over bridges from the nearest water arrival

point, making the proximity of the closest *vaporetto* stop another factor which may influence you.

Venice is very hot during the summer, so a courtyard or garden is a bonus, as are rooms away from the street. Bear in mind that noise bounces off water and narrow streets, especially if they are major thoroughfares.

WHAT YOUR MONEY BUYS

A star system operates in Venice, with five stars denoting the highest standards of comfort, luxury and convenience. Rooms at this level cost from around €350 for a single to €700–€2,000 for a double or suite per night. Four-star options range from around €280 to €400, three-star from €170 to €300, while two-star cost €150 to €220. At the low end of hotels proper, expect to pay between €50 and €150 for a simple room, which may well not have its own bathroom.

The last few years have seen a burgeoning number of boutique hotels and trendy bed-and-breakfast establishments opening in Venice, which are often housed in lovely old buildings tucked away from the main streets. They charge anything between €150 and €400 for a double and are extremely popular, with visitors returning time after time.

Most Venetian hotels include breakfast in the cost of the room; in smaller places, this may be served in your room. You can expect television (often satellite), telephone, a mini-bar and air-conditioning in three-star hotels; you may have to pay extra for the air-conditioning in cheaper places. If you want a room with a view, find out in advance how much of a view you'll be getting for your hefty surcharge; you could end up forking out a huge supplement for a glimpse of the Grand Canal from the bathroom window.

STAYING

MAKING RESERVATIONS

It pays to reserve well in advance, especially if you're planning a visit during peak periods. The city is packed during Carnevale, and you should reserve six months or more ahead to ensure plenty of choice, and at least two for much of the rest of the year. Venice's least busy month is January, virtually the only time when you could safely arrive without a confirmed reservation, though the choice will be limited, as many hotels close from after Christmas until Carnevale.

Do consult hotel websites for details of any special deals, or consider taking a package break to Venice. Tour operators usually have a fixed room allocation in some of the best hotels and their packages, which include flights and transfers, may be very competitively priced. If you haven't reserved ahead, ask to see the room before you commit yourself; this is perfectly acceptable in Italy. If you're making a reservation in advance

from home, get written confirmation and take it with you, or you may turn up and find all knowl- edge of your booking denied. It's a good idea to make sure your hotel has sent you directions for your arrival before you leave home, which should include a locator map, details of the nearest *vaporetto* stop and a local landmark such as a *campo* or church. Venice is a confusing city for first-time visitors and you don't want to have to carry your luggage farther than you have to or get lost before you've even arrived. If you come with- out a reservation, go to the accommodation desks run by the Associazione Veneziani Albergatori (Venetian Hoteliers' Association), who will do their best to help. These are at Santa Lucia railway station (tel 041 715 288); the arrivals hall at Marco Polo airport (tel 041 541 5017) and the Comunale parking area at Piazzale Roma (tel 041 522 8640). You can also telephone them on 041 523 8032 or 041 522 2264.

OTHER OPTIONS

If you're watching the budget, bear in mind that mainland hotels are cheaper than those in the city proper, though the Venetian experience won't be the same. Mestre, a 10-minute hop by bus or train across the water has plenty of hotel accommodation, much of which provides parking, useful if you're arriving by car. Padova (Padua), half an hour or so by train from Venice, has a lovely historic area, with a style of its own that's a good contrast to Venice itself.

If you're interested in the increasingly popular self-catering option see below for of camping on the edges of the lagoon.

ON-LINE HOTEL BOOKING

www.venicehotel.org
www.veniceinfo.it
www.venicehotel.com
www.web-venice-hotels.com
www.invenicehotels.com
www.hotelinvenice.com
www.veniceby.com
www.veniceclick.net

SELF-CATERING

An increasing number of visitors use self-catering when visiting Venice. The benefits are obvious: more space, independence, the flexibility of doing what you want, when you want, the chance to buy and cook your own food and really feel part of the city and, for many people the prime consideration, far lower prices. There are a number of both Venetian-based and international companies offering places in Venice, as well as numerous private owners letting their own holiday flats out while they're away from the city. If you're considering the rental option, there are a few points worth considering:

- Choose the location carefully, making sure there are food shops within easy reach—everything you buy has to be carried home.
- Check that linen, heating, air-conditioning, lighting, gas and end-of-stay cleaning is included in the rent.
- Check that there's an on-the-spot agent in case of emergencies—this is particularly important in the case of private rentals.
- If the rentals are on the third or fourth floors, bear in mind it's unlikely there will be access by elevator.
- Remember that Venetian buildings are old, and be prepared to trade state-of-the-art décor and facilities for the chance to stay in a historic house in a unique city.

The following companies are worth exploring:

Ca'Badoer dei Barbacani

Frari 2000 di Pasqualato Ketty & C, San Polo 2548
www.frari2000.it
There are five holiday apartments, accessible by elevator, on the top two floors of this wonderful old 15th-century *palazzo*, a stone's throw from the Frari. The apartments sleep from two to six, and some interconnect, making larger numbers feasible. Each 15th-century apartment has its own character; some have views towards the Frari, the Alps or over the rooftops, some have balconies. All are well equipped, with numerous extras, and offer excellent value for money. Contact the company via its website.

Holiday Rentals

www.holidayrentals.com
This Internet umbrella company acts on behalf of holiday-home owners all over the world. The site is easy to navigate and you'll find plenty on offer in Venice. Once you've made up your mind, links will lead you direct to the owners, with whom you make the reservation.

Venetian Apartments

403 Parkway House, Sheen Lane, London SW14 8LS
Tel 020 8878 1130; fax 020 8878 0982
www.venice-rentals.com
This long-established, British-based company has over 100 apartments in central Venice and on the Giudecca for rent. It specializes in beautiful, historic and luxuriously appointed *palazzi* and apartments so, if you're looking for a palace on the Grand Canal, this is the place to start your search. All the apartments, which vary considerably in size and décor, are fully equipped for self-catering.

Venice Central Apartments

Altra Vista srl, San Marco 3028
Tel 041 277 0318
www.nicevenice.it
This Venice-based company has a dozen or so apartments scattered around the city on its books. These sleep between two and six people and come with adequate kitchens and bathrooms, microwave and TV, though the décor varies considerably from place to place. A deposit is required and there is a charge for the final cleaning. Reserve via the website.

Views on Venice

San Marco 4267A
Tel 041 241 1149
www.viewsonvenice.com
Another Venice-based rental company, Views on Venice has a huge range of apartments, many of luxury standard. Reserve via the website.

CAMPING

If you are a family with kids, you may want to consider combining a beach and sea camping holiday with forays into Venice. The camping ground below is the nearest to the city, with regular *vaporetto* connections.

Camping Village Cavallino

Via delle Batterie, Cavallino 164
Tel 041 966 133
www.baiaholiday.com
This sprawling, well-equipped complex opens onto an attractive Adriatic beach, and has a pool, shop, newsagent, launderette, cash point, restaurant and bar on site. It costs €19 to pitch your tent in high season plus an additional €9 per person. Various bungalows and mobile homes are available: the cheapest 'Cavallino' (four-person) caravan has WC and kitchen facilities and costs €65, plus €9 per person, in high season.
Ⓒ Closed mid-Sep to early Mar

STAYING

The hotels listed below are scattered throughout the city, with a full range of price options and styles of accomodation in each *sestiere*. To help you choose, they have been listed by area, and it's worth deciding where you want to go before you make a reservation. In terms of transport links, hotels on the Grand Canal section of the route of the 1 or 82 *vaporetto* make sense, particularly if time is short, so bear in mind that hotels in northern Cannaregio or eastern Castello may be relatively remote, time-wise, from the major sites.

Pensione Accademia Villa Maravege, once a 17th-century private mansion

STAYING

CANNAREGIO
Al Ponte Antico
Giorgione
Grand Hotel dei Dogi
Minerva e Nettuno
Rossi
Villa Rosa

CASTELLO
Bisanzio
Campiello
La Colombina
Danieli
Foresteria Valdese
Locanda La Corte
Locanda Sant'Anna
Locanda Silva
Londra Palace
Metropole
Paganelli
Pensione Bucintoro
La Residenza
Scandinavia

DORSODURO
Agli Alboretti
La Calcina
Ca' Maria Adele
Ca' Pisani
Dinesen
La Galleria
Locanda Ca' Foscari
Locanda San Barnaba
Locanda San Trovaso
Palazzo dal Carlo
Pausania
Pensione Accademia Villa
   Maravege
Pensione Seguso

SANTA CROCE
Marin
San Cassiano Ca' Favretto

SAN MARCO
Al Piave
Antica Locanda al Gambero
Bauer Grunwald
Concordia

Europa & Regina
La Fenice et des Artistes
Flora
Gritti Palace
Locanda Art Déco
Locanda Orseolo
Luna Baglioni
Noemi
Novecento
San Clemente Palace
San Samuele

SAN POLO
Iris
Locanda Armizo
Locanda Ovidius
Locanda Sturion
Marconi

THE ISLANDS
Cipriani
Des Bains
Ostello di Venezia
Westin Excelsior

HOTEL LOCATOR

C   D   E   F

4

Canale delle Sacche

Canale delle Navi

SACCA DI
S ALVISE

Sant'Alvise

SACCA DI S
GIROLAMO

Campo
S Alvise

Sant'Alvise

5

Tre
Archi

PONTE D
TRE ARCHI

Campo
S Giobbe

San
Giobbe

CANNAREGIO

6

IL GHETTO

Campo
Ghetto
Nuovo

Guglie

Parco di
Savorgnàn

Rio Terrà S Leonardo

Villa Rosa

Rossi

PONTE
D'GUGLIE

Campo
S Leonardo

Minerva
e Nettuno

Campo
S Geremia

San Geremia
e Lucia

San
Marcuola

Campo
S Marcuola

San Marcuola

7

Rivi di Biasio

Museo
di Storia
Naturale

San Stae

Scalzi

STAZIONE FERROVIARIA
SANTA LUCIA

Canal Grande

Riva d Biasio

Campo
S Simeon
Grande

San Giovanni
Decollato

Campo
S Stae

San Stae

Ferrovia

PONTE
DEGLI SCALZI

Campo
S Simeon
Profeta

Museo del
Tessuto e
del Costume

Palazzo
Mocenigo

Ferrovia

Marin

San Giacomo
dell'Orio

Campo San
Giacomo
dell'Orio

Campo
S M Mater
Domini

Campo
N Sauro

Ruga Bella

8

Giardino
Papadopoli

Campo d
Lana

San Nicolò
da Tolentino

Scuola Grande di
San Giovanni
Evangelista

Campo
S Agostin

SAN POLO

9

Campo d
Tolentino

Archivio
di Stato

San
Rocco

Santa Maria
Gloriosa dei
Frari

Campo
del Frari

San Polo

Campo
San Polo

Scuola Grande
di San Rocco

Museo Casa
Carlo Goldoni

San
Pantalon

Iris

C   D   E

HOTEL LOCATOR

Map labels (reading order):

Upper inset — Murano

8 — 1, 2, 9, 3, 4

Campo Sportivo
Canale di Santa Maria
Cimitero Nuovo
C G M Ortes
C P Venin
C odorardo
Fond C Parmense
C s Coppa
C d Cimitero
R Cimitero
Campo del Cimitero
C S Bernardo
Fond S Salvi
C Convento
C Vigi
C Ghieri d'Figlietto
C Brussa
Fond S Lorenzo
C S Giuseppe
C S Radi
Venier
Canale degli Angeli
SACCA SERENELLA
Fond S Venier
C C d Vegro
C S Cristo
C S Bernardo
C S Misto
Campo S Donato
PONTE S DONATO
Canale Serenella
C d Vignani
PONTE VIVARINI
Fond S Maffa
C C d Mula
Fond Cavour
Canale Grande
Fond A Colleoni
Museo
Canale Ondello
Serenella
C S Pignano
C dietro gli Orti
Campo S Stefano
C S Giacomo
C Navagero
C Paradiso
Fond Serenella
C d Colonna
C Bercolini
C d Verrata
Fond d Vetrai
C Miotti
C Miotti
C lo turella
Via Briati
Navagero
Murano
Canale delle Navi
Fond S Piave
Faro
L — Colonna
M
N
Canale dei Marani

San Pietro

Lower map — San Pietro / Sant'Elena

Rio San Daniele
Campo S Daniele
Salizzada Stretta
C larga S Pietro
C d Terco
Calle di San Pietro
Campo di San Pietro
San Pietro di Castello
Ísola di San Pietro
10
C S Giovanni
C llo Figaretto
Campo di Ruga
C Sporca
C Marafani
C d Ole
C d Salamòn
C d Campanile
C d Pozzo Pozzi
Locanda Sant'Anna
C d Bianco
C S Anna
C llo Quintavalle
C llo Vigna
C d Mezo
C llo del Pomeri
Fond Casa Osono
C S Pietro
Fond San Gioacchino
Fond S Anna
C Quintavalle
C d Fari
C larga Quintavalle
C Pistor
Rio di Quintavalle
11
C Frisiera
C Corridòni
C d Angelo
C te Bassa
C d Strazza Sartori
Ramo del Nicoli
C San Gioacchino
C del Forno
C d Tiepolo
C te Correra
C Castagna
C te Ancore
C te Furlana
C d Scrini
Secco Marina
C te Martin Novello
C te Princi
C te d Colno
C te Sodoriera
C te Morosini
C te d Cenera
Fond San Giuseppe
Viale Trento
Campo San Giuseppe
Rio terrà San Giuseppe
C S Antonio
Paludo S Antonio
Biennale Internazionale d'Arte
C dentro il Giardino
Giardini Pubblici
Viale Trieste
Viale dei Giardini Pubblici
Rio d'Giardini
Darsena di Sant'Elena
12
Ísola di Sant'Elena
Ramo d Montello
Viale XXIV Maggio
C Asiago
C Nervesa
C del Forner
C d Pozzo
C d Montello
C d Fagare
C d Asolo
C d congregazione
Viale Piave
Fond Darsena
C del Pasubio
Campo d'Grappa
C Montesanto
C d'Sabotino
C dell'Hermada
Fond S Elena
C del Carso
C Podgora
Campo Sportivo
QUARTIERE SANT'ELENA
Campo d Indipendenza
C Gen Chinotto
C d Cottia
C Balnizza
C d Zugna
Sant'Elena
13
C Duca d Aosta
C del Rovereto
C del carnaro
Campo d Chiesa
Des Bains, Westin Excelsior
N
Parco delle Rimembranze
Viale IV Novembre
Viale S Elena
Rio di Sant'E
P
Viale Piave
Q

275

HOTELS

PRICES AND SYMBOLS

The hotels below are listed alphabetically and cover a range of budgets. Prices are the lowest and highest rate for a double room in high season and include breakfast, unless otherwise stated.

AGLI ALBORETTI
Map 272 E11
Rio Terrà Antonio Foscarini, Dorsoduro 884
Tel 041 523 0058
www.aglialboretti.com
This pretty little hotel, just a stone's throw from the Accademia, has long been popular with Venetians. Some of the rooms are rather small, but this is outweighed by the charming and helpful service and the pretty outdoor courtyard where breakfast is served in summer. It has most facilities, including 24-hour room service, satellite TV and internet connection.
€110–€190
23 rooms, 3 suites
Accademia

AL PIAVE
Map 273 J9
Ruga Giuffa, San Marco 4838–50
Tel 041 528 5174
www.hotelalpiave.com
This hotel is located near Campo Santa Maria Formosa and offers good value for Venice. A very sleek, art deco-inspired lobby welcomes guests and gives access to the public area, which includes a lounge bar, TV sitting room and a functional space for taking the buffet breakfast. The rooms are generally bright and very comfortable—expect flowery furnishings and cheerful artwork. Each one has a private bathroom, phone, climate control, safe and TV.
€115–€150
27
San Marco, Rialto

AL PONTE ANTICO
Map 271 G8
Calle dell'Aseo, Cannaregio 5768
Tel 041 241 1944
www.alponteantico.com

The frescoes and lovely old beams have been lovingly restored to form the backdrop for antiques, sumptuous drapes and chandeliers in this magnificent 15th-century *palazzo*. Public rooms have large windows with stunning views of the Grand Canal. Take breakfast or sip a restorative Bellini on the terrace or in the elegant *salone*. Guest rooms and junior suites are named after the city's bridges—they have bright, pleasant Venetian decorative flourishes and modern private bathrooms. Other facilities include safe, TV, minibar, hairdryer, internet and hydromassage bath.
€180–€520
9
Rialto

ANTICA LOCANDA AL GAMBERO
Map 273 H9
Calle dei Fabbri, San Marco 4687
Tel 041 522 4384
www.locandaalgambero.com
This well-run hotel is between the Rialto and San Marco. Public areas have dark wood furniture, marble flooring and a late Victorian-era ambience.

Renovation has improved the bedrooms, adding immaculate private bathrooms without drastically raising the prices. Other amenities include TV, telephone, safe, hairdryer and minibar. As with its sister hotel the Locanda Sturion, there are tea- and coffee-making facilities in each room. Discount meals are available in the excellent Le Bistrot downstairs.
€120–€180
27
San Marco

BAUER GRUNWALD
Map 273 G10
Campo San Moisè, San Marco 1459
Tel 041 520 7022
www.allluxuryhotels.net
The Bauer is a luxury hotel blessed with stunning rooftop and balcony views. It's split into a modern hotel, where most of the rooms are found, and the more evocative 18th-

century 'Palazzo at the Bauer', complete with palatial suites, furnished with elegant antiques, beautiful fabrics and Murano chandeliers, with state-of-the-art Jacuzzis and stunning views across the Grand Canal to Santa Maria della Salute. All rooms have TV and minibar. Breakfast is served in the Settimo Cielo (Seventh Heaven) salon, which opens onto a wonderful terrace. Facilities include health club and sauna. The Canal Grande restaurant serves a mix of international and Veneto fare.
€500–€1,300
196 rooms, 60 suites
Santa Maria del Giglio

BISANZIO
Map 274 K10
Calle della Pietà, Castello 3651
Tel 041 520 3100
www.bisanzio.com
The Busetti family has run this restored 16th-century *palazzo* hotel, near Vivaldi's church of La Pietà, since 1969. Guestrooms, some of which have charming balconies with rooftop views, have parquet flooring, beamed ceilings and unfussy Venetian décor. All have telephone, satellite TV, hairdryer and minibar. The Brown Lounge, bar and breakfast room all share a functional, understated

appearance. The continental breakfast may be taken in the old courtyard.

€110–€290
40
♿
San Zaccaria

LA CALCINA
Map 272 E12
Fondamenta Zattere ai Gesuati, Dorsoduro 780–83
Tel 041 520 6466
www.lacalcina.com
The excellent-value, classy Calcina, in its superb and secluded setting on the sunny Zattere looking across to the Giudecca, served in the 1870s as a lodging for the English writer John Ruskin and has been welcoming guests ever since. The airy, spacious rooms have parquet flooring and are simply furnished with attractive period touches. Each room has a private bathroom, telephone, hairdryer and safe. Breakfast is served inside or on a terrace above the water, and the roof terrace is another bonus.

€90–v240
32
♿
Zattere

CAMPIELLO
Map 273 J10
Campiello del Vin, Castello 4647
Tel 041 520 5764
www.hcampiello.it
This hotel, owned by the Bianchini sisters, is near the most popular San Marco sites.

The bright and cheery hall, breakfast room and bar have marble floors and elegant furnishings. Bedrooms are comfortable and functional, with private bathroom, safe, TV, internet point and telephone, and some attractive Venetian antique pieces.
Closed Jan
€115–€180
17
♿
San Zaccaria

CA' MARIA ADELE
Map 273 G11
Rio Terrà dei Catecumeni, Dorsoduro 111
Tel 041 520 3078
www.camariadele.it
Right next to the Salute and a minute's walk from the *vaporetto*, this luxurious little hotel provides the ultimate in sybaritic and romantic living. You can choose between one of the themed suites, where the décor ranges from cosy fireside to oriental, or relax in the comfort of a more conventional room. Breakfast is served in a charming room dominated by an over-the-top Murano glass chandelier.
€390–€500, excluding breakfast
7 rooms, 7 suites
♿
Salute

CA' PISANI
Map 272 E11
Rio Terrà Antonio Foscarini, Dorsoduro 979A
Tel 041 240 1411
www.capisanihotel.it
Ca' Pisani's stylish interiors are inspired by the 1930s and '40s—smooth lines, exposed beams and art deco furnishings mix with modern, minimalist décor. Each room is individually designed and has a relaxing, sophisticated charm. Facilities are excellent and bathrooms the most contemporary in town. La Rivista

restaurant continues this theme and serves simple, contemporary and classic Italian cuisine. There's a sauna and access to a nearby gym.
€190–€400
29
♿
Gym access
Accademia

CIPRIANI
Map 273 H13
Giudecca 10
Tel 041 520 7744
www.hotelcipriani.com
One of the world's great hotels, the Cipriani, set at the east end of the Giudecca across the water from San Marco, offers luxury, privacy and superb service. The Palazzo Vendramin and Palazzetto Nani Barbaro suites come with waterside views and your own private butler; all other rooms and suites are individually furnished with superb facilities. Within the extensive grounds there's a heated swimming pool, gym and beauty centre, red clay tennis court and vineyards. Dining at the Cipriani Restaurant is a well-heeled event, while the Cips Club is a more informal experience on a floating platform, with no jacket required. The hotel runs

a free shuttle boat service to and from San Marco.
The main hotel building closes between November and early April. Palazzo Vendramin and Palazzetto Nani Barbaro stay open year round
€813–€1,248
103 rooms and suites
♿ ☕ Outdoor Olympic size
Zitelle

LA COLOMBINA

Map 273 H9
Calle del Rimedio, Castello 4416
Tel 041 277 0525
www.hotelcolombina.com

This well-run hotel, named after the Carnival character, has superb views of San Marco and the Ponte dei Sospiri (Bridge of Sighs). Public rooms are filled with baroque decorative touches and furnishings, while guest rooms are typically Venetian, but not too overpowering—expect pastel patterned wallpaper, marble floors, dark wood antiques and chandeliers.

€170–€395
32
Zattere

CONCORDIA

Map 273 H10
Calle Larga, San Marco 367
Tel 041 520 6866
www.hotelconcordia.it

If you love being near the heart of things, the Concordia, just off Piazza San Marco, should fit the bill. Many of the rooms, furnished in a style veering towards 18th-century Venetian, have glimpses of the Basilica, while the suites have lighter, less overbearing furnishings; rooms at the back can be noisy. Every room has a telephone, TV, hairdryer and minibar. La Piazzetta restaurant serves Italian and Venetian cuisine. The service is very professional.

€190–€450
57 rooms and suites
San Zaccaria

DANIELI

Map 273 J10
Riva degli Schiavoni, Castello 4196
Tel 041 522 6480
www.danieli.hotelinvenice.com

This former home of Doge Dandolo ranks among the very best of Italian hotels, with a style and ambience that's hard to beat. Public rooms are sumptuous in every way, with marble floors, antique furnishings, sparkling glass and rich fabrics, while bedrooms and suites, though varying enormously in style and size, are equally well-appointed. Restaurants and bars offer exceptional food, drink and service, uniting to give the

ultimate Venetian experience. Make reservations well in advance for a room in the old building.

€390–€2,400
233 rooms and suites
San Zaccaria

DES BAINS

Lungomare Marconi, Lido 17
Tel 041 526 5921
www.starwood.com/sheraton/index.html

Des Bains is an art deco gem that featured in Visconti's film *Death in Venice*, and where Thomas Mann wrote the hauntingly atmospheric tale. Although this belle époque star has seen better days, it is still a popular Biennale haunt, with sumptuous public rooms, two restaurants, and well-equipped bedrooms and suites. The lush grounds have tennis courts, a gym, a sauna and a swimming pool, and there is access to the hotel's own private beach.

Closed mid-Nov to mid-Mar
€200–€900
191 rooms, 1 suite
Lido Casino Santa Maria Elisabetta

DINESEN

Map 272 E11
Fondamenta Bragadin, Dorsoduro 628
Tel 041 520 4733
www.hotelamerican.com

The balconies of the Dinesen, dripping with flowers, overhang the Rio di San Vio, one of the quietest and most attractive of Dorsoduro's canals. This refurbished hotel, formerly the American, has airy, spacious rooms, furnished and decorated in traditional Venetian style, a relaxing bar and pretty garden; the staff pride themselves on the level of service—booking tickets and tours and arranging baby-sitters—making this an excellent choice in a great part of town away from the crowds.

€100–€300
30
Accademia

EUROPA & REGINA

Map 273 G11
Off Calle Larga XXII Marzo, San Marco 2159
Tel 041 240 0001
www.westin.com

This Westin hotel occupies two adjoining and magnificent *palazzi*, overlooking the Grand Canal. The public rooms are full of marble, rich hues and

sumptuous fabrics, with a wonderful terrace for drinks and dining right on the Grand Canal. The bedrooms are simpler, well-furnished and equipped, but somewhat bland. All have marble bathrooms, TV, safe, hairdryer, minibar and 24-hour room service. Access to the Lido beach and sports facilities are included.

€270–€1,800
185 rooms, 17 suites
San Marco

LA FENICE ET DES ARTISTES

Map 273 F10
Campiello della Fenice, San Marco 1936
Tel 041 523 2333
www.fenicehotels.it

The old-established La Fenice et des Artistes, close to the Fenice and popular with musicians and opera aficionados, is a true Venetian institution with

a loyal clientele. Expect exposed beams, marble and antiques in the public areas, a theatre-style bar and bedrooms of varying size and décor—the best have balconies, and all have telephone, TV, private bathroom, hairdryer and safe. La Taverna restaurant serves classic Venetian dishes, and you can breakfast outside

STAYING

on sunny mornings in the central courtyard.

🛏 €140–€310
🛌 67
🅢
🚉 Sant'Angelo, San Marco

FLORA

Map 273 G11
Calle dei Bergamaschi, San Marco 2283A
Tel 041 520 5844
www.hotelflora.it

Hidden down a narrow *calle* a few minutes' walk from the Piazza, the Flora—family-run and brimming with character—is a wonderfully tranquil hotel, with a pretty garden and sense of peace. Room sizes vary greatly; some are extremely poky, and the quietest look onto gardens. They have small-ish private bathrooms, and TV and phone are included. The multilingual staff are friendly and helpful and can arrange baby-sitting.

🛏 €180–€250
🛌 44 rooms
🅢
🚉 San Marco

FORESTERIA VALDESE

Map 273 J9
Calle della Madonetta, Castello 5170
Tel 041 528 6797
www.chiesavaldese.org/venezia/foresteria/

The 18th-century Palazzo Cavagnis is near vibrant Campo Santa Maria Formosa, and run as a hostel by Waldensian Evangelicals, who also arrange concerts and

cultural events in the high-ceilinged public rooms, which have crumbling frescoes. The hostel provides something very special for those watching the budget, with accommodation ranging from dormitory beds (€22) and decent doubles, with TV and basic private bathrooms, to self-catering apartments. No credit cards

accepted.

🛏 €55–€75
🛌 75 beds
🚉 Rialto

LA GALLERIA

Map 272 E11
Rio Terrà Antonio Foscarini- Campo della Calità, Dorsoduro 878A
Tel 041 523 2489
www.hotelgalleria.it

Climb the stairs to this quirky little hotel and you'll find yourself in a timewarp, where Edwardian décor, lace mats and overstuffed sofas are the order of the day. But it's comfortable, well-run and the prices are excellent for this prime location. Reserve ahead to get one of the larger rooms on the Grand Canal—the best is No. 10, which sleeps four beneath its painted ceiling. Breakfast is served in your room.

🛏 €100–€150
🛌 12
🅢
🚉 Accademia

GIORGIONE

Map 271 G7
Campo Santi Apostoli, Cannaregio 4587
Tel 041 522 5810
www.hotelgiorgione.com

This 15th-century *palazzo* is down a tranquil *calle* off the Campo Santi Apostoli, and spreads its rooms between the old *palazzo* and a newer building, with the third floor reserved for non-smokers. There are some split-level rooms with terraces and

rooftop views; all have air-conditioning, minibars, satellite TV and internet connections. The public areas are welcoming and warm, and you can eat breakfast in the courtyard with its flowers and lily pond. Buffet breakfast included. The attached Giorgione pub/wine shop serves traditional Venetian cuisine.

🛏 €130–€330
🛌 76
🅢
🚉 Ca' d'Oro, Fondamente Nuove

GRAND HOTEL DEI DOGI

Map 271 F5
Fondamenta Madonna dell'Orto, Cannaregio 3500
Tel 041 220 8111
www.deidogi.com

Well off the beaten track, in the depths of a quiet corner of northern Cannaregio, this former French embassy *palazzo* and convent provides a water taxi service to San Marco for its guests. The hotel offers everything you'd expect in the way of luxury, with palatial accommodation, grandiose 18th-century décor in the public areas and a lush garden with sublime views across the water to Murano. The restaurant serves Venetian food.

🛏 €350–€522
🛌 68 rooms and 1 suite
🅢
🚉 Madonna dell'Orto

GRITTI PALACE

Map 273 F11
Campo Santa Maria del Giglio, San Marco 2467
Tel 041 794 611
www.starwood.com/grittipalace

One of Venice's great hotels, the Gritti was chosen by Queen Elizabeth II as her Venetian base. This is a beautiful, old-fashioned hotel, with elegance, style and service to match. There's a huge range of rooms, each uniquely deco-

rated and some overlooking the Grand Canal, while the dining room, bar and public areas are furnished with antiques and adorned with exquisite flowers; a drink on the terrace is one of the great Venetian experiences. A courtesy launch takes guests to the sports facilities, beach and pool of the Starwood group on the Lido.

STAYING

€450–€1,500
91 rooms and suites
Santa Maria del Giglio

IRIS
Map 272 E9
Fondamenta dei Forner, Calle del Cristo, San Polo 2910A
Tel 041 522 2882
www.irishotel.com
The Iris is in a quiet area of San Polo near the Frari church. The guest rooms, refurbished in

1997, are light and simply furnished; not all have private bathrooms, but each has a TV, hairdryer and telephone. Il Giardinetto restaurant is popular for its fish dishes, pizzas and live piano and jazz music.
€100–€140
30
San Tomà

LOCANDA ARMIZO
Map 271 G9
Campo San Silvestro, San Polo 1104
Tel 041 520 6473
www.armizo.com
Tucked under a *sottoportego* in the corner of the *campo* lies the Armizo, a small hotel housed in a converted merchant's premises, that offers excellent value and comfortable accommodation. Four big, airy and spacious rooms overlook the *campo*, and will sleep up to five; rates are per room not per person. Giancarlo and Massimiliano take trouble to look after their guests and it shows in the friendly welcome and well-presented breakfasts served in the bedrooms. All rooms have satellite TV.
€69–€249
7
San Silvestro

LOCANDA ART DÉCO
Map 272 F10
Calle delle Botteghe, San Marco 2966
Tel 041 277 0558
www.locandaartdeco.com
Sited near the Ponte dell'Accademia (Accademia Bridge), the Locanda will appeal to lovers of the belle époque, with both public rooms and bedrooms filled with assorted art deco antiques. Each attractive guest room has an orthopaedic

mattress, private bathroom, kettle, TV, hairdryer and phone. The buffet breakfast is served in the charming breakfast room.
€100–€170
6
Accademia

LOCANDA CA' FOSCARI
Map 272 E9
Calle della Frescada, Dorsoduro 3887B
Tel 041 710 401
www.locandacafoscari.com
The Ca' Foscari makes a great budget choice. As much a bed-and-breakfast as hotel, there's a cosy family feel to this pleasant guesthouse, well placed near the Frari. Not all rooms have their own bathrooms, but the warm welcome, spotless rooms, fresh flowers and excellent breakfast make this superb value for money. The *signora* will prepare dinner for groups.
€85–€100, excluding breakfast
11
San Tomà

LOCANDA LA CORTE
Map 271 J8
Calle Bressana, Castello 6317
Tel 041 241 1300
www.locandalacorte.it
This pleasant hotel is set in a quiet corner of Castello, near the huge bulk of Santi Giovanni e Paolo church. Guest rooms have typically elegant Venetian furnishings, high ceilings and exposed beams. Facilities include private bathroom, TV, hairdryer and phone.

The secluded courtyard is a great place to relax and take the buffet breakfast, which is included.
€115–€180
15
San Zaccaria or Fondamente Nuove

LOCANDA ORSEOLO
Map 273 G10
Corte Zorzi, San Marco 1083
Tel 041 520 4827
www.locandaorseolo.com
Just behind the Piazza San Marco, a wrought-iron gate shields tiny Campo Zorzi from the bustle of everyday life. Here you'll find the Locanda Orseolo, a charming hotel run by a welcoming young team. Public rooms are decorated in warm, rich shades and beautifully furnished; bedrooms echo the feeling, with hand-painted murals and canopied beds. Wonderful breakfasts are cooked to order by Matteo, one of the owners, and the rest of the staff will always make time for a friendly chat.
€210–€250, excluding breakfast
15
Vallaresso

LOCANDA OVIDIUS
Map 271 G9
Calle del Sturion, San Polo 677A
Tel 041 523 7970
www.hotelovidius.com

STAYING

There are great views of the Rialto and the Canal Grande from the terrace of this pleasant hotel, where the rooms have an 18th-century theme—expect parquet floors, traditional Venetian furnishings and exposed beams. The bathrooms, however, are firmly 21st-century, and the whirlpool baths do much to ease aching muscles after a long day's sightseeing. Public areas are similar in style to the bedrooms, though most guests head for the terrace for an evening drink. Some rooms have canal views; specify when you book and expect to pay a hefty premium.

🔲 €210–€265
🛏 18
🔲
🚤 Rialto

LOCANDA SAN BARNABA
Map 272 E10
Calle del Traghetto, Dorsoduro 2785-86
Tel 041 241 1233
www.locanda-sanbarnaba.com
Just a few steps from the Ca' Rezzonico *vaporetto* stop, the San Barnaba is acknowledged as one of the best hotels in this price range in this area. Every bedroom is different, but all are tastefully furnished with period pieces, lovely textiles and have parquet floors and exposed beams. Public areas are elegant, and there's a small courtyard and a rooftop terrace. The hotel has ground-floor rooms and there are no bridges between it and the *vaporetto*, making it a good option for visitors with disabilities.

🔲 €120–€200
🛏 13
🔲
🚤 Ca' Rezzonico

LOCANDA SANT'ANNA
Map 275 N11
Corte del Bianco, Castello 269
Tel 041 528 6466
www.locandasantanna.com
This out of the way hotel, near Via Garibaldi and San Pietro, is basic, comfortable and cheap for Venice. It is in the spacious, verdant and less touristy margins of the Castello *sestiere*, where most Venetians would prefer to live. Public rooms are functional and tidy, while the guest rooms are small. Air-conditioning is available on request. No credit cards accepted.

🚫 Closed Jan
🔲 €70–€130
🛏 10
🔲
🚤 Giardini

LOCANDA SAN TROVASO
Map 272 D11
Fondamenta delle Eremite, Dorsoduro 1350–51
Tel 041 277 1146
www.locandasantrovaso.com
This friendly, family-run hotel near the Zattere waterfront is good value for Venice. A small *altana* (roof terrace) allows guests to enjoy fantastic views and soak up the sunshine. The spacious and simple rooms have Venetian décor and fittings; their facilities include private bathroom with shower, though none have television. Air-conditioning is available on request, and there are some pretty rooms in the new annexe across the alley, which are payable by cash only; you can use credit cards in the main hotel.

🔲 €110–€160
🛏 7
🔲
🚤 Zattere

LOCANDA SILVA
Map 273 H9
Fondementa di Rimedio, Castello 4423
Tel 041 523 7892
www.locandasilva.it
The Silva is in the bustling *calle* between Santa Maria Formosa and San Marco. The public areas, including the breakfast room, are clean, with modern furniture and fittings, and vibrant artwork on the walls. Guest rooms have light wood furniture, basic amenities and a functional modern character. Some have pleasant canal views and the cheapest share a bathroom.

🔲 €65–€110
🛏 23
🔲
🚤 San Zaccaria

LOCANDA STURION
Map 271 G8
Calle del Sturion, San Polo 679
Tel 041 523 6243
www.locandasturion.com
The convivial Italo-Scottish management welcomes visitors to this well-run hotel, originally founded in the late 1200s as an inn for visiting merchants. Most of the rooms face a quiet *calle* and each has

a TV, safe, hairdryer, minibar and kettle. The luminous breakfast room and the most sought-after bedrooms have views of the Rialto action; many have marble floors, dark wood furniture and rich Venetian décor. There's no elevator, so getting your baggage in may be a challenge.

🔲 €120–€240
🛏 11
🔲
🚤 San Silvestro, Rialto

LONDRA PALACE
Map 273 J10
Riva degli Schiavoni, Castello 4171
Tel 041 520 0533
www.slh.com/londra or
www.hotellondra.it
The solidly elegant Londra Palace enjoys a prime location on the Riva overlooking St. Mark's Basin and the island of San Giorgio Maggiore. It was here that Tchaikovsky composed his Fourth Symphony, and the atmosphere of calm, restrained comfort has changed little since his day. The hotel received a major overhaul in the late 1990s, and the wide selection of bedrooms all have safe, TV, telephone, hairdryer, climate control, minibar and spacious pink marble bathrooms. The restaurant and terrace dining area serve regional food, there's a roof level terrace for sunbathing and the staff have a high degree of expertise and professionalism.

🔲 €270–€800
🛏 53 rooms and suites
🔲
🚤 San Zaccaria

STAYING

LUNA BAGLIONI

Map 273 G10
Calle Larga dell'Ascensione, San Marco 1243
Tel 041 528 9840
www.baglionihotels.com

Venice's oldest hotel, founded in the late 15th century, has had a major overhaul. More than a quarter of the bedrooms are front-facing, with views to the Giardini ex-Reali or across the water to San Giorgio Maggiore; all have stylishly opulent furnishings and marble bathrooms. Public areas are luxurious, and the Canova Restaurant features Venetian specialities. The conference room, sometimes used for the breakfast buffet, retains its original stucco and fresco decoration.

💶 €300–€600
🛏 100 rooms, 14 suites
🅂
🚤 San Marco

MARCONI

Map 271 G9
Riva del Vin, San Polo 729
Tel 041 522 2068
www.hotelmarconi.it

Only two of the rooms at this well-priced hotel have that coveted Grand Canal view, but the bonus of the others is their tranquillity. Public rooms are traditionally decorated and furnished, and there are outdoor tables for morning coffee with a close-up view of the Rialto bridge.

💶 €55–€228 single, €70–€325 double, excluding breakfast
🛏 26
🅂
🚤 Rialto

MARIN

Map 270 D8
Calle Muneghe, Santa Croce 670B
Tel 041 718 022
www.albergohotelmarin.it

Nadia, Bruno and their family will give you a warm welcome at their hotel, near the station, but removed from the crowds of the Lista di Spagna. Rooms are clean and functional; not all have private bathrooms, so specify when you book. Breakfast is served in an area full of plants and landscape pictures. Excellent value.

💶 €60–€100
🛏 17
🅂
🚤 Santa Lucia

METROPOLE

Map 274 K10
Riva degli Schiavoni, Castello 4149
Tel 041 520 5044
www.hotelmetropole.com

It may be right on the Riva, but the Metropole feels like an oasis of calm, largely thanks to its cool, spacious reading and sitting rooms, furnished with antiques from the owner's collection, and its wonderfully secluded garden. Bedrooms

are elegantly furnished in the Venetian style, with touches like heated bathroom floors and the occasional canopied bed. Many have views: choose from the lagoon, the canal behind or the garden. A buffet breakfast is included and you can eat in the courtyard restaurant in the evening.

💶 €220–€750
🛏 56 rooms, 14 suites
🅂
🚤 San Zaccaria

MINERVA E NETTUNO

Map 270 D7
Lista di Spagna, Cannaregio 230
Tel 041 715 968
www.minervaenettuno.it

The Minerva e Nettuno is more than a cut above many of the nearby establishments in the station area, with wood-beamed ceilings, and traditional furnishings in the spotlessly clean and simple bedrooms. Not all rooms have private bathrooms.

💶 €60–€110
🛏 30
🅂
🚤 Ferrovia

NOEMI

Map 273 G10
Calle dei Fabbri, San Marco 909
Tel 041 523 8144
www.hotelnoemi.com

This attractive and well-managed hotel is found in the long, straight, tourist-filled Calle dei Fabbri, near Piazza San Marco.

Step inside and you're in one of the best-value lodgings in this expensive area, complete with marble floors and bright fabrics in the public areas and well-appointed, traditionally beamed bedrooms. Not all have bathrooms; enquire when you book. All have satellite TV, telephone and safe, and air-conditioning available on request for an extra fee. No credit cards accepted.

💶 €50–€150
🛏 20
🅂
🚤 San Marco, San Marco (Vallaresso)

NOVECENTO

Map 272 F10
Calle delle Dose, Campo San Maurizio, San Marco 2683
Tel 041 241 3765
www.novecento.biz

The Novecento is another stunning boutique hotel that's right up with the best of Venice's new wave designer lodgings. The décor pays homage to Fortuny, using rich colours and textures with a multi-ethnic twist as the backdrop to fine old furniture. There's a tiny courtyard, a breakfast room and honesty bar, and rooms are equipped with every comfort, including Philippe Starck bathrooms.

💶 €130–€240, excluding breakfast
🛏 9
🅂
🚤 Giglio

OSTELLO DI VENEZIA

Map 273 G13
Fondamenta Zitelle, Giudecca 86
Tel 041 523 8211
www.ostellionline.org

Venice's youth hostel is on the Giudecca, a boat ride from San Marco, and has wonderful views across the water to Santa Maria della Salute and San Marco. Accommodation is cheap and basic, with dormitory beds and communal

STAYING

bathrooms. There is an 11pm curfew; check out time is 9.30am. A small continental breakfast is included and cheap meals are available (€8) in the evening. It is essential to reserve well ahead in writing, particularly during the summer. No credit cards accepted.

🎟 Closed 12 Dec–31 Dec
💶 €17
🛏 260 beds
🚤 Zitelle

PAGANELLI

Map 273 J10
Campo San Zaccaria–Riva Degli Schiavoni, Castello 4687
Tel 041 522 4324
www.hotelpaganelli.com
American novelist Henry James used the Paganelli as the setting for his *Portrait of a Lady*, and it remains a superbly sited

hotel, offering good-value accommodation in this busy area. Rooms come in two types: large and luminous facing the lagoon, and tiny, cheaper rooms in the annexe, looking onto the Campo San Zaccaria. Most rooms have private bathrooms and hairdryers, telephones, TVs and safes. The public areas are grand in the Venetian style—terrazzo floors, traditional furnishings and more than a touch of Murano glass. Breakfast is served in a functional 1970s-style room.

💶 €105–€195
🛏 22
🅂
🚤 San Zaccaria

PALAZZO DAL CARLO

Map 272 D11
Fondamenta Borgo, Dorsoduro 1163
Tel 041 522 6863
www.palazzodalcarlo.com
Beautifully restored Palazzo dal Carlo is among the best of the many fashionable bed-and-breakfasts that have recently opened in Venice. Lovely, elegant and spacious bedrooms,

each with its own glass and marble bathroom, are complimented by the sitting room, with its stucco ceiling, and cool terrazzo floors. Breakfast is served at a communal table by the warm and out-going hostess, Roberta.

💶 €110, excluding breakfast
🛏 3
🅂
🚤 Zattere

PAUSANIA

Map 272 D10
Fondamenta Gherardini, Dorsoduro 2824
Tel 041 522 2083
www.hotelpausania.it
This 14th-century *palazzo*, complete with quadruple lancet windows, stunning staircase and original well, has been tastefully refurbished. Public areas have marble floors, understated décor, Murano glass chandeliers and frescoed ceilings. The similarly decorated bedrooms are spacious and well-equipped: all have bathroom, telephone, TV, radio and minibar. The buffet breakfast is served in a room overlooking the garden—a rarity in Venice. Reserve early as this is a real gem.

💶 €130–€250, excluding breakfast
🛏 26
🅂
🚤 Ca' Rezzonico

PENSIONE ACCADEMIA VILLA MARAVEGE

Map 272 E11
Fondamenta Bollani, Dorsoduro 1058–1060
Tel 041 521 0188
www.pensioneaccademia.it
This lovely 17th-century villa, once the Russian embassy, is a popular choice with regular Venetian visitors. You'll need to reserve well ahead to experience this oasis of peace in the heart of the city. Two shady gardens surround the hotel buildings; bedrooms are comfortable and well-equipped and the public rooms are beautifully furnished with antiques. You can eat breakfast outside on a tranquil terrace overlooking a canal.

💶 €135–€200
🛏 27
🅂
🚤 Accademia

PENSIONE BUCINTORO

Map 274 L11
Riva San Biagio, Castello 2135
Tel 041 522 3240
www.hotelbucintoro.com
You can enjoy superlative views across St. Mark's Basin at a fraction of the cost of hotels nearer the Piazza at this friendly, family-run hotel near the Biennale. Not all the bedrooms have private bathrooms, so specify if you want one when you reserve. There are tables outside the breakfast room for sunny mornings and the staff are welcoming and efficient.

🎟 Closed Dec and Jan
💶 €70–€170, excluding breakfast
🛏 28
🅂
🚤 Arsenale

PENSIONE SEGUSO

Map 272 E12
Fondamenta Zattare ai Gesuati, Dorsoduro 779
Tel 041 528 6858
This wonderfully atmospheric old *pensione* has been packing in a loyal clientele for many years. The old-fashioned rooms, with their sloping floors and billowing white curtains, are simply and traditionally furnished, the public rooms dark and cosy, and there's a sunny terrace on the *fondamenta* for breakfast. Half board is obligatory and although the food's not great, staying here gives a real taste of what Venice used to be like.

🎟 Closed Dec–mid-Feb
💶 €180–€130, excluding breakfast
🛏 36
🅂
🚤 Zattere

LA RESIDENZA

Map 274 K10
Campo Bandiera e Moro, Castello 3608
Tel 041 528 5315
www.venicelaresidenza.com
La Residenza, a short walk from San Marco and overlook-

ing the tranquil Campo Bandiera e Moro, is a good choice for both location and price. It's housed in a handsome old *palazzo*, complete with stuccoed reading room, where breakfast is served, and furnished with some elegant pieces. The bedrooms have all been refurbished and facilities include private bathroom with shower, TV, safe and minibar.

€100–€155

15

Arsenale

ROSSI

Map 270 D6
Calle delle Procuratie, Cannaregio 263
Tel 041 715 164
www.hotelrossi.net

Rossi is a good value option if you need somewhere near the train station or Piazzale Roma. It's tucked away in a quietish

calle, slightly away from the Lista di Spagna crowds. Public areas are unassuming yet tidy; guest rooms are compact, comfortable and clean. Tranquillity can be sought in one of the rooms that look onto an adjacent garden. No credit cards accepted.

€70–€100

20

Ferrovia

SAN CASSIANO CA' FAVRETTO

Map 271 F7
Calle de la Rosa, Santa Croce 2232
Tel 041 524 1768
www.sancassiano.it

A 14th-century Gothic *palazzo* houses the San Cassiano—difficult to find, but worth the journey. The elegant reception rooms and lovely veranda overlook the Grand Canal, and bedrooms are spacious and well-equipped. This is a quiet part of town, and the hotel is particularly appealing if you want something special away from the crowds.

€60–€310, excluding breakfast

36

San Stae

SAN CLEMENTE PALACE

Map 273 off H14
Isola di San Clemente 1, San Marco
Tel 041 244 5001
www.thi.it

Venice's latest five-star hotel lies a 10-minute courtesy launch trip away from San Marco, on the island of San Clemente. First settled in 1131, when the church was built, its buildings have been converted into a luxury hotel set among 1.6ha (4 acres) of park and gardens. Rooms and suites are themed and equipped with everything imaginable; there are three restaurants, bars, terraces, a swimming pool, tennis courts, a spa and beauty centre and a three-hole practice golf course. With this level of facilities and service to match, you may well never make it as far as the city centre.

€190–€1,000, excluding breakfast

205

Private launch

SAN SAMUELE

Map 272 E10
Salizzada San Samuele, San Marco 3358
Tel 041 522 8045

This above average one-star hotel is blessed with a wonderful location near the San Samuele *vaporetto* stop. A lounge area has the usual Venetian trappings: patterned wallpaper, marble floors, antiques and chandeliers. For this price, the rooms are nothing special, but in contrast to the competition they are clean and comfortable. Most have shared bathrooms and basic facilities. No credit cards accepted.

€70–€110

10

San Samuele

SCANDINAVIA

Map 271 J9
Campo Santa Maria Formosa, Castello 5240
Tel 041 522 3507
www.scandinaviahotel.com

Set on one of Venice's great *campi*, the long-established Scandinavia offers cosy rooms

(all doubles) and a décor nudging well in the direction of the 18th century; expect plush furnishings and plenty of Murano glass. Staff are friendly, the bedrooms are comfortable and well-equipped, though prices soar if you want a room overlooking the *campo*.

€130–€310

37

San Zaccaria, Rialto

VILLA ROSA

Map 270 D6
Calle della Misericordia, Cannaregio 389
Tel 041 716 569
www.villarosahotel.com

By Venice's standards, this hotel is cheap and good value for money. It's also handy for the train station and parking areas. A cheery pink-hued lobby welcomes guests, and bedrooms have Venetian décor and decent facilities, including TV, hairdryer and telephone. Some look onto a pleasant courtyard, where the buffet breakfast is served in summer months.

€60–€115

34

Ferrovia

WESTIN EXCELSIOR

Lungomare Marconi, Lido 41
Tel 041 526 0201
www.starwood.com

Now part of the Starwood group, the pseudo-Moorish Excelsior was built in the early 1900s and still attracts hordes of celebrities during the Film Festival. Facilities, décor, rooms and service are everything you'd expect from a hotel of this standard, but the main attraction is the private beach with its luxurious Moorish-style cabanas. There are two restaurants, clay tennis courts, water sports and a beauty parlour. The hotel runs a launch service to San Marco.

Closed mid-Nov to mid-Mar

€300–€1,200

197 rooms and suites

Outdoor pool

Lido Casino

Planning

BEFORE YOU GO

CLIMATE

Venice's position, surrounded by sea and virtually in the foothills of the Alps, has a major influence on the climate, which, apart from the summer months, has more in common with central Europe than the true Mediterranean.

Spring comes around March, with frequent rain showers up to the end of April. Temperatures continue to rise during May, with rain getting less frequent until, by the middle of June, the summer weather systems are established; these bring high temperatures, occasional high humidity and sunshine. During the summer months of June, July and August fixed hot, dry weather is the norm, though this breaks down into dramatic thunderstorms and heavy showers at 2- to 3-weekly intervals. Temperatures begin to fall in September and October, and by the end of the month there is increasing rainfall and the likelihood of *acqua alta* (▷ 47) soars. November is wet and brings mist, foggy days and more *acqua alta*, and by December winter is setting in. The rain continues on and off up to Christmas, but there can be dry, crisp and sunny days. These are frequent in January and early February, accompanied by low temperatures and severe frost; snowfalls are not unknown. Late February and March see more rain, mixed with sunshine and rising temperatures as the Venetian spring starts.

WHEN TO GO

The best time to visit Venice is in the spring and autumn (fall), when the weather is pleasantly warm and there are frequent sunny days. The city is busy, but not too crowded, and away from the major sights you're likely to have districts, museums and churches virtually to yourself. The height of summer sees Venice at its worst—hot and packed with daytrippers. As elsewhere in Italy, August is the holiday month for the Venetians themselves, and it's not unusual for shops and restaurants to close for 2 to 3 weeks. If you are prepared to wrap warmly, January and February are superb months to visit; there are very few visitors and the city sparkles in the winter sun. Bear in mind though, that the fortnight of Carnevale (▷ 21 and 221), which generally falls in February, sees Venice as crowded as during high season.

WEATHER REPORTS

Weather reports are given during news bulletins on Italian TV, and the Italian local press has daily weather maps and forecasts. BBC World News and CNN news have websites (www.bbc.co.uk, www.CNN.com), and broadcast regular global weather updates in English, and The Weather Channel and the Met Office in the UK also have global weather websites (www.weather.com, www.metoffice.com).

WHAT TO TAKE

People dress smartly at all times. Skimpy T-shirts, vests, shorts and general scruffiness are not appreciated by the Venetians. You will need lightweight cottons and linens to wear during the

TIME ZONES

Italy is on Central European Time (CET), one hour ahead of GMT (Greenwich Mean Time) during the winter. In April, the clocks are put forward by one hour, and then put back again in October.

CITY	TIME DIFFERENCE	TIME AT 12 NOON IN ITALY
Amsterdam	0	noon
Auckland	+11	11pm
Berlin	0	noon
Brussels	0	noon
Chicago	-7	5am
Dublin	-1	11am
Johannesburg	+1	1pm
London	-1	11am
Madrid	0	noon
Montreal	-6	6am
New York	-6	6am
Paris	0	noon
Perth, Australia	+7	7pm
San Francisco	-9	3am
Sydney	+9	9pm
Tokyo	+8	8pm

summer, natural fabrics being more comfortable in hot and humid conditions. Remember, though, to bring clothes that cover your shoulders and knees for visiting churches; you won't be allowed in if you are improperly dressed. Spring and autumn call for heavier clothing, and 'layering' makes sense, as temperatures can fluctuate considerably throughout the day. If you're visiting in winter you will need warm clothing and a winter coat, and don't forget gloves, scarves and a hat as the weather can be bitter.

Bear in mind that *acqua alta* can occur anytime from mid-

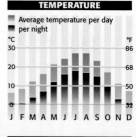

TEMPERATURE

Average temperature per day
per night

°C / °F

RAINFALL

mm / in

Average rainfall

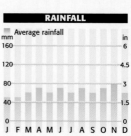

A tour guide with an umbrella leads her group round Venice

September until December (and even outside these months), and you will need waterproof boots (which you can buy in Venice) for negotiating flooded streets. Remember to pack:

- Waterproofs
- A folding umbrella
- A small bag for daily use
- Comfortable shoes
- Your address book, for emergency contacts or postcards
- Photocopies of all important documents: passport, insurance details, credit card, debit card and passport numbers and registration numbers for mobile phones, cameras and other expensive items
- A torch (flashlight) and binoculars—both are useful in dark churches and museums
- A first aid kit and any prescribed medication
- An Italian phrasebook—any attempt at Italian is appreciated
- Earplugs if you are a light sleeper—Venice is surprisingly noisy around dawn and church bells may wake you early
- Toiletries and sunscreen in screw-top containers inside plastic bags to guard against leakage

PASSPORTS

Officially visitors from EU countries need only a national identity card to enter Italy. In practice, you will need a passport. All other foreign visitors to Italy will need a passport, which should be valid for at least another six months from the date of entry into Italy. If you lose your passport, you should contact your embassy (▷ 296).

- Keep a note of your passport number or carry a photocopy of the information page separately from your passport.
- Alternatively, scan the information pages of your passport and any other important documentation and email them as attachments to a web-based email account you can access from anywhere in the world.

Duty-paid guidelines for non-EU citizens

US citizens can bring home up to $800 of duty-paid goods, provided they have been out of the country for at least 48 hours and haven't made another international trip in the past 30 days. This limit applies to all members of the family, regardless of age, and exemptions may be pooled.

- 200 cigarettes; or
- 100 cigarillos; or
- 50 cigars; or
- 250g smoking tobacco
- 1 litre of spirits or strong liquors

- 2 litres of still table wine
- 2 litres of fortified wine, sparkling wine or other liquors
- 60cc/ml of perfume
- 250cc/ml of toilet water

Duty-paid guidelines for EU citizens

European Union citizens can take home unlimited amounts of duty-paid goods, as long as they are for personal use. In the UK, HM Customs and Excise consider anything over the following guidelines as for commercial use:

- 3200 cigarettes; or
- 400 cigarillos; or
- 200 cigars; or
- 3kg of tobacco
- 110 litres of beer

- 10 litres of spirits
- 90 litres of wine (of which only 60 litres can be sparkling wine)
- 20 litres of fortified wine (such as port or sherry)

VISAS

If you are an EU national, or from Australia, Canada, New Zealand or the US, you do not need a visa for stays of up to 90 days. To extend your visit you can, one time only, apply to any police station for an extension of a further 90 days. This extension cannot be used for studying or employment, and you will have to prove that you can support yourself financially.

Regulations can change at short notice so check before making travel arrangements. If you are a citizen of a country other than those mentioned above, you should contact the Italian Embassy in your home country to check visa requirements.

DUTY-FREE AND DUTY-PAID GUIDELINES

Anything that is clearly for personal use can be taken into Italy free of duty. It is worth carrying receipts for valuable items in case you need to prove on your return home that they haven't been bought in Italy. For up-to-date information on duty-free and duty-paid allowances, see the HM Customs and Excise website (www.hmce.gov.uk) or that of the US Department of Homeland security (www.customs.treas.gov). You cannot buy goods duty-free if you are touring within the EU.

Whatever your entitlement, you cannot bring home goods for payment (including payment in kind) or for resale. Such goods are considered for commercial use, and duty is payable.

TRAVEL INSURANCE

Take out travel insurance when you book your trip. If you leave it too close to your departure date you may not be covered for delays. Most policies cover cancellation, medical expenses, accident compensation, personal liability and loss of personal belongings (including money). They should also cover the cost of getting you home in case of medical emergency. If you have private medical cover, check your policy, as you may be covered while you are away.

ITALIAN EMBASSIES ABROAD		
COUNTRY	**ADDRESS**	**WEBSITE**
Australia	12 Grey Street, Deakin ACT 2600, tel 02 6273 3333,	www.ambitalia.org.au
Canada	275 Slater Street, 21st Floor, Ottawa (ON), KIP 5HP, tel 613 2322401,	www.italyincanada.com
Ireland	63–65 Northumberland Road, Dublin 4, tel 1 6601744,	www.italianembassy.ie
New Zealand	34–28 Grant Road, PO Box 463, Thorndon, Wellington, tel 4 4735339,	www.italy-embassy.org.nz
South Africa	796 George Avenue, Arcadia 0083 Pretoria, tel 012 4305541/2/4/4,	www.ambital.org.za
UK	No. 14 Three Kings Yard, London W1Y 2EH, tel 020 73122200,	www.embitaly.org.uk
US	3000 Whitehaven Street NW, Washington DC 20008, tel 202/612-4400,	www.italyemb.org

PLANNING

PRACTICALITIES

ELECTRICITY

The electricity supply in Italy is 240 volts. Plugs have two round pins. If your appliances operate on 240 volts, you just need a plug adaptor. If your voltage is different (such as in North America), you will need an adaptor and transformer; bring these with you as they hard to find in Venice.

LAUNDRY

• Most visitors use the hotel laundry, where clothes are returned to your room and the (often high) charge added to your bill.
• Self-service launderettes (*la lavandaria automatica*) are few and far between in Venice. The best places to find one are in the university areas of San Polo and Santa Croce. A wash will cost around €4.
• Dry cleaning (*lavasecco*) starts from around €3 for a shirt, up to €7.50 for larger items such as jackets and coats, but the quality of the service varies immensely.

MEASUREMENTS

Italy uses the metric system, with all foodstuffs sold by the kilogram or litre. Italians also use the *ettogrammo* (100g or just under 4oz), usually abbreviated to *etto*.

LAVATORIES

• Venice has public lavatories at the railway station and in larger museums.
• There are public lavatories, marked with blue and green signs, throughout the city, with a flat rate of 50¢ for entrance. They are clean and well run and the most useful ones are at: Accademia—underneath the bridge on the Galleria side (open daily 8–8)
Rialto—Campo Rialto Nuovo (open daily 7–5)
Campo San Bartolomeo—Calle della Bissa (open daily 8.30 – 8)
San Marco—Giardinetti (open daily 9–8)
• You can also use lavatories in bars and cafés, which are legally obliged to let you use their facilities. However, it's considered good form to buy a coffee or glass of water at least before you

Venice's streets and squares can become very busy

use their facilities. Sometimes there is only one lavatory for both men and women, and in some places there is a dish for gratuities—you should tip around 25¢. Where separate facilities exist, make sure you recognize the difference between *signori* (men) and *signore* (women).

SMOKING

• Smoking is still very common in Italy, but is no longer permitted indoors in any public places, on public transport, inside airport buildings and in most public offices and buildings.
• Smoking is banned in all bars and restaurants.
• Cigarettes and other tobacco products can only legally be sold in *tabacchi* (tobacconists) to over 16s. Stand-alone *tabacchi* are open during normal shop hours (▷ 297). Those attached to bars stay open longer.

CONVERSION CHART		
FROM	**TO**	**MULTIPLY BY**
Inches	Centimetres	2.54
Centimetres	Inches	0.3937
Feet	Metres	0.3048
Metres	Feet	3.2810
Yards	Metres	0.9144
Metres	Yards	1.0940
Miles	Kilometres	1.6090
Kilometres	Miles	0.6214
Acres	Hectares	0.4047
Hectares	Acres	2.4710
Gallons	Litres	4.5460
Litres	Gallons	0.2200
Ounces	Grams	28.35
Grams	Ounces	0.0353
Pounds	Grams	453.6
Grams	Pounds	0.0022
Pounds	Kilograms	0.4536
Kilograms	Pounds	2.205
Tons	Tonnes	1.0160
Tonnes	Tons	0.9842

CLOTHING SIZES

Use the clothing sizes chart below to convert the size you use at home.

UK	Metric	US	
36	46	36	SUITS
38	48	38	
40	50	40	
42	52	42	
44	54	44	
46	56	46	
48	58	48	
7	41	8	SHOES
7.5	42	8.5	
8.5	43	9.5	
9.5	44	10.5	
10.5	45	11.5	
11	46	12	
14.5	37	14.5	SHIRTS
15	38	15	
15.5	39/40	15.5	
16	41	16	
16.5	42	16.5	
17	43	17	
8	36	6	DRESSES
10	38	8	
12	40	10	
14	42	12	
16	44	14	
18	46	16	
20	46	18	
4.5	37.5	6	SHOES
5	38	6.5	
5.5	38.5	7	
6	39	7.5	
6.5	40	8	
7	41	8.5	

VISITING VENICE WITH CHILDREN

Venice is by no means a child-friendly city and the nature of the city makes travelling with very young children in pushchairs (strollers) difficult. If you're bringing your kids, it's worth

PLANNING

If you are Catholic you will have no problem finding somewhere to celebrate your faith in Venice. Mass times vary from church to church, but details of Sunday services can be found on all church doors. The Sunday 11am High Mass in the Basilica di San Marco is a superb occasion for Catholics and non-Catholics alike, and provides a chance to experience this unique building functioning as a living church. Sunday Mass is celebrated in English at 9.30am from May to September in San Zulian. Other denominational services are listed below.

St. George's Anglican church in Dorsoduro

Anglican
St. George's, Campo San Vio, Dorsoduro 870, tel 041 520 0571
Eucharist Sunday 10.30am
Lutheran
Campo Santi Apostoli, Cannaregio 4448, tel 041 522 7149 Morning service 10.30am on 2nd and 4th Sunday of the month
Methodist (Valdese)
Fondamenta Cavagnis, Castello 5170, tel 522 7549 Sunday service 11am
Greek Orthodox
San Giorgio dei Greci, Fondamenta dei Greci, Castello 3412, tel 041 522 5446
Services Sunday 9.30 and 10.30am
Russian Orthodox
San Giovanni Decollato, Campo San Giovanni Decollato, Santa Croce 1670, tel 041 524 0672 Morning service Sun 11am
Jewish
Services are held after sunset on Friday in different synagogues depending on the time of year. Contact the Museo Ebraico for further information:
Campo Ghetto Nuovo, Cannaregio 2902, tel 041 715 359

booking accommodation on the Lido, from where sightseeing can be judiciously mixed with the pleasures of sea and sand. For further ideas and information see page 171.

● Children are welcomed at most hotels and in almost all restaurants. Family-run and more modest restaurants will serve small portions, and will often produce simple meals such as pasta in tomato sauce, pizza or fish and chips. Hotels will provide extra beds in your room if asked; this normally adds another 33 per cent to the room price.

● Disposable nappies (diapers) and baby foods are available in many food shops (*alimentari* or *supermercati*). If your child is still bottle-fed, bring the milk powder (formula) with you as you may not be able to find it in Venice.

● Remember that the lack of public lavatories and changing facilities, most of which may not be as clean as you are used to, can make things difficult for people with very young children. Always carry tissues or wipes, as not all establishments will provide toilet paper.

● Italian children stay up late—if parents are eating out, the kids go too. This means that most hotels do not offer a baby-sitting/listening service.

● Put on high-factor sunscreen and keep children covered up until they acclimatize to the sun. If they're swimming or on the beach at the Lido, persuade them to cover up and swim in a T-shirt.

● Children are susceptible to heat stroke, so seek shade in the middle of the day and keep their heads and necks protected.

● Many Venetian hotels are unheated until the end of October.

● If you're planning an excursion out of the city, children between 4 and 12 qualify for a 50 per cent discount on trains; those under 4 go free.

● For ideas on how to keep children occupied see pages 219–220 or ask for suggestions at the tourist information offices.

● There is an excellent children's guide to Venice in English available at good book shops (*Viva Venice* by Paolo Zoffoli and Paola Scibilia, published by Elzeviro, 2002). Look out, too, for *Venice for Kids* by Elisabetta

Protect children against sunburn

Pasqualin (Fratelli Palombi 200), one of a series covering the major Italian cities.

VISITORS WITH DISABILITIES
Venice presents unique problems to people with disabilities, but should not be crossed off the holiday list. For full information on visiting Venice, see page 56. The city council runs an information service for people with disabilities, which is availably in English. Contact: Informahandicap
Piazzale Candiani 5, Mestre, tel 041 274 8144 (Venezia), 041 274 6144 (Mestre), www.comune.venezia.it/handicap

USEFUL CONTACTS
Tourism for All
The Hawkins Suite, Enham Place, Enham Alamegn, Andover SP11 6JS, tel 0845 124 9971,
www.tourismforall.org.uk
A UK-based company that produces publications and information on accessibility

RADAR
12 City Forum, 250 City Road, London EC1V 8AF, tel 020 7250 3222, www.radar.org.uk

SATH
347 5th Avenue, Suite 610, New York City, NY 10016, tel 212/447-7284, www.sath.org

PLANNING

MONEY

Tip in restaurants if the service has been good

CREDIT AND DEBIT CARDS

● MasterCard, Diners Club, American Express and Visa credit cards (*carte di credito*) are widely accepted in Venice, though not for relatively small payments and purchases, and some smaller establishments still do not take them.
● Look for the credit card symbols in the shop window or on the restaurant door or check with the staff.
● You can also use your credit card to make cash withdrawals, although your credit card company will charge it as a cash advance. Contact your credit card company before you go to get a PIN number if you do not already have one.
● Credit cards are not accepted for food purchases, though debit cards can be used in some supermarkets, providing they are the chip and pin type.
● Notify your credit card company that you will be using your card abroad as some place blocks on use overseas for security reasons.

TRAVELLERS' CHEQUES

● Travellers' cheques are accepted almost everywhere. To avoid additional exchange rate charges, take them in euros, pounds sterling or US dollars.
● You can exchange travellers' cheques without commission at American Express, Salizzada San Moisè, San Marco 1471 (tel 041 520 0844) and Travelex, Piazza San Marco, San Marco 142 (tel 041 277 5057), or at the Rialto branch at Riva del Ferro, San Marco 5126 (tel 041 528 7358).

LOST AND STOLEN CARDS AND TRAVELLERS' CHEQUES

● If your credit card or bank card is stolen, report it to the police and the appropriate emergency number. All are open 24 hours a day and have English-speaking staff.
● If your travellers' cheques are stolen, notify the police, then follow the instructions given with the cheques. You can contact the Venice office of American Express or telephone the following toll-free numbers:

BANKNOTES AND COINS

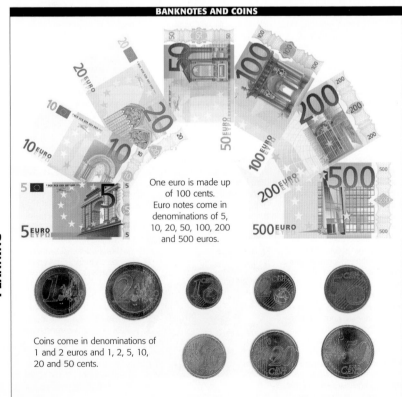

One euro is made up of 100 cents. Euro notes come in denominations of 5, 10, 20, 50, 100, 200 and 500 euros.

Coins come in denominations of 1 and 2 euros and 1, 2, 5, 10, 20 and 50 cents.

PLANNING

A typical ATM in Venice

For American Express travellers' cheques, call 800 872 000
For Thomas Cook's travellers' cheques, call 800 872 050

CASH MACHINES/ATMS

● Cash machines, or Bancomats in Italy, are plentiful and many are accessible 24 hours a day.
● Most have instructions in English and other languages, as well as Italian.
● You avoid commission and the exchange rates are better when you withdraw cash with a debit card (Cirrus/Maestro/Delta) from ATMs rather than using a bureau de change.
● Check with your bank before leaving home that you will be able to take cash out with your card while in Venice.

CURRENCY EXCHANGE AND BANKS

Travellers' cheques, cheques and foreign money can be changed at banks, the railway station and the airport, and very often at major hotels (generally at a poorer rate). Many banks in your home country have differing exchange rates depending on the denominations of currency being bought or sold. Check with banks for details and shop around before you buy. Banks are listed in the *Pagine Gialle* (Yellow Pages) under *Banche e Istituti di Credito*. Banks offer a better rate of exchange than the numerous bureaux de change *(cambio)* in Venice, many of which advertise 'no commission' but offer poor exchange rates. If you are using a bank to change travellers' cheques or draw money on your credit card across the counter, you will need to produce your passport. Remember that bank transactions in Italy are slow and cumbersome, so allow plenty of time.

CURRENCY RESTRICTIONS

The import and export of local and foreign currency is limited to €10,329.14, but check with your embassy before departure if you need to bring large sums into the country. Amounts greater than this should be declared and validated in Italy.

WIRING MONEY

● Wiring money is quite a lengthy process and the bureaucracy involved means that it is probably not worthwhile unless you are planning to spend quite a long time in Italy.
● Ask your bank at home for a list of affiliated banks. You can get money wired out to any bank from home, but if your bank is already in contact with certain banks in Italy it will make the process a lot easier. Always ask for a separate letter, telex or fax confirming that the money has been sent and ask that it be sent to Swift. It can take up to a week for the money to transfer.
● If you have a bank account in Italy and at home, you can transfer money directly if both the banks are part of the Swift system of international transfers.

Again it takes about 5 to 7 days, if not longer.
● American Express, Moneygram and Western Union Money Tranfers are faster from the US, but more expensive. Citibank can transfer money for a flat fee of $10 to anywhere in the world (www.c2it.com). Do not wire more money than you need.

TAX REFUNDS

All non-EU shoppers are entitled to an IVA (sales tax) refund on major purchases. Ask for an itemized *fattura* (invoice) when shopping, then present this at customs for stamping when leaving the EU. Return the stamped invoice to the store within four months of the date of purchase and the shop will refund the IVA direct.

DISCOUNTS

● Over 65s can often get discounted admission charges to museums and galleries—use your passport as proof of age.
● Children's admission charges are usually available up to the age of 18, and reductions also exist for people between 18 and 26.
● If you are a student, you will qualify for some reductions; see page 297 for details of specifically Venetian student and young people's cards.

10 EVERYDAY ITEMS AND HOW MUCH THEY COST	
Takeaway sandwich	€3
Bottle of water	€1–€2
Cup of coffee (outside/inside)	€1/€2–€8
Beer—half a litre (outside/inside)	€1.50/€3–€10
Glass of house wine (outside/inside)	€1.50/€3–€12
Daily newspaper (Italian)	€1
Roll of camera film	€5
20 cigarettes	€2.50
Ice cream (takeaway)	€1–€4
ACTV *biglietti a tempo* (24 hours)	€10.50

TIPPING

Italians do not tip heavily. Service is often included in your hotel or restaurant bill, although a little extra is appreciated if the service has been good. The following is a general guide:

Pizzerias/trattorias: round up to the nearest euro
Expensive restaurants: 10%
Bar service: up to 25c, or 5–10% for table service
Taxis: round up to nearest 50c
Porters: 50c–€1 per bag
Chambermaids: 50c–€1 per day
Cloakroom attendants: 50c
Toilets: 25c

HEALTH

BEFORE YOU GO

● No vaccinations are necessary for a trip to Italy, unless you are coming into the country from an infected area. If you have any doubts, contact your doctor before you leave. It is a good idea to check when you last had a tetanus injection, and, if more than 10 years ago, have a booster before you travel.

● You should always take out health insurance, and most people do so as part of their travel insurance. Ensure that it covers the cost of getting you home in an emergency. If you already have health insurance to cover treatment at home, check with your insurer before you leave that you will be covered while abroad.

● In addition to health insurance, European citizens should carry an EHIC (European Health Insurance Card), which you should get before departure. This replaces the old E111, and is obtainable from post offices and travel agents. Italy has a reciprocal health agreement with the rest of the EU, Iceland, Liechtenstein and Norway, which allows reduced-cost dental and medical (including hospital) treatment on presentation of the EHIC. A fee must be paid, though, plus part of the cost of any prescribed medicines. For specialist treatment you will need medical insurance.

● It is essential for non-EU visitors to carry health insurance.

● Visitors from the US and Canada may find that their existing health policy covers them while they are abroad. Check with your insurance company before you travel, and remember to bring your policy identification card.

● Check with your doctor or pharmacist for the chemical name for any prescription drugs you need, in case you need to

A gondolier gives way to a water ambulance with a casualty on board

replace them while you are away. Brand names often change from country to country.

● For up-to-date information, visit the Department of Health's website, www.doh.gov.uk (in the UK), or the National Center for Infectious Diseases, www.cdc.gov/travel, in the US.

● It is a good idea to take photocopies of all important documentation, which should be kept separate from the originals. You could scan the photocopies and send them to an email address that can be accessed anywhere in the world.

HOW TO GET A DOCTOR (UN MEDICO)

● To get in touch with a doctor, ask at your hotel or consult the Yellow Pages (*Pagine Gialle*) under Unità Sanitaria Locale.

● For an ambulance, call 118. Ambulance boats in Venice will come to the nearest *fondamenta* to your hotel; the number to call is 041 523 0000.

● If you need emergency

treatment, go directly to the *pronto soccorso* (casualty department/emergency room) of the nearest hospital.

HOW TO GET TREATMENT WITH YOUR EHIC

● If you need medical treatment while you are away, take your EHIC to the USL (Unità Sanitaria Locale) office, which will give you a certificate of entitlement.

● Take this to any doctor or dentist on the USL list to receive free treatment. If they need to refer you to a hospital, they will give you a certificate that entitles you to free treatment.

● If you go to hospital without being referred by a doctor, you should give the EHIC to them.

● If you do not have a USL certificate, you will have to pay for treatment and it may be difficult to get the money back afterwards, and then you will probably only receive a partial refund.

● If you are charged in full for medicines, keep the receipts—you will not get a refund without them.

● It is advisable to carry a photocopy of your EHIC, as some doctors and hospitals may keep it. If they do, you can pick up another form when you get home.

FOR EMERGENCY TREATMENT

If you need emergency treatment you can go straight to the *pronto soccorso* (casualty department or emergency room) at the following hospitals:

Ospedale Civile (main hospital, English spoken), Campo Santi Giovanni e Paolo, Castello 6777, tel 041 529 4588 (information department), 041 529 4111 (main switchboard), 041 529 4516 (casualty department).

Ospedale al Mare (subsidiary hospital, English spoken), Lungomare d'Annunzio 1, Lido, tel 041 529 4111 (main switchboard), 041 529 5234 (casualty).

PLANNING

HOW TO GET TREATMENT WITH INSURANCE

● If you have health insurance at home it is likely that it will cover you for medical treatment abroad. Check your policy before you leave home.
● Take a copy of your insurance documents to the doctor or hospital—they may be able to bill your insurance company direct.
● If you have to pay for treatment, keep all of your receipts for your insurance claim.

PHARMACIES (FARMACIE)

● Pharmacies sell toiletries as well as a wide range of over-the-counter medicines.
● Pharmacists are well-trained and can deal with minor ailments and provide some medicines that are only available on prescription in the UK and US.
● Most pharmacies are open during normal shop hours (8.30–1 and 4–8), but a rota system operates outside opening hours in Venice so there is at least one open at all times—a copy of the rota is displayed in pharmacy windows.

DENTISTS (DENTISTI)

● If you have an EHIC, contact the USL, as above.
● If you do not have an EHIC, contact a private dentist (in the Yellow Pages under *Dentista*). Again, take a copy of your insurance details and keep your receipts.

OPTICIANS (OTTICHI)

● Opticians can usually carry out minor repairs to your glasses, such as replacing screws on the spot for little or no charge.
● Lenses can often be replaced overnight.
● If you really cannot survive without your glasses or contact lenses, bring a copy of your prescription with you so that you can have replacements made up if necessary.

TAP WATER

Venice's tap water is safe to drink, but you should look out for signs (often on public fountains) that say *acqua non potabile*, which means the water is not drinkable.

SUMMER HAZARDS

● From April to the end of September the sun is extremely strong and you will need to wear a high-factor sunscreen (broad spectrum of factor 15 or above is recommended).
● Insect bites are irritating rather than dangerous. There are no malaria-carrying insects in Italy, but there is an ongoing and severe mosquito problem in Venice from April through to November.
● Do not open the bedroom window after dusk and ask your hotel for a plug-in electric mosquito repellent; tablets for these are available in supermarkets, *alimentari* and hardware stores.

The familiar green cross

HEALTHY FLYING

● Visitors to Italy from as far as the US, Australia or New Zealand may be concerned about the effect of long-haul flights on their health. The most widely publicized concern is deep vein thrombosis, or DVT. Misleadingly called 'economy class syndrome', DVT is the forming of a blood clot in the body's deep veins, particularly in the legs. The clot can move around the bloodstream and could be fatal.
● Those most at risk include the elderly, pregnant women and those using the contraceptive pill, smokers and the overweight. If you are at increased risk of DVT see your doctor before departing. Flying increases the likelihood of DVT because passengers are often seated in a cramped position for long periods of time and may become dehydrated.

To minimize risk:
Drink water (not alcohol)
Don't stay immobile for hours at a time
Stretch and exercise your legs periodically
Do wear elastic flight socks, which support veins and reduce the chances of a clot forming

EXERCISES

1 ANKLE ROTATIONS	2 CALF STRETCHES	3 KNEE LIFTS

Lift feet off the floor. Draw a circle with the toes, moving one foot clockwise and the other counterclockwise

Start with heel on the floor and point foot upward as high as you can. Then lift heels high, keeping balls of feet on the floor

Lift leg with knee bent while contracting your thigh muscle. Then straighten leg, pressing foot flat to the floor

Other health hazards for flyers are airborne diseases and bugs spread by the plane's air-conditioning system. These are largely unavoidable, but if you have a serious medical condition seek advice from a doctor before flying.

CALL CHARGES

● There are several call bands for telephone charges. Peak time is between 8am and 1pm, off-peak between 1pm and midnight, and cheaper international rates between 6.30pm–8am (in two price bands—up to midnight and after) and at weekends.

● Free phone numbers (numeri verde) usually begin with 800 and national call rate numbers begin with 848 or 199.

● Hotels tend to overcharge for long-distance and international calls, so it is best to make calls from public phones, using telephone cards.

PAYING FOR CALLS
Public telephones and phone cards

● Public telephones can be found all over Venice, both in street booths and bars.

● Most public telephones now take phone cards (carte telefoniche) rather than cash. These are available in denominations of €2.50, €5 and €7.50 from tabacchi, newsstands and some bars.

● Tear off the corner of the card and slide it in the appropriate slot to get a dialling tone. Dial the number. The display will show how much remaining credit you have on the card. After you hang up, the card is returned so you can use it until it runs out.

● If you are calling abroad it's cheaper to buy an international rather than a Telecom Italia phone card. These operate like

Most public telephones take phone cards rather than cash

a scratch card with a hidden number you dial when you start using the card, and can be used with public, private and mobile phones.

● Interglobal Card 5, Planet, Welcome and Europa are some of the best-value cards.

Reverse-charge (collect) calls

You can place a direct call abroad from Venice by reversing the charges or by using a phone credit card number. To reverse the charges, call the International Operator on 170 or, for a cheaper alternative, dial the country's operator direct on one of the free numbers in the chart below.

MOBILE PHONES

● British, Australian and New Zealand mobile phones can be used in Italy without any problem. You may need to unbar

your phone for overseas use; contact your service operator for details.

● Due to their different frequency, American cell phones can only be used if they are triband.

● It can be very expensive to use your mobile phone abroad and you will often be charged to receive calls as well as make them; check with your service provider before you leave.

● If you travel abroad frequently and intend to use your phone,

consider swapping your SIM card to a card from an alternative provider—either a foreign network or a dedicated provider of international mobile phone services. You can buy these at mobile phone shops before you leave.

● Text messages are often a cheaper alternative to voice calls, but check the charges for making calls and text messages with your service provider. Italian mobile numbers begin with 330, 335, 347, 368 etc.

● If you are using your mobile without changing the SIM card you will need to dial the Italian international code (00 39) to call local Venetian numbers.

INTERNET CAFÉS

● These are relatively widespread in Venice and reasonably cheap—you can expect to pay around €5 an hour. The netcafeguide.com website (www.netcafeguide.com/countries/italy/htm) has an impressive searchable directory of internet cafés in Italy and throughout the world.

● You do need a web-based email account if you want to send or receive email from abroad (hotmail, yahoo etc.).

● Remember to log out once you have finished browsing or emailing at an internet café and close the browser completely to dump your session cookies (temporary files where your personal info is sometimes stored). These are shared computers and you don't want someone else reading your mail or accessing your personal files.

LAPTOPS

● If you intend to use your own laptop in Italy, remember to bring a power converter to recharge it and a plug socket adaptor. A surge protector is also a good idea. To connect to the internet you need an adaptor for the phone socket.

● If you use an international internet service provider, such as AOL or Compuserve, it's cheaper to dial up a local node rather than the number in your home country.

● Wireless technology, such as Bluetooth or Blackberry, allows you to connect to the internet using a mobile phone.

● Dial-tone frequencies vary

POSTAGE RATES			
Airmail (via aerea)	Letter (20g)		Delivery time
Europe	65c		up to 2 weeks
USA and rest of World	70c		up to 2 weeks
Posta Prioritaria	Letter (under 50g)	Letter (50–100g)	Delivery time
Europe	62c	€1.80	3 days
US and rest of World	€1	€2	4–8 days

Post office in San Marco

from country to country, so set your modem to ignore dial tones.

POST OFFICES

● Venice's main post office is at Salizzada del Fontego dei Tedeschi, San Marco 5554, tel 041 271 7111, open Mon–Sat 8.30–6.30. It provides a full range of post office services and operates a *fermo posta* (poste restante) service.

● Each city district also has its own post office. These are open Mon–Fri 8.10–1.30 and Sat 8.10–12.30.

POSTAL SERVICES

● You can buy stamps (*francobolli*), send letters and packages, faxes and telegrams from Venice's post offices. Italy's postal service, Poste Italiane (tel 803 160; www.poste.it), has improved considerably in recent

years, and you can be sure your letters will arrive in reasonable time.

● Use the *posta prioritaria* service to ensure quick delivery. This promises delivery within 24 hours in Italy, 3 days for EU countries and 4 to 5 for the rest of the world. Stamps for this service cost 62¢ for Italy and the EU and 77¢ for the rest of the world.

● Stamps are also available from tobacconists, denoted with an official *tabacchi* sign, a large 'T'. If you need to send a heavy letter or a package, you are better off taking it to a post office, where it can be weighed.

● Post boxes are red (see below) and have two slots; *per la città* is for Venice, and *tutte le altre destinazioni* for everywhere else, including international destinations.

POSTCARDS

● These are classed as low-priority post, so if you want them to arrive at their destination within a couple of weeks, send them *prioritaria*.

SENDING ITEMS OF VALUE

● You can use the registered post (*raccomandato*) to send valuable items; add and extra €2.60 on top of the price of normal postage.

● The cost of insured mail (*assicurato*) depends on the value of the items (€5.15 for packages up to €55.65 in value).

● Insured mail services are not available to the US.

PLANNING

EMERGENCY PHONE NUMBERS

Police (*carabinieri* & local police) 112/041 271 5511
Ambulance 118/041 523 0000
Fire brigade 115/041 257 4700
Coast guard 041 240 5711

Police on duty in Venice

PERSONAL SECURITY

Venice is one of Italy's safest cities, and serious crime against visitors is extremely rare. Be aware of pickpocketing, which can occur in the more crowded city areas, at the railway station or on crowded *vaporetti*. Taking a few sensible precautions to help prevent becoming a victim.
● Passports, credit cards, travel tickets and cash should not be carried together in handbags or pockets. Only carry what you need for the day and use the safety deposit facilities in hotels.
● Never carry money or valuables in your back pocket. Always keep them secure in a money belt or something similar.
● Do not flaunt your valuables. Leave expensive jewellery in hotel safes and, if you are a woman walking around on your own, consider turning any rings with stone settings or similar around so that only the band is visible and not the jewels.
● Never put your camera or bag down on a café table or on the back of a chair, from where it could be snatched.
● Keep a close eye on your possessions in crowded areas.
● Wear handbags across your body, rather than just over your shoulder, from where they can be easily snatched.

REPORTING THEFT

Report thefts to a police station, where you will need to make a statement (*denuncia*). It is unlikely that you will get your belongings back, but you need the statement to claim on your insurance.
● In Venice, you will need to go to the office in Campo San Zaccaria. The process may be time-consuming and the duty officer may not necessarily speak English, but the process is essential as insurance companies will not consider a claim unless it is backed by a police report.

● If your passport is lost or stolen, report it to the police and your consulate. Getting a replacement is easier if you have kept a copy of your passport number or a photocopy of the information page safe (▷ 287).
● If your credit card or bank card is stolen, report it to the police and phone the appropriate bank card/credit card emergency number to cancel your card. All are open 24 hours a day and have English-speaking staff.
● If your travellers' cheques are stolen, see page 290.

LOST PROPERTY

Venice has three main *uffici oggetti smarriti* (lost property offices). If you lose something try whichever seems the likeliest.
● ACTV: Piazzale Roma, tel 041 2723 2179. Open daily 7.30–6. For items lost on *vaporetti* and buses.
● Comune (City Council): Riva del Carbon, San Marco 4136, tel 041 274 8225. Open Mon–Fri 8.30–12.30. For items lost in public places.
● Stazione Santa Lucia: Centro Accoglienza Clienti, Stazione Santa Lucia, tel 041 785 670. Open daily 7am–9pm. For items lost on trains and in the station.

POLICE

There are three branches of the police in Italy, any of which should be able to help you if you are in difficulty.
● The *carabinieri* are military police, easily recognizable by the white sash they wear across their bodies. They deal with general crime, including drug control.
● The *polizia* is the state police force, whose officers wear blue uniforms. They also deal with general crime, and if you are unfortunate enough to be robbed (or worse) they are the ones you will need to see.
● The *vigili urbani*, the traffic police, wear dark blue uniforms and white hats. You will only need to deal with them if an incident occurs while you are away from Venice.

WHAT TO DO IF YOU ARE ARRESTED

If you are taken into custody by the police, you could be held for up to 48 hours without appearing before a magistrate. You can also be interviewed without a lawyer present. You do, however, have the right to contact your consul, who is based at your country's embassy, but you are still bound by Italian law. Your consul will not be able to get you out of prison, but will visit you and put you in touch with English-speaking lawyers and interpreters, offer advice and support and contact your family on your behalf. Try to keep hold of your passport and contact your travel insurance company, as your insurance may cover you for legal costs.

CONTACTING YOUR EMBASSY IN ROME

American Embassy	Via Vittorio Veneto 119a, 00187, tel 06 46741, www.usis.it
Australian Embassy	Via Antonio Bosio 5, 00161, tel 06 852721, www.italy.embassy.gov.au
British Embassy	Via XX Settembre 80a, 00187, tel 06 4220 0001, www.fco.gov.uk
Canadian Embassy	Via G.B. de Rossi 27, 00161, tel 06 445981, www.canada.it
Irish Embassy	Piazza di Campitelli 3, 00186, tel 06 697 9121, www.europeanirish.com
New Zealand Embassy	Via Zara 28, 00198, tel 06 441 7171, www.nzembassy.com

PLANNING

OPENING TIMES AND TICKETS

BANKS
Mon–Fri 8.30–1.30. Some larger branches might open on Sat.

POST OFFICES
Mon–Fri 8.30–6, Sat 8.30–noon or 2.

PHARMACIES
Pharmacies are usually open the same hours as shops, but take turns to stay open in the afternoon and late in the evening. Look for the list in the shop window of other pharmacies in the area and their opening times.

MUSEUMS AND GALLERIES
Opening times for museums and galleries vary greatly. Many close one day each week, usually Monday.

CHURCHES
Some churches open around 7 for Mass, then close for much of the rest of the day, though some with important artworks may be open between 10–12 and 4–6. Some are only open on Sundays. Times are displayed on the main door of individual churches. Churches in the Chorus group (see right) are open from 10–5 Mon–Sat and 1–5 on Sun.

CAFÉS AND BARS
Opening times vary considerably from place to place. Some are open for breakfast, others open for lunch, and some are only open in the evenings. Wine bars usually close at midnight or later.

RESTAURANTS
Restaurants that serve lunch open from 11am and usually close in the afternoon, though some are open all day. Those that close after lunch reopen, along with those that only serve dinner, sometime after 7pm and stay open late. Pizzerias usually only open in the evening. Many restaurants close for August—look for the sign *Chiuso per ferie*.

SHOPS
Traditionally shops open between 8 and 9 and close for lunch at 1. They reopen in the afternoon at 3.30 or 4 and close at 8. Most are closed Sundays and Monday mornings, but shops in central Venice are beginning to stay open all day—look for the sign *Orario continuato*.

NATIONAL HOLIDAYS
Shops and banks generally close on national holidays. There is a limited public transport service on Labour Day and the afternoon of Christmas Day. However, with the exception of Labour Day, Assumption and Christmas Day, most bars and restaurants remain open.

VENICE COMBINED MUSEUM TICKETS AND DISCOUNT CARDS
There are two types of combined museum ticket for the civic museums, both valid for 3 months and allowing one visit to each museum.
● The Museum Pass gives entrance to the Musei di San Marco (Palazzo Ducale, Museo Civico Correr and Museo Archeologico, Biblioteca Marciana), Musei del Settecento (the 18th-century museums—Ca' Rezzonico, Palazzo Mocenigo, Casa Goldoni), Musei delle Isole (Island Museums—Museo del Vetro on Murano, Museo del Merletto on Burano) and Ca' Pesaro (Galleria d'Arte Moderna and Museo d'Arte Orientale). Full price €15.50; reduced (students aged 15–29, holders of Rolling Venice cards) €10.
● The Museum Card gives entrance to groups of themed museums: the Musei di San Marco (full price €11, reduced €5.50), Musei del Settecento (full price €8, reduced €4.50) and Musei delle Isole (full price €6, reduced €4).
● The Gallerie dell'Accademia has a combined ticket for the Accademia, Ca' d'Oro and Museo d'Arte Orientale; full price €11, reduced €5.50.
● The Chorus Pass allows entry to 15 of the city's most artistically important churches. Single ticket €2.50; full price €9, reduced €6 (includes audioguide). It is valid for a year. You can buy the pass at any of the Chorus churches or by telephoning 041 275 0462 (www.chorusvenezia.org).

VENICE CARD
There are two types, the Blue Card and the Orange Card.
● The Blue Card is valid for all public transport, with free access to public toilets and baby-changing facilities. 1 day: full price €11, reduced (under 30s) €7; 3

days: full price €23 reduced €17; 7 days: €41 reduced €39.
● The Orange Card is valid for all public transport, entrance to all Musei Civici (civic museums) and the casino, with free entrance to public toilets. 1 day: full price €26, reduced (under 30s) €16; 3 days: full price €42 reduced €30; 7 days: €58 reduced €51.
● The Venice Card must be bought at least two days before, either by phoning 899 90 90 90 within Italy or (39) 041 271 4747 from abroad or online at www.venicecard.it. You will be given a reservation number, then collect the ticket from the VeLa offices or the Alilaguna ticket office at the Tronchetto parking area or at Piazzale Roma.

ROLLING VENICE
This discount card is issued to people aged 14 to 29. It gives discounts on selected hotels, restaurants, shops, museum entrances, some cultural events and a reduction on the 72-hour *vaporetto* pass (€15 rather €22). It costs €3 and is valid for 1 year. It is obtainable from VeLa and APT offices; take 2 passport-size photos and an identity document.

OTHER DISCOUNTS
Most museums and attractions have concessions for students (with an international student card), and EU citizens over 65 and children under 5 or 6 who are generally admitted free. Children under 10 are only occasionally admitted free, but there tend to be discounts available for youngsters up to 18, and sometimes under 20. Some attractions admit people with disabilities and a carer free and charge less for groups of more than 15, teachers and visitors from EU countries.

PLANNING

TOURIST OFFICES

Venice's main tourist office is underneath the arcade in the southwest corner of Piazza San Marco (San Marco 71f; tel 041 529 8711; open daily 9.30–3.30). The staff have city maps and the APT also publishes the *Leo Bussola*, an invaluable pamphlet, every three months, which details useful numbers, museum and church opening times, exhibitions, lectures and guided tours, and includes a day-by-day cultural What's On. The tourist office can also give you information on sightseeing, guided tours and is the place to pick up the *Planet Audioguide*, a GPS city audioguide. The staff speak good English and, if things are fairly quiet, are extremely helpful. There are other APT offices around the city, the best of which isin the Palazzina del Santi by the Giardini ex-Reali. This office also doubles as a ticket agency for concerts, opera and theatrical performances, and has an excellent bookshop with a good range of English-language guidebooks, picture books, Venice-related literature and souvenirs. There are APT offices at the following addresses:
- Aeroporto Marco Polo (arrivals hall)
- Stazione Ferrovia Santa Lucia
- Piazzale Roma (Garage ASM)
- Gran Viale 6a, Lido di Venezia (May–Sep)
- Cavallini Treporti, Punta Sabbioni (May–Sep).

ITALIAN GOVERNMENT TOURIST OFFICES ABROAD			
Level 26, 44 Market Street, NSW 2000 Sydney, tel 92 621666	175 Bloor Street East, Suite 907 South Tower, Toronto, Ontario M4W 3R8, tel 416 925-4882, fax 416 925-4799; www.italiantourism.com	1 Princes Street, London W1B 2AY, tel 020 7489 1254/020 7355 1557, fax 020 7499 3567; www.enit.it	630 Fifth Avenue, Suite 1565, New York NY 10111, tel 212 245-5618/245-4822, fax 212 586-9249; www.italiantourism.com Also offices in Chicago and Los Angeles

USEFUL WEBSITES

GENERAL WEBSITES
www.turismovenezia.it
The APT official site includes details of accommodation, transport, eating and drinking, and sightseeing.
www.comune.venezia.it
The official site of Venice's city council gives comprehensive transport, accommodation and cultural listings. The FAQ section is particularly useful for first visits.
www.museicivicineveneziani.it
Excellent site covering all the civic museums.
www.chorusvenezia.org
Comprehensive information on churches in the Chorus group.
www.veneto.org
An American-based site that specializes in the history, culture and language of the city.
www.veniceguide.net
All the tourist information and listings you'll need and some quirky articles on aspects of Venetian life.

www.venezia.net
Another good independent site that offers interesting snippets of history, news and culture as well as the usual listings. Good shopping links.
www.venicefinder.com
A huge site, popular with locals, covering tourist information, eating, sleeping, shopping, events, entertainment and sport.
www.venetia.it
This site is worth a glance for its history and articles.

www.carnevale.venezia.it
Everything you need to know about the Carnival, and a huge photo library.

TRANSPORT
www.veniceairport.it
Full details of both Marco Polo and Treviso airports.
www.actv.it
The official site of ACTV gives full timetables, routes and prices for *vaporetti* and mainland bus services.
www.trenitalia.it
Full train information and online booking for the national rail network.

MISCELLANEOUS
www.weather.com
www.bbc.co.uk/weather
Weather for Venice and elsewhere.
www.paginegialle.it
Italian Yellow Pages.
www.vestaspa.net
Full list of public lavatories in Venice.

NEWS
La Repubblica
www.repubblica.it
Il Messaggero
www.ilmessaggero.it
Corriere della Sera
www.corriere.it
Il Gazzettino
www.gazzettino.it

KEY SIGHTS QUICK WEBSITE FINDER		
SIGHT	PAGE	WEBSITE
Ca' d'Oro	70–71	www.cadoro.org
Ca' Pesaro	72–73	www.museicivicineveneziani.it
Ca' Rezzonico	74–75	www.museicivicineveneziani.it
Collezione Peggy Guggenheim	92–93	www.guggenheim-venice.it
Gallerie dell'Accademia	94–100	www.gallerieaccademia.org
Museo Correr	108–109	www.museicivicineveneziani.it
Palazzo Ducale	112–117	www.museicivicineveneziani.it
Santa Maria Gloriosa dei Frari	144–147	www.basilicadeifrari.it

PLANNING

MEDIA

TELEVISION
● Italy has three state-run television stations (RAI-1, -2 and -3); three stations run by Berlusconi's Mediaset group (Italia Uno, Rete Quattro and Canale Cinque); and a number of local channels. RAI-3 has international news broadcasts, including an English-language section. It starts at 1.15am.
● Italian television usually comprises a mixture of soaps, chat shows and American imports dubbed into Italian.
● Most hotels, from mid-range upwards, have satellite television, so you can keep up to date with the news and sport on BBC World, CNN and Eurosport.

RADIO
● RAI Radio 1, 2 and 3 (89.7FM, 91.7FM and 93.7FM), the state-run stations, have a mixture of light music, chat shows and news—all in Italian.
● Radio Italia Network (90–108FM) is the best national radio station for dance music and Radio Deejay (99.7–107FM) plays a variety of popular music and chat shows.
● You can pick up three local radio stations in Venice. Radio Venezia (100.95 and 92.4 FM) offers pop music and light news; Radio Capital (98.5 FM)

alternates local news and advertising with 1980s and '90s hits; and Radio Padova (103.9 and 88.4 FM) plays non-stop popular chart music.
● You can get BBC radio stations including Radio 1, 2, 5 Live and 6 Music on the internet via www.bbc.co.uk. The BBC World Service frequencies in Italy are MHz 12.10, 9.410, 6.195 and 0.648.
● Visit www.radio-locator.com to find US radio stations online.

MAGAZINES
● *Amica* is a stylish Italian read with articles on all that is fashionable and cutting edge in Italy, and there are also Italian-language versions of glossies such as *Vogue* and *Marie Claire*.
● English-language magazines are few and far between; if you read a little Italian, magazines

such as *Panorama* and *L'Espresso* are good for news.
● *Casa Bella* showcases the best of Italian homestyle, while *Bell'Italia*, a beautiful travel magazine in the National Geographic style, has regular features on different parts of Italy.

NEWSPAPERS
English-language
● The *Financial Times*, the *Wall Street Journal*, *USA Today*, the *International Herald Tribune* and most British and European dailies are available in Venice from about 2pm on their day of publication.
● The best places to find them are at the airport, the railway station, the Rialto, the newsstand just outside the west end of Piazza San Marco and the one at the foot of the Accademia Bridge.

Italian-language
● *La Repubblica*, *Corriere della Sera* and *La Stampa* are the main national newspapers.
● Venice has two daily newspapers: *Il Gazzettino* and *La Nuova Venezia*.
● There are two daily sports papers—*La Gazzetta dello Sport* (pink paper) and the *Corriere dello Sport*. *La Gazetta* also publishes a supplement on Saturday called *Sport Week*.

BOOKS, FILMS AND MAPS

BOOKS
For more Venetian background than your guidebook can provide, there's a choice of books on both the art and history of the city. *Venice: A Maritime Republic* by Frederick C Lane is a scholarly, in-depth history; for something lighter, but no less thorough, try John Julius Norwich's *A History of Venice* or Jan Morris' seminal and impressionistic *Venice*.

The best companion guide to Venice is J G Links' *Venice for Pleasure*, a series of city walks annotated with fascinating and idiosyncratic information. If the city as a fictional protagonist appeals, you'll find it wonderfully evoked in *The Wings of the Dove* by Henry James, while the edgy corruption of 20th-century Venice is marvellously portrayed in *Death in Venice* by Thomas Mann.

Other 20th-century writers who've featured the city include Ian McEwan, whose *The Comfort of Strangers* employs Venice as the backdrop to a disturbing tale of a dysfunctional marriage. The sinister undertones induced by the city's atmosphere contribute to the tension in Barry Unsworth's *The Stone Virgin*, an art history romance spreading across the centuries, and there's a touch of the same in Sally Vicker's *Miss Garnett's Angel*, the story of the effect of Venice on a staid English spinster.

On a lighter note, two crime writers capture the very essence of everyday Venice and its inhabitants. Michael Dibdin's *Aurelio Zen* is a world-weary and all too human detective from an old Venetian family, while Donna Leon's series of detective stories starring Commissario

Guido Brunetti draw the reader into the city behind the tourist face.

FILMS
Venice has provided the perfect stage set for a series of romantic and historical movies. Among the best known are David Lean's *Summertime*, starring Katherine Hepburn, *Death in Venice* with Dirk Bogarde, the sumptuously filmed *The Comfort of Strangers* with Helena Bonham Carter and Nicholas Roeg's disturbing 1973 *Don't Look Now*.

In the 21st century *The Talented Mr. Ripley* included an evocative portrait of Venice in the 1950s, while *Casanova* (2005) conjured the hedonism of the 18th century (see also page 35).

MAPS
See page 47.

PLANNING

ITALIAN WORDS AND PHRASES

Once you have mastered a few basic rules, Italian is an easy language to speak: It is phonetic, and unlike English, particular combinations of letters are always pronounced the same way. The stress is usually on the penultimate syllable, but if the word has an accent, this is where the stress falls.

Vowels are pronounced as follows:

a	casa	as in	mat short 'a'
e	vero closed	as in	base
e	sette open	as in	vet short 'e'
i	vino	as in	mean
o	dove closed	as in	bowl
o	otto open	as in	not
u	uva	as in	book

Consonants as in English except:
c before i or e becomes ch as in church
ch before i or e becomes c as in cat
g before i or e becomes j as in Julia
gh before i or e becomes g as in good
gn as in onion
gli as in million
h is rare in Italian words, and is always silent
r usually rolled
z is pronounced tz when it falls in the middle of a word

All Italian nouns are either masculine (usually ending in o when singular or i when plural) or feminine (usually ending in a when singular or e when plural). Some nouns, which may be masculine or feminine, end in e (which changes to i when plural). An adjective's ending changes to match the ending of the noun.

Help!
Aiuto!

Stop, thief!
Al ladro!

Can you help me, please?
Può aiutarmi, per favore?

Call the fire brigade/police/an ambulance
Chiami i pompieri/la polizia/un'ambulanza

I have lost my passport/wallet
Ho perso il passaporto/il portafoglio

Where is the police station/police station?
Dov'è il commissariato/l'ospedale?

I have been robbed
Sono stato derubato

I need to see a doctor/dentist
Ho bisogno di un medico/dentista

Excuse me, I think I am lost
Mi Scusi, penso di essermi perduto

SHOPPING

Could you help me, please?
Può aiutarmi, per favore?

How much is thi/thats?
Quanto costa questo/quello?

I'm looking for …
Cerco …

Where can I buy…?
Dove posso comprare…?

I'll take this
Prendo questo

Are the instructions included?
Ci sono anche le istruzioni?

Do you have a bag for this?
Può darmi un sacco?

Can you gift wrap this please?
Può farmi un pacco regalo?

Do you accept credit cards?
Accettate carte di credito?

I'd like a kilo of …
Vorrei un chilo di …

When does the shop open/close?
Quando apre/chiude il negozio?

GETTING AROUND

Where is the train/bus station?
Dov'è la stazione ferroviaria/degli autobus (dei pullman—long distance)?

Does this train/bus go to …?
È questo il treno/l'autobus (il pullman—long distance) per…?

Where are we?
Dove siamo?

When is the first/last bus/vaporetto to …?
Quando c'è il primo/l'ultimo autobus/vaporetto per …?

Do you have a vaporetto map?
Ha una piantina degli vaporetti?

Do I have to get off here?
Devo scendere qui?

Please can I have a single/return ticket to …
Un biglietto di andata/andata e ritorno per …

I would like a standard/first class ticket to…
Un biglietto di seconda/prima classe per…

Where is the timetable?
Dov'è l'orario?

Where can I find a taxi?
Dove sono i tassì?

Please take me to …
Per favore, mi porti a …

How much is the journey?
Quanto costerà il viaggio?

I'd like to get out here please
Vorrei scendere qui, per favore

Is this the way to…?
È questa la strada per…?

HOTELS

I have made a reservation for…nights
Ho prenotato per…notti

Do you have a room?
Avete camere libere?

How much per night?
Quanto costa una notte?

Double/single room/Twin room
**Camera doppia/singola/
Camera a due letti**

With bath/shower
Con bagno/doccia

May I see the room?
Posso vedere la camera?

I'll take this room
Prendo questa camera

Could I have another room?
Vorrei cambiare camera

Is there a lift in the hotel?
C'è un ascensore nell'albergo?

Is the room air-conditioned/heated?
C'è aria condizionata/riscaldamento nella camera?

Is breakfast included in the price?
La colazione è compreso?

When is breakfast served?
A che ora è servita la colazione?

The room is too hot/too cold/dirty
La camera è troppo calda/troppo fredda/sporca

I am leaving this morning
Parto stamattina

Please can I pay my bill?
Posso pagare il conto?

MONEY

Is there a bank/currency exchange office nearby?
C'è una banca/un ufficio di cambio qui vicino?

Can I cash this here?
Posso incassare questo?

I'd like to change sterling/dollars into euros
Vorrei cambiare sterline/dollari in euro

Can I use my credit card to withdraw cash?
Posso usare la mia carta di credito per prelevare contanti?

TOURIST INFORMATION

Where is the tourist information office, please?
Dov'è l'ufficio turistico, per favore?

Do you have a city map?
Avete una cartina della città?

Can you give me some information about…?
Puo darmi delle informazioni su …?

What sights/hotels/restaurants can you recommend?
Quali monumenti/alberghi/ristoranti mi consiglia?

What is the admission price?
Quant'è il biglietto d'ingresso?

Is there an English-speaking guide?
C'è una guida di lingue inglese?

Do you have a brochure in English?
Avete un opuscolo in inglese?

Could you reserve tickets for me?
Mi può prenotare dei biglietti?

RESTAURANTS

Waiter/waitress
Cameriere/cameriera

I'd like to reserve a table for … people at …
Vorrei prenotare un tavolo per … persone a …

A table for …, please
Un tavolo per …, per favore

Could we sit there?
Possiamo sederci qui?

Are there tables outside?
Ci sono tavoli all'aperto?

We would like to wait for a table
Aspettiamo che si liberi un tavolo

Could we see the menu/wine list?
Possiamo vedere il menù/la lista dei vini?

Do you have a menu/wine list in English?
Avete un menù/una lista dei vini in inglese?

What do you recommend?
Cosa consiglia?

What is the house special?
Qual è la specialità della casa?

I can't eat wheat/sugar/salt/pork/beef/dairy
Non posso mangiare grano/zucchero/sale/maiale/manzo/latticini

I am a vegetarian
Sono vegetariano/a

I'd like…
Vorrei…

May I have an ashtray?
Può portare un portacenere?

I ordered …
Ho ordinato …

Could we have some salt and pepper?
Può portare del sale e del pepe?

The food is cold
Il cibo è freddo

This is not what I ordered
Non ho ordinato questo

Can I have the bill, please?
Il conto, per favore?

Is service included?
Il servizio è compreso?

The bill is not right
Il conto è sbagliato

We didn't have this
Non abbiamo avuto questo

on/to the right **a destra**	I live in … **Vivo in …**	castle/palace **castello/palazzo**	canal **rio**
on/to the left **a sinistra**	cross over **attraversi**	museum/gallery **museo/galleria**	island **isola**
around the corner **all'angolo**	in front of/behind **davanti/dietro**	monument **monumento**	river/lake **fiume/lago**
opposite **di fronte a...**	north/south/east/west **nord/sud/est/ovest**	town **città**	street/avenue **via/viale**
straight on **sempre dritto**	free **gratis**	old town **centro storico**	no entry **vietato**
near **vicino a**	open/closed **aperto/chiuso**	square **piazza/campo**	entrance/exit **ingresso/uscita**
Where do you live? **Dove abita?**	cathedral/church **cattedrale/chiesa**	bridge **ponte**	

CONVERSATION

What is the time? **Che ore sono?**	Hello, pleased to meet you **Piacere**
I don't speak Italian **Non parlo italiano**	Good morning **Buongiorno**
Do you speak English? **Parla inglese?**	Good afternoon/evening **Buonosera**
I don't understand **Non capisco**	Goodbye **Arrivederci**
Please repeat that **Può ripetere?**	How are you? **Come sta?**
My name is **Mi chiamo**	Fine, thank you **Bene, grazie**
What's your name? **Come si chiama?**	I'm sorry **Mi dispiace**

TIMES, DAYS, MONTHS

Monday	**lunedì**
Tuesday	**martedì**
Wednesday	**mercoledì**
Thursday	**Giovedì**
Friday	**venerdì**
Saturday	**sabato**
Sunday	**domenica**
day	**giorno**
week	**settimana**
today	**oggi**
yesterday	**ieri**
tomorrow	**domani**
January	**gennaio**
February	**febbraio**
March	**marzo**
April	**aprile**
May	**maggio**
June	**giugno**
July	**luglio**
August	**Agosto**
September	**settembre**
October	**ottobre**
November	**novembre**
December	**dicembre**

NUMBERS

0 zero	6 sei	12 dodici	18 diciotto	40 quaranta	100 cento
1 uno	7 sette	13 tredici	19 diciannove	50 cinquanta	1000 mille
2 due	8 otto	14 quattordici	20 venti	60 sessanta	million milione
3 tre	9 nove	15 quindici	21 ventuno	70 settanta	quarter quarto
4 quattro	10 dieci	16 sedici	22 ventidue	80 ottanta	half mezza
5 cinque	11 undici	17 diciassette	30 trenta	90 novanta	three quarters tre quarti

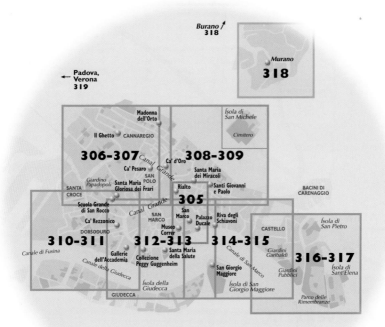

Burano
318

Murano
318

← Padova,
Verona
319

Madonna
dell'Orto

Isola di
San Michele

Il Ghetto   CANNAREGIO

Cimitero

306-307   Canal Grande   Ca' d'Oro   **308-309**

Ca' Pesaro   SAN POLO   Santa Maria
dei Miracoli

SANTA CROCE   Giardino Papadopoli   Santa Maria Gloriosa dei Frari   Rialto   Santi Giovanni e Paolo

Canal Grande   **305**

BACINI DI CARENAGGIO

Scuola Grande di San Rocco   San Marco   Riva degli Schiavoni

SAN MARCO

Ca' Rezzonico   Museo Correr   Palazzo Ducale

DORSODURO

Isola di San Pietro

310-311   **312-313**   **314-315**   CASTELLO

Canale di Fusina   Gallerie dell'Accademia   Collezione Peggy Guggenheim   Santa Maria della Salute   Giardini Garibaldi   **316-317**   Isola di Sant'Elena

Canale della Giudecca   Canale di San Marco

Giardini Pubblici

San Giorgio Maggiore

Isola della Giudecca   Isola di San Giorgio Maggiore

GIUDECCA   Parco delle Rimembranze

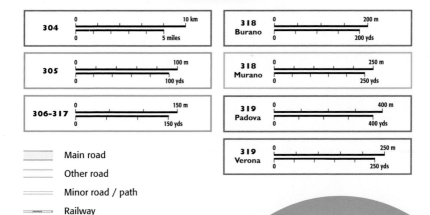

| 304 | 0 ————————— 10 km |
| | 0 ————————— 5 miles |

| 305 | 0 ————————— 100 m |
| | 0 ————————— 100 yds |

| 306-317 | 0 ————————— 150 m |
| | 0 ————————— 150 yds |

| 318 Burano | 0 ————————— 200 m |
| | 0 ————————— 200 yds |

| 318 Murano | 0 ————————— 250 m |
| | 0 ————————— 250 yds |

| 319 Padova | 0 ————————— 400 m |
| | 0 ————————— 400 yds |

| 319 Verona | 0 ————————— 250 m |
| | 0 ————————— 250 yds |

Main road

Other road

Minor road / path

Railway

Park

Railway station

Important building

⬤ Featured place of interest

● Monument / statue

🛈 Tourist information office

✝ Church

✉ Post office

○ Vaporetto stop

🅿 Parking

Maps

Carbonera
Treviso
San Biagio di Callalta
Ceggia
Noventa di Piave
Fossalta di Piave
San Dona di Piave
Roncade
Meolo
Musile di Piave
Preganziol
Casale sul Sile
Caposile
Zero Branco
Quarto d'Altino
Portegrandi
Mogliano Veneto
San Liberale
Jesolo
Martellago
Palude Maggiore
Spinea
Mestre
Aeroporto Marco Polo
Torcello
Cavallino
Mirano
Marghera
Burano
Porto di Piave Vecchia
San Francesco del Deserto
Murano
Treporti
Litorale del Cavallino
Oriago
PONTE DELLA LIBERTÀ
Vignole
Mira
VENEZIA
Sant' Erasmo
San Lazzaro degli Armeni
Lido
Litorale di Lido
Lido
Lova
Laguna Veneta
Alberoni
Porto di Malamocco
Golfo di Venezia
Litorale di Pellestrina
Pellestrina
Conche
Porto di Chioggia
Chioggia
Sottomarina
Ca' Bianca
Foce d Brenta
Foce d Adige
Martinelle
Canale Gorzone
Sant'Anna
Rosapineta
San Pietro di Cavarzere
Tornova
Caleri
Rosolina
Ísola Albarella
Loreo
Foce del Po d Levante
Ca' Cappello
Porto Levante
Foce del Po d Maistra
Donada
Porto Viro

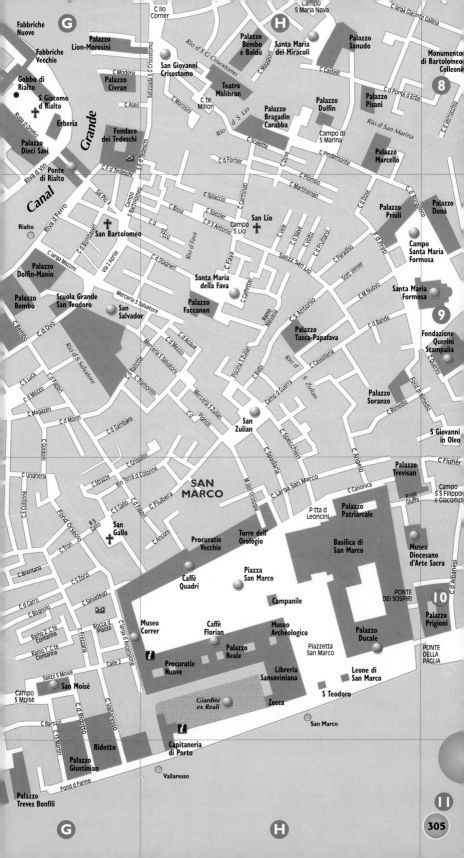

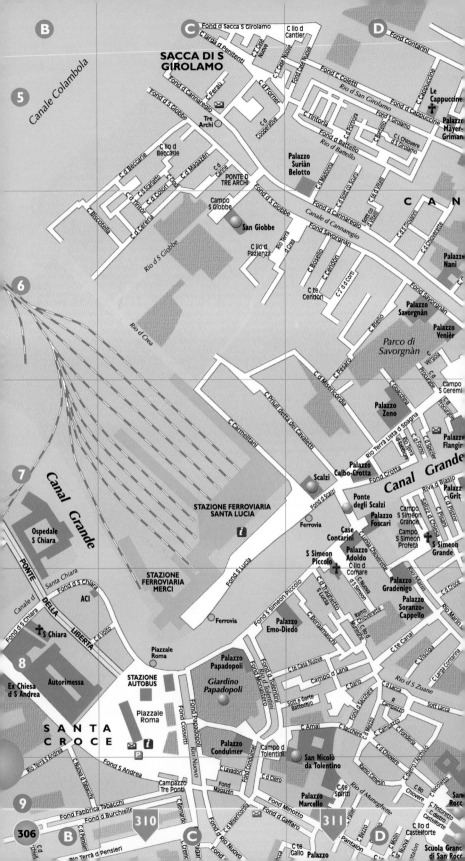

4

5

Cimitero ○   San
Michele

5

Cimitero

6

6

*Ísola di
San Michele*

K   L

7

ondamenta Nuove

Santa Lázzaro
'ei Mendicanti

Fondamente Nuove

Ospedale
Civile

8

Santa Maria
del Pianto

Calle Nicolò Massa

R Moschette

C d Mezzo

C delle Cappuccine

spedaletto
Santa Maria
ei Derelitti)

Barbaria delle Tole

C d Forno

C d Caffetièr

C Cavalli

Rio di Santa Giustina

Fondamenta di Santa Giustina

Celestia

F Case Nuove

C d Orti

C Assisi

C 2° Sagredo

C d Pietà

azzo
agnis

C zen

C s Francesco

C Tedeum

C d Cimitero

Ex Chiesa
di S Giustina

Rio d S Giovanni Laterano

Campo
S Giustina

Palazzo
Gritti o d
Nunziatura

San Francesco
della Vigna

C d
Sagredo

C d
Oratorio

C te del
Muneghe

CASTELLO

Campo della
Confraternita

Ex Ospizio
San
Lorenzo

Palazzo
Gradenigo

Palazzo
Contarini

Rio d S Francesco

C d Cimitero

Campo
d Celestia

Salizzada S Giustina

Ramo d
Francesco

Campo
San Lorenzo

Rio de S Agostin

C Morión

C te
d Vida

Campo
S Ternità

C Nuova

C d Vida

314

K

315

L

309

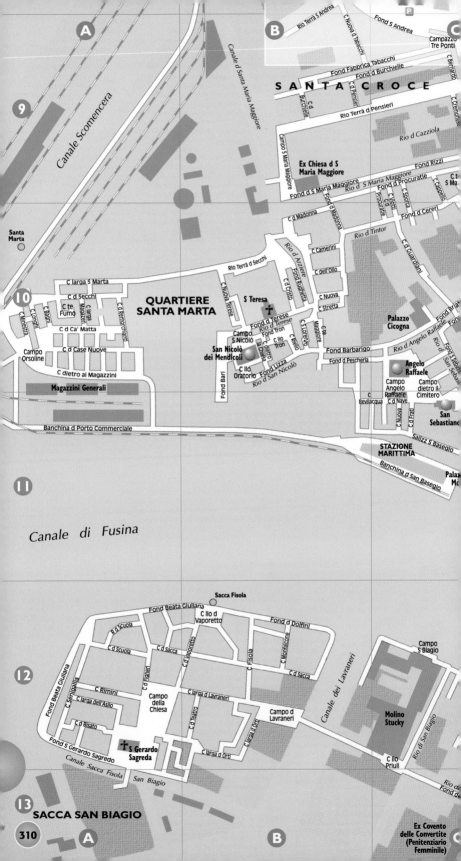

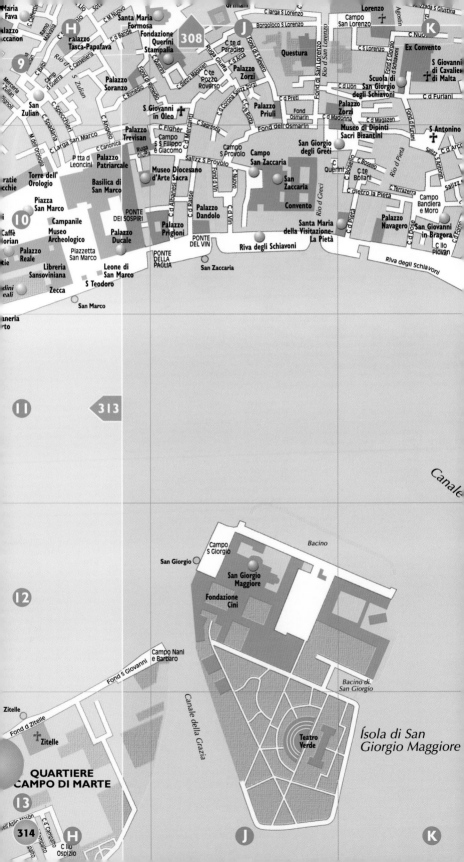

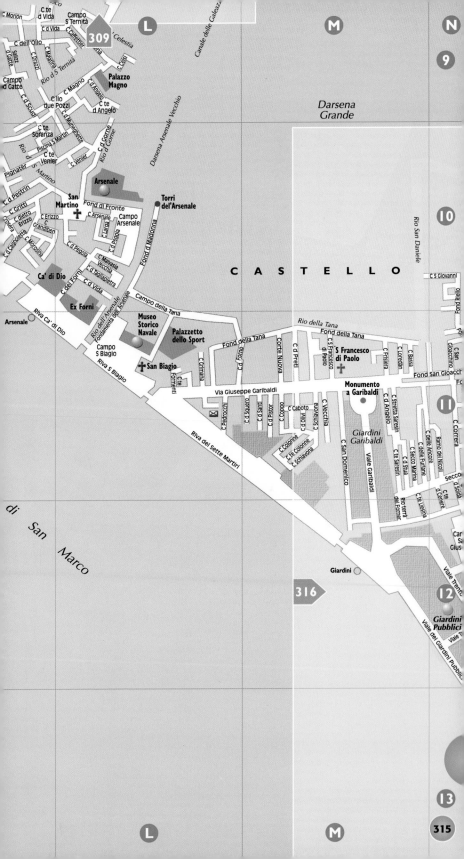

Dursena Arse

Torri
dell'Arsenale

10

am
ser

Fond d Madonna

Campo della Tana

Museo
Storico
Navale

Palazzetto
dello Sport

San Biagio

C te
Formenti

C Grimana

Riva del Sette Martiri

11

315

Giardini

12

13

14

C A S T E L L O

Rio San Daniele

Campo
S Daniele

C larga S Pietro

Salizzada Stretta

C d Terco

Campo d
San Pietro

Canale di San Pietro

C d
Campanile

C S Giovanni

C llo
Figaretto

Campo
di Ruga

C Sporca

C Marafani

C d Ole

C Salamòn

Oslo Forno

Forno Forni

Fond Quintavalle

C d Bianco

C Croce

C Calafotolo

C S Anna

C Riello

C San
Gioacchino

Fond Forno

C d Ole

Rio della Tana

Fond della Tana

Fond della Tana

Corte Nuova

Forno d 2

C d Preti

C S Francesco
di Paolo

S Francesco
di Paolo

C Frisiera

C Loredan

C Bassa

Fond San Gioacchino

Fond S Anna

C Quintavalle

Ex Chiesa
di S Anna

Monumento
a Garibaldi

Via Giuseppe Garibaldi

C Pedrocchi

C Squero

C d Santi

C d Pistor

oddo C

C d Polo

Caligo d O

C Caboto

C Vecchia

C d Angelo

C Strada Saresin

C Stretta Saresin

Giardini
Garibaldi

C Colonne

C te Colonne

C te Schiavona

C San Domenico

Viale Garibaldi

C te Saresin

C delle Ancore

C delle Furlane

Rio del Nicoli

C Correra

C te B Tiepolo

C Cattapan

Ramo del Nicoli

Secco Marina

C te
d Mazzan

C te
d Savona

C te
Sabbionera

C te
d Cisto

C te
Martin
Novello

Rio terra
del Forner

C te Lesina

C te
d Cenere

C te
d Sola

Fond San Giuseppe

San Giuseppe
di Castello

Campo
San
Giuseppe

Rio terra San Giuseppe

Paludo S Antonio

C dentro il Giardino

Biennale
Internazionale
d'Arte

Viale Trento

Giardini
Pubblici

Viale Trieste

Viale dei Giardini Pubblici

Rio d Giardini

San Pietro

*Ísola di
San Pietro*

**San Pietro
di Castello**

**Ex Palazzo
Patriarcale**

C unga Quintavalle
C d Mezzo
C llo
Vigna
Fond Castel Olivolo
C llo dei
Pomeri
an

Rio di Quintavalle

*Darsena
di Sant'Elena*

Viale XXIV Maggio
Ramo d
Montello
C Asiago
C Nervesa
C d
Fontei
C d
Pozzo
C d Cengio
C d
Olisto
C d Pasubio
C d Congregazione
Viale Plave
C d Montello
C del Pasubio
Campo
d Grappa
C Montesanto
C Ostaria
C dell'Hermada
C del Carso
C dei Sabotino
C Podgora
Viale Plave
Campo d
Indipendenza
Fond S Elena
Fond Darsena
*Campo
Sportivo*

C Gen Chinotto

**QUARTIERE
SANT'ELENA**

C Cordia
C zugna
C Bainsizza
C Duca d Aosta
C Rovereto
C dei Carnaro
C Buccari
Viale Plave
Viale S Elena

Sant'Elena

Campo
d Chiesa

*Ísola di
Sant'Elena*

*Parco delle
Rimembranze*
Viale IV Novembre

Viale Vittorio Veneto
Sant Elena

Rio di Sant'Elena

BURANO

Murano   Treporti

Burano

I

Strada di Corte Comare
Calle di Saladi
Fond Pontinello Sinistro
Fond Pontinello Destro

Fond S Mauro

Fond di Cao di Rio

2

Fond Cavanella
Fond Cao Moleca
Via Baldasarre Galuppi

Fond della Peschiera
Fond della Giudecca

Museo del Merletto

Piazza Galuppi

Fond d Terranova

San Martino

Burano

a   **b**   **c**

MURANO

Campo Sportivo

Canale di Santa Maria

I

C P Venini
C G M Ortes
Fond C Parmense
C d Odorado

S Maria d Angeli

Cimitero Nuovo

Fond S Santi
C d Convento
C Volpi

Strada Comune del Cimitero
R Cimitero
C S Bernardo
Fond Andigiano
C S Salvado
C S Giuseppe
Fond L Radi

Venier

C S Bernardo
C Brussa
C d Cristo

2

SACCA SERENELLA

Canale Serenella

C A Vivarini

Fond S Venier

C d Mistro

Fond da Mula

PONTE VIVARINI

Fond Cavour

Santa Maria e Donato

C Contarie
Fond S Lorenzo
Campo S Donato

Museo del Vetro

Fond Giustinian

C A Maschio
PONTE S DONATO

Palazzo Trevisan

Canale Ondello

Palazzo da Mula

Canale Grande di Murano
Fond A Colleoni
Campo S Stefano

Museo
C S Giacone

Fond A Navagero

S Pietro Martire

C llo Turella

3

Serenella

C S Cipriano
R Cipriano
C Bertolini

Fond Serenella

C dietro Gli Orti

Navagero

C P Paradiso

Fond D Manin
Fond della Gallia
Fond d Vetrai
C Miotti
C Milotti
Fond d Olio
Calle Cimballo
Via Briati
Fond P Piave

Murano

Faro

4

Canale delle Navi

Colonna

Canale dei Marani

L   **M**   **N**

PADOVA

Via Savonarola
Via San Fermo
Via Dante
Stazione
Corso Garibaldi
Cappella degli Scrovegni
Musei Civici Eremitani
Piazza Eremitani
Chiesa degli Eremitani

VIA MORGAGNI

Piazza Insurrezione
Via Verdi
Via S Lucia
Riv Ponti Romani
Via Zabarella
Via Altinate

Via S Nicolo

Via S Sofia

Riviera A Musato
Palazzo del Capitano
Piazza dei Signori
Piazza della Frutta
Piazza Cavour

Via Tadi
Palazzo della Ragione
Caffè Pedrocchi
Via Cesare Battisti

Piazza Duomo
Piazza dell'Erbe
Battistero
Duomo
Via D Manin
Via S Francesco

Riv S Benedetto
Via Vescovado
Via S Martino
San Francesco

Via San Rosa
Via Marsala
Riv Tito Livio
Via del Santo

Via S Tomaso
Via G Barbarigo
Via XX Settembre
Via Umberto I
Via G Galilei

Riviera T Camposanpiero
Riv Ruzzante
Via Rudena
Statua Gattamelata
Piazza del Santo
Basilica di Sant'Antonio

Via Riello
Via Belludi
P Pontecorvo

Via Dimesse
Via Acquette

A   **B**   **C**

VERONA

Via N Bixio
VIA S ALESSIO
Porta S Giorgio
San Giorgio in Braida
Santo Stefano
Castel San Pietro

Via del Mille
PONTE GARIBALDI
PONTE PIETRA
Museo Archeologico

VIA IV NOVEMBRE
Via M Todeschini
Via Prato Santo
Duomo
Via Duomo
Teatro Romano

Via S Chiara
Lungadige G Matteotti
Adige
Via Garibaldi
Via Pigna
Sant' Anastasia

Via Mamaso
Via Forti
Corso S Anastasia
Palazzo degli Scaligeri
Via Sottoriva

Via E Emilei
Casa Mazzanti
Santa Maria Antica
LUNG RE TEODORICO

S Eufemia
Loggia del Consiglio
Arche Scaligere

PONTE D'VITTORIA
Corso Porta Borsari
Piazza dell'Erbe
Piazza dei Signori
Via Nizza
PONTE NUOVO

Lungadige Campagnola
San Lorenzo
Porta Borsari
Via Mazzini
Casa di Giulietta

Ponte Scaligero
Via Oberdan
Via Stella
Via Cappello
Via Leoni
Via Zambelli
LUNG SAMMICHELI

Castelvecchio
CORSO CAVOUR
Via Cattaneo
Via Anfiteatro
Interrato dell'Acqua Morta

San Zeno Maggiore
Via Roma
Piazza Brà
Arena
Via Leoncino
PONTE NAVI

Via Manin
Palazzo del Municipale
STR S FERMO
San Fermo Maggior

CORSO PORTA NUOVA
Stazione
Adige

a   **b**   **c**

Page numbers in bold indicate the main reference.

ACKNOWLEDGMENTS

Abbreviations for the credits are as follows:
AA = AA World Travel Library, t (top), b (bottom), c (centre), l (left), r (right), bg (background)

UNDERSTANDING VENICE

4 AA/A Mockford & N Bonetti; **5cl** AA/A Mockford & N Bonetti; **5c** AA/C Sawyer; **5cr** AA/S McBride; **6/7, 8cl, 8cr, 8/9, 9t, 9r, 9b, 10tr, 10cl, 10crt** AA/A Mockford & N Bonetti; **10crb** AA/C Sawyer; **10b** AA/A Mockford & N Bonetti; **11tlt** AA/A Mockford & N Bonetti; **11tlb** AA/C Sawyer; **11tr** AA/A McBride; **11clt, 11clb, 11b, 12trt, 12trb** AA/A Mockford & N Bonetti; **12crt** AA/C Sawyer; **12crb** AA/C Sawyer; **12l** AA/A Mockford & N Bonetti; **12b** AA/A Mockford & N Bonetti

LIVING VENICE

13 AA/A Mockford & N Bonetti; **14/15bg** AA/S McBride; **14tl, 14tc, 14tr** AA/A Mockford & N Bonetti; **14c** AA/S McBride; **14/15** AA/S McBride; **14b** AA/C Sawyer; **15tl** AA/C Sawyer; **15tr** AA/R Walford; **15c** AA/C Sawyer; **15cr** AA/A Mockford & N Bonetti; **16/17bg** AA/A Mockford & N Bonetti; **16tl** AA/S McBride; **16tr, 16cl, 16cr** AA/C Sawyer; **16b** AA/S McBride; **17tl** AA/C Sawyer; **17tr** AA/A Mockford & N Bonetti; **17ctl** AA/C Sawyer; **17ctr** AA/D Miterdiri; **17cbl** AA/S McBride; **17cbr, 17b, 18/19bg, 18tl, 18tr, 18cl** AA/A Mockford & N Bonetti; **18cr** Rex Features; **18b** Venice in Peril; **19tl, 19tctl, 19ctl** AA/A Mockford & N Bonetti; **19tc** © Sunset Boulevard/Corbis Sygma; **19cl** AA/A Mockford & N Bonetti; **19cr** Venice in Peril; **20/21bg** AA/A Mockford & N Bonetti; **20l** Getty Images; **20r, 20/21, 21tc** AA/A Mockford & N Bonetti; **21tr** AA/S McBride; **21cl** AA/D Miterdiri; **21c** AA/D Miterdiri; **21cr** AA/A Mockford & N Bonetti; **22/23bg** AA/A Mockford & N Bonetti; **22tl** AA/S McBride; **22t**r Francis Model Handbags; **22cl** AA/S McBride; **22c** AA/S McBride; **22cr** AA/A Mockford & N Bonetti; **23tl** AA/S McBride; **23tr** AA/C Sawyer; **23cl** AA/A Mockford & N Bonetti; **23c** AA/A Mockford & N Bonetti; **23cr** Thierry Tronnel/Corbis; **24bg** AA/S McBride; **24tl** Venice Marco Polo Airport; **24tr** AA/S McBride; **24cl** © Michele Crosera/Reuters/Corbis; **24cr** AA/A Mockford & N Bonetti; **24b** Rex Features

THE STORY OF VENICE

25 AA/C Sawyer; **26/27bg** AA/R Newton; **26t** AA; **26bl** AA/C Sawyer; **26/27** AA/T Souter; **27cl** AA/A Mockford & N Bonetti; **27c** AA; **27bc** AA/C Sawyer; **27br** AA/C Sawyer; **28/29** AA; **28t** AA/C Sawyer; **28c** AA; **28bl** AA/C Sawyer; **28bc** Mary Evans Picture Library; **28/29** Museo Correr, Venice, Italy/Bridgeman Art Library; **29cl** AA/S McBride; **29cr** AA/C Sawyer; **29b** AA; **30/31** AA; **30cr** Bibliotheque Nationale, Paris, France, Giraudon/Bridgeman Art Library; **30cb** AA; **30bl** AA/D Miterdiri; **30/31** AA; **31cl** AA; **31c** Biblioteca Marciana, Venice, Italy/Bridgeman Art Library; **31bc** Private Collection, The Stapleton Collection/Bridgeman Art Library; **31br** AA/S McBride; **32/33bg** AA; **32t** AA/A Mockford & N Bonetti; **32c** Galleria degli Uffizi, Florence, Italy/Bridgeman Art Library; **32bl** AA/A Mockford & N Bonetti; **32bc** AA/A Mockford & N Bonetti; **32/33** Palazzo Vescovile, Prato, Tuscany, Italy/Bridgeman Art Library; **33cl** AA/D Miterdiri; **33c** AA/D Miterdiri; **33bc** AA/C Sawyer; **33br** AA/A Mockford & N Bonetti; **34/35bg** AA; **34t** AA; **34c** © Bob Krist/Corbis; **34bl** Mary Evans Picture Library; **34bc** AA/A Mockford & N Bonetti; **34/35** © The Bowes Museum, Barnard Castle, County Durham, UK/Bridgeman Art Library; **35c** AA; **35cr** Mary Evans Picture Library; **35cb** Illustrated London News; **35br** AA/A Mockford & N Bonetti; **36/37bg** AA; **36t** AA/A Mockford & N Bonetti; **36bl** Mary Evans Picture Library; **36cb** Private Collection, The Stapleton Collection/Bridgeman Art Library; **36/37** Rex Features; **37cl** AA; **37c** Illustrated London News; **37cr** AA/C Sawyer; **37cb** Getty Images; **37b** AA; **38bg** AA/A Mockford & N Bonetti; **38t** AA/D Miterdiri; **38cbl** AA/S McBride; **38bl** AA/S McBride; **38br** AA/C Sawyer

ON THE MOVE

39 AA/A Mockford & N Bonetti; **40t** Digital Vision; **40b** AA/C Sawyer; **41** Digital Vision; **42t** Digital Vision; **42c** AA/A Mockford & N Bonetti; **43t** Digital Vision; **43b** AA/S McBride; **44t** AA/A Mockford & N Bonetti; **44c** AA/C Sawyer; **45t** AA/A Mockford & N Bonetti, **45ct** AA/C Sawyer; **45b, 46t, 46c, 47t, 47c, 48t, 48/49, 48c, 48bl, 48br, 49cl, 49cr, 49bc, 49b, 50t, 50b, 51, 52t, 52c, 53t, 53b, 54t, 54c, 55** AA/A Mockford & N Bonetti; **56** AA/N Sumner

THE SIGHTS

57 AA/A Mockford & N Bonetti; **64l** AA/S McBride; **64r** AA/A Mockford & N Bonetti; **65l** AA/S McBride; **65r** AA/C Sawyer; **66l, 66r, 67l, 67r, 68l, 68r** AA/A Mockford & N Bonetti; **69bg** AA/C Sawyer; **69tl** AA/A Mockford & N Bonetti; **69tr** AA/S McBride; **70t, 70cl, 70c, 70cr** AA/A Mockford & N Bonetti; **71t** Ca' d'Oro, Venice, Italy/Bridgeman Art Library; **71c** AA/A Mockford & N Bonetti; **72t** AA/S McBride; **72cl, 72cr, 72b, 73l, 73r** AA/A Mockford & N Bonetti; **74t** AA/C Sawyer; **74cl** AA/A Mockford & N Bonetti; **74c** AA/C Sawyer; **74cr** AA/C Sawyer; **75l** AA/A Mockford & N Bonetti; **75r** AA/C Sawyer; 76tl AA/A Mockford & N Bonetti; **76tr** AA/A Mockford & N Bonetti; **77tl** Caffe Florian; **77tr, 77b, 78t, 78b, 79tl, 79tc, 79tr, 79b** AA/A Mockford & N Bonetti; **80tl** AA/C Sawyer; **80tc** AA/S McBride; **80tr** AA/S McBride; **81tl** AA/A Mockford & N Bonetti; **81tr** AA/A Mockford & N Bonetti; **81b** AA/S McBride; **82t** AA/C Sawyer; **82cl** AA/S McBride; **82c** AA/A Mockford & N Bonetti; **82/83** AA/S McBride; **82b** AA/S McBride; **83** AA/A Mockford & N Bonetti; **84tl** AA; **84/85, 84c, 84bcl, 84bl, 84br, 85t, 85c, 85b, 86c** AA/A Mockford & N Bonetti; **86t** AA/S McBride; **86b** AA/A Mockford & N Bonetti; **87t** AA/A Mockford & N Bonetti; **87c** AA/C Sawyer; **87b, 88t, 88cl** AA/A Mockford & N Bonetti; **88c** AA/C Sawyer; **88cr** AA/A Mockford & N Bonetti; **88b** AA/C Sawyer; **89l, 89r, 90/91, 91, 92t** AA/A Mockford & N Bonetti; **92cl** AA/S McBride; **92cr** AA/S McBride/© DACS 2005; **93t** Getty Images; **93b** Peggy Guggenheim Foundation, Venice, Italy, Alinari/Bridgeman Art Library/© ARS, NY and DACS, London 2005; **94/95** AA/A Mockford & N Bonetti; **94b** AA/S McBride; **96/97** AA/A Mockford & N Bonetti; **96** Galleria dell'Accademia, Venice, Italy, Cameraphoto Arte Venezia/Bridgeman Art Library; **97cl, 97cr, 98cl, 98c, 98cr, 99** AA/A Mockford & N Bonetti; **100** Galleria dell'Accademia, Venice, Italy, Giraudon/Bridgeman Art Library; **101tl** AA/C Sawyer; **101tr** AA/S McBride; **101b** AA/A Mockford & N Bonetti; **102t** AA/D Miterdiri; **102cl, 102c, 102cr** AA/S McBride; **103** AA/A Mockford & N Bonetti; **104tl** AA/C Sawyer; **104tr** AA/S McBride; **105tl** Museo d'Arte Moderna, Venice, Italy/Bridgeman Art Library; **105tr** AA/A Mockford & N Bonetti; **105b** AA/A Mockford & N Bonetti; **106t** AA/C Sawyer; **106cl** AA/S McBride; **106c** AA/D Miterdiri; **106cr** AA/C Sawyer; **107** AA/C Sawyer; **108t** Museo Correr, Venice, Italy/Bridgeman Art Library; **108cl** AA/S McBride; **108c** AA/D Miterdiri; **108cr** AA/C Sawyer; **109t**

Scala, Florence; **109b** Museo Correr, Venice, Italy/Bridgeman Art Library; **110tl** Museo della Fondazione Querini Stampalia; **110tr** AA/Mockford & N Bonetti; **111t** AA/S McBride; **111b** AA/C Sawyer; **112t** AA/Mockford & N Bonetti; **112cl** AA/C Sawyer; **112c** AA/S McBride; **112cr, 113, 114/115, 114b, 115, 116cl, 116c, 116cr, 117cl, 117cr, 118tl, 118tc, 118tr, 119tl, 119tc, 119tr, 120t, 120cl** AA/A Mockford & N Bonetti; **120c** AA/C Sawyer; **120cr** AA/A Mockford & N Bonetti; **120b** AA/A Mockford & N Bonetti; **121** AA/C Sawyer; **122t** AA/B Rieger; **122lcl** AA/S McBride; **122cl** AA/D Miterdiri; **122cr** AA/S McBride; **122/123** AA/D Miterdiri; **123l** AA/S McBride; **123r** AA/S McBride; **124tl, 124tr, 125tl, 125tr, 126t, 126c, 127tl** AA/A Mockford & N Bonetti; **127tc** AA/C Sawyer; **127tr, 128t, 128b, 129tl, 129tr, 130t** AA/A Mockford & N Bonetti; **130cl** AA/S McBride; **130c** AA/C Sawyer; **130cr** AA/S McBride; **130b** AA/A Mockford & N Bonetti; **131c** AA/A Mockford & N Bonetti; **131cb** AA/A Mockford & N Bonetti; **132t** AA/R Newton; **132cl** AA/S McBride; **132c** AA/S McBride; **132/133** AA/S McBride; **133, 134t, 134cl** AA/A Mockford & N Bonetti; **134c** AA/C Sawyer; **134cr** AA/S McBride; **135** AA/A Mockford & N Bonetti; **136** AA/S McBride; **136/137** AA/A Mockford & N Bonetti; **137** AA/S McBride; **138** AA/A Mockford & N Bonetti; **139cl** AA/C Sawyer; **139c** AA/A Mockford & N Bonetti; **139cr** AA/A Mockford & N Bonetti; **139b** AA/C Sawyer; **140** AA/C Sawyer; **140/141, 142tl, 142tc, 142tr, 143t, 143b** AA/A Mockford & N Bonetti; **144t** AA/C Sawyer; **144cl** AA/C Sawyer; **144c** AA/C Sawyer; **144cr** AA/D Miterdiri; **145** AA/C Sawyer; **146/147** AA/S McBride; **147** AA/S McBride; **148t, 148lcl, 148cl, 148cr, 148/149, 149t, 149b, 150t, 150cl** AA/A Mockford & N Bonetti; **150c** AA/C Sawyer; **150cr, 151cl, 151cr, 151b, 152tl** AA/A Mockford & N Bonetti; **152tr** AA/C Sawyer; **152b, 153tl, 153tr** AA/A Mockford & N Bonetti; **154t** AA/D Miterdiri; **154c** AA/S McBride; **155t, 155c, 156tl, 156tc, 156tr, 157t, 157c, 158t, 158b, 159tl, 159tr** AA/A Mockford & N Bonetti; **160t** AA/D Miterdiri; **160c** AA/C Sawyer; **161t, 161b, 162, 163, 164t** AA/A Mockford & N Bonetti; **164cl** AA/D Miterdiri; **164c** AA/A Mockford & N Bonetti; **164/165** AA/D Miterdiri; **165** AA/S McBride; **166/167 strip** AA/C Sawyer; **166/167, 166b, 168tl** AA/A Mockford & N Bonetti; **168tr** AA/S McBride; **168b** AA/C Sawyer; **170t** AA/C Sawyer; **170c** AA/S McBride; **171t** AA/A Mockford & N Bonetti; **171c** AA/A Mockford & N Bonetti; **172t** AA/C Sawyer; **172lcl** AA/S McBride; **172cl** AA/C Sawyer; **172cr** AA/C Sawyer; **172/173** AA/S McBride; **172b** AA/S McBride; **173** AA/C Sawyer; **174t, 174cl, 174c, 174cr, 175, 176tl** AA/A Mockford & N Bonetti; **176tc** AA/D Miterdiri; **176tr** AA/D Miterdiri

WHAT TO DO

177 AA/D Miterdiri; **178t** AA/A Mockford & N Bonetti; **178cl** AA/C Sawyer; **178cr** AA/C Sawyer; **179l** AA/A Mockford & N Bonetti; **179r** AA/A Mockford & N Bonetti; **180l** AA/C Sawyer; **180r, 181l, 181r** AA/A Mockford & N Bonetti; **182l, 182r, 183l** AA/S McBride; **183r** AA/C Sawyer; **190t, 190c, 191t, 191c, 192t** AA/A Mockford & N Bonetti; **192c** Liberia Studium; **193t** AA/A Mockford & N Bonetti; **193c** AA/C Sawyer; **194t** AA/A Mockford & N Bonetti; **194c** Pantagruelica; **195t** AA/A Mockford & N Bonetti; **195c** AA/S McBride; **196t** AA/A Mockford & N Bonetti; **196c** Photodisc; **197t** AA/A Mockford & N Bonetti; **197c** Bevilacqua; **198t** AA/A Mockford & N Bonetti; **198c** Francis Model Handbags; **199t** AA/A Mockford & N Bonetti; **199c** La Fenice Atalier; **200t** AA/A Mockford & N Bonetti; **200c** AA/M Chaplow; **201t** AA/D Miterdiri; **201cl** Ateneo Veneto; **201cr** La Fenice/Michele Crosera; **208t** AA/D Miterdiri; **208c** Ateneo

Veneto; **209t** AA/D Miterdiri; **209c** Digital Vision; **210t** AA/D Miterdiri; **210c** Ristorante Giorgione; **211t** AA/D Miterdiri; **211c** Digital Vision; **212t** AA/D Miterdiri; **212cl** AA/A Mockford & N Bonetti; **212cr** Bacaro Jazz; **213t** AA/D Miterdiri; **213c** AA/A Mockford & N Bonetti; **214t** AA/D Miterdiri; **214c** J Wyand; **215t** AA/A Mockford & N Bonetti; **215cl** Photodisc; **215cr** AA/A Mockford & N Bonetti; **216t** AA/A Mockford & N Bonetti; **216c** Circolo Golf Venezia; **217t** AA/A Mockford & N Bonetti; **217c** Photodisc; **218t** Image 100; **218c** Image 100; **219t** AA/D Miterdiri; **219c** AA/D Miterdiri; **220t** AA/D Miterdiri; **220c** AA/A Mockford & N Bonetti; **221t** Photodisc; **221c** AA/A Mockford & N Bonetti; **222t** Photodisc; **222c** AA/S Day

OUT AND ABOUT

223, 225tl, 225tr, 225cbl, 225bl AA/A Mockford & N Bonetti: **227t** AA/S McBride; **227c** AA/S McBride; **227ctr** AA/C Sawyer; **227cbr** AA/A Mockford & N Bonetti; **227b** AA/S McBride; **229t** AA/A Mockford & N Bonetti; **229ctl** AA/A Mockford & N Bonetti; **229ctr** AA/D Miterdiri; **229c** AA/A Mockford & N Bonetti; **229b** AA/S McBride; **231t** AA/C Sawyer; **231c** AA/A Mockford & N Bonetti; **231b** AA/A Mockford & N Bonetti; **233t, 233cr, 233c, 233cb** AA/S McBride; **233b** AA/D Miterdiri; **234** AA/C Sawyer; **235tl** AA/C Sawyer; **235tr** AA/S McBride; **235bl** AA/C Sawyer; **235br** AA/S McBride; **236** AA/A Mockford & N Bonetti; **237** © ImageState/Alamy; **239t** © Bob Krist/Corbis; **239ct** AA/A Mockford & N Bonetti; **239cb** AA/C Sawyer; **239b** Yann Arthus-Betrand/Corbis; **240** AA/C Sawyer; **241t** © CuboImages srl/Alamy; **241c** AA/T Souter; **242, 243t, 243ct, 243c, 244l, 244c, 244r** AA/A Mockford & N Bonetti

EATING AND STAYING

245, 246cl, 246c, 246cr AA/A Mockford & N Bonetti; **247l** AA/C Sawyer; **247c** AA/A Mockford & N Bonetti; **247cr** Caffe Florian; **248cl, 248c** AA/A Mockford & N Bonetti; **248cr** AA/C Sawyer; **249cl** AA/C Sawyer; **249c** AA/A Mockford & N Bonetti; **249cr** AA/C Sawyer; **250cl** AA/E Meacher; **250c** AA/A Mockford & N Bonetti; **250/251** AA/C Sawyer; **251c** AA/A Mockford & N Bonetti; 251cr AA/S McBride; **258t, 258c, 258b, 259tl, 259tr, 259b, 260c, 260cl, 261t, 261b, 262tl, 262tc, 262cr, 263cl, 263cr, 263b, 264c, 264cl, 264b, 265t, 265b** AA/A Mockford & N Bonetti; **266lcl** AA/C Sawyer; **266cl** AA/C Sawyer; **266c** AA/D Miterdiri; **266cr, 266rcr, 267c, 267r, 269, 276t, 276b, 277tl, 277bl, 277bc, 278t, 278b, 279bl, 279bc, 279br, 280l, 280c, 281, 282c, 282r, 283l 283r, 284** AA/A Mockford & N Bonetti

PLANNING

285 AA/A Mockford & N Bonetti; **286** AA/C Sawyer; **288** AA/C Sawyer; **298t** St. George's Church, Venice; **289b** AA/M Langford; **290t** Caffè Florian; **291t** AA/A Mockford & N Bonetti; **291b** AA/C Sawyer; **292** AA/C Sawyer; **293, 294, 295t, 295b, 296** AA/A Mockford & N Bonetti; **297** AA/C Sawyer; **298** AA/A Mockford & N Bonetti; **299** AA/A Mockford & N Bonetti

Every effort has been made to trace the copyright holders, and we apologise in advance for any unintentional omissions or errors. We would be pleased to apply any corrections in any following edition of this publication.

Project editor
Karen Kemp

Interior design
Kate Harling

Picture research
Vivien Little

Cover design
Tigist Getachew

Internal repro work
Michael Moody, Susan Crowhurst, Ian Little

Production
Lyn Kirby, Helen Sweeney

Mapping
Maps produced by the Cartography Department of AA Publishing

Main contributors
Sally Roy (author); The Content Works (contributions to Eating and Staying); Tim Jepson (verifier);
Marie Lorimer (indexer); Stephanie Smith (proofreader)

Copy editor
Karen Kemp

See It Venice
ISBN: 1-4000-1655-X
ISBN-13: 978-1-4000-1655-6

Published in the United States by Fodor's Travel Publications and simultaneously in
Canada by Random House of Canada Limited, Toronto.
Published in the United Kingdom by AA Publishing.

Color separation by Keenes
Printed and bound by Leo, China
10 9 8 7 6 5 4 3 2 1

A02355
Mapping produced from map data © New Holland Publishing (South Africa) (Pty) Ltd, 2005
Relief map images supplied by Mountain High Maps ® Copyright © 1993 Digital Wisdom, Inc
Weather chart statistics supplied by Weatherbase © Copyright (2005) Canty and Associates, LLC
Transport map © Communicarta Ltd, UK

Important note: Time inevitably brings changes, so always confirm prices, travel facts, and other
perishable information when it matters. Although Fodor's cannot accept responsibility for errors,
you can use this guide in the confidence that we have taken every care to ensure its accuracy.

Fodor's Key to the Guides

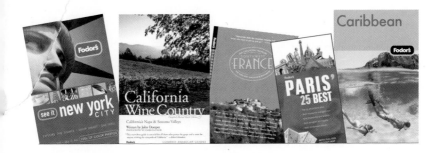

AMERICA'S **GUIDEBOOK LEADER** PUBLISHES GUIDES FOR **EVERY KIND OF TRAVELER**. CHECK OUT OUR MANY SERIES AND FIND YOUR **PERFECT MATCH**.

FODOR'S GOLD GUIDES
America's favorite travel-guide series offers the most detailed insider reviews of hotels, restaurants, and attractions in all price ranges, plus great background information, smart tips, and useful maps.

COMPASS AMERICAN GUIDES
Stunning guides from top local writers and photographers, with gorgeous photos, literary excerpts, and colorful anecdotes. A must-have for culture mavens, history buffs, and new residents.

FODOR'S 25 BEST / CITYPACKS
Concise city coverage in a guide plus a foldout map. The right choice for urban travelers who want everything under one cover.

FODOR'S AROUND THE CITY WITH KIDS
Up to 68 great ideas for family days, recommended by resident parents. Perfect for exploring in your own backyard or on the road.

SEE IT GUIDES
Illustrated guidebooks that include the practical information travelers need, in gorgeous full color. Perfect for travelers who want the best value packed in a fresh, easy-to-use, colorful layout.

FODOR'S FLASHMAPS
Every resident's map guide, with 60 easy-to-follow maps of public transit, parks, museums, zip codes, and more.

FODOR'S LANGUAGES FOR TRAVELERS
Practice the local language before you hit the road. Available in phrase books, cassette sets, and CD sets.

THE COLLECTED TRAVELER
These collections of the best published essays and articles on various European destinations will give you a feel for the culture, cuisine, and way of life.

At bookstores everywhere.   www.fodors.com/books

Dear Traveler

From buying a plane ticket to booking a room and seeing the sights, a trip goes much more smoothly when you have a good travel guide. Dozens of writers, editors, designers, and cartographers have worked hard to make the book you hold in your hands a good one. Was it everything you expected? Were our descriptions accurate? Were our recommendations on target? And did you find our tips and practical advice helpful? Your ideas and experiences matter to us. If we have missed or misstated something, we'd love to hear about it. Fill out our survey at www.fodors.com/books/feedback/, or e-mail us at seeit@fodors.com. Or you can snail mail to the See It Editor at Fodor's, 1745 Broadway, New York, New York 10019. We'll look forward to hearing from you.

Tim Jarrell
Publisher